OPERATING SYSTEMS THEORY AND PRACTICE

OPERATING SYSTEMS THEORY AND PRACTICE

Paul Massie

George Cheng

St. John's Univ

Dec 1st 1987

Macmillan Publishing Company
New York

Collier Macmillan Publishers
London

To my wife, Esther

Macmillan Publishing Company
866 Third Avenue
New York, N.Y. 10022
Collier Macmillan Canada, Inc.

Library of Congress Cataloging-in-Publication Data

Massie, Paul, 1955 —
Operating systems theory and practice.

Includes index.
1. Operating systems (Computers) I. Title.
QA76.76.063M37 1986 005.4'3 86-934
ISBN 0-02-303602-8

Printed in the United States of America

Printing 2 3 4 5 6 Year 7 8 9 0

CONTENTS

APPENDICES

PREFACE

This is an introductory text on operating systems theory. It presents both theoretical principles and the ways those principles are used in the implementation of actual operating systems. Students in the operating systems course will normally have completed one or more courses in computer science and be familiar with the concepts of computer programming. While not absolutely necessary since the text does not assume these prerequisites, such a background will greatly facilitate comprehension of the material in this text.

General Approach

Most of the coverage of memory management is devoted to virtual memory systems, occasionally at the expense of covering more traditional memory management algorithms. Although it is necessary to understand basic memory management algorithms, few modern operating systems use them. Virtually all modern operating systems use virtual memory algorithms. The exceptions to this rule are either operating systems that are still evolving, such as PC-DOS, or operating systems for specialized purposes, such as real-time processing.

Considerable emphasis is placed on operating system performance throughout the text. This is a practical issue with little theory surrounding it, but one that is critical in all large computer installations. Attaining maximum possible performance is emphasized throughout the text, from memory management to scheduling jobs.

The demands made on computers are growing at such an explosive rate that computer design cannot keep pace. One of the best ways to alleviate this problem is to provide greater throughput with existing computer technology. Such throughput requirements dictate that a major focus of operating system design be on enhancing performance. Not only must the design of the operating system enhance performance—the way that system is installed must be planned to achieve maximum performance.

To date, operating system technology has not reached a level sufficient to allow systems to be self-tuning. A systems programmer must monitor and change the way the system is installed to achieve maximum possible performance. Thus, it is increasingly important that any course on operating systems contain at least an introduction to primary performance issues confronting the system and programmers.

Many of the smaller computer systems, such as single-user microcomputers, are not yet made with operating systems designed to enhance performance. However, even in this area, performance is at a premium—witness the increasing sales of the IBM PC-AT versus the IBM PC-XT. As small computer systems become larger and support more tasks, performance optimization will become more important.

Most texts on operating systems concentrate exclusively on theory, perhaps because the details of specific operating systems are constantly changing. The specifics of a particular release of an operating system can always be learned by studying its manuals. It is not possible for a textbook to always be current, so the common approach is to include no details at all. The logic behind this approach is that it is better to provide no details than to provide details that may prove to be incorrect when applied to the current release of an operating system.

This underestimates the difficulty many students experience when trying to apply theoretical constructs to the actual details of operating systems. This problem is increased by the fact that operating system manuals are not designed as tutorials, but rather to provide specific information to the expert user. Consequently, these are often very difficult to understand and require considerable experience on the part of the reader.

The latter half of this text is designed to assist students in applying theoretical ideas to specific operating systems. Considerable effort has been made to link this section of the text with the earlier part of the text on theory. Students should find it easier to identify theoretical concepts as actually implemented in common operating systems. Every attempt has been made to clearly identify the theoretical idea underlying each practical system, subsystem, or algorithm in actual operating systems.

A common mistake made by students after studying operating systems theory is to assume that all operating systems use only the very best theoretical ideas. It is important for students to see that many operating systems features may not be included in specific operating systems, even though theory states that those features are good or necessary. Students need to see that practical considerations governing the release of operating systems frequently make it difficult to include desirable theoretical features.

Students should be cautioned, however, against assuming that the specific details of the operating systems covered in this text will always be true. Operating systems change frequently and any feature can be subject to change at any time. For this reason, the specific release number of each operating system is specified. The details should be accurate for that release of the operating system, but not necessarily for any other release of the same operating system.

Organization

The text is divided into two major sections: theory and the application of that theory. Under normal circumstances, Section One should be covered before Section Two. The chapters in each section are arranged in logical order; they are independent enough, however, that the order can be determined by the instructor with no significant problems.

Chapter One provides a chapter-by-chapter description of the plan of the text. Chapter Two provides an overview of the history and functions of operating systems. Successive chapters in Section One cover all the major theoretical issues regarding operating systems. The coverage is as general as possible, although the slant is inevitably toward IBM and DEC operating systems concepts. Such a slant is unavoidable since the two vendors have dominated the commercial arena for operating systems. While their offerings have not always been the most technically advanced, IBM and DEC have had the most commercial success.

Section Two is devoted to actual operating systems as they are implemented today. The sequence of chapters shows increasing complexity in the operating systems covered. This section is useful in showing how theoretical features are implemented, and in demonstrating that few operating system designers consider the same features equally important. Features that receive major attention on some operating systems are barely available on other systems. The high-level focus (interactive vs. batch vs. software development vs. . . .) of the operating system frequently determines which features are emphasized, although some features are always present.

Each chapter in Section Two is organized to cover the corresponding theoretical material presented earlier in the text. This makes it easy for students to see how various theoretical concepts are actually implemented in each operating system. It also makes it easier to compare implementations between operating systems.

The two appendices cover subjects that were not appropriate for earlier chapters, but which may be of interest to some instructors. A brief summary of analytic modeling is presented; those wanting a more in-depth presentation should consult various mathematical textbooks. The presentation on RAM memory is designed for those not already familiar with the organization of computer memory.

Learning Aids

Each chapter has key terms presented at the head of the chapter. The terms represent the most important concepts presented in that chapter. Key terms are also boldfaced when first presented and defined in the text. In addition, each chapter begins with an introduction that provides motivation for the material, and a summary where the key concepts are briefly recapped.

A variety of exercises are presented throughout the text for students to test comprehension of the material. These consist of true/false, multiple-choice, and discussion questions. Most of the important concepts presented in each chapter are covered in these questions.

A glossary of important terms is presented at the end of the text.

Paul Massie
Half Moon Bay, California
March 1986

ONE

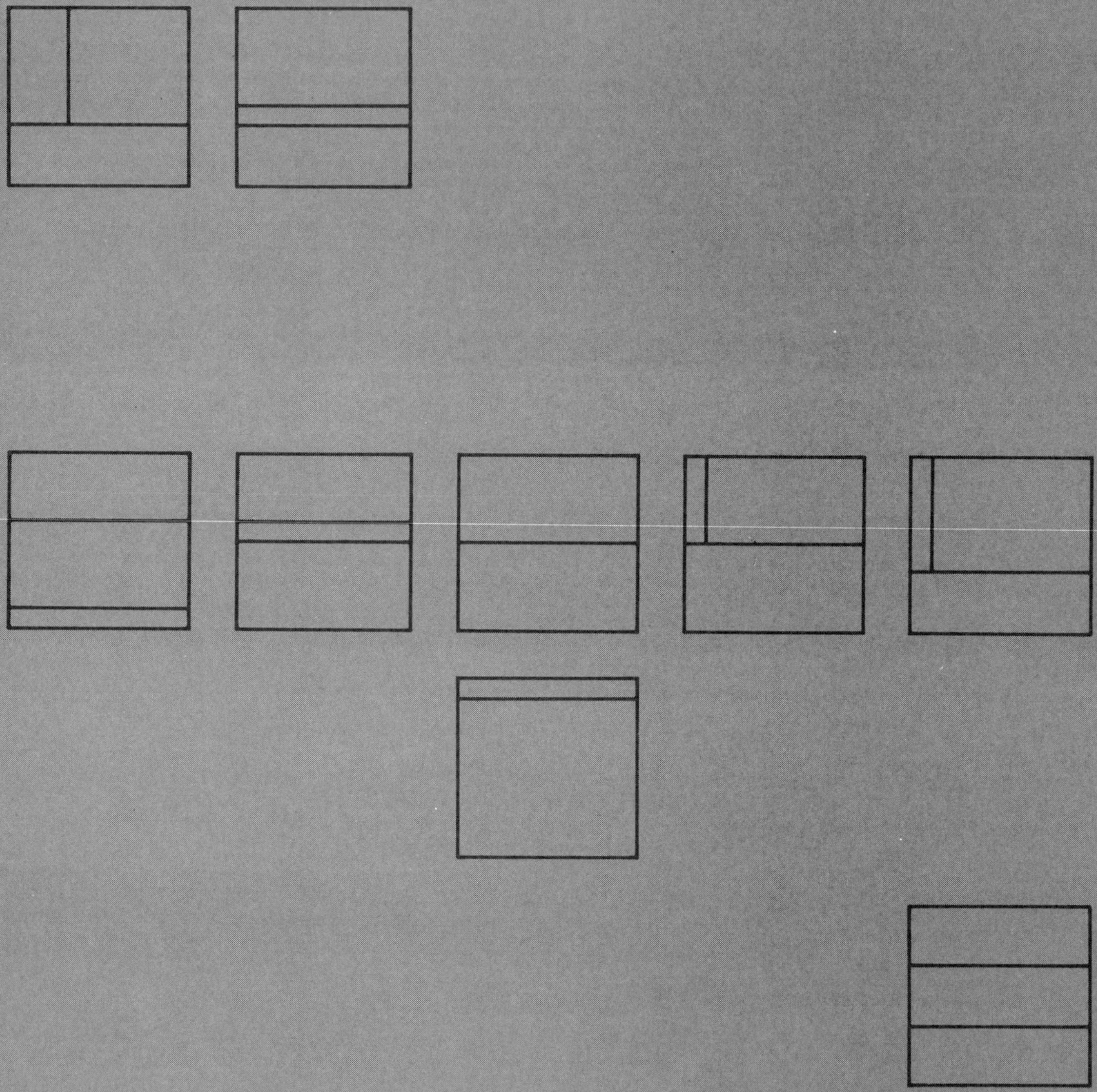

INTRODUCTION

1

This is an introductory text on operating systems as they are currently used in industry. The text is divided into two sections; Section One covers operating system theory, and Section Two describes how that theory is implemented in five current operating systems.

A course on operating systems may seem unnecessary to many students, since very few of those students will ever be in a position to modify or write a new operating system. Many of them, however, may become systems programmers supporting an operating system. These students must be very familiar with operating systems. The majority of students will never become systems programmers of any type, so the course may seem to have little direct applicability to them. It has tremendous indirect effect, however, since any computer user constantly uses the operating system.

Any person who is writing large applications must be familiar with the operating system on the computer being used.e It is not necessary to have the same degree of skill as possessed by a systems programmer, but it is necessary to have enough knowledge to write the application so that it will make full use of the available facilities. An application written by a person not familiar with the operating system may use far more computer resources than is necessary. Along with its inefficiency, the program may also be much less usable than it should be, simply because some available features of the operating system were not used.

Even persons who are only using the computer to run applications should be somewhat familiar with operating systems. A user who is familiar with operating systems is better able to make fullest use of all the available options on the application that he or she is using, and is also more likely to use that application efficiently.

It is important to understand the theory behind the design of operating systems, but it is equally important to see the way that theory is actually implemented in real operating systems. For this reason, the text is designed so that operating system theory is presented first, followed by an in-depth look at several operating systems. It is instructive to see when certain theoretical constructs are adopted in operating systems, and when they are not.

OPERATING SYSTEM ISSUES

The question of which operating system is the best is guaranteed to generate controversy among systems programmers. Since there are several very important operating systems in existence, each of which has its devotees, it is likely that there is no one single best operating system. The perceived quality of the various operating systems is dependent on a variety of factors. For instance, the age of the system is a factor, since new systems are often designed with modern principles, whereas older systems may have difficulty adopting some of the modern principles. The primary objective of the system is another major factor, since a system designed to optimize batch processing will not usually be very good for user interaction.

Operating systems are extremely complex assemblies of programs. Many person-years of effort are invested in developing even a relatively simple operating system, and a system such as IBM's MVS is awe-inspiring. Some systems programmers may spend years working on only one small part of a particular operating system, and other systems programmers may know the basics about several different systems but not know the intimate details of any one system. Because of the complexity of the systems, operating systems always have some errors in them. This leads to an on-going support task as bugs are fixed, features are added, new bugs are fixed, etc.

Operating systems programmers can be divided into a few different job types. Some systems programmers actually write a new system. These programmers are relatively rare, and usually work for a few selected computer vendors. Many more programmers maintain or support existing systems. They spend their time fixing bugs, adding new features, fixing the bugs they just fixed, fixing the bugs in the new features they just added, etc.

One of the most important areas for support systems programmers is performance measurement and tuning. On large computer systems, in particular, as much as twenty to fifty percent of the total system performance may be lost or regained through performance tuning. Some systems do not require very much performance tuning, while other systems require a vast amount. Usually, smaller computer systems do not require as much tuning as large systems.

The difficulty of operating system support tends to vary considerably, depending upon the size and complexity of both the operating system and the computer. Smaller computers tend to have less complex operating systems, while the very large computers have more complex systems. As operating systems become more complex, they also tend to generate more operating overhead. Managing the resources of a minicomputer tends to be much simpler than managing the resources of a large mainframe, so the operating system can be much simpler.

Complex operating systems require a large amount of physical computer resources in order to run. This resource consumption varies depending upon the load on the computer, but much of the overhead is still used even when the load is quite small. A small computer can be totally saturated by just the operating system overhead if that operating system is complex. That same complex operating system, when placed on a large computer, may use the same amount of resources, but those resources are only a small part of the total available on a large computer.

The systems programmer who is developing an operating system needs to understand the support issues in order to design the features that are necessary for the support programmer. Supporting an operating system can be relatively easy or very difficult, depending upon the level of support features built into the operating system. Certain tools make systems maintenance much easier, while the absence of those tools can change systems maintenance from a simple task to a black art.

Support systems programmers need to know how the operating system is designed since they may need to make modifications to various areas of the operating system. If modifications are attempted without a thorough understanding of how the operating system is designed, more harm may be done than good. Similar considerations apply to performance tuning. Without a good understanding of the design of the operating system, it is quite likely that misguided tuning might make the performance worse instead of better.

There are many constraints in real operating systems that may have nothing to do with the theory of operating systems. Many operating systems are designed as revisions or outgrowths of an older operating system, and consequently are forced to retain many of the structures of that older operating system, even though these structures may be completely obsolete.

Another frequent constraint is the overall purpose of the operating system and the computer on which it runs. It is useless to develop a highly sophisticated algorithm for interactive users if the operating system is going to be used to monitor an assembly line. Some operating systems deliberately do not implement sophisticated algorithms simply because the operating system may fail in the purpose for which it was designed.

There is not an operating system that is able to be the "best" operating system on all sizes of computers and for all tasks. Any operating system that is designed to serve more than one purpose must have compromises in its design, and the more functions that operating system must serve, the more compromises are necessary in the design.

LAYOUT OF THIS TEXT

This text is structured in such a way as to give the student a good grasp of the fundamental theoretical concepts, then to illustrate how those concepts are used in operating systems that are in use today. The operating systems that are covered are chosen to represent both a wide variety of approaches and to cover the majority of the installations in use today. It is not a coincidence that three of the five operating systems are from IBM, while the remaining two are from DEC. These two vendors dominate the industry. IBM clearly dominates the field in revenue, but not necessarily in the number of computers installed, since DEC computers are often cheaper than IBM computers.

These operating systems are continually evolving and changing, so the characteristics covered here may be changed at some future date. Nevertheless, the concepts presented are still valid. Even if the details of the implementation of one operating system change, the concepts presented here should still be studied. Many of the reasons for new developments only become understandable when the previous problems are studied. Because operating systems change, the particular release level is specified for each operating system.

A historical perspective

This is a brief history of operating systems which traces some of the major developments from their beginnings in the 1950's, to the current state of the art in operating systems in the 1980's. The major functions of current operating systems are briefly mentioned, including an explanation of how the functions developed and why they were needed.

Systems services

An operating system is divided in two general parts. The first part performs internal functions, such as scheduling jobs and managing resources. This is the part of the operating system that tends to receive the most attention. The second part consists of those programs that provide specific functions to users, such as compiling programs. These functions are often called **system services.** This part tends to be just a loose collection of programs.

The systems services are very important to the functioning of the operating system, even though they frequently do not seem as vital as the services provided by the kernel of the operating system. In many cases, these services are more important than the kernel because the users see and use the services regularly, while they seldom see the kernel. The way the system services are designed and presented to the users often dictates how the system is perceived by the users.

There is no clear consensus on just what system services are, but for the purposes of this text we shall assume that any service offered by the operating system, that is not part of the kernel, is a systems service. Some systems services are closely tied to the file system and will be covered in the section on file systems. Other systems services qualify for an entire chapter; such things as security and networking. Only those systems services that are included in a wide variety of systems, yet are not large enough components to warrant a complete chapter, are covered in chapter 1.

Example 1-1:

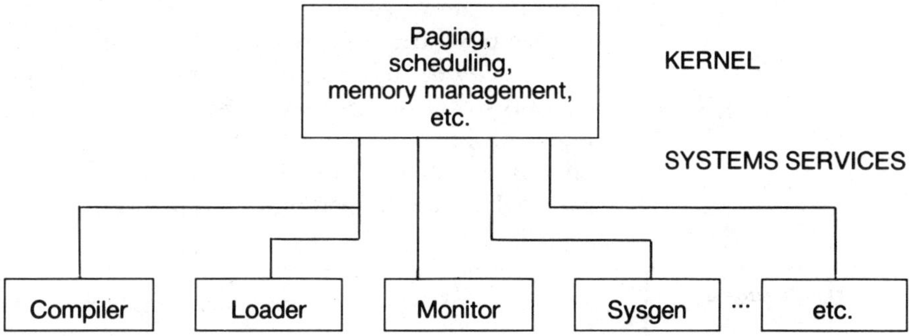

File systems

Computers are designed to process data. All other operations performed by a computer are support operations that allow more or better processing of data. The requirements for handling data differ between applications, but all applications have such requirements. It is therefore very important that the operating system allow data to be manipulated easily and quickly.

The file system of an operating system plays a crucial role in determining how fast and how easily the data can be manipulated. The file system should be designed to match the design objectives of the operating system itself. This is why, for example, the file system for a production-oriented operating system is not designed the same way as the file system for an interactive software development system.

Multiprogramming

One of the most useful aspects of many computers is their ability to interleave the execution of programs, so that one program is executing while another is waiting on something, such as an I/O operation. This prevents the processor from wasting time while slower operations are being done independently. The primary goal of multiprogramming is to have one program executing in the processor at all times, which is only possible by having several programs take turns at the processor. Another goal is to allow several users access to the system at the same time. The value of multiprogramming is probably best demonstrated by looking at current microcomputers, most of which do not now support multiprogramming. Anyone who has ever had their computer tied up for thirty minutes while printing a large file is very aware of the value of multiprogramming.

The ability to interleave program execution is provided almost exclusively by the operating system, although modern computer hardware has several features that improve the performance of multiprogramming. The processor in the computer can only execute one instruction at a time, so only one program can actually be run at a time. However, multiprogramming operating systems take advantage of the characteristics of executing programs to allow several different programs to appear to be executing at the same time. This function of operating systems is contained in the heart of the operating system and is integral to the smooth operation of the computer.

Example 1-2:

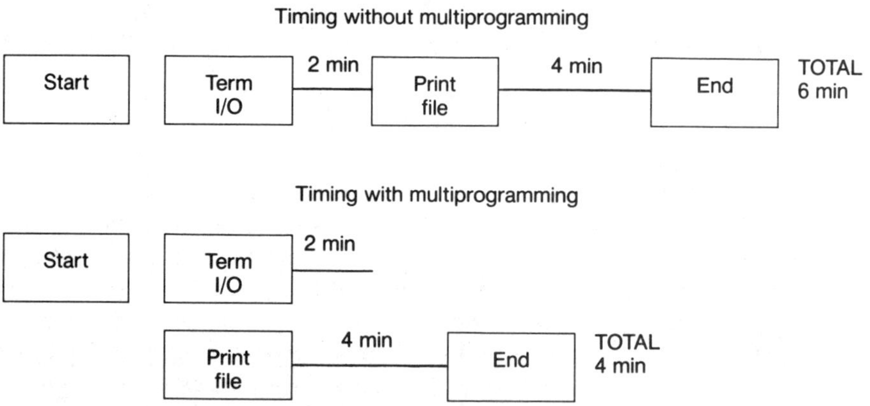

Job and task scheduling

The part of the operating system that does the job and task scheduling is the real heart of the operating system. These functions are contained primarily in the kernel of the operating system. There are really three different levels of scheduling, which are sometimes known as low, middle or intermediate, and high level scheduling. All three of these functions must be performed by the operating system, although not all of them need be contained within the kernel of the system.

Example 1-3:

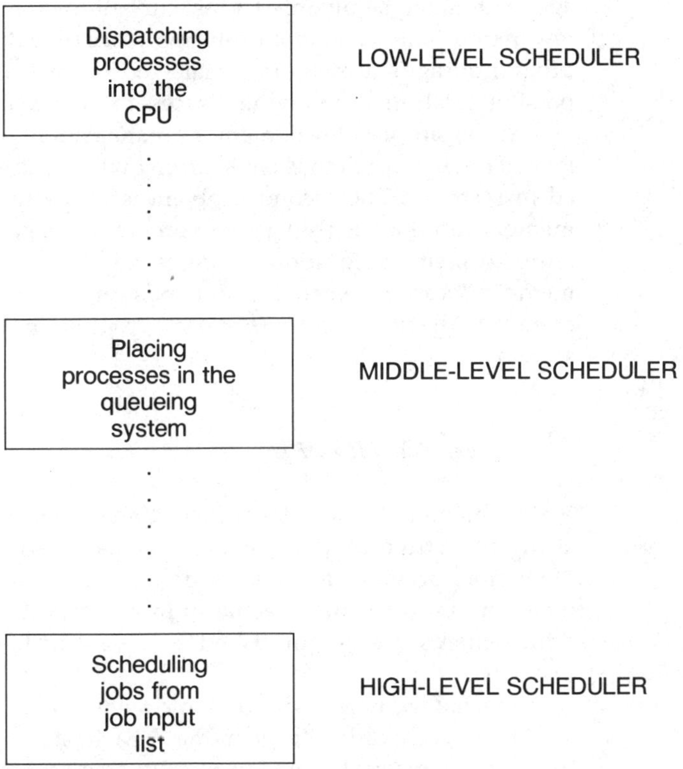

There are many features that must be shared by all schedulers. Predictability is very important; a given job should execute in about the same amount of time each time it is run if the system load is approximately the same. Schedulers should be set up to maximize both system resources and job throughput. They should be designed to optimize processing of those jobs the system is designed to handle. There are also other, less important, features to provide, such as the ability to continue functioning correctly when the system is heavily loaded.

Real memory management

The concept of multiprogramming causes great difficulties in the management of resources that must be shared between programs, and the most crucial of these resources is the internal memory of the computer. Historically, very little memory management was needed as long as operating systems serviced only one program. As soon as multiprogramming began appearing, memory management had to be invented. Most current microcomputers, for example, have few memory management problems, since they do not usually support multiprogramming. The memory is managed just by loading the program at the first possible location, then giving it access to the rest of the memory.

At the simplest level, memory management consists of solving two problems. The first problem is determining where a given program should be loaded in memory. The second problem is properly setting up all references to memory locations within a given program. Every program makes many references to memory locations, such as for variables and constants. The actual memory location referred to depends on where the program is loaded into memory. All such references in each program must be set up by the operating system.

Virtual memory

Virtual memory is a system of providing each program access to memory that, at any given time, may or may not be actual internal memory. The total amount of memory provided to all users, or to any one user, may be far in excess of the total amount of memory actually in the computer. Such seemingly magical achievements are accomplished by using disk drives to emulate internal memory.

Internal memory is divided into small pieces, normally two to four thousand bytes each, called "page frames". Each page frame may be occupied at any time by a memory allocated to an executing process. When the demand for internal memory exceeds the total amount available, some of memory is copied to a disk drive. The program using that memory is completely unaware of any difference, although it cannot actually execute until any memory it needs is actually in internal memory. This allows each of the programs to run as though it had exclusive use of a large physical memory.

Memory is copied onto **paging devices,** which are usually disk drives. In certain computers, special devices have been developed expressly for the purpose of providing storage for pages. These devices are usually similar to disk drives, but use more expensive hardware to achieve higher data transfer speeds.

Example 1-4:

PAGE FRAMES

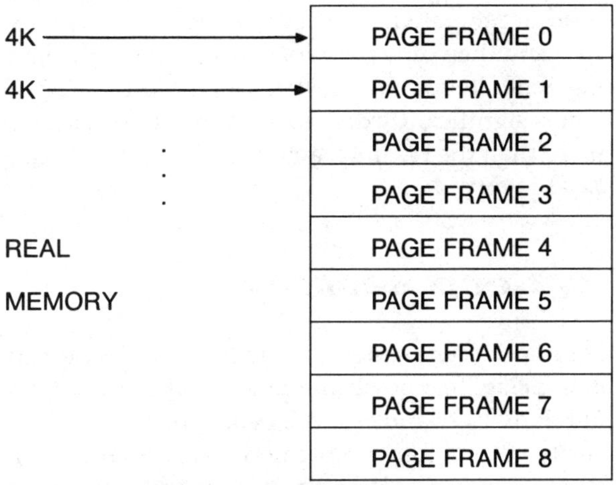

System performance

Systems performance, which consists of both monitoring and optimization, is a subject that must be considered both when the system is designed and continuously after the system is installed. Contrast this to most of the subjects covered previously, which have been exclusively concerned with the theory behind the design of operating systems. Both monitoring and optimizing must be considered, since optimizing the performance of the system is impossible without knowing its current performance characteristics.

There are only three basic areas of any computer where improvement can be made: the processor, the memory, and the I/O. The only way to improve the processor performance is to get a more powerful processor, but extensive monitoring of the processor performance can be used to determine when it is necessary to use a more powerful processor. The memory and I/O utilizations, however, are subject to vast performance changes. These two areas are closely tied together in most modern operating systems, since most of them use virtual memory, and thus the memory performance is closely tied to the I/O performance.

Monitoring can be invaluable if used properly, but can cause a disaster if used improperly. The monitoring process inevitably adds a certain amount of overhead to the system. The more in-depth the monitoring is, the more overhead is generated in the system. Some types of monitoring should be seldom run, and then only for very short periods of time, since those types of monitoring generate so much system overhead that the performance of the whole system is significantly degraded. A careful evaluation must be made before doing more than the minimal amount of monitoring due to the possible system overhead involved.

Systems security

For many years, systems security was an issue only to few people, such as those doing classified government research. As computers invade more and more of our daily lives and as more people become skilled computer programmers, security both becomes more necessary and more difficult to maintain. Computer systems now maintain records on virtually every person in the country, and those records become more complete every year. Computer systems also now control more functions of business and government than ever before. The increased usage of computers makes them more vital to everyone's lives, and also means that more and more information and power is contained in computers every year, which in turn makes those computers more attractive to the criminal or merely curious.

The advent of cheap, popular microcomputers has caused a computer revolution where a relatively sophisticated computer is available to anyone. This becomes important to security because the best way to gain access to one computer is with another computer. Computers were relatively secure as long as only computer programmers with access to an expensive mainframe computer were a danger, but as soon as microcomputers became available to millions of people, the pool of potential security violators became much larger.

Security systems can be either a part of the operating system or another system added on top of the operating system. Most operating systems, particularly those designed for multiple users, have some level of security built into them. Operating systems developed in recent years tend to have more security than those developed earlier. Very few operating systems, however, have a complete security system. When a complete security system is deemed necessary it is usually achieved by placing another system on top of the basic operating system.

Multiprocessing

Multiprocessing is the concept of putting more than one central processing unit in a computer. This is a common solution to the need for more computing power since many problems exist with developing faster single processors. The physical limitations, such as the speed of light, or heat buildup, are causing a great deal of difficulty in increasing the speed of processors. New generations of processors are being developed constantly, with speeds much faster than the best available only three to five years ago, but this is still not enough to satisfy users' demand. Most of the largest general purpose computers now use a multiple-processor configuration.

The operating system must be able to efficiently manage all processors and allocate resources between them in the best possible way. This becomes an extremely difficult task for the operating system. The overhead associated with keeping track of which processor is using which resource, or is running which process at any time, is significant even when the management itself is done well.

Example 1-5:

SAMPLE DUAL PROCESSOR CONFIGURATION

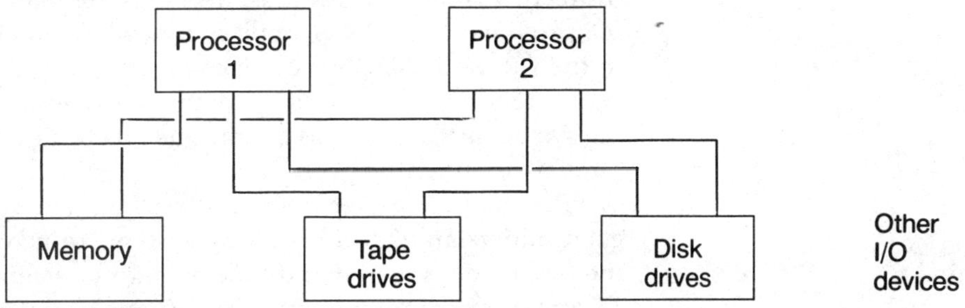

The memory, disk drives, tape drives, and all peripherals are shared by both processors.

Networking systems

One of the most important areas in the computer industry today is setting up and maintaining telecommunications networks between computers. This was not always so. For many years, putting facilities in operating systems to allow them to communicate with other computers was not considered very important. Only a relatively small number of companies had computers, and those that did have computers usually had only one specialized computer, so it was rarely necessary or desirable to have computers communicating with one another. This has changed, and now there are so many computers in use that one of the most critical areas in operating systems is communication between computers.

One special case of computer communication that is becoming very well known is **local area networks,** or **LANs.** This is a network set up between various computers, all of which are relatively close physically to one another. Most of the topics of interest in local area networks are in linking groups of personal computers. These networks are most commonly used to share information and expensive peripherals with one another.

Current data communications developments are focused in the areas of linking mainframes or minicomputers to one another, linking personal computers to one another, and linking personal computers or terminals with mainframes or minicomputers. The technology used to link different sized computers tends to vary, since smaller computers usually require much less sophisticated and expensive technology than do the larger computers.

PC-DOS

The first operating system covered, PC-DOS, is for microcomputers. Many of the features that are considered necessary for mainframe operating systems are not provided in PC-DOS, but it is almost inevitable that they will be included in the future. PC-DOS is quite common and is evolving quite rapidly. Many people tend to think of it as less than a real operating system, but it is an operating system just as much as mainframe operating systems, and is faced with the same requirements.

Personal computer operating systems are very useful for developing a good understanding of operating systems in general, since they often reflect the same evolution as mainframe operating systems. The process that required thirty years of development in mainframe operating systems, and fifteen years in minicomputer operating systems, is being covered by the personal computers in only seven or eight years. Many of the functions that are normally contained in operating systems on larger computers are tied into a specific application on personal computers, so that the user may never need to use the operating system at all.

PC-DOS is a version of the popular MS-DOS operating system used on the IBM personal computers. The system was written by a software company called Microsoft, and is slightly modified and sold by IBM with their personal computer. Release 3.1 of PC-DOS is used in this book.

PC-DOS is a complete operating system, and provides most of the functions of any normal operating system. The primary features currently absent from it are multiprogramming and multi-user capabilities. The personal computer was originally designed as a single-user system, so the operating system was also designed to be single-user. This will change as the personal computers become more powerful. The multiprogramming capabilites are needed even if the system is only single-user, so that should be one of the first features to be implemented in the future.

UNIX

The second operating system covered is DEC's implementation of UNIX, called Ultrix. UNIX is becoming much more popular, but it still does not have the maturity of many other commercial operating systems.

UNIX is unique in several respects. It is the only operating system that is currently supported at the same time on microcomputers, minicomputers, and mainframes from different vendors. It is also unique in that it appeared as one programmer's spare-time tool, not as a planned project. Devotees of UNIX swear it is the answer to all operating systems needs; devotees of other operating systems sometimes swear that UNIX is completely useless. The truth is probably somewhere in between.

UNIX is a very powerful system; it allows experienced users to quickly and easily do things that are difficult or impossible on other systems. One of the primary strengths of the system is that it was designed by a programmer for the express purpose of aiding in program development. It is probably the best system available for program development since almost all of the features in the system are designed to make program development easier.

UNIX is perhaps the most flexible of all the major operating systems, and has more potential than many of the other major operating systems, since its structure is not as tightly locked into one form. The recently increased support that AT&T is giving to UNIX may be the impetus needed to give it the features it is lacking. With such major vendors as AT&T, IBM, and DEC supporting UNIX, (and supporting versions with similar features), the support needed should soon become available.

VM

The third chapter in section Two covers the "Virtual Machine," or "VM" operating system from IBM. This operating system presents each user with a virtual computer, hence the name. Each of the physical features of a real computer, such as disks, tapes, card readers, etc., are simulated by VM, so that the user is able to use each of those features as though they were real.

VM is unique in that it is one of the very few operating systems that runs virtually unchanged on computers ranging in size from very large mainframes to microcomputers. The actual implementation of VM across machines varies, but there are only minor differences in the features the user sees. It runs on

IBM's 3090-200 mainframe, which is an extremely large computer, and it also runs on the IBM Personal Computer XT/370, which is a modified version of the IBM Personal Computer XT.

The version of VM covered in this chapter is VM/SP High Performance Option system, or VM/SP HPO, which is based on VM/SP, but contains enhancements and modifications to support very large mainframe computers with the highest possible performance level. The information in this chapter is relevant to VM/SP HPO Release 3.4.

VM consists of two major components; the "control program," or "CP," and the "conversational monitor system," or "CMS." The control program is the basic operating system. It manages all the real computer hardware, and presents each user with a fully-configured virtual machine (computer). That virtual machine does not have many of the functions required by normal users. It does not have any file system, no compilers, no editor, and none of the other commonly required features. All of those features must be provided by whatever program is running in that virtual machine.

MVS

The IBM MVS operating system is the operating system of choice for many installations using large IBM or IBM-compatible mainframes. IBM concentrated much of their systems development effort on MVS for several years at the end of the 1970's, apparently in an effort to encourage a complete migration to MVS as the only major IBM operating system. If this was the purpose, it was not successful, since many major installations continue to use VM and other less-popular systems. Nevertheless, MVS has been the subject of a tremendous amount of development during the last ten years.

The MVS operating system has evolved tremendously from its early beginnings, as a primarily batch-oriented system, to the current implementation, called MVS/XA. It still has a very highly developed batch system, but it also supports many interactive users through a variety of subsystems.

MVS is only used on relatively large computers, since the system is so large and complex that there is a significant amount of overhead involved in running it. Small computers just do not have sufficient processor power and memory size to allow the necessary overhead involved in running MVS.

The acronym XA stands for "eXtended Architecture", which is a comprehensive series of changes to both hardware and software that is designed to provide a clear path for development during the next decade. The primary change is to the addressing modes used in both the hardware and the software. All IBM systems previously used 24-bit addressing, meaning all addresses in the system consisted of a maximum of 24 bits. The maximum address possible with 24 bits is 16 megabytes, which is no longer large enough. The new addressing mode has 31 bits, which allows addresses of up to 2 gigabytes, or 2 billion bytes.

Another major change for MVS/XA is greatly increased performance in the I/O system. Many changes have been made in both the hardware and software to improve I/O performance. Much of the processing necessary to handle I/O was previously done only in the primary processor. Many of these functions have now been off-loaded to subsidiary processors that are dedicated just to I/O. Other changes improve the way I/O is handled on computers with many central processors, so that an I/O operation started on one processor may sometimes complete on the other processor. This reduces the wait time necessary to actually complete the operation.

VMS

The last operating system covered is the VMS system. It is designed to run on the Digital Equipment Corporation's VAX series of computers. It is one of the youngest operating systems considered in this text, since it did not come into existence until the middle to late 1970's, although many of its features are an extension and outgrowth of similar features in earlier DEC operating systems.

DEC operating systems have traditionally been oriented toward interactive users instead of batch usage. This tradition is continued in the VMS operating system, since it is very well designed to enhance interactive usage. In many respects, the relative youth of the operating system is an advantage since it was designed with modern concepts in mind and was not tied to older, sometimes inefficient designs.

The VMS system runs only on VAX computers, so it was designed with the architecture of those computers in mind. This allows it to make efficient use of the hardware features available. The VMS system is similar to the VM system in that it runs on a range of computers from microcomputers to mainframes. The largest mainframes that it runs on are not as large as the largest mainframes that VM runs on because DEC does not manufacture mainframes as large as those IBM manufactures.

VMS runs on computers as small as the MicroVAX and as large as the VAX-Cluster. The goal of these systems is that an application developed on any of the systems will run equally well on any of the other systems.

VMS may very well be the best current compromise between all the necessary features of an operating system. It seems the primary operating system that DEC will make a mainstay for years to come.

EXERCISES

DISCUSSION QUESTIONS

1. List the common types of systems programmers and give a brief explanation of the primary job functions of each type.
2. Discuss performance measurement and tuning.
3. Why should operating system designers study system support issues?
4. Discuss some of the constraints on operating system development.
5. Briefly discuss a single, all-purpose system.
6. Why is studying a microcomputer operating system useful?
7. Summarize the strengths and weaknesses of UNIX.
8. Summarize the strengths and weaknesses of VM.
9. Summarize the strengths and weaknesses of MVS.
10. Summarize the strengths and weaknesses of VMS.

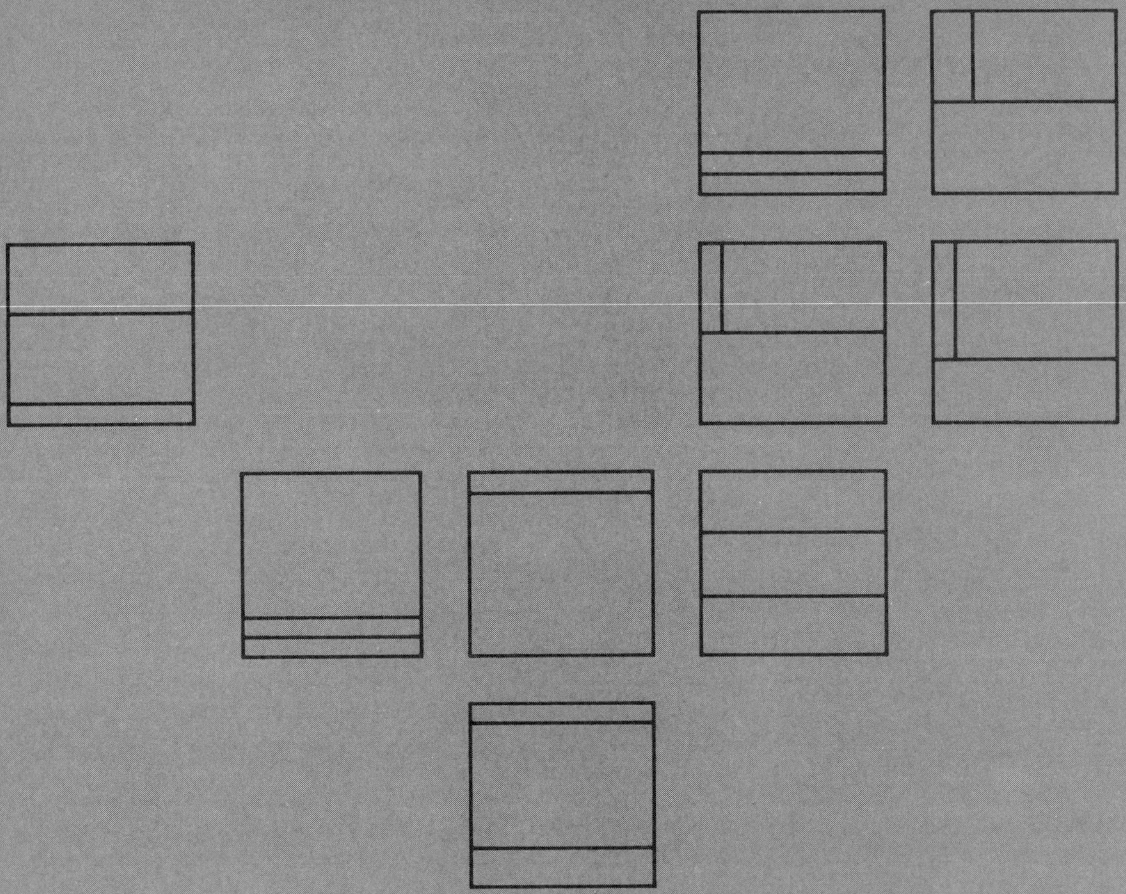

A HISTORICAL PERSPECTIVE

2

KEY TERMS

Batch processing systems	*Batch*
Multiprogramming	*Single-threading*
Multitasking	*Concurrency*
Central processing unit (CPU)	*Peripheral I/O devices*
Scheduling	*Device independence*
Time sharing	*Real-time systems*
Job control language (JCL)	*Virtual memory*
Interactive systems	*Unbundling*
User-friendliness	*Firmware*

THE FIRST GENERATION

One of the most important features of any computer system is the operating system that runs on that computer. In the early days of computers, operating systems were non-existent. They are now so important that, in many cases, they control the design of the hardware.

An operating system is a collection of programs that allows one or more people to use computer hardware efficiently. This sounds like a very simple task, but is enormously difficult. Some of the operating systems that have been used are among the largest, most complex, most expensive, and most error-prone collections of programs that have ever been written. An operating system may be compared to the brain that activates the body (in this case, the computer hardware). The body is virtually useless unless the brain is also healthy. Similarly, computer hardware is relatively useless without an operating system to activate it.

Operating systems that are in common usage today cover a wide range of complexity, from the massive IBM MVS system to the much simpler microcomputer systems such as CP/M or MS-DOS. The size of the systems and the features provided vary widely, yet each has the same basic function; to provide the best possible use of the computer hardware on which that system is running.

The earliest computers existed only as hardware, with no operating systems. There were very few computer programs at all when computer hardware was first developed in the 1940's and early 1950's. Running a program was very difficult. The computer had switches that allowed the programmer to display and modify the computer memory. The programmer used those switches to manually load the program, in machine language, into memory. The program was executed by starting the computer at the beginning of the memory area just loaded.

The first generation of operating systems was developed and used during the 1950's. These operating systems were a huge leap forward from the previous arrangement. The first step was to have a setup program placed in memory with the manual switches, and then to have that setup program read the real program from an input device such as punched cards or paper tape. The setup program was relatively small and easy to load, whereas the real program might be much larger. Thus, having such a setup program made programming much easier.

This setup program became the first primitive operating system. Developing ways to allow one program to remain constantly in memory, and to run other programs, raised the first problems of operating system development. Those problems are still faced today, although both the problems and the algorithms to handle them have been developed considerably.

The first operating systems only mechanized the setup procedure for programs to be input and reset the computer hardware to an initial state after each program finished executing. These systems could automatically input the next program after resetting the hardware. The first **batch processing system** read in programs in "batches" or groups, whereas previously each program required manually setting up the hardware and resetting it after the program executed. Only one program was allowed to access the computer at any one time, and any processor time not used by the program in the computer was wasted.

The state-of-the-art in operating systems remained the same until the early 1960's, when operating systems were developed that were similar to operating systems used today. Several concepts that are common today were first developed during this period.

Tracking the history of operating systems is, in many ways, tracking the history of IBM, since IBM has been the most powerful influence in the development of commercial operating systems. IBM has not always been the first to introduce particular features in operating systems, but it has almost always been the first to make those features industry standards. The major exceptions to this rule lie in the introduction of interactive operating systems by Digital Equipment Corporation, and in the support for vector processing pioneered by Control Data Corporation and Cray Research.

Multiprogramming

The first concept that was introduced in the first generation of operating systems was **multiprogramming.** This means that several programs can be in the computer at the same time and the computer takes turns executing each of the programs. This replaces the previous concept of **single-threading,** where each program had to finish executing before the next program could begin. The terms **multitasking** and **concurrency** are sometimes used as synonyms for multiprogramming. Each of these terms has slightly different definitions, but the overall concept is always that of allowing several different programs to be resident in the computer at the same time. Most microcomputer systems do not support multiprogramming, although it is one of the most necessary improvements to such systems.

Example 2-1:

SINGLE-THREADING

JOBS WAITING

Job n

.
.
.

Job 3

Job 2

JOB IN COMPUTER

Job 1

JOB 1 remains in the computer until it finishes, regardless of whether it is actually able to execute during all that time.

MULTIPROGRAMMING

JOBS WAITING

Job n

.
.
.

Job 5

Job 4

JOBS IN COMPUTER

Job 1 | Job 2 | Job 3

JOB 1, JOB 2, and JOB 3 take turns executing, (when ready). Whenever one of them is not ready, one of the other jobs executes in its place.

The multiprogramming concept is based on the idea that some parts of a computer run much faster than other parts. The fastest part of a computer is the part that actually executes the instructions. This is called the **central processing unit** or **CPU.** Sometimes it is just known as the processor. The computer receives information via **peripheral** I/O devices which communicate with the rest of the world. These peripheral devices are always much slower than the CPU, which causes the CPU to have to wait while a program is communicating with the rest of the world.

Example 2-2:

MULTIPROGRAMMING

RUN FIRST	***RUN SECOND***	***RUN THIRD***
RUN FOURTH	***RUN FIFTH***	***RUN SIXTH***
etc.		
Job 1	Job 2	Job 3
READY	READY	READY

When all jobs are ready, they are executed in turn.

RUN FIRST	***NOT RUN***	***RUN SECOND***
RUN THIRD	***NOT RUN***	***RUN FOURTH***
etc.		
Job 1	Job 2	Job 3
READY	WAITING	READY

When a job is not ready, the remaining jobs take turns, and it is not given a turn until it is ready.

Multiprogramming allows several programs to be in the computer at the same time, so that while one program is performing I/O, another program can be using the CPU. If none of the programs is delayed by such communication, then the CPU takes turns processing each of the programs. This is a concept that is still at the heart of most minicomputer and mainframe operating systems.

The part of the operating system that decides which program will get a share of CPU time is called the **scheduler** or **job scheduler.** A great deal of care must be spent in developing and implementing algorithms for the scheduler since its performance is critical to the overall performance of the operating system. The scheduler can make or break the performance of an operating system.

Device independence

Another concept that was developed in the early 1960's is **device independence.** This means that a program can do input from or output to a "generic" type of device without having to know specific information about that device. Before device independence existed, a program that needed to read in punched cards had to specify the actual card reader to be used. Device independence allows programs to specify only that input is desired from a card reader, and the operating system then found and used a specific card reader. The concept of device independence is now extremely important for devices such as tape drives and disk drives, where dozens of different types with different operating specifications may exist.

Human interface

Most of the human interaction with computers today is performed by terminal. This is much easier than either the front panel of a computer or punched cards. Terminal support is considered essential for modern operating systems, but it was not until the early 1960's that such support was first developed.

The terminals used previously were quite different from those existing today. Ergonomic features were not considered, and the terminals were often hard-copy devices that printed each character on paper. The first terminals used were actually teletype devices developed for long-distance communication.

Accessing a computer system from terminals is called **time-sharing** because each terminal user has to share the computer time with all the other users. Some dramatic changes were necessary in operating systems when humans began interacting directly with computers. When computers ran only batch, the share of time allocated to each program running was not too important as long as the total time allocated to the program was sufficient; that is, one long period was as good as several short periods. Terminal users have different requirements, however, and require many short slices of time, since they access the system frequently. This required a different algorithm for time-sharing users than for programs running in batch. Some operating systems were developed expressly for supporting time-sharing users.

Real-time systems

A different type of operating system that developed in the early 1960's was the **real-time system.** This is an operating system designed to allow a computer to monitor and control some conditions as they happen. These are normally conditions that require very rapid responses. An example of such an application is a computer that monitors an assembly line. In general, such a computer should have reserve computing capacity available at any time to react to an emergency.

THE SECOND GENERATION

The decade from the middle 1960's to the middle 1970's was a period during which operating systems developed much futher. Probably the most significant development of this period was IBM's introduction of the System/360 family of computers. This was the first time a major vendor had introduced a family of computers, as opposed to several individual computers. The family concept meant that several computers were available at the same time that had the same name and would run the same software. This allowed customers to purchase a small computer and later upgrade to larger models of the same computer without having to rewrite any software.

The idea of integrating the computers into a single family today seems like an obvious concept, but at the time it was revolutionary. Even today, this practice has not always been followed by some manufacturers. The more successful ones, however, have followed this practice even with microcomputers. Ironically, the vendor who has done the best job of integrating a wide range of products into a single family is not IBM; instead, Digital Equipment Corporation has this distinction with its family of VAX computers.

The 360 family of computers also brought the first successful large, general purpose, operating system. This system combined batch processing facilities, time-sharing facilities, and, sometimes, real-time facilities. The development of such operating systems was a monumental task which took far longer and was far more expensive than anyone had expected. The programming principles that are today used to manage huge software projects were then in their infancy. In fact, development of these huge systems, with their attendant problems, contributed greatly to the current theory of programming management techniques. The inability of manufacturers other than IBM to develop and support such systems probably contributed more than anything else to IBM's domination of the mainframe computer market.

Operating systems became so complex that large groups of people were necessary to support them. Only experienced programmers who knew the intricacies of the specific operating system were able to answer questions about it and fix the numerous bugs that showed up in it. Operating systems development and support, for the first time, began occupying a significant amount of the vendor's development efforts.

The development and support efforts were complicated by the users demand for several different functions from the operating systems. This led to most vendors maintaining several different operating systems since any one operating system could not completely provide all desired features. Some of these systems were huge, and were aimed at the customer who had a large computer and wanted as many features as possible in one system. Others were smaller and were aimed at the customer who did not need as many features.

The largest systems were so complex that the overhead generated by the operating system itself was too great to run that system on a small computer and still get user programs to run.

Job control language

One of the most important events during this period was the development of a structured language for communication between the program and the operating system. Previous systems had concentrated on allowing the programs to run, without paying much attention to allowing those programs to request services from the operating system.

The language developed was similar to a programming language and was called **job control language,** or **JCL.** Many programmers regarded JCL as black magic and trembled at its mention, but JCL was a tremendous step forward in operating systems development. Most operating systems today use some form of JCL, although few of them actually call it that. Most modern operating systems provide the features of the original JCL, without most of the complexity and mystery associated with early JCL.

JCL solved the serious problem of scheduling the resources needed for a job without making the job wait. The programmer was able to specify any special resources needed for the program to run, and the operating system then made those resources available before the job started executing. This prevented the program from being delayed while it was waiting on some scarce resource.

JCL allowed the user to specify many other things such as the time or conditions under which a program was allowed to run. It also promoted device independence, since the device could be specified in the JCL instead of in the program itself. This allowed devices to be changed without requiring the program to be re-built.

Support programmers

The complexity of the systems, difficulties in maintaining the systems in good condition, and the intricacies of JCL led to the development of another type of systems programmer. These differed from systems programmers who actually wrote the operating systems. They worked for companies who were using computers and specialized in supporting operating systems. Many of them had been involved in the writing of a particular operating system, and were hired because that was the only way a company felt able to effectively use that operating system.

THE THIRD GENERATION

Many of the computer vendors who had successfully competed with IBM in the early 1960's dropped out of the competition by the middle 1960's due to the introduction of the 360 computers and operating systems. In the early 1970's, IBM introduced the next generation of computers and systems. The computers again comprised a complete family, from small to large, which IBM called the System 370. These systems were considerably advanced over the 360 systems but were not complete departures. Some features were added, and the performance was dramatically enhanced, but the changes were not as great as the 360's had been from the previous computers.

Virtual memory

With this third generation of computers, IBM introduced the concept of **virtual memory** on all systems. Vitual memory means that the physical memory of the computer is not a constraint, since the operating system can use disk storage to emulate memory to the users. The virtual memory concept was used by Burroughs in the early 1960's, but it did not become generally accepted until IBM announced it with the System 370. The operating systems running on the System 370 supported virtual memory, and the 370 computer was designed to use hardware functions to support virtual memory. This tying of the virtual memory to the computer hardware provided sufficient performance to make the system universally accepted.

Example 2-3:

VIRTUAL MEMORY

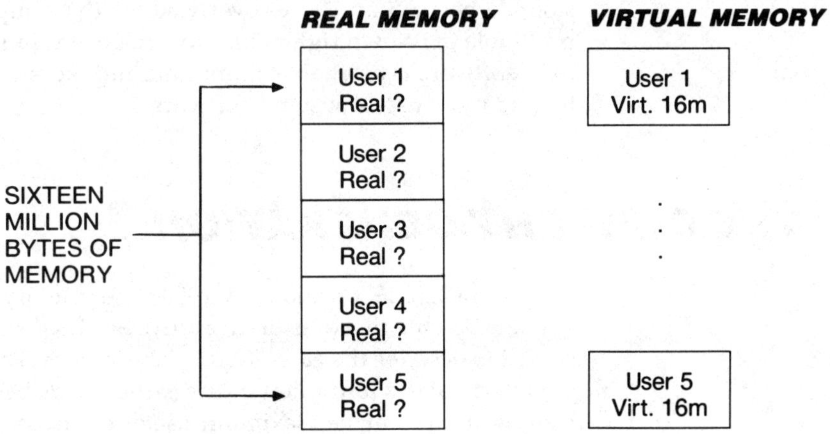

Interactive systems

One of the most significant developments of this period was the change in orientation of operating systems from batch processing to direct terminal interaction. This development was mostly spurred by the minicomputer manufacturers who needed to make their systems easy to use in order to compete in the marketplace. During the 1970's, the majority of computer users ceased to use punched cards and hard-copy terminals to access computers and began using video terminals.

Example 2-4:

GENERAL TYPES OF OPERATING SYSTEMS

Batch	Interactive	Real-time

Software unbundling

Another major event in the 1970's was **unbundling** of systems software. Before, the computer manufacturers were in business solely to sell computer hardware. They provided operating systems and systems support only because it was necessary in order to convince customers to buy their hardware. Systems software was generally given freely to customers with no charge. In effect, it came "bundled" with the computer hardware, since it was only available with the hardware.

With unbundling, the systems software could be separated from the computer hardware and each could be sold separately. The systems software stopped being simply sales overhead for the computer hardware and became profitable in its own right. One advantage of unbundling is that, since the systems software is profitable, more time and money can be spent to develop better and more useful systems software.

THE CURRENT GENERATION

During the late 1970's and early 1980's the primary consideration for operating systems became that of **user-friendliness.** User-friendliness is a term that was coined to describe the ease-of-use of the system. This idea had not been considered particularly important in the earlier years because the operating systems were written to make maximum use of the existing computer hardware, and any hardships this imposed on the programmers were accepted as necessary.

By the late 1970's, the computer hardware developed enough power for the primary bottleneck experienced by computer users not to be lack of computer power, but difficulty in using the computers.

Therefore the primary thrust of operating systems research is now to provide more tools for programmers and other users, and generally to make computers easier to use. This almost always leads to some inefficiencies in usage of the computer hardware, but the price of computer hardware has come down enough so that the primary expense lies with the users and not with the hardware. Consequently, the customers are willing to accept the losses in efficiency in order to optimize people time.

The primary recent advance in computers is the introduction of the microcomputer as a common tool. This has made computing available to almost anyone, and has caused increased attention on making systems easy to use by people other than programmers.

Other significant recent advances are the introduction by IBM of the Extended Architecture series of mainframe computers and systems, and the recent hardware and software products from DEC that unite almost all of their computers. The Extended Architecture series heralds many more capabilities offered to the user, and the DEC announcements foretell a time when a piece of software developed on one computer may run on any other computer.

The advent of microcomputers has greatly increased the number of people that have some experience with an operating system. Since many of these operating systems do not yet implement some of the more advanced concepts such as multiprogramming and virtual memory, people who have only experienced microcomputer operating systems tend to have a somewhat biased view of the capabilities of computers and systems.

FUNCTION OF OPERATING SYSTEMS

There are several functions that each operating system must provide, depending upon the sophistication and design objectives of the system. These requirements range widely in scope, as some systems have many more than do other systems. The services available may also differ depending upon the class of the user. That is, a systems programmer maintaining the system probably has access to services that are not available to the general user of that system. These services can be as simple as allowing a user to check the load on the system or as complex as a multi-step process for updating the system itself.

The file system

The part of the operating system with the most impact on the users is the **file system.** The file system for an operating system should be carefully designed to provide maximum performance for the functions provided by that system. The file system may be set up in different ways depending on the primary function of that operating system.

The design of the file system determines to a large extent the degree of compatibility between one operating system and another. This is why the file system has such a large impact on the users. If the file systems are compatible between two different operating systems, the data from one system can usually be transferred to the other system. If the file systems are different, then the data transfer becomes impossible or very difficult.

File systems tend to vary widely between operating systems, even when those operating systems are from the same vendor. For example, IBM's VM operating system supplies each user with a dedicated section of disk on which to store all files and does not normally allow any other users to write into that dedicated area. Since each user has his own dedicated area, of which only a small part is probably used, the total amount of disk space in the system that is not used tends to be rather large. IBM's MVS system, on the other hand, stores user files in shared disk areas, which allows it to manage the total disk area with much less wasted disk space. The VM design allows an individual user much greater flexibility with dedicated disk space, whereas the MVS system places more restrictions on file use.

Multiprogramming

Multiprogramming is so important to the operating system that scheduling algorithms are at the core of those operating systems which use multiprogramming. These algorithms determine which program will be allowed to execute at which time and for how long. The greatest degree of correctness is necessary in these algorithms, since only slight mistakes in this area can significantly affect the performance of the computer.

Many theoretical technical papers have been written on scheduling algorithms, but much care still must be taken in selecting the algorithm that will maximize performance on a particular computer, for the particular types of tasks that operating system is designed for, and for the particular mix of programs that the customer is running on the computer. In practice, some compromises are always necessary on general purpose computers running general purpose operating systems. Operating systems with a specific design goal, such as IBM's Transaction Processing Facility (which is designed to handle a large number of small transactions in real time) use very different scheduling algorithms than those used by a general purpose operating system such as IBM's MVS.

Memory management

One of the implications of multiprogramming is that the memory given to each program must be very carefully managed. Since several programs may be in memory simultaneously, great care must be taken to ensure that each program uses the correct memory location when it is executing, and that one program does not have access to memory belonging to another program.

There are two levels to basic memory management. One level ensures that memory is managed to allow correct execution of each program; the other level provides security to each program so that there is no possibility of its memory being accessed by another program. The security issue can be very important when the computers are being used for critical programs such as banking at the same time non-critical programs are being run. If the security is not adequate, a user could put a program into memory that could alter a payroll program, for example.

Virtual memory allows the users on the system to use far more memory than is physically in the computer. For instance, a computer may have only sixteen megabytes of internal memory, but twenty users may be executing simultaneously, each with what seems to them to be four megabytes of memory. Obviously, sixteen megabytes cannot become eighty (4 * 20) megabytes of memory; the system is able to use other storage to emulate memory.

System maintenance

A large percentage of the jobs available today for systems programmers lie in the installation and maintenance of operating systems. One of the reasons for this is that the ratio of customers to vendors tends to be rather high. Each operating system vendor has many customers but not much competition. Since there are a small number of vendors but a large number of customers who needs operating systems installed and maintained, there are many jobs in installation and maintenance.

There are several major tasks in maintaining an operating system, but one task that is sometimes overlooked is performance measurement and tuning. This is a task that is critical in the case of large installations that have heavily-loaded computers. Even if all the internal algorithms in the operating system have been well written, the performance is still heavily dependent on how the system is installed and maintained. The performance of the system should be monitored at all times, since operating system loads are seldom constant and regular. Whenever the load changes, the layout of the operating system must be changed to compensate for it. Failure to measure and tune systems can quickly result in a performance degradation, which is equivalent to wasting a good portion of a multi-million dollar computer.

Systems security

As more of the critical functions of the nation's businesses become computerized, and as more computers become cheaply available to everyone, the issues of providing systems security becomes more critical. There was a time when the only businesses with security concerns were banks and the military, and only a programmer working on some large computer had the possibility of illegally accessing computers. Those days are long past. Virtually every business today has critical information on computers. This ranges from new product designs to the company financial records. When this amount of important information maintained on computers is combined with the widespread proliferation of computers, the subject of systems security becomes very critical. The best place to begin installing some degree of security is in the operating system.

Multiprocessing

Using multiple processors in a single computer allows a dramatic increase in computing power with very little increase in subsidiary costs (such as power, cooling, software, etc.) However, this causes a new series of problems for the operating systems. With multiple processors, the operating system has to be aware of which processor is doing a particular task, it must allocate resources and jobs properly between the processors, and always give the correct response to the correct processor. All of this greatly complicates the task of managing resources.

Network systems

The next step beyond computers with multiple processors is the concept of setting up a virtual computer that consists of several real computers networked together to appear as one computer to all the users. This has several advantages, particularly in availability; a failure on any single computer will not cause the virtual computer to be unavailable, and therefore, only a major failure of many components of the network will cause the virtual computer to be unavailable. The primary disadvantage of this concept is the difficulty and overhead generated in managing the various resources. The links between the nodes of the network are critical for performance, as is the efficiency of the network operating system.

The network concept frequently provides a cheap way of obtaining large amounts of computing power, but this computing power is not always usable. Since this power is obtained in several small processors instead of one large processor it is very efficient at running several small programs simultaneously, but not efficient at all in running one very large program.

Example 2-5:

OPERATING SYSTEM FUNCTIONS

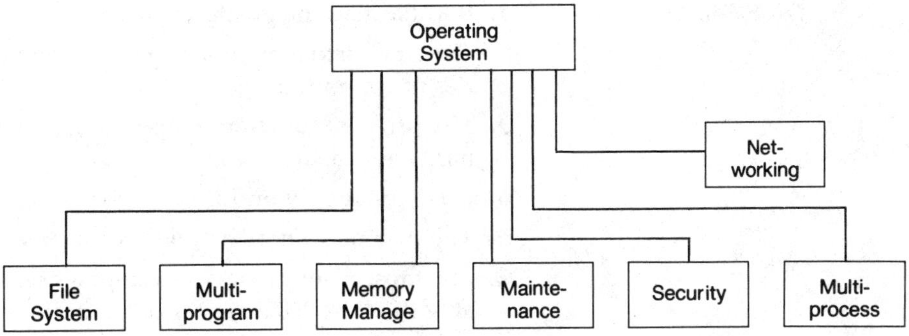

Firmware

Many of the operating system and hardware functions are today being combined in a medium that is neither. There is a trade-off between putting functions in hardware or in software. Hardware is much more difficult to modify, but it provides much greater performance levels. There is an intermediate level, called **firmware** or microcode. This usually is software that is provided on a floppy disk and is loaded into microprocessors running within the computer. These microprocessors then control many of the subsidiary functions the computer must accomplish. Such firmware is more easily modified than hardware, but not as easily as the operating system software. It also provides higher performance than software functions but not usually as good as hardware.

SUMMARY

This chapter has provided a brief overview of the history of operating systems and the major functions that an operating system must provide. The history is somewhat biased in favor of IBM, partly because IBM has always had a tremendous impact on the computer marketplace, and partly because their systems provide a good representation of the evolution of commercial operating systems.

EXERCISES

TRUE/FALSE

1. IBM has had the greatest impact on computer systems development.
2. The first virtual memory operating system was with the IBM 370 series of computers.
3. The primary function of operating systems is to make the computer hardware easily usable.
4. JCL is used only on IBM computers.
5. The first computers had only primitive operating systems.
6. The most revolutionary development in computer history was probably the IBM 360 series of computers.
7. The IBM 360 series of computers provided many opportunities for competitors of IBM to increase their market share.
8. Most operating systems developments during the 1980's were in the area of improved scheduling algorithms.
9. Disk scheduling is almost solely devoted to improving performance.
10. The same job scheduling algorithm, if it is well developed, can be used for time-sharing and batch operating systems.

MULTIPLE CHOICE

1. The practice of "bundling" refers to:
   a) Selling computers alone
   b) Selling peripheral devices with computers
   c) Selling software to run on computers
   d) Giving away software with a computer purchase

2. User-friendly systems are:

a) Common among traditional mainframe operating systems

b) Easy to develop

c) Required for batch-oriented processing

d) Becoming more common

3. The primary purpose of an operating system is:

a) To make the most efficient usage of the computer hardware

b) To allow people to use the computer

c) To keep systems programmers employed

d) To make computers easier to use

4. Real-time systems are:

a) Primarily used on mainframe computers

b) Used for monitoring events as they occur

c) Used for program development

d) Used for real-time interactive users

5. Multiprogramming systems are:

a) Easier to develop than single programming systems

b) Execute each job faster

c) Execute more jobs in the same time period

d) Only used on large mainframe computers

6. Virtual memory is:

a) Simple to implement

b) Used on all major commercial operating systems

c) Less efficient in utilization of memory

d) Useful when fast I/O devices are not available

7. Memory management is:

a) Not used in modern operating systems

b) Replaced with virtual memory on current systems

c) Not used on multiprogramming systems

d) Critical for even the simplest operating systems

8. Scheduling is:

a) Allowing jobs to use the processor

b) Unrelated to performance considerations

c) Quite simple to implement, even on large mainframes

d) The same regardless of the purpose of the system

9. Multiprocessing:
   a) Makes the operating system simpler
   b) Allows multiple processes to run simultaneously
   c) Is completely understood by all major computer vendors
   d) Allows the same computer to have multiple processors
10. Device independence:
    a) Allows the computer to run without I/O devices
    b) Allows programs to be written much more easily
    c) Makes all devices look the same to the operating system
    d) Allows tape drives to be substituted for disk drives

DISCUSSION QUESTIONS

1. Briefly describe the first operating system.
2. What is the concept of multiprogramming?
3. What is device independence?
4. Discuss real-time systems.
5. Discuss the introduction of the first general-purpose operating systems to achieve wide commercial acceptance.
6. What is JCL and why is it important?
7. Briefly discuss virtual memory.
8. Discuss the concept of unbundling.
9. Briefly describe the primary functions of an operating system.
10. List five important functions performed by operating systems.

SYSTEMS SERVICES

3

KEY TERMS

Kernel	*Capacity planning*
Operands	*Systems services*
HELP facilities	*Mnemonics*
Source program	*Context-sensitive HELP*
Line editor	*Prompts*
Compile	*Full-screen editor*
High-level language	*Assemble*
Machine language	*Assembler language*
Linker	*Object code*
Internal references	*Loader*
Load module	*External references*
Command interpreter	*Load map*
Systems generation	*I/O sysgen*

INTRODUCTION

The part of the operating system that handles internal functions is known variously as the core or **kernel** of the operating system. The functional programs are frequently called **systems services,** since they provide services to users.

USER INTERFACE

One of the most important parts of any operating system is the way it appears to the person using it. This is often called the **user interface.** The user interface controls the way the user makes requests and the way the operating system responds to those requests. A good user interface may not improve the performance of the operating system such as a better scheduling algorithm would, but it frequently makes the difference in whether or not the system is accepted or even usable by the users.

On some systems, the user interface is maintained as part of the kernel of the operating system. On other systems, it is supported by a separate program that interprets JCL and arranges for requested services to be provided. The complexity of the user interface depends largely on the amount of flexibility, freedom, and help given to the users. Systems that provide many features are often user friendly, that is, they are easy for the user to learn and operate. The greater the degree of user friendliness the system possesses, the greater the complexity that is necessary in the user interface routines.

Most user interfaces are interactive and allow the user to work closely with the operating system. Interactive interfaces usually use a **prompt** to signal that they are ready for additional input. A prompt is a character or group of characters that is written on the screen; various characters are used by different operating systems, such as: ">" and "R;".

A simple user interface is one where all commands have a pre-determined format, each command is represented by only one mnemonic, all commands are the same length, and each command can do only one very simple function. Such a user interface is relatively easy to program, but is not easy to use. In contrast to this, a good user interface allows the user to enter commands in a format similar to the English language or any language they are familiar with. Such an interface is often difficult to develop, but a great deal of research has been done on developing those features.

A key part of all user interfaces is the way that commands are given, since a major portion of the interaction necessary by the user consists of entering commands. These commands are usually represented by code words, called **mnemonics,** that are a representation of the command. One of the most difficult aspects of setting up the command structure is making it useful to both the experienced and inexperienced users, since their needs are quite different.

Providing different mnemonics for the same command is a good way to make the same system useful to both neophyte and experienced users. Less experienced users do not want to have to remember cryptic mnemonics, but prefer to spell out the command, preferably in something that looks like English. Experienced users, on the other hand, do not want to always have to use several keystrokes to enter a command that they are very familiar with, so they prefer a short, sometimes cryptic, mnemonic. The solution to this problem is to provide at least two mnemonics for all common commands; one that is similar to English, and one that is a short abbreviation of the English command.

Providing many functions for one command is another good way to increase productivity and make the system easier to use. There are many cases where a series of commands must be repetitively executed; it is very useful to have just one command that will execute the entire series of commands. An example of this is the process of compiling and running a program. Even though three or more separate operations may be involved, it is very useful to have one command that will do all those operations in the proper order.

Most commands require information describing how the requested function is to be performed, or on which objects it is to be performed. These pieces of information are included in the command itself, and is called **operands** or **arguments** to the command. The arrangement that the user must give the operands should be structured as carefully as the commands themselves, with all possible effort made to keep the operands as simple and few in number as possible.

One implication of having commands that do complex functions is that they frequently require large numbers of operands. It is usually good to keep the number of operands to a minimum, both because it makes the system easy to use, and because it makes the system easy to develop. This is not always possible, however, in a system that tries to minimize the number of different commands that must be executed to do a particular function.

The basic structure of commands in most operating systems is a format such as:

```
COMMAND OPER1, OPER2, ..., OPERn
```

The "COMMAND" is the operation to be performed, and "OPER1, . . . OPERn" are the operands that supply additional information to allow the operation to be performed correctly. Such operands are sometimes optional and tend to vary in number between commands.

Example 3-1:

SAMPLE COMMANDS

LISTFILE	English — lists all files
L	Abbreviation — also lists all files
LOAD	Loads program into memory
START	Starts program executing
RUN	Both loads and starts program

A very important part of the user interface is the way errors are reported to the user. All users make errors at some time, but novice users tend to make far more of them. An error that may be immediately obvious to an experienced user may cause a novice many hours of frustration before being able to correct the error. Clear, explicit, and easy to understand error messages are critical when a user is attempting to understand and correct errors. Such error messages should appear whenever an error is discovered, and should both explain the error and suggest corrective action.

The trend today is toward various specialized tools to improve the user interface. Such tools have not yet achieved widespread acceptance. Examples of such tools are **cursor keys, touch-screens,** and **mice.** Virtually all terminals today include special keys that improve the user interface. These keys may be quite simple, such as keys that move the cursor around on the screen. They may also be more complex in function, such as programmable function keys, where the user assigns a series of keystrokes that is typed by the keys.

One set of keys that are quite specialized are used to recall and edit the last command entered. Some systems do not support this function at all, others assign it to commonly used keys, while still others have special keys dedicated to it. However the function is supported, it is quite valuable. There are many everyday cases where the next command to be entered is the same as, or a slight variation of, the last command entered. Many keystrokes are saved by being able to recall and edit the last command instead of having to enter the command all over again.

The mouse input device tends to create a love/hate relationship with many users. Some users love using a mouse, while others hate it and prefer using the keyboard. One compromise is to use the keyboard for traditional command entering, but to make the mouse available for those who prefer to use it. When both options are available, each can be used for the application for which it is best suited.

No discussion of user interfaces would be complete without mentioning the unusual user interface implemented on the Apple Macintosh computer. This is an icon-based system where commands are entered by pointing to the appropriate icon on a graphics screen. An **icon** is a pictorial representation of a function, such as a filing cabinet representing the function of storing data.

The Macintosh interface has many good features and a few bad ones. It is unquestionably easy to learn to use. No sophisticated knowledge of computers is necessary to use it, only a little observation and common sense. The penalty exacted for the interface is the complexity involved in developing software to implement that interface. The primary complaint voiced about the interface is that experienced users must still use it, even though they might be faster and more comfortable bypassing the friendliness and using the keyboard in a more traditional manner.

HELP facilities

A very important feature of any operating system that is designed to service novice users is some means of on-line instruction. This on-line instruction is usually called a **HELP facility,** because it can be accessed by entering the word HELP. Such a facility is used frequently by novice users, and surprisingly often by experienced users. There are many occasions when even experienced users need some additional information on some operating system features.

A HELP facility is designed to provide information about commands in the operating system. There are two different types of such facilities. The older type is hierarchically structured, so that both general and specific information about commands can be obtained.

The newer, and better, form of the HELP facility is known as "context-sensitive" HELP. This provides information on whatever command the user is attempting to execute whenever a special key is pressed. If information on a particular command is desired, all that is necessary is to enter that command and then press the HELP key.

Summary

There is an inverse but almost constant relationship between the degree of user friendliness and the complexity of the system. Almost every feature added to increase user friendliness increases the complexity of the system. Despite the added complexity, the marketplace in the 1980's requires a relatively high degree of user-friendliness. It is likely that the systems developed in the future will all require a very high degree of user-friendliness as a prerequisite to selling them.

Operating systems twenty years from now may be quite different from today in the way the user interface is handled. Commands might use a language very similar to English so that users actually talk to the system instead of just entering commands. If artificial intelligence is able to develop fast enough, the system, when first used, might understand a simple natural language and be able to learn from each user. After a short period, the language users use would be tailored just for them.

PROGRAM DEVELOPMENT

One of the most common usages of operating systems is developing programs, so the services provided for program development are quite important. These services fall into two different areas. The first concerns providing tools to make development easier, and the second concerns providing tools to allow the program to be executed.

Before a program can be executed, it must be translated from some programming language, such as FORTRAN or COBOL, into a language the computer can execute, called **machine language.** This process is broken down into several distinct steps, each of which requires services from the operating system. The number of steps varies between operating systems, but the basic functions remain the same.

Example 3-2:

PROGRAM PREPARATION

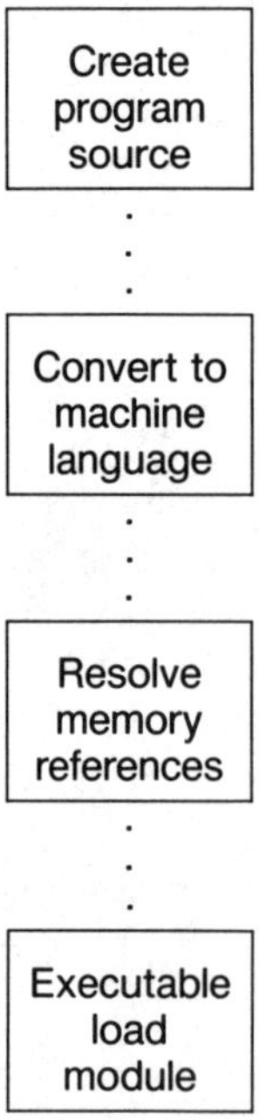

Full-screen editor

The first step in developing any program is to input it to the system. This can be done in a variety of ways, although the most frequent way today is with a **full-screen editor** on a video display. This editor is often a service provided by the system. After the program has been input to the system, it is called a **source program,** because this is the beginnings of the program. It is also sometimes known as "source code", "source module", or just "source".

A full-screen editor is much faster and easier to use than a **line editor.** A line editor is designed to operate on a single line of a program, although some commands function on many lines. Specific commands are required to cause a line editor to display more than one line. The only way to change to line in the program is to move to that line and use a change command. A full-screen editor always displays many lines of source code, which is usually twenty to twenty-four lines. Any character displayed on the screen can be changed by just moving the terminal cursor to that position on the screen and typing in the new character.

Example 3-3:

FULL-SCREEN EDIT SAMPLE

```
NAPPLIC PLIOPT A1   F 80  TRUNC=72 SIZE=220 LINE=169 COL=2 ALT=0
====>

00169     MONTH='12' & DAY='25'
     ....+....1....+....2....+....3....+....4....+....5....+..>
00170     MONTH='12' & DAY='30'
00171     MONTH='12' & DAY='31' THEN NSHIFT = 2;
00172    SHIFT2:
00173     TEMP = TOTCPU;
00174     IF NSHIFT = 1 THEN DTOTAL = DTOTAL + TEMP / 1000;
00175     ELSE OTOTAL = OTOTAL + TEMP / 1000;
00176
00177     IF CPUREC.BATCH<BATNAME THEN DO;      /* UNKNOWN */
00178        IF NSHIFT = 1 THEN DAYTOTU = DAYTOTU + TEMP;
00179        ELSE OFFTOTU = OFFTOTU + TEMP;
00180        GO TO READCPU;
00181     END;
00182
00183     IF CPUREC.BATCH=BATNAME THEN DO;      /*  MATCH */
00184        IF NSHIFT=1 THEN DAYTOT = DAYTOT + TEMP;
00185        ELSE OFFTOT = OFFTOT + TEMP / 1000;
00186        NUMREC = NUMREC + 1;
00187        GO TO READCPU;
00188     END;
```

Compilation

After writing source code, you **compile** or **assemble** the program. If the program is in a **high-level language** such as FORTRAN, it will be compiled, but if it is in **assembler language** then it will be assembled. Either process takes a source program and converts it into a form of machine language, which is the most basic form of instruction input to the computer. Machine language is just a series of numbers that the computer interprets and executes as instructions.

The process of preparing a program to execute is similar whether the program is written in assembler or a high-level language. Assembler language is very similar to machine language. It uses the same instructions, but the instructions are in alphabetic characters instead of numbers. Each instruction is specified by a mnemonic abbreviation. High level languages, such as FORTRAN or Pascal, use a much more English-like structure. The distinction between assembler language and a high level language is that each assembler language instruction is converted into one machine language instruction, whereas each high level language instruction may be converted into several machine language instructions.

The compilation or assembly results in **object code,** which is almost, but not quite, ready to execute. The mnemonic instructions in the program have been converted to machine language instructions, but references to internal memory, such as variables and constants, are not set up by the compiler or assembler.

Linking

The program that finishes the program preparation process is called a **linker** or **loader.** It is also sometimes known as a "link editor" or "linking loader." The linker takes the object code module created by a compiler or an assembler, finds all of the unresolved memory references in it, and puts the correct memory values in.

Memory references resolved by the linker are "internal" and "external". Internal memory references are references to variables, constants, or subprograms that are defined in the program itself. External memory references are references to variables, constants, or subprograms that are defined in some other program or in the operating system.

Resolving external memory references requires that the program in which those references are defined be found and included in the same final machine language program. Any such other programs must be defined to the linker, and must already be compiled or assembled separately. These separate object code modules are combined together into one larger machine language program. Each of the programs must be written so that such a combination is possible.

The final output of the linker is the executable program. This is called a **load module.** The load module can be stored and executed in the future. Every executable program on the systems is a load module and has gone through the same preparation process.

A **load map** is also generated by the linker. The load map is most useful when several different programs are combined to form one final program, because it shows how the programs were combined. It shows the address at which the program is to start executing, and the address of each of the major components, such as external memory references within the module. It is very useful in debugging the program, since debugging may require tracing the instructions executed, or viewing the contents or some variable, both of which require knowing specific memory locations for certain component programs or variables.

The distinction between loaders and linkers is sometimes blurry, because some operating systems use only one of the two. In operating systems that support both a linker and a loader, the primary distinctions are that a linker supports more functions than a loader but also uses more overhead. The loader usually will only resolve memory references, link modules together, and load and execute the program. The linker will do those things as well as creating a load module, and usually has more options available.

Example 3-4:

PROGRAM PREPARATION

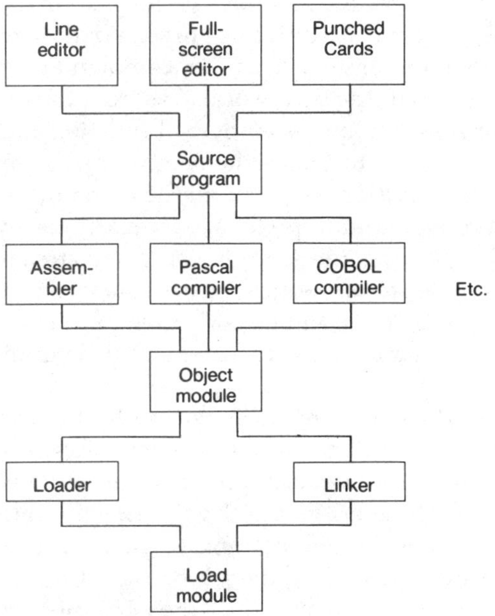

Development tools

The services covered in the previous section are sufficient to develop programs, but some operating systems provide a number of other software tools that enhance the development. Many of these tools are only used on a few operating systems, but any system that is used for software development would do well to supply at least some of these tools.

The design goal of such software development tools is to provide some of the common functions that are needed only by software developers and to provide the building blocks of programs. A software library maintenance system, for example is quite useful for a group of software developers who maintain libraries of programs, although such a tool is of limited usefulness in the general marketplace. Another category of tools, building block programs, provide functions that are frequently needed for programs. These functions can be incorporated into new programs without writing a program to perform that function.

JCL OR COMMAND INTERPRETER

Each system that has a form of JCL must have a part of the operating system devoted to translating that JCL into a form understandable by the operating system and executing it. This function is performed by a module, or group of modules, called a JCL interpreter or **command interpreter.**

An example of the functions performed by such a command interpreter is specifying an area on a disk drive to store data. Some systems require a detailed specification for all such areas. The command interpreter removes the burden of actually specifying such work areas from the programmer. Instead, the programmer merely requests an overall function such as compilation. The command interpreter then takes the programmer's request and expands it into the detailed specifications required by the operating system.

The command interpreter acts similarly to any other language processing utility. It first reads in the input command stream and scans it for syntactical errors. If there are such errors, they are flagged by the interpreter and the job is returned to the programmer for correction. If there are no syntactical errors, the interpreter analyzes each statement to determine what, if any, action is required.

Those statements requiring action by the command interpreter are processed and the requested facilities are made available. If there are any non-syntactical errors in the statements, they are found when the requested action is performed. These errors are flagged and the interpreter either immediately aborts the job stream or attempts to guess at what correct action was desired and continues processing the job stream. If there are no detectable errors, all requested services are set up and the job is queued for execution.

Example 3-5:

SAMPLE JCL

```
//DITCOR    EXEC PGM=SORT
//SORTLIB   DD   DSNAME=SSY1.SORTLIB,DISP=SHR
//SORTIN    DD   DSN=&DSNQ..CARPSI,DISP=OLD
//SORTWK01  DD   UNIT=SYSDA,SPACE=(550,(100),,CONTIG)
//SORTWK02  DD   UNIT=SYSDA,SPACE=(550,(100),,CONTIG)
//SORTWK03  DD   UNIT=SYSDA,SPACE=(550,(100),,CONTIG)
//SORTOUT   DD   DSN=&&SORTOUT,DISP=(NEW,PASS),UNIT=SYSDA,
                 SPACE=(550,(100,200)),
                 DCB=(BLKSIZE=550,LRECL=55,RECFM=FB)
//SYSOUT    DD   &OUTA
//SYSUDUMP  DD   &OUTA
//SYSIN     DD   DSN=&DSNQ..OS.CTLCARD(CORPSRT),DISP=SHR
//
```

SYSTEM PREPARATION

A large number of services are necessary to set up and run an operating system. These services are seldom visible to the user (except in the case of a single-user system), but are critical to the user or systems programmer that must set up and maintain the system. These services can be as simple as using PC-DOS to format a diskette, or as complex as using the SMP program to maintain MVS.

There is almost always some procedure necessary to initially tailor an operating system to a specific hardware environment. This process is called **systems generation,** or **sysgen.** The major part of the tailoring is describing to the operating system the exact specifications of the peripheral devices which are attached to that computer. The operating systems must operate all of the peripheral devices attached to that computer, and the exact type of attachment of each physical device is important.

Forcing each individual application program to handle the devices would be wasteful, both in duplicating programming between applications (the device handling features) and in time spent configuring several programs identically. Sophisticated operating systems control all of the peripheral devices themselves; instead of individually configuring each new software package when it arrives, the systems programmer configures the operating system for all application programs. This allows the configuration effort to be done fewer times and eliminates the device-handling programming from the applications.

The process of configuring an operating system for all of the available physical devices is sometimes called an "I/O sysgen", or **iogen.** A full systems generation frequently has several additional considerations, such as specifying characteristics of the computer itself. For example, with an operating system that runs on more than one type of computer, the type of the current computer must be specified. Other physical characteristics of the computer, such as the amount of memory available, must also be specified.

The first systems generation performed on a particular operating system frequently requires much more than just configuring the system. The current trend is to build the system as completely as possible before distributing it to the customers, but this trend has not yet achieved complete success. Many operating systems are distributed to customers in a piecemeal fashion, somewhat similar to "some assembly required" toys. These systems are distributed with their component parts on computer tapes, and those parts must be used to build a complete system.

On some operating systems, putting the components together is a very complex process that takes an experienced systems programmer several days to complete successfully. The length of time and difficulty in building the system is partially determined by the number and type of systems tools or services that are available to help build the system. A good system will have sufficient services available so that the system generation process is largely automated, and the systems programmer need only specify certain parameters and monitor the process to ensure that it completes successfully.

Systems that have a large number of complex components and sub-systems required tend to take much longer to put together. Many of the sub-systems are themselves of a considerable size and complexity, and may require hours or days to install. A system with a large number of complex sub-systems can take several weeks to install.

A system with such a large number of components also increases the testing requirements. Whenever a new or updated operating system is installed, it should be thoroughly tested to ensure correct functioning. All the major manufacturers carefully test their systems for problems before distributing them, but there are enough different system configurations available so that there is no guarantee that that system will work correctly in all environments. Thorough testing of both an operating system and all related sub-systems may sometimes require several additional weeks to complete. It is not uncommon for large installations to schedule several months for the installation and testing of new operating systems.

Example 3-6:

SYSTEM GENERATION

1. Prepare the disk drive(s) to receive the system
2. Download the components from tape
3. Load the distributed system
4. Configure the I/O part of the system
5. Configure the computer part of the system
6. Combine the components to build a new system
7. Load the new system

SYSTEM MAINTENANCE

It is unfortunate that operating systems are never completely free from bugs. This is not a reflection on the programmers writing the system, but rather on the complexity of the system. The existence of these bugs requires that the vendor maintain a large support staff to constantly fix problems in the operating system. This staff is often separate from the systems programmers who are constantly developing enhancements and new features for the system.

Both the enhancements and the problem fixes must be distributed to the customers, and the systems programmers at the customer sites must apply those fixes to the operating system. The process of applying the fixes and enhancements to the operating system can be extremely difficult or relatively easy, depending largely upon the services available.

A well-designed operating system has services available that make applying changes a semi-automated, relatively error-free process. These services should allow systems programmers to receive a tape with changes from the vendor, easily view documentation on the specifics of the changes, decide which changes to apply to their system, run a single program that automatically applies specific changes, and then test the results of the changes. A system that requires much more than this from the systems programmers can lead to some necessary changes not being applied or to the systems programming staff being larger than it needs to be.

One of the reasons for the large number of fixes being distributed is that operating systems inevitably fail at some time. When a systems "crash" occurs, everything possible should be done to avert a recurrence of the crash. This, of course, means that the cause of the crash must be determined. Some system crashes are the result of the failure of something not a part of the operating system (such as the hardware or electrical power), and it is relatively easy to find the cause of these crashes. Other crashes are not so easy to diagnose.

The cause of system crashes due to a failure of the operating system itself can seldom be determined while the crash is occurring, since the system is often no longer responding. Frequently, all the information that can be obtained about the systems crash is a **dump** (or picture) of memory taken at the time of the crash. A very useful service an operating system can provide is a program to aid in analyzing dumps. Such a utility can greatly expedite the analysis of dumps.

SYSTEMS PERFORMANCE

One of the primary tasks of systems programmers is that of monitoring and improving system performance. Systems changes can sometimes result in significant improvements in overall performance. This is an improvement that can save millions of dollars that might have been spent to buy larger computers.

The task of improving systems performance is dependent on knowledge of the characteristics of current systems performance. This knowledge requires tools or services that supply information about the performance of the operating system. These tools should provide a high level overview of systems performance, but should also have much more detailed information available. Such tools are covered in detail later in this text.

Capacity planning

An area that is closely tied to performance enhancement is that of **capacity planning.** While performance enhancement is the attempt to get the most possible performance from the existing hardware and software, capacity planning is making sure that adequate hardware and software are available for the amount of resources needed in the future. Since this is basically a prediction of the future, it is not possible to be totally accurate. With the aid of certain tools, it is possible to be accurate to within a relatively small margin.

The accuracy of the prediction is dependent upon the type and accuracy of the data and the accuracy of the tool used to make the prediction. The information used is taken from that collected by the performance monitoring tools, and must be over a relatively long period of time. The information must also represent times when the load on the system is normal and when it is extreme.

Capacity planning tools use models of computer performance to predict the future load, and whether or not the capacity at that time will be adequate to handle that load. It is usually also necessary to input estimates of workload growth. The planning tool correlates current performance statistics, estimates of future loads, and the computer configuration, to predict whether the available capacity will be sufficient to meet the need at some time in the future. From this prediction comes decisions about when to add additional computing power or I/O peripherals.

MISCELLANEOUS

Many of the functions that are standard and part of the kernel of the operating system on one system are auxiliary and more of a systems service on other systems. An example of this is the batch monitor, which is provided as a systems service on IBM's VM operating system but not on other computers. Other systems that were initially developed as batch systems have this capability as part of the normal scheduling algorithms in the kernel.

Other functions that are provided by some operating systems cannot properly be called systems services since they are the size and complexity of operating systems themselves. These products are designed to supply additional features not included in that particular host operating system, although they might be included in another operating system.

SUMMARY

Systems services mean different things for each operating system. Systems services is a very loose term that can be used to refer to a wide variety of operating system features. This chapter has taken the approach that systems services can be defined as some service offered by the operating system that does not clearly fit into any other category.

Many of these systems services control the way the operating system interfaces with the user. This is perhaps the most important feature of the operating system, although it has frequently been neglected in the past. Some of the necessary and important features of the user interface include a full-screen editor, a command structure designed for both novice and experienced users, a simple HELP facility, and a large number of software tools.

Another category of systems services is designed to assist the systems programmers in setting up and maintaining the operating system. Other features that allow the performance of the system to be monitored are also necessary. Maintaining and improving systems performance is critical, particularly on large systems, and this requires system tools be provided to the systems programmer. Additional tools are sometimes available to assist in capacity planning.

EXERCISES

TRUE/FALSE

1. Systems services are normally supplied as part of the kernel of the operating system.
2. Programs can be executed as soon as they have been compiled.
3. Both a linker and a loader are necessary for program preparation.
4. System generation is the process of writing an operating system.
5. One of the most important parts of systems programming is putting bug fixes on systems.
6. Improving systems performance requires extensive monitoring of the operating system functions by programs not associated with the operating system.
7. A systems monitor should have only a general display.
8. The most important of a modern operating system is the user interface.
9. A compiler is used to generate machine language if the resulting program is to be saved; otherwise an assembler is used.

MULTIPLE CHOICE

1. The user interface is:
   - **a)** Relatively unimportant
   - **b)** Slanted toward novice users
   - **c)** Supports both novice and experienced users
   - **d)** Easy to provide, even with good support
2. Full-screen editors:
   - **a)** Are common in current major systems
   - **b)** Are only a frill, and not really useful
   - **c)** Are not considered important by the users
   - **d)** Are useless on real-time operating systems
3. Most systems provide:
   - **a)** Only one compiler
   - **b)** Several compilers and an assembler
   - **c)** Either compilers or an assembler
   - **d)** An assembler, with several compilers available, but not included
4. System generation:
   - **a)** Is always quite simple
   - **b)** Is always very difficult

c) Varies in difficulty between systems

d) Requires extensive tools to be understandable

5. Systems maintenance:

a) Is usually not necessary

b) Is not required if the system is well-written

c) Is necessary on all systems, regardless of how good

d) Always requires several programmers

6. Object code:

a) Is ready to execute

b) Is the output of compilers, but not assemblers

c) Must be loaded before execution

d) Must be re-written before execution

7. The command interpreter:

a) Is usually the primary user interface

b) Requires fixed-format commands

c) Is menu-driven

d) Is quite different from the JCL interpreter

8. Capacity planning:

a) Is not needed in small installations

b) Requires detailed system performance information

c) Is independent of the operating system

d) Does not depend upon the monitoring tools available

9. The linker:

a) Is the same as the loader

b) Is required to create a load module

c) Uses source code as input

d) Is always used before programs are executed

10. Assembler language:

a) Is a mnemonic version of the RPG language

b) Is another name for machine language

c) Is a mnemonic form of machine language

d) Must be compiled before it is executed

DISCUSSION QUESTIONS

1. List four types of major system services and explain the function of each.
2. Briefly describe the concept of "user friendly".
3. Explain context sensitive help and why it is useful.
4. List and explain the steps in preparing a program for execution.
5. Why is a full-screen editor better than a line editor?
6. Explain the function of a command interpreter.
7. Explain the term "iogen".
8. List the major steps in a full system generation.
9. Explain the primary functions of system maintenance tools.
10. Explain the primary functions of capacity planning tools.

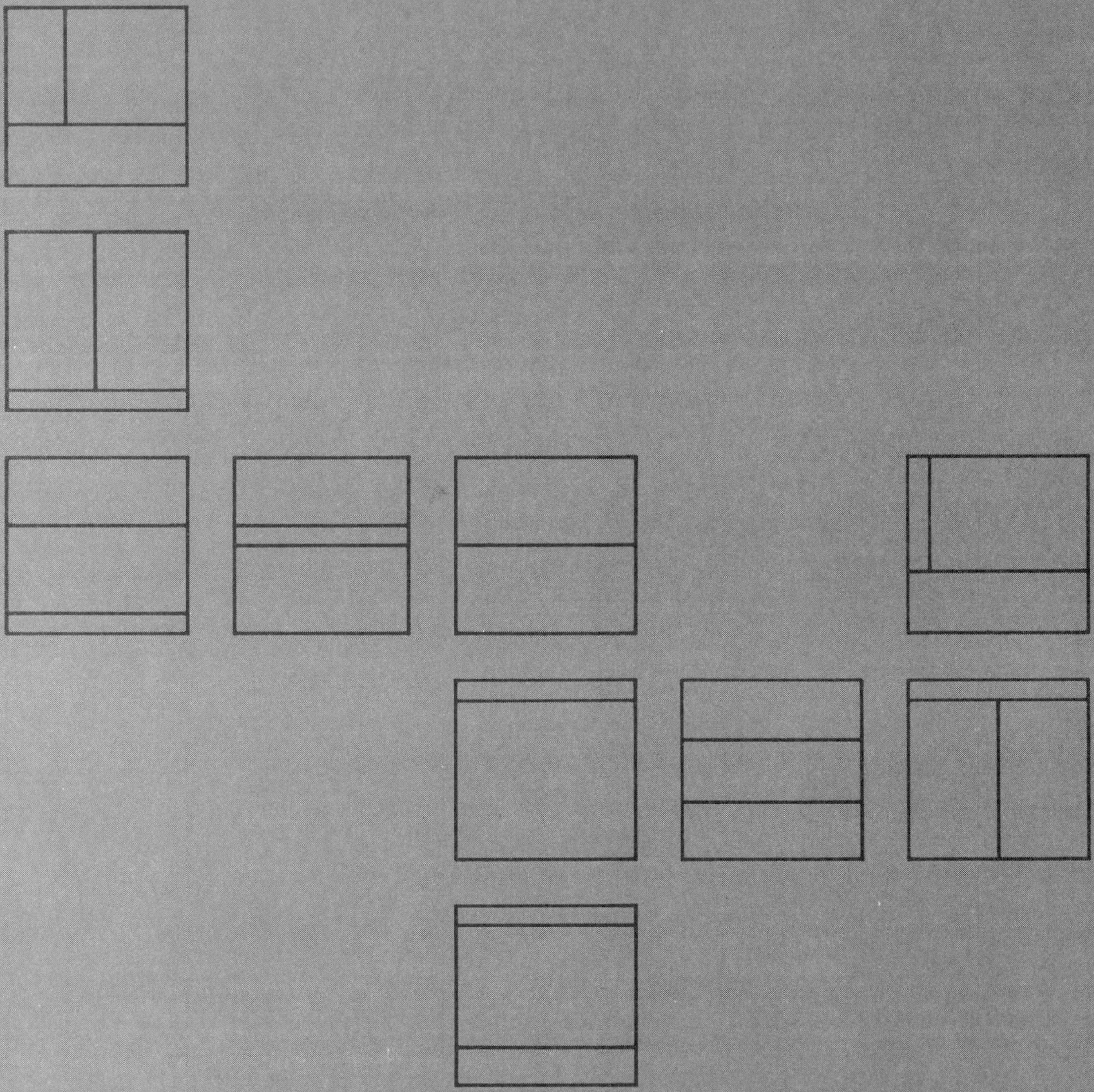

FILE SYSTEMS

4

KEY TERMS

Data set	*Disaster recovery*
Direct access storage devices (DASD)	*File*
Seek time	*Rotational delay*
File records	*Sequential data sets*
Indexed sequential data sets	*Partitioned data sets*
Direct data sets	*Fixed length records*
Record formats	*Undefined length records*
Variable length records	*File descriptor block*
Fragmentation	*Allocation map*
Directory	*Incremental backup*
Wild-card specifiers	*File compression*

INTRODUCTION

Computers are designed to process data. All other operations performed by a computer are support operations that allow more or better processing of data. The requirements for handling data differ between applications, but all applications have such requirements. It is therefore very important that the facilities provided allow data to be manipulated easily and quickly.

The file system of an operating system plays a crucial role in determining how fast and how easily the data accessed via that operating system can be manipulated. The file system should be designed to match the design objectives of the operating system itself. This is why, for example, the file system for a production-oriented operating system is not designed the same way as the file system for an interactive software development system.

FILES

Data is usually organized in collections called **data sets** or **files.** It is therefore important to understand what constitutes a file and how the data in a file can be formatted. A file can be regarded simply as a collection of logically related data. This can be a stack of punch cards, a group of information on a magnetic tape, etc. As long as the data in a particular collection is logically related in some way, it can be thought of as a file. Most operating systems, however, have specific types of files where the data must adhere to much stricter rules to be considered a file.

Virtually all files in a modern computer system are maintained on two different physical media. One media, which has a low cost and high capacity, is magnetic tape. The magnetic tapes used by computers are very similar in appearance to the magnetic tapes used in reel-to-reel recorders, and are used in the same way to record and playback data.

The primary problem with magnetic tape is that access is relatively slow. The tape must be physically mounted onto a tape drive before the data on it can be accessed. The necessary handling of the tape also tends to cause reliability problems. This problem has been addressed by the new cartridge tape drives, which promise to revolutionize the computer tape industry the same way cassette tape drives did the consumer industry, but the slow access time remains a problem.

The other major media used to maintain files is **direct access storage devices,** or **DASD,** or **disk drives.** These are very similar to the fixed disks used in microcomputers, except that the disk drives used on large computers have much greater speed and capacity than those used in microcomputers. They are called "direct access" because a file maintained on such a device can be accessed randomly, or "directly". For example, it is not necessary to begin reading such a file at the beginning; any part of it may be accessed at any time.

The files discussed in this text will be assumed to be on disk drives. There are two reasons for this assumption. Most files do indeed reside on disk drives, and files on other physical devices can usually be treated similarly to files on disk drives.

Knowledge of how disk drives work is critical for understanding many of the performance items presented later. A disk drive consists of aluminum platters coated with iron oxide that rotate at very high speeds. Data is recorded on them by modifying the orientation of the magnetic particles on the surface (very much like tape). Reading and writing data is performed by "heads" which are on an arm extending in a straight line from the edge of the platters to the hub.

The head can access any location on a platter by moving forward or backward until oriented over the circle that contains the desired location. Once the head is over the proper circle, that location is accessed by waiting until the rotation of the platter brings it under the head.

The primary delays when accessing data on a disk drive stem from the forward and backward motion of the head, called **seek time,** and the time until the location rotates under the head, called **rotational delay.** Data that is physically contiguous on the disk drive is usually quicker to access since the seek time and rotational delays are reduced.

File Format

The data within a file is not usually randomly organized, but is instead grouped into logically related collections. These collections of data are called **records.**

Each record has the same type of information as all other records, although the information in the records varies. A good comparison is a checkbook register. Each entry in the register keeps the check number, amount, date, etc., so that each entry keeps the same type of information. These smaller items are called **fields.** Similarly, each record in a file keeps the same type of information.

The simplest and most common file format is **sequential files.** This is the format adopted by all non-direct devices, such as magnetic tapes, cards, printout, etc., and by some files on direct access devices. If the location of the current record is known, then the location of the next record is known as well, since it immediately follows the current record. This is a very simple format, although it is seldom the most efficient. This is the only type of file that does not require a direct access device.

Example 4-1:

SEQUENTIAL FILE ORGANIZATION

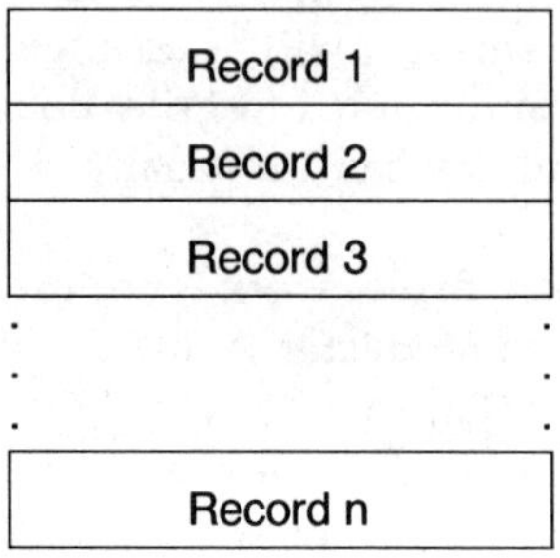

A more efficient organization is **indexed sequential files,** often called **ISAM files.** These files are arranged in a complex manner that allows more efficient access by a program. Each record in the file has a part of it defined as a **key field.** This key must be unique for each record and must be in the same location on each record. The operating system keeps an index of the record keys and allows each record to be accessed either sequentially or by specifying the unique key for that record.

Example 4-2:

INDEXED SEQUENTIAL FILE ORGANIZATION

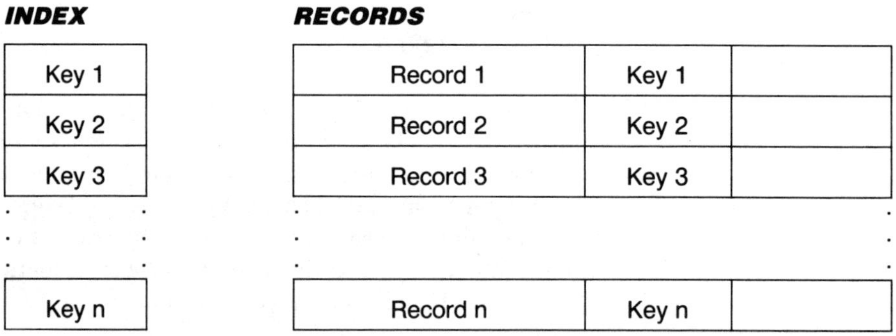

Another type of file is a **direct file,** sometimes known as a **direct access file.** These files allow tremendous flexibility in formatting. The records are not set up to be accessed in a sequential fashion. The address of each record is maintained by the program. When access to a particular record is desired, the program must determine the address of that record and issue the proper command to access it. This address may be maintained in a variety of different ways, each of which is the responsibility of the program.

Example 4-3:

DIRECT FILE ORGANIZATION

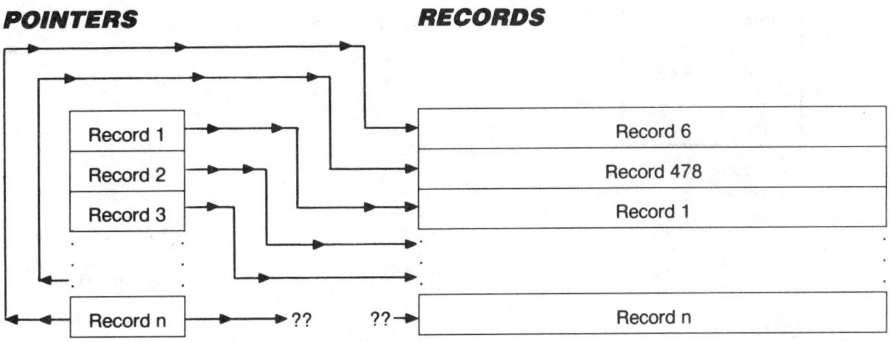

A more specialized file format is used by **partitioned files,** sometimes known as **partitioned data sets** or **PDS**'s. They incorporate many of the characteristics of both sequential and indexed files. They consist of a group of members, each of which is a sequential file. The PDS has an index that contains the location of the beginning of each member. This index is maintained by giving each member a simple name. Partitioned files are frequently used to store groups of programs and are thus sometimes known as libraries. Each member can be accessed by specifying the name of the partitioned file and then the member name.

Example 4-4:

PARTITIONED DATA SET

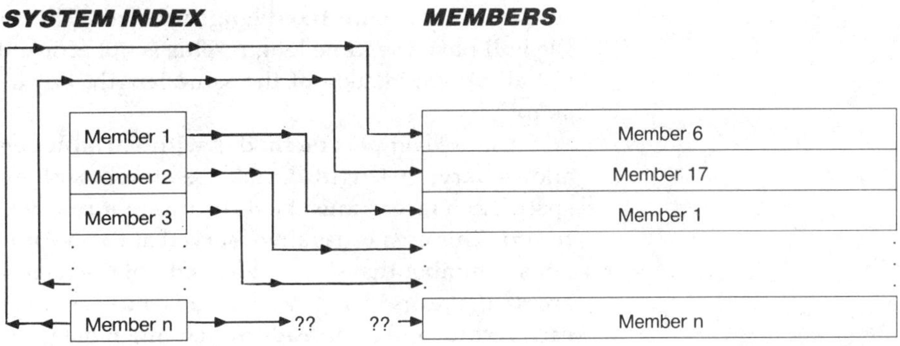

(Continued on page 64)

Example 4-4:
Continued from page 63

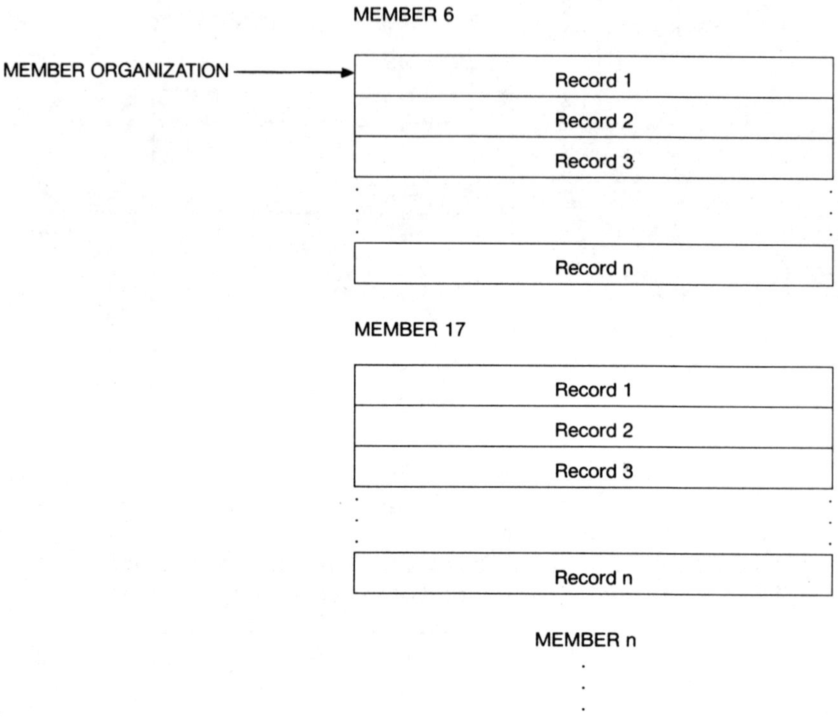

RECORD FORMATS

The records within each file can be formatted in several different ways. The simplest way is with **fixed length** records. This means that each record in the file will have the same length. This is not efficient if the data in the records is not all approximately of the same length, but it has the advantage of being simple.

A more complex method is with **variable length** records in the file. This allows varying length data to be stored without wasting large amounts of space. Each record must have an area in it reserved to contain the length of the record. This area is usually reserved at the beginning of each record, and contains a number that shows the length of the record. Whenever such records are accessed, the operating system reads the specified record from the beginning of each record, and then reads in that much data.

The last method is with **undefined length** records. In this case each record may be of any length and no length checking is performed by the operating system. This format allows more flexibility in the file format but it requires the program to do more processing than would otherwise be done by the operating system.

File efficiency

The way the file is organized has a tremendous impact on the efficiency with which it can be accessed. In general, the most efficient technique is to allow the operating system to do as much as possible of any necessary error checking and file maintenance. In cases where the records are of widely varying lengths, fixed length records are very wasteful of space, so those cases should use variable length records. Undefined length records should be used only when some other programming reason requires their use.

Another very critical element in improving the efficiency of file accesses is the way records are set up to be transmitted to and from the peripheral devices. Direct access devices usually operate most efficiently on large volumes of data, and data records are usually too small be efficient. The most efficient way to transmit these records is to group them into "blocks", and then transmit a whole block at a time. This greatly reduces the overhead inherent in both the operating system and the computer hardware.

The blocking of records is done by the operating system, although it can be requested by an application program. The operating system sets up buffers to save output records until several have been collected, then outputs them as a block. A similar technique can be used on input, so that several records are read at once, even though the user program has only requested one record. This particular technique works best on sequential files. If the file is being accessed randomly, the extra records the operating system read in the block may never be used. All of the operating system blocking of records should be completely transparent to the user programs.

FILE SYSTEM STRUCTURE

Many of the systems services that the user sees are connected with the file system. These services include the ability to create, modify, delete, copy, change the name, and display the contents of a file. The file system must have a directory that maintains information on the various files accessible by a particular user, and many services related to this directory. These services should provide the capability to list the files owned, display information about each file, and perform various file functions directly from the list. A facility that allows users to share data with each other in a controlled manner is also useful, as are other features such as providing a backup and recovery facility for files and security for files.

There are two primary considerations for file system services. The first is the implementation of the file structure. This implementation may be completely invisible to the user, but it is critical for operating systems performance.

The second is the user interface to the file system. This is the way the user sees the file system, and may be quite different from the internal construction of the file system.

The average file size and the average activity of a file must be considered before designing the file system. A system devoted to timesharing usage, such as program development, may have from fifty to several hundred users, each of whom uses from twenty-five to two hundred files. Each of these files will probably be rather small, and only a few of them will be used often. On the other hand, a system devoted to large batch applications such as financial systems, may have fewer than ten users, each of whom has only five to ten files, but each of these files may be huge and will see high daily activity.

Contiguous allocation

Files can be allocated on a disk in several different ways. The simplest way is to allocate the file in contiguous disk space. This means that the entire file is contained in one physical area on the disk. This system has several advantages and disadvantages. The first advantage is that there is much less overhead associated with this allocation, since there is very little processing involved with locating each record of the file. Locating the file in one physical area tends to enhance the performance of the system by reducing location calculations in the operating system and seek time on the disk. This allocation is most appropriate on operating systems with a few large, inactive files where the emphasis is on improving performance and reducing operating system overhead and complexity.

There are two primary disadvantages with contiguous allocations. The first is the difficulty of finding a large, contiguous, unused area of disk space when creating a file. Even when such large amounts of disk space exist, the allocations tend to be rather wasteful of disk space. This is because of a problem that is known as **fragmentation.**

Fragmentation is a process where areas of disk space become unusable because of they are too small to hold full files. Such areas can quickly accumulate until a large part of the total disk space is unusable. The problem develops as many files are allocated so that they occupy areas close to one another. Whenever one of these files needs to increase in size, it must be allocated somewhere else, since there is not enough space near it on the disk to allow growth. The old space that file occupied is now free, but may be too small for any other file to be allocated. The same condition arises when a file is erased.

Whenever a file is erased, or moved, the old area it occupied becomes an unused area on the disk surrounded by used areas. This area can be allocated to another file the same size or smaller than the old file, but very rarely will a file or combination of files be available to exactly fill the unused area. This means that some disk area is permanently unused because of the inability to fit a file into that area. As this process continues, a significant part of the total available disk area may become unusable (sometimes as much as half). This condition can only be avoided by periodically running a cleanup program that goes through the entire available disk area and moves each file into adjacent areas, thus consolidating the used disk space into one area and the unused space into another area.

Example 4-5:

FRAGMENTATION

File 1
Unused
File 2
Unused
File 3
Unused
File 4
Unused

Since the files are all much larger than each of the unused areas, those unused areas will not be usable unless a smaller file appears, even though the total unused area is easily large enough to contain another file.

A second disadvantage of contiguous file allocations is that they require the user to know how large the file is to be before it is first allocated. This leads to either large allocations that waste a large amount of disk space, or to smaller allocations with frequent re-allocations. The first approach can easily lead to a great deal of disk space being wasted, and the second can lead to a large amount of overhead associated with frequent disk consolidations.

Linked files

A much more flexible approach to file allocation is to use a system that allocates non-contiguous areas of disk space to a file. This can be accomplished in several ways, and allows efficient utilization of disk space. More operating system overhead and complexity is required to maintain a non-contiguous file system, but the increased flexibility of the file structure is completely justified for almost all operating systems.

One way of implementing a non-contiguous file system is by using links between the different blocks which make up a file. In a system like this, the first block of a file has an area that holds the address of the physical location of the next block in the file. That block in turn has the location of the next block, and so on.

Example 4-6:

CHAINED LINK FILE

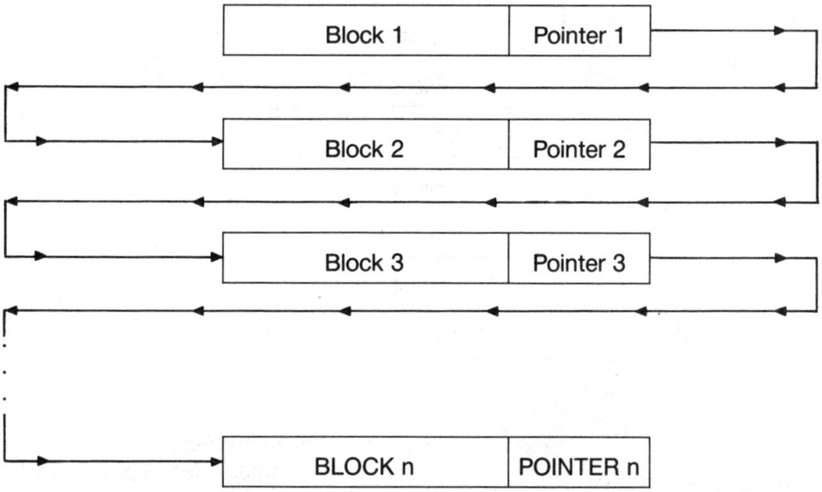

Another technique that can be used to allocate file blocks is similar to that used in direct data sets. In this case, a pointer to all blocks in a file is kept in a **file descriptor block.**

Example 4-7:

FILE ORGANIZATION

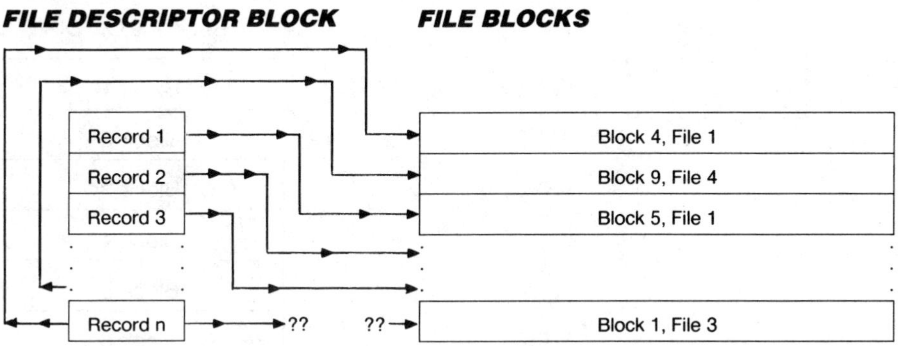

Allocation map

The operating system must flag which areas of the disk are used and which areas are available, regardless of the allocation method used for the file system. The method of tracking the disk space allocations is frequently done with an **allocation map.**

The most common allocation method is to use a combination of the contiguous and non-contiguous methods. The process is to divide the total available disk area into blocks that are relatively small. Frequent choices for block sizes are 512, 1,024, or 2,048 bytes. Each file is then put into as many blocks as it needs, and the only space wasted is some portion of one block. The allocation map is set up with one bit for each block. If that block is allocated to a file, then the bit is turned on; otherwise, the block is available and the bit is not on.

Example 4-8:

BIT MAP

110100 . . .1

BLOCKS ON DISK

IN USE	Block 1
IN USE	Block 2
FREE	Block 3
IN USE	Block 4
FREE	Block 5
FREE	Block 6
	. . .
IN USE	Block n

Directory

The **directory** of a file system is somewhat like a telephone directory. It maintains the name and characteristics of the files in that file system. Most of the information in the directory is based on information in the file descriptor block. Some systems use the directory and the file descriptor block interchangeably, but other systems keep separate entities. The directory usually maintains information about the files that is useful to the user, while the file descriptor block maintains information that is useful to the operating system. Some of this information (such as the size of the file) is the same, but other things, such as the allocation bit map, are only useful to the operating system.

The directory should contain the name of all of the files in the file system. This is the name by which the user references each file. The presence of all of the file names in the directory provides a quick and easy way of listing all of the files in that area of the disk. Various other information about the files should also be included in the directory, such as the date and time the file was last modified, the size of the file, the type of file (data, FORTRAN, memos, etc.), and the way the file is organized (sequential, direct, PDS, etc.). There are other features that are not as necessary but also might be useful, such as the creation date of the file, the type of disk device on which the file resides, the type of access allowed to that file, and the number of accesses made to that file.

Example 4-9:

SAMPLE VM/CMS DIRECTORY FILE LISTING (SORTED BY DATE)

FILENAME	FILETYPE	Fm	FMT	LRECL	RECORDS	BLOCKS	DATE	TIME
RESPONSE	ASSEMBLE	A1	F	80	43	1	1/10/85	12:47:44
TYPECON	ASSEMBLE	A1	F	1024	7	2	7/31/84	11:32:06
TAPECOPY	ASSEMBLE	A1	F	1024	20	5	7/31/84	11:32:05
DISKZAP	ASSEMBLE	A1	F	1024	25	7	7/31/84	11:32:04
SUPERID	ASSEMBLE	A1	F	1024	2	1	7/31/84	11:32:04
CLASS	ASSEMBLE	A1	F	1024	9	3	7/31/84	11:32:03
TRIVRESP	ASSEMBLE	A1	F	80	39	1	6/06/84	8:38:06
3081RIO	ASSEMBLE	A1	F	80	451	9	6/05/84	8:54:35
3081SYS	ASSEMBLE	A1	F	80	45	1	6/05/84	8:53:20
3081SNT	ASSEMBLE	A1	F	80	256	5	6/05/84	8:53:19
EXTTAPE	ASSEMBLE	A1	F	80	33	1	5/23/84	9:22:47
TRAIN	ASSEMBLE	A0	F	80	323	7	4/12/84	15:50:15
PROBLEM	ASSEMBLE	A1	F	80	144	3	1/20/84	12:11:19
ANALYST	ASSEMBLE	A1	F	80	177	4	12/29/83	16:18:37

FILE SYSTEM SERVICES

The basic file services are the ability to create, modify, delete, copy, change the name, and display the contents of a file. Each of these functions should be provided in a way that is both efficient and easy to use.

Creating files

Creating a file can be done in several different ways. Each way should be as easy as possible. One way is to create output from a program. Facilities should be provided that allow a file to be created with default characteristics and requiring only the fewest possible parameters, such as the file name and type. For the programmer who desires to carefully tailor the characteristics of the file, other facilities should be provided that allow the file to be created with each characteristic carefully listed. The general principle is that simple, easy-to-use facilities should be available to the programmer who just wants a file without worrying about setting it up in any particular way, and other facilities should be available for the programmer who desires to set a file up in a particular fashion.

Files can also be created by capturing input from other peripheral devices, such as tape drives or card readers. In this case, the same general rules should be followed as in creating a file with a program. The most frequent method of file creation is with an editor, such as those discussed earlier.

It is very helpful if the same command with the same arguments can be used to create files from each of the different input sources. This allows users to become effective without having to learn several different ways of creating files.

Modifying files

Files are usually modified in ways very similar to the way they are created. A file that is created with an editor is usually modified with an editor. The same features useful in creating files are therefore also useful in modifying files.

Deleting files

Deleting files should also be as simple as possible, but here options should be available for deleting a group of files at once. Some checking should also be provided to prevent files from being accidentally deleted. One way of preventing accidents is to force confirmation of the deletion request, such as requiring the user to answer affirmatively the question: "Do you really want to delete this file?" before the file is deleted. Another method is to not actually delete the file when the delete command is given, but to just mark it as "to be deleted", then not do the actual deletion until later. This allows the file to be re-created at any time until it is actually deleted. The actual deletion usually consists of simply marking the directory block previously used by that file as free.

Copying files

Copying a file is a seemingly simple task that can actually have a large number of options. The copy process is a good way to change many of the file characteristics, such as variable length records to fixed length records, or direct organization to sequential organization. The copy process can also be used to change the record length of the file, such as from 100-byte records to 80-byte records. New files can be built by selecting only certain portions of the old file, such as all records between 1,000 and 5,000.

Renaming files

The copy command can be used to change the name of a file by copying it to a new file with a different name, then deleting the old file, but that is not efficient. A single command should be used to change only the name of the file. This is a frequently needed function and should be available without the additional overhead of copying and deleting the old file.

Viewing files

The editor can be used to look at the contents of some files, but different methods should be available for the cases when editing the file is not desired. Most operating systems provide a facility for displaying the contents of files either on a printer or on a terminal. These commands tend to be rather simple, but some have options such as putting formatting codes into files to be printed, or displaying only selected portions of a file on a terminal.

Directory services

A well-designed system provides a large number of file services based on the directory. Most of these services are mostly for the purpose of making the system user-friendly, not for providing just a means of performing some function. Since one of the most important characteristics of a system is user-friendliness, these services are very important.

The most basic directory service is a display of the name of the files in that directory. This display should be full-screen, just like the editors, and allow file functions to be performed on files directly from the display. For example, to erase a file it should only be necessary to display the name of the file, and enter the erase command next to the file name. This is particularly useful when the same function is to be performed on several files in a group.

The directory display should be available from a single command that displays all files in a specific category. The display command should allow the use of **wild-card specifiers.** Wild-card specifiers are used in the file names on the display command to denote any characters in that position in file names to be displayed. The common wild-card is an asterisk (*) in the place of the unknown characters.

Example 4-10:

USE OF WILD-CARD FILE SPECIFICATION

In a case where file names are shown as "filename.ext", wild-card specifiers can be:

*.BAS — all files with ext of BAS such as

FILE1.BAS

FILE3.BAS

TEMP.BAS etc.

ACC*.DAT — all files with ext of DAT who begin with ACC

ACCT.DAT

ACCOUNT.DAT

ACC.DAT etc.

. — all files

Another useful feature of directory displays is the ability to sort the listed file names in various ways. The most common choices are to sort the listed files alphabetically by the file name, numerically by the creation date, numerically by the date last modified, numerically by the size of the file, or alphabetically by the type of file. These sorts are very useful when searching for a file or files with certain characteristics, such as the biggest files, or the most recently modified files.

The file services provided from the directory display should encompass, as far as possible, the entire list of file services offered.

File sharing

A well designed file system allows extensive sharing of files between the system and users, and between individual users. Files can be shared at several different levels. The simplest level of data sharing is none, that is, all data is owned by a specific user and is not available to any other user. This is not very efficient because there are many system data areas that should be available to all users, and even if these areas are made available to all users, there are still many cases where users may need to share data with one another. The concept of allowing every user to view all data is equally impractical however, since computers tend to be the repository of much confidential information. Some middle ground between these two extremes must be achieved.

Most forms of data sharing are accomplished by defining an owner for the file, who is usually the user that created the file, and then allowing other users to access that file. This allows the data sharing to be controlled by controlling the access other users have to that data.

Four basic levels of file access can be defined. The top, most free level is to allow users to view and copy the file, execute the programs, and modify or erase the data. The next level down provides all these functions except modifying or erasing the data. The next level below this is to allow the file to be viewed and the programs executed, but to prevent copying the data or programs. The lowest level is to allow the programs to be executed without allowing either the data or programs to be viewed or copied.

Granting access to write to files is certainly the most difficult aspect of file sharing. The primary difficulties are in ensuring that each person receives only the latest copy of a file. Updating a file must be done in a sequential fashion; otherwise, two different users could try updating a file at the same time. This inevitably leads to lost data, since both users read the old copy of the file, add their updates, and write out the new copy. Unfortunately, since both users updated the old copy, the user who writes the file first has his updates wiped out when the other user writes out his copy of the file, since the first updates were not already incorporated in the file. Because of these problems, shared write access is usually achieved by locking any file, or part of a file, that is accessed for writing. That lock prevents any other user from accessing that file until it is released.

Data access, at any level, can be provided to four different classes of users. The first level, which is always provided, is to allow the owner access to his files. The next level is to allow the owner and some other specified user access. The extension of this is to allow the owner and a specified group of users, who need not be individually defined, access. The last level is to allow all users access to the data.

File compression

One other service that is useful for maintenance of the system, but is rarely seen by the user, is a **file compression** utility. Even when file allocation algorithms are quite efficient, disk space has a tendency to become fragmented. The file compression utility copies the files on a specified area of disk to a temporary area, and then recopies them to the original area, with the files allocated in contiguous areas. Running this program periodically groups all of the file blocks in a given area at the beginning of that area, and thus reduces fragmentation.

FILE BACKUP AND RESTORATION

It is sad but true that accidents do happen to data contained in computers. These accidents range from a user hitting the wrong key and accidentally erasing an important file, to a fire that wipes out the entire computer room. The accidents differ, and consequently the responses should differ, but they all require that a file or files be restored, which requires that the files first must have been backed up.

The degree and type of backup needed are determined both by the scale of the disaster being avoided, and by the availability requirements of files being backed up. Such requirements may differ greatly. A system with a large number of time-sharing users who are constantly modifying a large number of important files may need to have all files backed up several times a day, while another system might have only a very few important files that get modified only once per week.

There are several different ways of doing backups, but the two most common techniques involve backing up either an image of every disk drive in the system, or just backing up those files that have been changed since the last time a backup was performed. The latter type of backup is known as an **incremental backup,** since it can be thought of as an "increment" to the last backup. The advantage of the latter method is that much less time and computer resources are involved. The disadvantage is that in the case where all of the files on an entire disk must be restored, it may take many different backups to actually retrieve all of the lost files.

Example 4-11:

DISK IMAGE

File A	Block 1
File B	Block 2
File A	Block 3
File C	Block 4
File D	Block 5
File B	Block 6
File D	Block 7
File A	Block 8
File A	Block 9
File C	Block 10

In this example, the blocks belonging to each of the files are interspersed with blocks belonging to the other files. A file backup groups blocks 1, 3, 8, and 9 into file A, blocks 2 and 6 into file B, blocks 4 and 10 into file C, and blocks 5 and 7 into file D. Each file, is then written on tape. In an image backup, the blocks are written out to tape in exactly the same order as they are stored on disk, with no attempt to group them into files.

Most computer centers use a combination of the two backup methods. A regular incremental backup is done at short intervals (often daily), and an image backup is done at longer intervals (such as weekly). Doing backups in this fashion provides a full backup for the cases when it may be needed, but most of the backups still do not require the large amounts of computer time and tape as a full backup.

The timing of backups is a subject of some controversy. The basic rule is that any backups are too many when no files need to be restored, while no backup is recent enough when files do need to be restored. The trade-off between too many and not enough backups must be made constantly. An analysis of how often files are changed and how important those files are is important. This information must then be weighed against the expense and difficulty of more backups. The timing of the backups must be such that no vital data is ever lost.

Incremental backups can be done by reading the directory and comparing the date and time of the last backup with the date and time of the last time each file in the directory was modified. Only files that have been modified since the date and time of the last backup should be backed up. The actual backup can be performed by writing each of the files out to tape or a removable disk in a normal fashion. This process requires that the date and time of each backup be stored in some location where the next backup can read that date and time.

The full backups can be done more efficiently than is possible with the incremental backups. Since all of the data in a specified area must be backed up, it is not necessary to actually read each of the files in that area; instead, it is possible to sequentially read each block in the area and write it to the tape. This process is much more efficient than following all of the file chains through to find the blocks in each file.

It is possible to do full backups in this fashion because when the data is restored, it will be restored in exactly the same location as it currently exists on the disk.

The efficiency obtained by doing an image-copy backup is significant, but the fact that this type of backup can only be restored as a complete area severely limits the usefulness of this type of backup. It is quite proper to do such a backup at weekly or monthly intervals, but it is seldom proper to use such a backup for the regular, daily backups, since most restoration requests are for individual files, not the entire disk. It is very difficult to restore individual files from an image backup, since the backup process did not distinguish between files. Incremental backups, however, write out files instead of blocks, so it is quite easy to restore individual files from them.

Full backups, on the other hand, allow the entire disk drive to be easily restored, which is most useful in case of a hardware failure on the disk drive. Such catastrophic failures do occur, but are rather unusual.

Before deciding which type of backup to use and how often to use it, it is necessary to understand the usual causes for needing file restoration. One case is where a user accidentally erases one or more files, and needs those files restored. Another case is where an entire area of a disk is lost (this is generally due to some type of hardware failure). If there are many users with individual files being lost, an incremental backup should always be available to restore those files. If there are many cases of hardware failure, a recent image backup should be available to restore those disks.

The next issue that must be resolved is how long should each of the individual backups be kept. File backups that are erased just before a user needs a file that was on one of those backups could be a new application of Murphy's law. Backups should usually be kept somewhat longer than seems reasonable.

The basic rule here is that files must be kept as long as it is possible that they might be needed. In the case of some financial data, this may be as long as ten years. In the case where the system is devoted to processing data and then sending it to another system, the files may not be needed for more than a few days.

Another issue that should be addressed when the backup process is being set up is that of **disaster recovery.** This subject encompasses such areas as having another computer system available in case of disaster striking the main system. A somewhat more common case is simply ensuring that all data in the computer center is available for recovery in case some disaster strikes the computer system and destroys all the data. A simple way to implement this is to use one of the many commercial systems that provide storage of computer tapes in sealed vaults. These companies usually have systems for picking up and delivering computer tapes at regular intervals, and their vaults are designed to withstand anything up to and including a major earthquake.

Recommended backup strategies

Probably the most common backup system is to do incremental backups daily and image backups once per week, usually on the weekend. In this way the oldest image backup is one week old, so if there is a disk failure the area can be restored from the last image backup, and then the files saved on the incremental backups done since the last image backup can be restored on top of the data restored from the image backup. This system also provides an incremental backup for users, since the image backup is done on the weekend, when most users are not modifying their files. The needs for saving files at an off-site vault can be achieved by making a duplicate copy of one of the image copies each week or month and sending that backup to the vault.

A common system for saving backups is to save each daily backup for eight weeks, the weekly backups for twenty-six weeks, and monthly backups for many years. This allows users to restore a file as much as eight weeks old from any day during those eight weeks. Files that are more than eight weeks old can be restored at weekly intervals, so that the most that would be lost in any of these files is one week's worth of data. Files that are more than six months old can be restored with no more than one month of data lost. The monthly backups can then be saved for one year to five years, depending on the importance of the data. A duplicate copy of each weekly and monthly backup can be made and sent to a vault, to be saved for the same length of time as the other backups. This is a good system for a typical time-sharing system developing and running programs.

Example 4-12:

SAMPLE BACKUP STRATEGY

DAILY	DATE
FILE + WEEKLY IMAGE (ARCHIVAL)	Sunday
FILE	Monday
FILE	Tuesday
FILE	Wednesday
FILE	Thursday
FILE	Friday
IMAGE	Saturday

WEEKLY	DATE
IMAGE	Week 1
IMAGE	Week 2
IMAGE	Week 3
IMAGE + MONTHLY IMAGE	Week 4
IMAGE	Week 5
IMAGE	Week 6
IMAGE	Week 7
IMAGE + MONTHLY IMAGE	Week 8

Catalogs

The backup system must have some way of keeping track of the files that have been backed up. This is normally done with a catalog system. The catalog must contain the names of the files backed up, the date and time when each file was backed up, the owner of each file, and which tape or tapes that file is backed up on.

In a large system with many files and users, the catalog system frequently becomes unbearably large. Many systems may have a thousand different users, each with perhaps one hundred files. Many of these files are not modified regularly, and so are not backed up in the incremental backups, but all of them are backed up in the image backups, and there are certain to be several thousands of files to be backed up each week.

This huge number of files adds up to a very large data storage requirement just for the backup system catalogs. The decision must then be made as to how much data should be retained in each backup. A system similar to that described above will lead to one hundred or more separate backups being maintained at all times, with each catalog containing information on hundreds or thousands of files. If the information to be retained for each file is extensive, then the catalog system quickly grows to the point where it occupies hundreds of millions of bytes of disk storage. Some middle ground must be achieved which will allow necessary information on backed up files without the catalogs becoming impossibly large.

One such system is to maintain a complete catalog for all recent backups, such as those performed in the last eight weeks. This is the period, on most systems, from which most restorations are requested. For backups that are older than eight weeks, it is sufficient to maintain in the catalog only the list of disks that were backed up and the list of tapes containing those backups. This requires that the tapes themselves contain a complete catalog of the files backed up on that tape. Each tape can have the catalog for itself, or one tape from the group can contain the catalog from the entire group. Another requirement of using the reduced catalog is that some service be available that will process normal catalogs, with complete information on each file, and convert them to the simple catalog.

Even the reduced directory system still requires a large amount of disk space, since complete information is retained for all backups done in the last six weeks, which could be as many as fifty different catalogs. This is certainly far less than keeping complete catalogs of all backups, however, and may be necessary in systems where the catalogs are occupying too much disk space.

SUMMARY

Data sets or files can be set up in four major ways: sequential, indexed sequential, direct, and partitioned. Sequential organization is the best if the file is to be processed from start to finish, indexed sequential organization is useful in particular cases where the records in the file have a key field available, and direct organization is appropriate where the records are to be accessed randomly. Partitioned data sets are best for setting up libraries where each member of the data set contains a complete sequential file.

Records within files can be of fixed length, which is best if all the records in the file are of the same length, or variable length, which works best when the records in the file are of different lengths. Undefined length records should only be used when no record processing is desired by the operating system.

File systems can be designed so that each file exists in one contiguous disk area. This is easy, but usually not very efficient. Other allocation schemes use small blocks of data scattered about the available disk area, with either a pointer in each block to locate the next block, or a central index containing the location of each block in the file. This is a more complex allocation, but the increased flexibility is so useful that this is a nearly universal allocation method.

File system fragmentation is the problem encountered when the available disk area consists of scattered, small pieces. This problem is serious in contiguous allocation schemes because it prevents allocating some files, but it also exists in the chained block allocation scheme, since performance can be seriously degraded if a file is scattered all over the disk.

The directory is the index to the files available in a disk. It contains information about each file. Some of this information is used only by the system, such as the physical location of the file. Other information is available to the user, such as the length of the file.

The basic file services provide the ability to create, modify, delete, copy, change the name, and display the contents of a file. Each service should be as easy to use as possible. One of the most user-friendly and useful features of directory services is to allow most file services to be performed directly from directory displays. A full-screen display of all files should be available. Options should allow all files in a specific category to be displayed, such as all of the programs.

File backup and restorations systems are necessary and should provide the ability to do both an incremental file backup, and a complete image-copy backup. An incremental backup should be performed frequently, and the full backup should be performed at less frequent intervals.

EXERCISES

TRUE/FALSE

1. A sequential file organization is the simplest but never the most efficient.
2. The most common record format is fixed length records.
3. Variable length records cannot be used in direct data sets.
4. Fragmentation refers to the process where parts of files get lost.
5. The disk allocation map shows which files are currently active.
6. The directory display information is maintained in the directory.
7. Each file should be backed up daily in every system.
8. File compression is not useful with non-contiguous file allocations.
9. The backup system should be linked with disaster recovery plans.
10. Wild-card file specifiers should be available for file services.

MULTIPLE CHOICE

1. A file is sometimes called a:
   a) Collection of input data
   b) Data set
   c) Temporary place to store data
   d) Program
2. The most efficient data set organization is:
   a) A sequential file
   b) An ISAM file
   c) Varies depending upon the usage of the data set
   d) A partitioned data set
3. A partitioned data set is mostly used for:
   a) Storing program data
   b) Storing ISAM files
   c) A program or source library
   d) Storing backup information
4. Fragmentation of the file system:
   a) Can always be prevented
   b) Only occurs if the file system is used improperly
   c) Can be temporarily removed by compaction
   d) Is a characteristic of all file systems

5. File record length:
   a) Should always be fixed
   b) Should always be variable
   c) Depends upon the size of the file
   d) Should be chosen to match the data characteristics
6. An incremental backup:
   a) Uses more tapes
   b) Should be done each month
   c) Saves only files that have recently changed
   d) Saves all files
7. Backups should be done:
   a) Daily for most installations
   b) Weekly for most installations
   c) As several image copies, followed by an incremental
   d) As several incrementals, followed by an image copy
8. Disaster recovery:
   a) Is needed by every installation
   b) Is never needed
   c) Varies in degree between installations
   d) Requires off-site computers for immediate use
9. Wild-card specifiers:
   a) Provide an easy way of finding groups of related files
   b) Are only used when printing the contents of files
   c) Can be used when writing a file
   d) Allow several files to be read simultaneously
10. The allocation map:
    a) Is used to store program data
    b) Specifies which blocks are used by which file
    c) Is updated by application programs
    d) Allows programs to erase files

DISCUSSION QUESTIONS

1. Describe the most common file format.
2. Describe variable length records.
3. Discuss fragmentation of files.
4. Explain how linked files are set up.
5. Describe an allocation map.
6. List five necessary file system services.
7. Explain how wild card specifiers are used with file directories.
8. List and explain the four basic levels of data access.
9. Describe a recommended backup strategy.
10. Describe a backup catalog system.

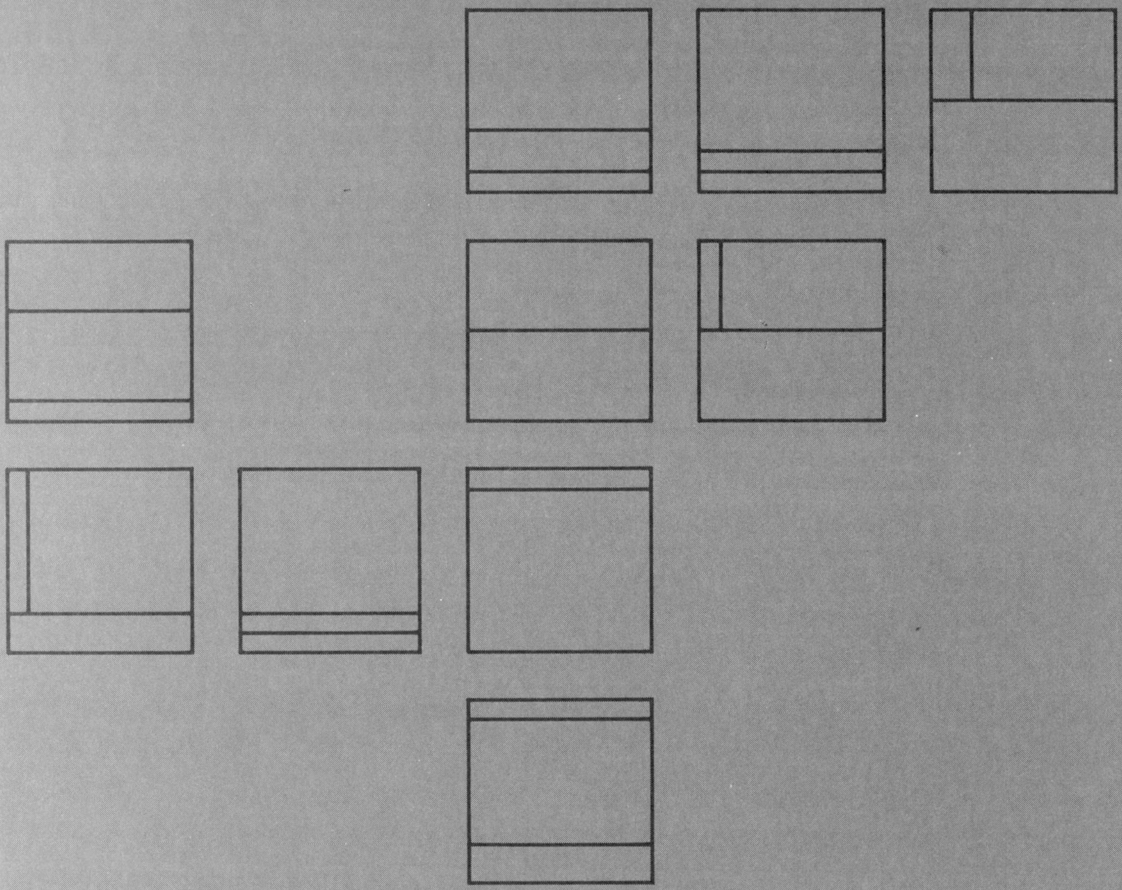

MULTIPROGRAMMING

5

KEY TERMS

Task	*Process*
Ready state	*Blocked state*
Primitive	*Fork*
Quit	*Interrupts*
Priorities	*Suspended task*
Context switching	*Interrupt handler*
Polling	*Serializing resources*
Critical sections	*Locks*
Semaphores	*P-semaphore*
V-semaphore	*Deadly embrace*
Local locks	*Global locks*
Deadlock	*Indefinite postponement*
Spinning	*Delaying on locks*
Locking hierarchies	*SEND*
RECEIVE	

INTRODUCTION

One of the most useful aspects of computers is their ability to interleave the execution of programs, so that one program is executing while another is waiting on something such as an I/O operation. This prevents wasted processor time while slower operations are being done independently of the processor. The primary goal of multiprogramming is to have one program executing in the processor at all times, which is only possible by having several programs take turns at the processor. Another goal, of course, is to allow several users access to the system at the same time.

The ability to interleave program execution is provided almost exclusively by the operating system, although modern computer hardware has several features that improve the performance of such operating systems. Multiprogramming operating systems take advantage of the characteristics of executing programs in order to allow several different programs to be executed during the same time period. This function of operating systems is contained in the kernel of the operating system and is integral to the smooth operation of the computer.

An additional function provided by multiprogramming is the ability to perform utility functions without the user having to wait for those functions to complete. An example of this is printing at the same time as using a terminal. Both the printing operation and the terminal operation are much slower than the processor and can both be serviced by the processor at the same time. If these functions are not multiprogrammed, the user at the terminal must wait while the file is printed.

Example 5-1:

Timing without multiprogramming

Timing with multiprogramming

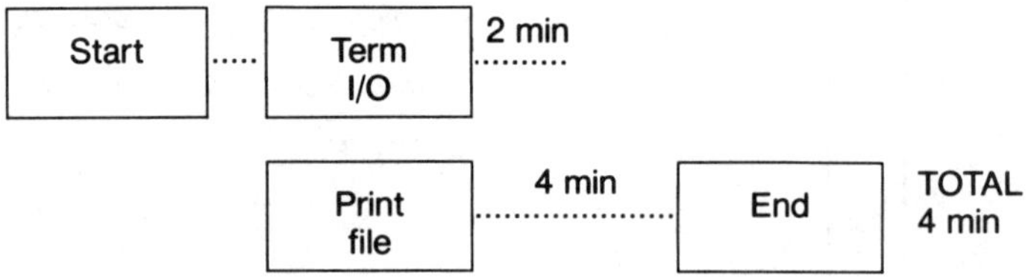

There are several issues when attempting to interleave the execution of several programs. The major issues lie in the area of competition for resources between the different programs. These resources consist primarily of main memory, the processor, and disk areas, although any peripheral device may be a resource that several programs are trying to access at the same time. Some method must be set up to allocate resources between competing programs in a way that both prevents errors caused from overlapping requests, and provides each program with a fair share of that resource.

An additional requirement, although comparatively minor, is providing a means where programs can communicate with one another. Such a facility allows programs to synchronize their execution, and can be used to improve resource sharing. For example, if two programs both need to utilize the same resource then it may be possible, if both are part of the same system, for the programmers to be aware of that need, and to write the programs so that they communicate with one another, and only have one of them request the resource at any time.

PROCESS CHARACTERISTICS

The execution of a program can usually be broken down into discrete steps which can be analyzed separately. Each of these steps is called a **task.** It is somewhat difficult to obtain general agreement on what actually constitutes a task, but a general rule of thumb is that a task is the smallest discrete step in a job. A job may then consist of several different tasks. For example, the compilation and running of a program can be broken down into a step of compiling the program, a step of loading the compiled program into memory, and a step of executing the program.

Another term that is sometimes used interchangeably with "task" is **process.** It is even more difficult to obtain agreement on the proper definition of this term than it is with task. Definitions of the term process tend to vary with the different operating system implementations. A general working definition of process is that it is some task that is executing or trying to execute.

A process can be in one of two primary states at any time. One state is that of **running,** or actually in possession of the processor and executing. The other state is **waiting,** which means that the process is attempting to run but cannot. There are two major reasons why a process might be waiting. The first reason is that another process is currently executing on the processor. This state is sometimes called the **ready** state. The second reason is that the process is waiting on some other activity to complete, such as an I/O operation. This is sometimes known as a **blocked state.**

There are typical steps that most jobs go through in the system. Some of the steps vary depending upon whether the job is time-sharing or batch, but most of them are the same. Batch jobs tend to have more steps, so a better example is a batch job.

The first step is to read the job into the input stream. This is done by an operating system process that transfers the job from its location (such as on disk) to a temporary staging area. The next step is to read and interpret the JCL included with the job to set up certain parameters for execution of the job. Once this information is determined, the job is placed in a scheduling queue, and waits there until it is actually scheduled to execute.

When it is determined that the job is ready to execute, a process is started that sets the job up for execution. The setup process then branches to the beginning of the job to start it executing. At any time during the execution of the job, it may go into a blocked state (if it needs some resource) or into a ready state (if it is removed from the processor while still needing processor time). A process in blocked state moves from there into ready state, and then to running state, instead of directly from blocked state to running state.

When the job needs services, it cycles between running, blocked, and ready states. When it loses control of the processor, it cycles between running and ready states. When the job is complete, another system process deallocates the resources used by that job and sends the completed job back to the user or into a completed jobs list.

PROCESS MANAGEMENT

There are many terms to describe how processes are managed. **Primitive** is used to describe a function similar to a process, but generally somewhat narrower in scope. A primitive is almost always part of the operating system instead of being part of a user program, and generally has less overhead and function than a process. A primitive can almost be regarded as a subset of a process. Examples of primitives are the functions that bring processes into the processor and remove processes from the processor. The term for creating a new process is **fork,** and for ending a process is **quit.**

The task of managing the processes in the system is not very easy. Processes are constantly changing states, and some methods must control which process is in which state and know when it is time to perform some function for a process. There are two tools used by most modern operating systems to manage processes. These tools are **interrupts,** and **priorities.**

Most of the features of multiprogramming are made possible through the use of interrupts. An interrupt is a condition where the task using the processor is interrupted and forced into ready state while some other task moves into

Example 5-2:

LIFE CYCLE OF A SAMPLE PROCESS

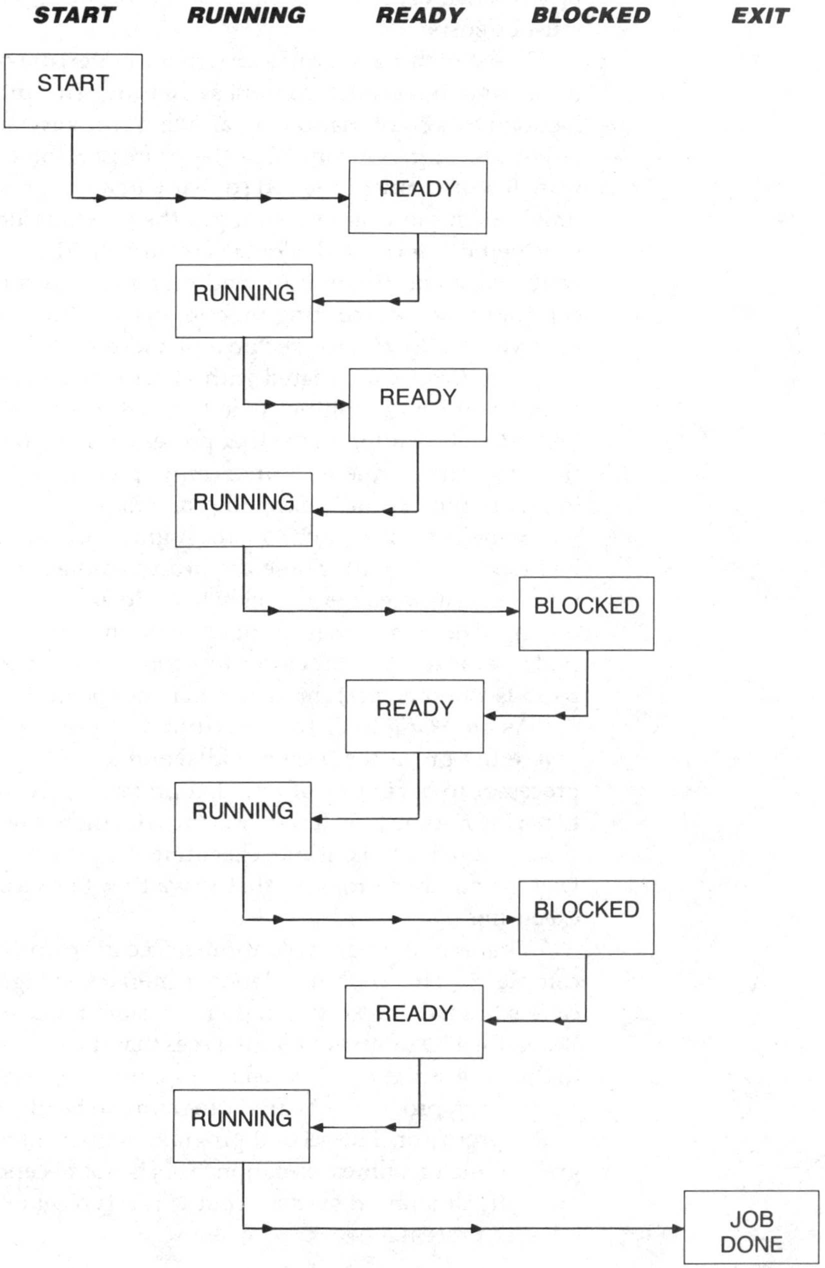

the running state. The task that was forced into the ready state is **suspended,** and will resume executing at some time after the interrupting task has completed whatever it was doing. An interrupt is a signal that current processing must be suspended.

The switching of processes when an interrupt occurs or in normal scheduling is sometimes called **context switching.** This process, on most computers, is handled by a combination of hardware and software features. Whenever a different task is given control of the processor, the current state of all the hardware features must be saved so that when the previous task is returned to the processor, it can begin executing at the previous location with no indication of ever being interrupted. This is accomplished by having the computer hardware save all pertinent information from an executing task before transferring control to the interrupting process. Placing this function in hardware instead of software allows it to execute much faster.

Priorities are associated with interrupts. Each process or task is assigned a priority which determines whether that process should be allowed to execute immediately or after some other process has finished. Priorities allow control of the interrupt sequence, since only processes with a higher priority can interrupt the currently executing process.

Some processes, such as some highly specialized systems processes, cannot be interrupted at all. These are processes that are performing functions that must be completed very quickly to avoid errors, such as some types of I/O processing. These processes cannot remain in control of the processor for long periods, because if the processor in a condition of not being interrupted for long periods, other critical interrupts may not be noticed.

As an example of the interrupt and priority structure consider the case where the processor becomes idle, and a waiting program is loaded into the processor to begin execution. That program executes for a while until it needs to perform some I/O. It requests the I/O, then must wait until that I/O is complete before it can continue executing. Its priority is lowered while it is in I/O wait, so another program that is waiting to execute interrupts it and begins executing.

The second program continues executing until the I/O of the first program completes. The I/O completion generates a high-priority interrupt, which causes the I/O interrupt handler, a system process, to take over the processor. When the I/O interrupt handler sees that the I/O is complete, it returns control to the program it interrupted (the second program), and causes the priority of the waiting program (the first program), to be higher than that of the program in the processor. The second program is then interrupted by the waiting program, which resumes execution. This is not necessarily the way this process is implemented on all systems, but it is a typical example of the interrupt and priority process at work.

Example 5-3:

PRIORITIES AND INTERRUPTS

SAMPLE PRIORITIES (1-10)

RUNNING	**READY**	**BLOCKED**
	Job 1 Priority 5	

The processor is idle, so the waiting job (Job 1) is loaded.

RUNNING	**READY**	**BLOCKED**
Job 1 Priority 5		

The job (Job 1) executes for a period of time.

RUNNING	**READY**	**BLOCKED**
Job 2 Priority 5		Job 1 Priority 1

Job 1 is waiting on I/O, so it becomes blocked with a low priority. A job (Job 2) with a higher priority begins executing.

RUNNING	**READY**	**BLOCKED**
I/O Priority 10	Job 2 Priority 5	Job 1 Priority 1

When the I/O completes, the I/O handler (with a very high priority) takes over the processor, while Job 2 becomes ready.

RUNNING	**READY**	**BLOCKED**
Job 2 Priority 5	Job 1 Priority 6	

The I/O handler is done, so Job 2 regains the processor. Job 1 is now ready with a higher priority.

RUNNING	**READY**	**BLOCKED**
Job 1 Priority 5	Job 2 Priority 5	

Finally, Job 1 is back with its old priority.

Most production operating systems have far more than the ten priorities possible in the previous example. Priorities are divided into classes, usually with different priorities possible within each class. The class is determined by function of the process, and whether that function can afford to wait on another process. If there are several processes in the same class all waiting, then they can be given different priorities in that class, so that they are scheduled separately, but ahead of any lower priority classes. Many of the interrupts received are generated by the computer hardware.

For example, a user program desiring to execute is given a relatively low priority because there is no serious impact on the system if that program is delayed. Servicing an I/O interrupt from a disk drive is given a higher priority since that interrupt must be serviced within a given time period or an error may result. The highest priority of all is given to an interrupt generated by a failure in the computer processor or memory since there is very little time to service that interrupt before the whole computer fails.

Several interrupts may be received at almost the same time, so some technique must nest interrupt processing routines, or to prevent interrupts from being received. The usual way this is implemented in operating systems is to allow the system to temporarily disable interrupt reception. This must be done to allow the original interrupt to be processed properly before being interrupted by some other process and because some interrupts require that their processing be completed before another interrupt is processed. A routine that disables interrupts must, of course, be extremely short and efficient, because it is dangerous to have a computer running for any length of time with the interrupts disabled.

Example 5-4:

INTERRUPT SOURCES

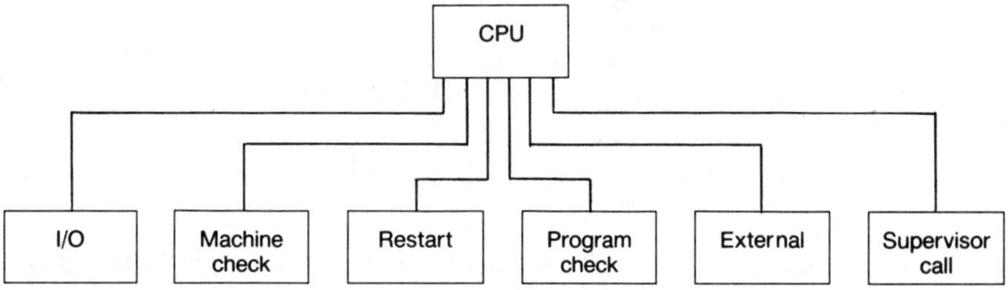

Specific routines are designed solely for processing a particular type of interrupt. These routines are called **interrupt handlers** and are divided up into several different areas, depending upon the type of interrupt. The interrupt handler for a specific interrupt is given control of the processor when that particular interrupt is encountered.

Interrupt handlers are usually accessed by having specific locations in memory that contain the address of each interrupt handling routine. When an interrupt of a particular type is received, the computer automatically looks at a specific memory location and branches to the address stored at that location. This address should be the beginning of the appropriate interrupt handling routine.

As an example of the interrupt handling process, assume that the address of the I/O interrupt handling routine is stored at physical location X'48' in memory. (If memory addresses are new to you, see Appendix B.) Also assume that the I/O interrupt handler begins at location X'1000', which then is the address stored in location X'48'. Whenever an I/O interrupt is received, the computer looks in location X'48' and fetches its contents. It then branches to that location and begins executing there. The I/O handler determines the type of the I/O interrupt, and branches to the appropriate subroutine. When the interrupt processing is complete this subroutine returns to the interrupt handler, which in turn allows the system to restore execution to the program it interrupted.

Some computers also provide facilities for allowing certain programs to generate interrupts of their own. These interrupts are at a lower priority than hardware generated interrupts, but are nevertheless serviced in the same fashion. This can be an efficient means of transferring control, since much of the transition process is handled by the hardware. User-generated interrupts are usually needed only in very large programs.

Polling

There are some systems that do not use interrupts to drive systems activities, but instead use a **polling** process. This is a technique where a process that is waiting for something to happen periodically checks to see if it has happened yet. It is very difficult to determine just how often the polling should occur. If the process checks too often it generates excessive overhead, but if it does not check often enough, some critical element may not be serviced in time. A polling system usually tends to be less efficient than an interrupt driven system, so most modern systems are interrupt driven.

RESOURCE MANAGEMENT

The primary difficulty to overcome when setting up multiprogramming is allocating the system resources properly between the processes that are contending for those resources. Some of these resources may be external, such as I/O devices, while others may be internal, such as control blocks. The interrupt and priority schemes, normally used for process management, cause a potential problem with managing the various resources.

Critical Sections

One particular resource that must be managed, just like disk and tape drives, is access to memory areas that are shared between processes. It is not immediately apparent that this is such a resource that must be managed, since it is physically possible for several processes to access memory very rapidly with no errors of failures occurring. The problem arises when one of those processes is changing the data in the shared area. If another process accesses the shared area while the update is only partially complete, then the information read may be completely useless. Worse yet, if the second process accessing the data is also trying to update it, the final information written may be severely garbled.

Such areas of shared memory are known as **critical sections** because they are sections of memory that are critical to the performance of both individual processes and the overall system. Any section of a process that accesses data shared by another process qualifies as a critical section. Critical sections are subject to the same management and control as any other system resource.

The critical sections of processes should be made as short as possible in order to reduce the amount of memory that must be managed. Reducing the size of the critical sections tends to increase throughput on the system, since any memory in a critical section is periodically not available to some processes.

Locks

Many system resources must be shared between processes, but cannot be used by one process until another process is finished. Therefore, some method must be developed that **serializes** the usage of those resources. Serializing a series of events forces those events to occur in sequence, instead of any two events occurring simultaneously. Serializing the usage of resources prevents a second process from using that resource until the first process is finished.

The technique most often used for serializing resources is to **lock** those resources. The state of the lock determines whether the resource is currently in use by a process. The simplest case of locks is simply a bit that is set to 1 when the resource is in use and set to 0 when the resource is not in use. No process can use a resource as long as the lock for that process is set. Only when the first process has completed its use of the resource does it release the lock, and allow other processes to use that resource.

Locks are implemented with the use of **semaphores.** A semaphore is a flag that is used to indicate whether a lock is set for a particular resource. The name for the operation to set a resource lock is a **P-semaphore.** The companion name to indicate the resource is no longer in use is **V-semaphore.** These names originated from a computer scientist called Dijkstra, who has done much work in the field of semaphores.

An example of the use of semaphores is in a process that is writing data into memory. This task requires that the data be placed in a physical location in memory, so it is necessary that no other process access that memory location while the first process is running. This is accomplished by setting a P-semaphore on the area in memory that is in use. When the operation is complete and the memory is no longer needed, a V-semaphore is set indicating that the memory is now available for other processes.

Example 5-5:

SEMAPHORE USAGE

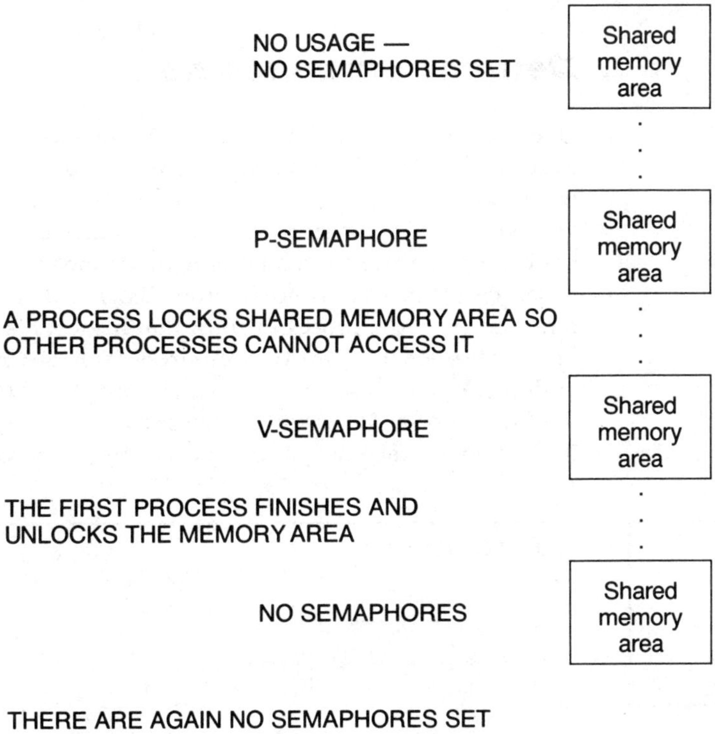

The timing in setting semaphores is very important, since it would be catastrophic if one process tested the semaphore and found the resource available, but another process managed to seize the resource before the first process could set its own semaphore. This would lead to the semaphore system not working, since it would not be successful in preventing many processes from accessing the same resource at the same time. This problem can be circumvented by implementing a single hardware instruction, such as "TEST-AND-SET", that will check the condition of the semaphore and set it if it is not currently set. By putting this operation into a single instruction it guarantees that no other process can get between the testing and setting operations.

Two general types of locks are used in most operating systems. A **local lock** can be used by a process in a small, local area. This type of lock does not require the operating system lock-processing routines to handle it. The lock that does require the normal lock-processing routines then becomes known as a **global lock.** Whenever a global lock can be converted to a local lock, it reduces the number of potential blocked processes and the overhead of processing both the lock and the blocked processes.

Deadlock management

One of the worst problems that must be avoided when using locks is known as **deadlock, indefinite postponement,** and **deadly embrace.** This is the case where a process has locked some system resource (Resource A), and requested a lock on some other system resource (Resource B). It waits for Resource B, but it has been blocked from receiving it; in the meanwhile, it maintains the lock on Resource A. Since the process is then blocked on Resource B, it consequently is removed from the processor until that resource is available. Another process, however, needs the same two resources. It already has locked Resource B and is itself blocked on Resource A. It is therefore placed in the blocked list along with the first process. Thus, both processes are on the blocked list and will remain there forever, since each of them needs the resource the other has locked.

Example 5-6:

DEADLOCK

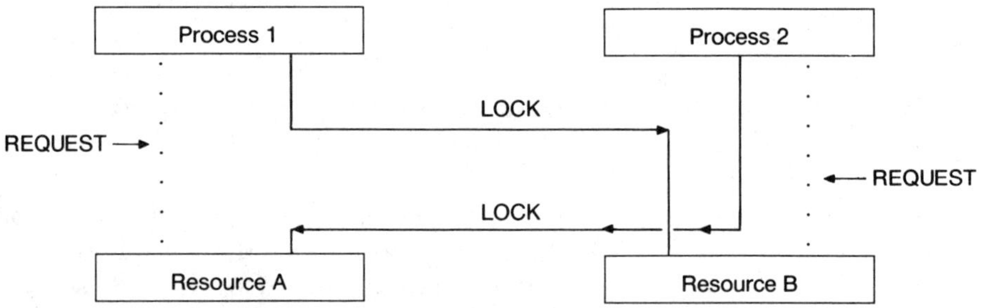

Several techniques are available to avoid the deadlock problem, but there is usually no single solution that is best. Most systems implement a variety of different techniques. One technique is to prevent any process that has a lock from leaving the processor. This is simply not possible in the general case, since there are some operations that must have access to the processor as soon as they request it.

Another technique that is more successful is to prevent most processes from displacing a process that has a locked resource, and for those processes that do displace it, to ensure that it is restored to the processor as soon as possible after being displaced. Instead of being placed on the ready list, as is usually the case, the displaced process is given a special priority that ensures that it regains the processor as soon as possible. This prevents the case where some critical process fails because it is locked out of the processor, but still does not completely address the issue of another process waiting (perhaps for a long time) until a locked resource is freed.

A better technique is one that is known as **spinning,** or **spinning on the lock.** This is a technique similar to the polling technique described previously, where the process that needs the locked resource continues querying the state of the lock until that lock is freed. This uses more resources to do the regular querying, but sometimes uses fewer resources than some more sophisticated algorithms.

There are also cases where the most efficient technique is to use a **delay on the lock** to cause the process in the processor to pause while waiting for a lock to free. This is somewhat inefficient in resources, since the processor is doing nothing else while it is delaying, but in the case of short locks the lost time may actually be less this way than by spinning or other algorithms. Delaying on the lock can be made more efficient by allowing the process requesting the locked resource to search for and perform any other functions possible that do not require the locked resource.

The practical solution to the lock problem usually lies with determining how long the lock is expected to be held. "Short" locks should be treated differently than "long" locks. A solution that is implemented in some systems is to spin on short locks and to displace the process from the processor on long locks. The displaced process is placed in the blocked list. The obvious difficulty with this technique is that the length of the lock must be determined with some degree of accuracy in order to have this technique work. In fact, it is not usually too difficult to determine the length of the lock, since most functions have typical lock times. For example, I/O performed to a terminal is almost always slow, and accesses to small system tables are almost always very fast.

Blocking a process with a lock leaves the possibility of encountering a deadlock condition, and something must be done to prevent this. One technique is to refuse to block any process that has a lock and is requesting another lock. This is very limiting, but can be improved by doing additional checking of the blocked process list to determine if the requested lock is held by another blocked process. If it is, then some additional checking reveals whether the blocked process is requesting the lock held by the current process. If so, then the current process cannot be blocked. This prevents the simple deadlock case, but does not handle the circular case in which three or more processes reach deadlock.

The general deadlock issue can be handled by checking the blocked process list to see if any process is requesting the resource the current process has locked. If so, then the current process cannot be blocked, and either spinning or delay should be used. This checking uses processor resources, but, as with most queueing problems, the more complex the solution, the more processor resources used.

The operating system can improve the performance of locked processes by carefully observing the blocked process list. Each process that is blocked because of a denied resource lock has information stored on both the reason for the blocking, and the name of the requested resource. Each process also has a priority associated with it. It is sometimes possible to juggle the priorities of the blocked processes to quickly free locks that otherwise would cause processes to remain locked for a long period of time. This can greatly enhance the throughput of blocked processes with only a relatively small cost, from the additional checking that is necessary.

Most operating systems avoid the deadlock problem by setting up "locking hierarchies". This assigns a hierarchy to all possible locks in the system. The system then prevents any process from obtaining a lock on any resource that is equal to or higher in the hierarchy than the lock currently held. As long as the locking hierarchy is carefully chosen, this prevents deadlock.

A feature that assists in lock management is setting the locks so that the system is notified whenever a lock is freed. Since there may be several processes blocked at any one time waiting for locks, it is important that the operating system be notified as soon as a lock is freed, so that it can scan the blocked processes to see if any of them are waiting on the freed lock. If so, then the highest priority blocked process waiting on that lock is placed in the ready list.

INTERPROCESS COMMUNICATION

There are many cases where it is necessary for one process to communicate with another process, such as when trying to synchronize access to some area containing data. This communication may involve sending a message and waiting for a reply, or it may be just setting up a job for a subsequent process. In either case, some communication is necessary. As with most other forms of communication, some way of sending a message (called **SEND**) is required, as is a way of receiving a message (called **RECEIVE**).

The SEND and RECEIVE functions are implemented in many ways. One of the simplest techniques requires that both the sending and receiving processes must be prepared for such a communication, and that both processes be related in some fashion. If both processes are expecting such a communication to take place, all that is necessary for the operating system is to provide a means for the message to be physically transferred from one process to another. This is a much simpler case than the general one, where the two processes may be neither related nor expecting the communication.

The general requirement for any communication between processes is that the message have a destination specified, and a means of reaching that destination. This usually takes the form of a process name, with sometimes an address as well. In some systems, an address must be specified that locates the receiving process for the operating system. In other systems there are general queueing and searching techniques that allow the operating system to find the recipient process.

More complicated systems keep track of the name of each process in the system, together with the current location of the process. When a message is sent by a process it is placed in a queue and the name of the intended receiver is read. This name is then used to index into a table of processes and the current location of the intended receiver is read from there. The message is then transferred to the receiving process, which must have some way of reading the message.

The communication system between processes frequently results in one or more processes being locked while waiting for a message to be received from another process, or while waiting for another process to receive a message that this process has sent. For this reason, it is necessary that there be a facility available that will notify the sending process when its message has been received.

Example 5-7:

SEND and RECEIVE

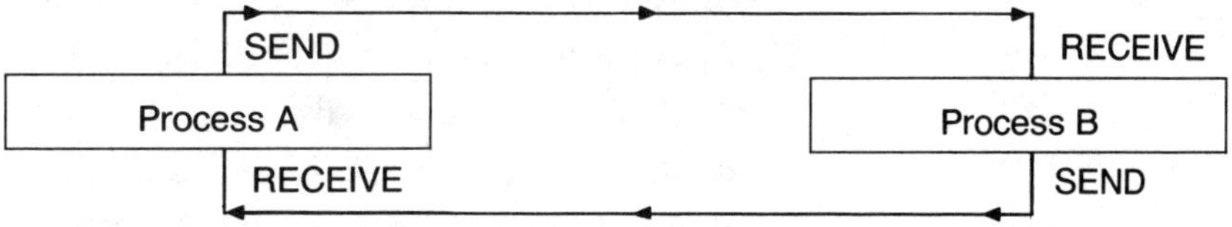

SUMMARY

This chapter has covered multiprogramming capabilities in an operating system. The first concept is that of a task or process, which is a step within a program. These steps may be contained within a user program, or within some part of the operating system itself.

A process can be in one of two general states at any given time. These states are running and waiting. There can be several reasons for the process to be waiting. The two waiting states that processes can be in are "ready" and "blocked". When the process is ready, it is available to execute, but another process is actually using the processor to execute. A blocked process is one that cannot execute because of some resource that it needs that is not available.

Most operating systems schedule processes by assigning priorities to each of them. The priority is determined by the function performed by that process. Processes critical to the continued functioning of the operating system have high priorities, while user processes tend to have lower priorities. Any process that is executing in the processor can be interrupted by a higher priority process at any time. The interrupt technique allows high priority processes temporary access to the processor when needed.

P-semaphores and V-semaphores are used to sequence resources between different processes. They are flags that show when a resource is in use. Using semaphores to schedule resources prevents a deadlock condition, which is when two different processes lock each other out permanently by locking and requesting each other's resources. A variety of techniques are used to prevent deadlock, but the usual techniques are spinning, where the process desiring the resource continually checks for the availability of the resource, and delaying the process needing the resource.

EXERCISES

TRUE/FALSE

1. A task and a process sometimes are the same.
2. A process can be in four different states.
3. A process can be waiting for either I/O or paging.
4. An interrupt-driven system is very common.
5. Interrupts driven systems frequently use priorities for scheduling.
6. A primitive is the same as a task.
7. Polling is more efficient than interrupts.

8. Deadly embrace is where neither process can be freed.
9. Beginning a new process is also known as a "fork."
10. The critical section of processes should be as large as possible.

MULTIPLE CHOICE

1. A task is:
   - **a)** The smallest discrete step in a job
   - **b)** A piece of work
   - **c)** Part of I/O
   - **d)** A collection of jobs
2. A process is another name for:
   - **a)** A job
   - **b)** A task
   - **c)** Paging
   - **d)** The operating system dispatcher
3. Fork is:
   - **a)** The creation of a new job
   - **b)** The dispatching of a task
   - **c)** Increasing the priority of a task
   - **d)** The creation of a new process
4. A task in a blocked state:
   - **a)** Is executable
   - **b)** Must still be placed in the run queues
   - **c)** Is waiting for some temporarily unavailable resource
   - **d)** Is running
5. Semaphores:
   - **a)** Are used to do I/O
   - **b)** Synchronize critical resources to prevent contention
   - **c)** Synchronize critical resources to prevent deadlock
   - **d)** Allows processes to communicate with one another
6. Priorities:
   - **a)** Are used to schedule processes
   - **b)** Increase as a process remains in the processor
   - **c)** Are attached to each page in the system
   - **d)** Are assigned by the user

7. Resource locking:
   a) Allows multiple tasks to simultaneously use resources
   b) Force only one task to use any resource at any time
   c) Can easily cause a deadlock condition
   d) Is not used for disk drives
8. Inter-process communication:
   a) Is never necessary
   b) Allows processes to synchronize activity
   c) Is required for all processes
   d) Is usually done via disk drives
9. Spinning:
   a) Requires several processes
   b) Uses very little processor time
   c) Requires the processor to keep trying until successful
   d) Should be used for all resources
10. Global locks:
    a) Are used to avoid local locks
    b) Synchronize access to global resources
    c) Synchronize access to local resources
    d) Prevent access to global resources

DISCUSSION QUESTIONS

1. Briefly discuss the major difficulties with multiprogramming.
2. Show the life cycle of a sample process.
3. Explain the functioning of context switching.
4. Give an example of how interrupts and priorities function.
5. Briefly describe the interrupt handling process.
6. Describe critical sections.
7. Describe locks and how they are used.
8. Show how P- and V-semaphores are used.
9. Describe a resource deadlock.
10. Explain spin and delay locks.

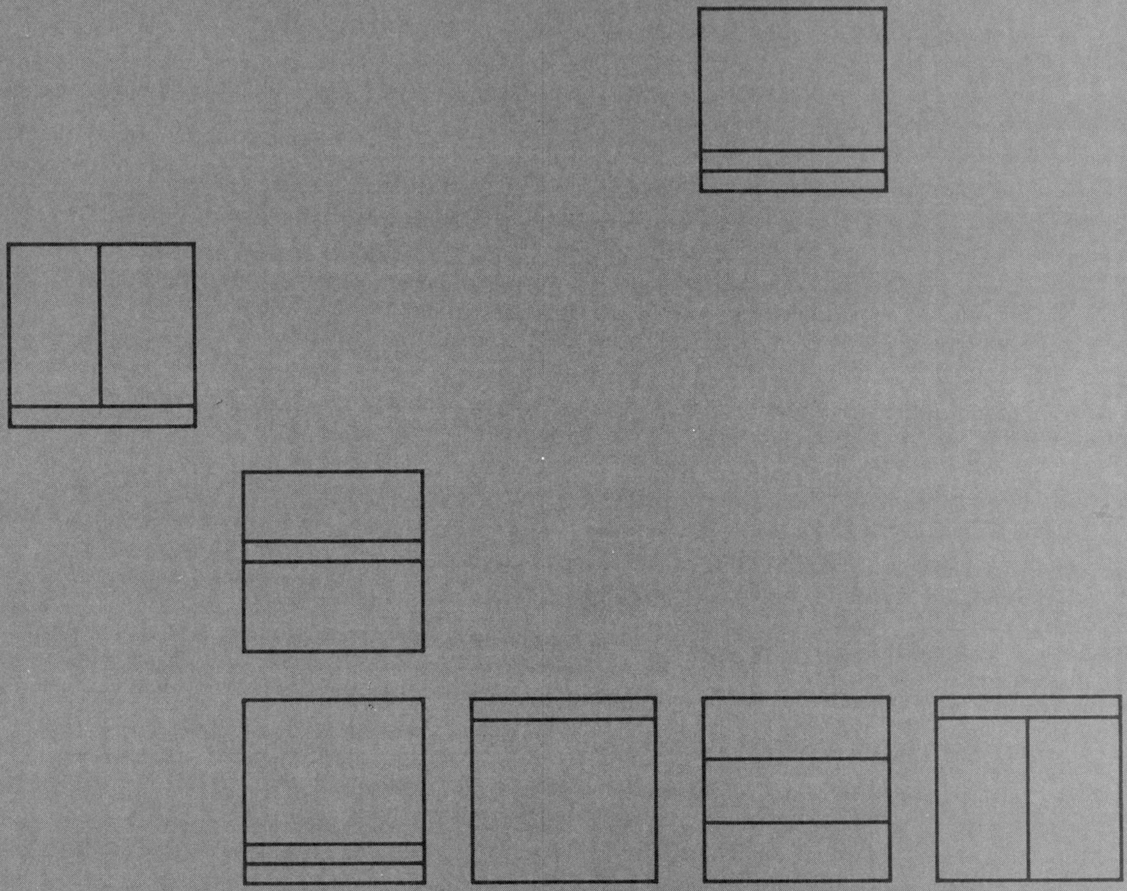

JOB AND TASK SCHEDULING

6

KEY TERMS

Dispatcher	*Round-robin*
Feedback queues	*Service level*
CPU-intensive	*Memory-intensive*
I/O-intensive	*FIFO (First In First Out)*
SJF (Shortest Job First)	*Checkpoint*
HRN (Highest Response Ratio Next)	

INTRODUCTION

There are three levels of scheduling, sometimes known as low, intermediate, and high level scheduling. Low-level scheduling is concerned with allowing a process to run on the processor. This is controlled by a mechanism within the kernel of the system known as the **dispatcher.** The dispatcher monitors both the processes in the ready queue and the process that is running. From this, the dispatcher determines when the processor should be given to another process and which process should be given control.

Intermediate-level scheduling is primarily concerned with setting up the processes in the ready queue. This can be a very complex scheduling system, although it may not even be necessary on some simple operating systems. The intermediate-level scheduler is concerned with many things, such as attaining acceptable performance levels on the computer, best utilizing available memory, providing certain guaranteed levels of performance for specific programs, etc.

High-level scheduling is sometimes known as job scheduling. This is the scheduling that is done when a job enters the system. Many of the concerns that the high-level scheduler must handle relate to scheduling physical resources, such as disk drives and tape drives. The high-level scheduler handles jobs, each of which later becomes one or more processes.

LOW-LEVEL SCHEDULING

Low-level schedulers are concerned with giving a process control of the processor. There are some events that help the scheduling process, such as when the process currently in control of the processor becomes blocked, or decides to voluntarily give up the processor. When this occurs that process is removed from the processor and another process given control. Another possible event is that a higher priority process that was previously blocked suddenly becomes free and ready to run. When this happens the higher priority process is given control of the processor.

In the absence of other events occurring, another process should still be given control of the processor after a certain amount of time has elapsed. When the computer is lightly loaded and there are no other processes waiting, the current process should remain in the processor. As long as other processes of similar priority are waiting, however, no process should remain indefinitely in the processor.

Example 6-1:

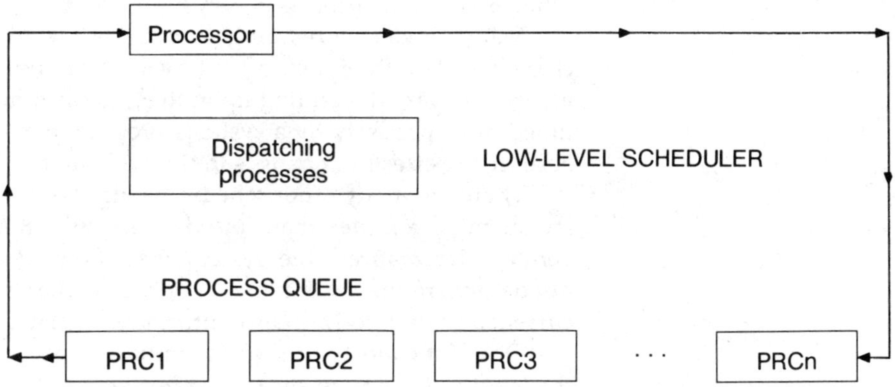

One of the simple, yet effective, scheduling algorithms commonly used is **round-robin** scheduling. This is a system whereby all available processes are placed on a list. The process in the processor is allowed to remain there for the specified time interval, then it is removed from the processor and placed back at the end of the list. The process at the head of the list is next allowed into the processor for the same time interval, then the next process, etc. After the last process in the list has had its turn in the processor the first process that ran in the processor is again allowed into the processor. This continues in a cyclic fashion until all processes are satisfied. The previous diagram example illustrates a round-robin queue, where the process at the top of the list is the next process to get control of the processor, and the process that last had control of the processor is returned to the back of the queue.

Round-robin scheduling is most appropriate for time-sharing systems, where each process should be allowed access to the processor at regular, short, intervals. Batch systems can function very well with forcing some processes to wait for long periods of time, since the jobs do not need immediate access to the processor, and the total job turnaround time may be the same. Time-sharing users, however, expect to get access to the processor within a very short time period.

The difficult part of round-robin scheduling is in deciding the length of time that each process has access to the processor. If the time is too short, much of the work done by the system is moving processes into and out of the processor, instead of by the processes themselves. If the time slice is too long, some processes may not get access to the processor for a very long time, which is inappropriate when that process needs only a very small amount of processor time, or when the process is very high priority.

Many modern operating systems allow the systems programmers to change the length of the time interval when tuning the system. Time requirements may vary depending upon the jobs running on that system, so it can be tuned most precisely by a systems programmer who is on-site and is able to observe the effects of changes in the time interval.

There are many other scheduling algorithms that are used. Most of these are far more complex than round-robin, and often purport to produce much better performance. One system that shows good potential is a **feedback queue,** where the scheduling algorithm is changed dynamically, based upon current and past performance information on the processes to be scheduled.

One of the most successful examples of feedback queues is in determining the length of the time-slice a process gets in the processor. Some overhead is involved in allocating processes to the processor and in removing them from the processor, so it is good to reduce the number of times a long job is cycled in and out of the processor. For this reason, many modern operating systems have many queues; one is for very short jobs such as time-sharing users, and another is for longer jobs such as major batch applications. There may also be different queues between these two extremes. Processes in the short queue get frequent, short, slices of time in the processor, while processes in the long queue get fewer accesses to the processor, but remain in longer when they get there. This allows the processor resource to be optimized somewhat.

The processes are placed in the queues based on two factors. The first factor is information about that process supplied by the user with the original job. This may or may not be accurate (and may not even exist), but it is a good beginning point for placing processes in queues. The other, and better, method is a feedback technique, based on the actual performance characteristics that process has previously exhibited.

The feedback process is relatively simple. The process queues are based on the amount of processor time used by each process, so all that is necessary is to keep track of the total processor time consumed by each process. Once this value passes some threshold amount, the process is automatically placed in the next longer process queue. As processes use more and more of the processor, they are automatically moved into longer and longer process queues, until they are in the queue for the longest processes.

Whenever a process is blocked, it is removed from the run queues. For this reason there must be some way to handle the case where a process re-enters the queues. There are two methods to handle this case. One method is to cause all processes re-entering the queues to re-enter in the short-process queue. This has the advantage that processes that get blocked frequently spend most of their time in the short-process queue, so they are quickly able to receive the little processor time they need. The significant disadvantage is that a process that uses a large amount of processor time will be placed in the wrong queue whenever it returns from what may have been a very small amount of I/O. The process then must go through the entire feedback mechanism before it is returned to its proper queue.

An advancement on this system is to tag each process with the name of the queue it was last in whenever it is removed from the queueing system. When that process is then returned to the queueing system, it re-enters the queue that it was last in. This allows processes that need a large amount of processor time to perform occasional small bits of I/O without being placed in the short-process queue, and therefore enhances performance.

The only problem with this system is that it does not allow for processes that change characteristics. The above queueing system allows processes to only move to queues with longer and longer processor times. This is correct when the process maintains the same performance characteristics throughout its life, but fails when a process changes from being mostly a processor user to being blocked frequently.

Example 6-2:

MULTIPLE QUEUES WITH FEEDBACK SCHEDULING

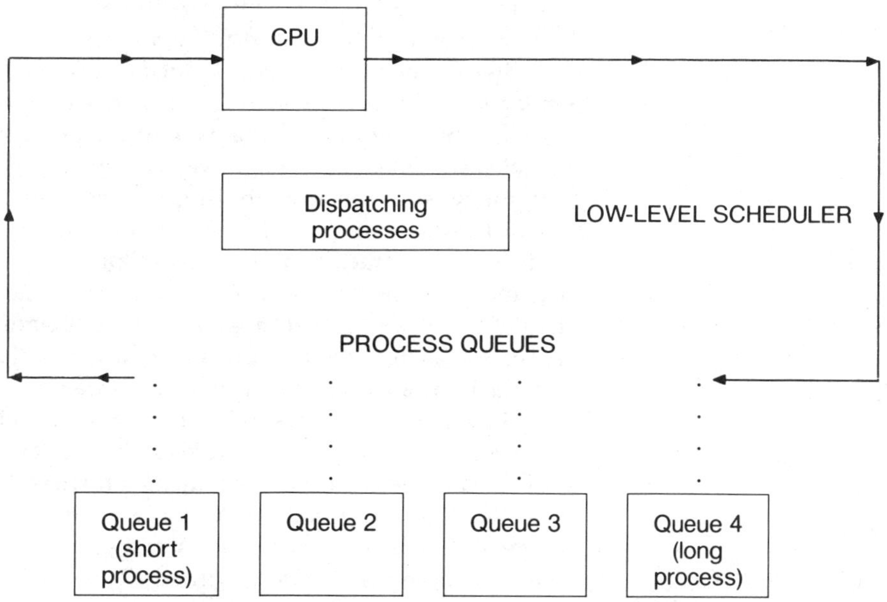

To handle the case where a process changes its performance characteristics, the operating system must keep track of not only which queue a process last inhabited, but its actual performance when in the processor. This information allows the queueing system to know if the process last used only a small portion of the allocated time-slice in the processor. If the process repeatedly uses only a small portion of its processor time-slice, it is clearly in the wrong queue.

A process that is frequently blocked remains in the queues designed for short processes. A process that uses a large amount of processor moves steadily toward the queues designed for longer processes, and remains there as long as it continues to use large amounts of processor time. If it then changes characteristics, and starts being blocked frequently, it is moved back up to the queues designed for processes requiring less processor time.

INTERMEDIATE-LEVEL SCHEDULING

The intermediate-level scheduler controls which processes are allowed into the queueing system and which are removed from it. The low-level scheduler controls the disposition of processes once they arrive in the queueing system, but does not have any influence on how they arrive in the queueing system or when they are removed from it. Only the more complex operating systems even have intermediate-level schedulers, since the primary purpose of such a scheduler is to balance and optimize the workload on the computer, and simple systems usually do not concern themselves with optimizing the workload.

The efficiency of a heavily-loaded computer is greatly affected by the particular mix of processes running. It is usually not possible to vary the basic types of jobs in the system; that is, a time-sharing system always has time-sharing jobs, and a batch system always has batch jobs. It is, however, possible to vary the types of processes in the queueing system at any given time.

Processes can usually be divided into different categories based on their performance characteristics. Almost all processes do some I/O, use some memory, and use some processor time, but most processes use more of one resource than of the others. Sometimes a process uses significantly more of one type of resource than the others. In this case, it is possible to refer to that process as **processor-intensive, I/O-intensive,** or **memory-intensive.**

The best mix of processes to have in the queueing system at any one time is a mix that fully utilizes the processor, the I/O, and the memory. Processes that are I/O-intensive tend to need many short slices of time in the processor, while processes that are processor-intensive or memory-intensive need fewer, but longer slices of time in the processor. If all the processes in the queue are I/O-intensive, then the processor will be idle or switching much of the time while the processes are waiting on I/O. If all the processes in the queueing system are memory-intensive, then they are not all likely to fit in memory at once, and

Example 6-3:

INTERMEDIATE-LEVEL SCHEDULER

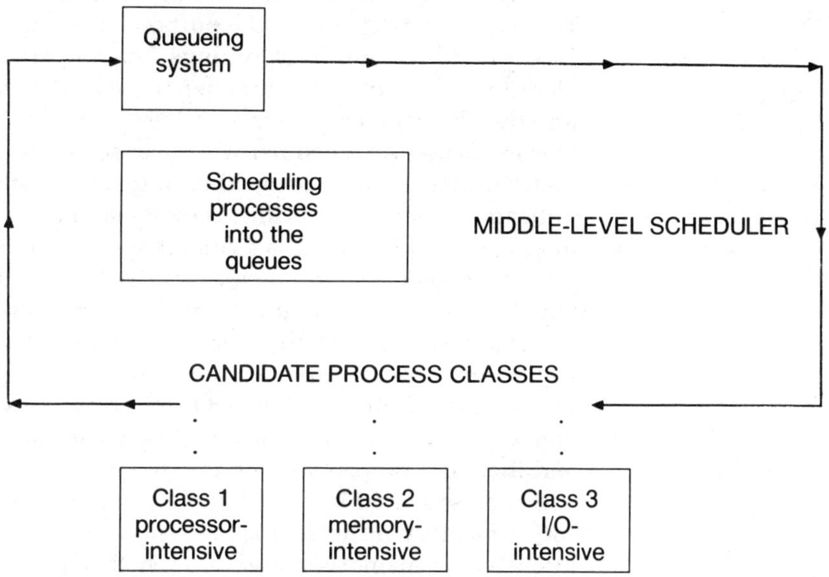

consequently much of the processor time will be spent moving them in and out of memory. Either condition is inefficient in processor utilization and should be avoided whenever possible.

The queueing system should contain enough memory-intensive processes to fully utilize the memory, enough processor-intensive processes to fully utilize the processor, and enough I/O-intensive processes to fully utilize the I/O system. Attaining this perfect mixture is very difficult and requires, in addition to a good scheduling algorithm, the ability to correctly determine whether a process is processor-intensive, I/O-intensive, or memory-intensive. Since many processes use a large amount of more than one type of resource, these processes must also be understood in order to attain a proper mixture of processes in the queueing system.

A tracking technique similar to the feedback mechanism used with the low-level schedulers is used to track the performance of different processes and to determine the current characteristics of each. Care must be taken when setting up this tracking mechanism to ensure that enough information is retained about each process to allow determination of the characteristics of that process, but not so much that too much overhead is generated by the tracking. It is very important that the tracking system be simple enough so that only a very small amount of overhead is generated by it. Once the tracking mechanism is in place each process can be flagged by type. This information can then be used in balancing the workload.

The intermediate-level scheduler should run only at certain intervals. These intervals depend on the purpose of the operating system and the complexity of the scheduling algorithms. The simplest method is to have the scheduler run at fixed intervals, although this may tend to frequently leave processes unscheduled for a longer period than is desirable. Another method is to run the intermediate-level scheduler whenever some resource is significantly over- or under-utilized. The latter method implies a method of monitoring resource utilization, but this is usually necessary anyhow. Probably the best method for intermediate scheduling is a combination of both; that is, run the scheduler whenever some resource is significantly over- or under-utilized, and to run it anyhow if a certain amount of time has passed since the last time it was run.

Intermediate schedulers are similar to other schedulers in that several algorithms exist for implementing them. The simpler algorithms just monitor the processor utilization, the I/O activity to the various I/O devices, and the memory utilization. If the activity in a particular part of the I/O system is low, and there is a process waiting that requires that part of the I/O system, then that process should be placed in the queueing system. Similarly, if the processor or memory utilization is low, and a process is waiting that is processor-intensive or memory-intensive, then that process should be placed in the queueing system.

This simple algorithm works well with lightly-loaded computers, but tends to break down when the load is high because some processes may seldom get into the queueing system if their particular characteristics do not fit the current load. Some means must be available to guarantee a minimum level of service provided to all processes.

This "minimum level of service" concept is used in many of the more complex algorithms. It is called, not surprisingly, **service levels** for processes. This simply means that different types of processes may receive different levels of service, and the same process may receive different levels of service depending upon the overall load on the computer at any given time. It is reasonable to have a processor-intensive process spend a long time in the queueing system when the computer is lightly loaded, but that same process should spend much less time in the queueing system when the computer is heavily loaded.

Service levels are selected for each type of process at several different load levels. This then allows the scheduler to ensure that each process has received a fair share of time in the queueing system. Such levels ensure that each process will get access to the processor even when the system load is very high. The amount of service given to each process may be greatly reduced from the normal level, but at least some service is provided.

The addition of service levels makes the scheduler seem complete, but experience has shown that such schedulers sometimes tend to not work well when the system load is very high. The scheduler can over-compensate and spend too much time moving processes into and out of the queueing system without allowing any one process enough time in there.

Example 6-4:

SERVICE LEVELS

Queue 1 — Interactive jobs — Time slice .1 second
Queue 2 — Intermediate jobs — Time slice .8 second
Queue 3 — CPU intensive jobs — Time slice 6.4 seconds

Jobs that complete one time slice in Queue 1 without performing any I/O are moved into Queue 2. Jobs in Queue 2 are only dispatched one-eighth as often as jobs in Queue 1, but have a time slice eight times as long. Jobs that complete six time slices in Queue 2 without performing any I/O are moved to Queue 3. Jobs in Queue 3 are only dispatched one-eighth as often as jobs in Queue 2, but again have a time slice eight times as long.

The problem of over-compensation can be partially avoided by adding some additional sophistication to the scheduling algorithm. One way to do this is to classify the processes more accurately. If the process classification is not extensive enough, merely adding or re-defining service levels for certain classes of processes sometimes makes a significant difference in the performance of the scheduler.

Another way is to change the service levels for some of the different load levels within a specific process class. Seemingly small changes in these areas can sometimes make very significant differences in the success of the scheduler. The services levels and process classifications are sometimes made available to a systems programmer maintaining the operating system as parameters that can be used to tune the performance of the system.

Some operating systems have an option that allows certain privileged users, such as systems programmers, to specify that a certain process or group of processes is guaranteed to be in the queueing system a certain percentage of the time that process is in the computer. If no processes in that category are available to use the processor, then other processes are scheduled normally. Whenever processes of the specified category are available, they are kept in the queueing system until the specified percentage of processor time has been met for that time interval. Once the percentage has been met, those processes are then scheduled normally for the remainder of that time period.

Each step forward in the development of intermediate-level schedulers has demonstrated that some problem can be addressed by just adding slightly more complexity to the scheduler. The trap that must be avoided is adding so much complexity to the scheduler that is causes an excessive amount of system overhead. In many cases, it is advantageous to use a simpler scheduling algorithm, even though certain problem areas may not be addressed well, just to control the complexity of the scheduler.

HIGH-LEVEL SCHEDULING

A high-level scheduler, sometimes also known as a job scheduler, processes the list of jobs input to the system, analyzes the expected performance characteristics of each job, breaks the jobs up into individual processes where possible, and prepares those processes to be input to the intermediate-level scheduler. These schedulers were initially developed for use with batch systems and are usually more effective in a batch environment than in a time-sharing environment.

Example 6-5:

HIGH-LEVEL SCHEDULER

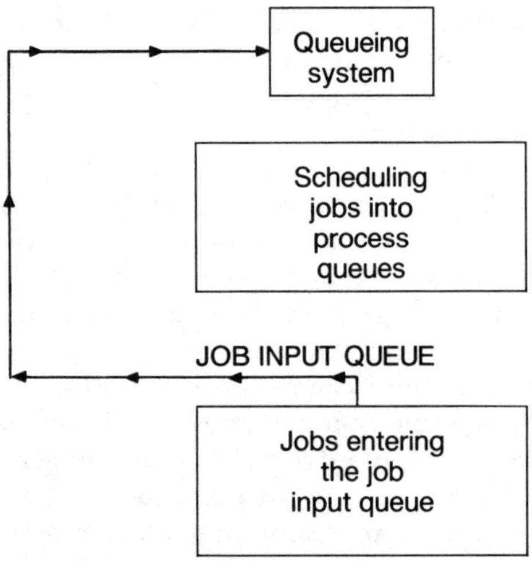

The first thing such a scheduler must do is correctly select the jobs from the input list. There are several different algorithms for determining which job should be selected first from the input list. The simplest algorithm is **FIFO,** which stands for **first in first out.** This is a very simple algorithm which says that the job that has been in the input list the longest is the job which is selected, or that the first job that entered the input list (of the jobs now in it), is the first job to be removed from the list.

The FIFO algorithm is simple and it ensures complete fairness to all jobs, but it does nothing to optimize system throughput. FIFO may mean that a job requiring only ten seconds of computer time must wait until a job requiring ten hours has completed, even though running the ten-second job first helps its turnaround time immensely without significantly affecting the turnaround time of the ten-hour job.

Example 6-6:

FIFO ALGORITHM

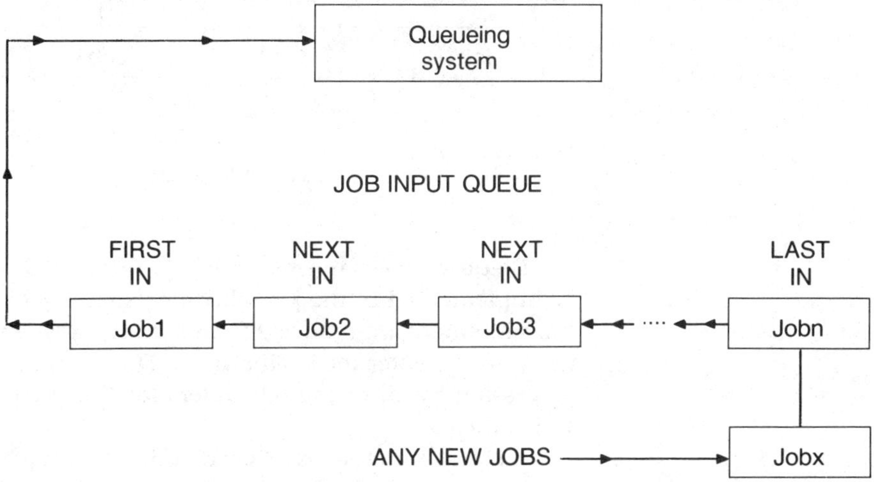

An algorithm to solve the case of the short job waiting on the long job is called **SJF, or Shortest Job First.** This algorithm involves the job scheduler regularly scanning the input job list and always scheduling the shortest job on that list. This algorithm works very well in allowing many short jobs quick throughput, but it has a couple of major problems. It may cause a long job to never get scheduled if there are many short jobs in the system, and it requires some reliable way of determining the length of time each job is expected to require.

The only way of determining the estimated job length when that job is still in the input job list is to have the user estimate the length and input that estimate with the job. It is very difficult for the average user to make even a rough approximation of the time required for jobs, and the scheduling algorithm breaks down completely when several jobs that are estimated to be short actually turn out to be very long. This is complicated by the fact that knowledgeable users may deliberately under-estimate the time required for their jobs so that those jobs will be scheduled for execution sooner.

Example 6-7:

SJF ALGORITHM
THE SHORTEST JOB IS THE NEXT TO BE SCHEDULED, REGARDLESS OF POSITION IN THE INPUT QUEUE

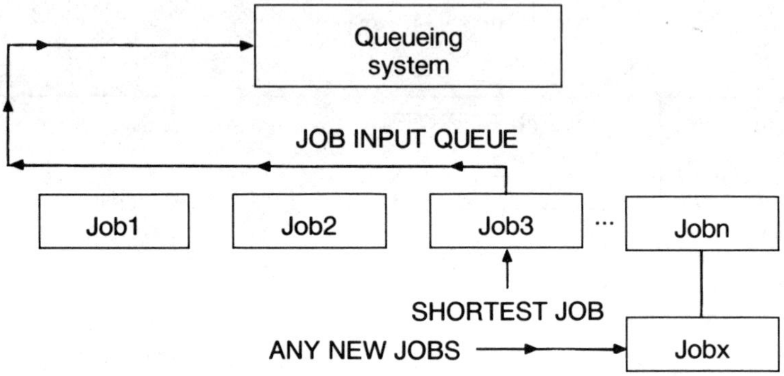

Feedback mechanisms similar to those used by low-level schedulers may be implemented in the job scheduler, so that jobs that exceed their estimated time allotment are returned from both the low- and intermediate-level schedulers, and re-enter the job input list. This technique requires a large amount of processing by all of the schedulers for this purpose, and the gain is seldom worth the cost.

A simpler method is to just halt the execution of the job after the estimated time has elapsed. The job is aborted (the execution is halted with no restart possible) and the result returned to the user; this solves the scheduling problem but can lead to unhappy users. The job can also be **checkpointed** (the current status saved in a fashion that allows continued execution at a future time) and then re-scheduled, but this also causes users to be angry.

A more complex job scheduling algorithm is known as **HRN,** or **highest response ratio next.** This was developed by Hansen, and is a modification of the SJF algorithm that solves the problem of long jobs waiting excessively. This algorithm operates in a fashion similar to SJF, except that instead of just picking the shortest job to schedule next, the algorithm also calculates the length of time each job has been waiting. The longer a job has waited, the more likely that it will be scheduled. Long jobs do not get scheduled immediately, but are more likely to be scheduled as they wait longer.

The true priority of the job is calculated by calculating the normal priority for a job of that length class, and then calculating wait time, and adding the two priorities. The separate priority is calculated by adding the estimated job length to the time waiting and dividing by the estimated job length. This ratio equals 1 when the wait time is 0 and grows as the wait time grows. Eventually the ratio is high enough so that the job gets scheduled ahead of shorter jobs.

Example 6-8:

HANSEN'S HRN ALGORITHM

$$\text{HRN priority} = \frac{\text{(estimated job length)} + \text{(time waiting)}}{\text{(estimated job length)}}$$

$$\text{final priority} = \text{(normal SJF priority)} + \text{(HRN priority)}$$

One of the likely functions of the job scheduler is to ensure that all necessary resources are available when a particular job is scheduled. Jobs require additional resources, such as memory or specific data files. Some of these resources are easier to allocate than others, but all must be available during job execution.

The simple approach is for the scheduler to acquire all required resources before the job is allowed out of the input queue. This ensures that the job will not spend a long time in the queueing system waiting for a file or memory to become available. The problem with this technique is that it requires that several different resources all be available at the same time, which is sometimes difficult to achieve. Attempting to make all necessary resources available at the same time may require that some of those resources remain allocated to that job for a long period of time while waiting for the last few resources to be collected. Because of this, it is not efficient to have resources allocated to a job before it actually begins executing, so this characteristic should be controlled as much as possible.

Another algorithm is to ignore the resources requested by the job when scheduling the job, and only attempt to allocate each resource when it is actually required by the job. This method prevents a resource remaining allocated for a long period of time. It may, however, lead to a job remaining in a blocked state for a long period of time while waiting for some resource to become available.

Probably the best method is some combination of the above two techniques. Each of the jobs in the input job list should be scanned for resources that are known to need a long lead time for allocation, such as file requests. The job then waits in the input queue until those scarce resources have been allocated to it, while other resources, such as memory, are not allocated until the job actually requires them. The difficulty with this method, of course, is determining which resources are difficult to acquire. In the absence of a clear definition of which resources are difficult to acquire, the better algorithm is to allocate the resources only when specifically requested.

Checkpointing

Checkpointing a job and then restarting it later is not a particularly simple task. It is first necessary to ensure that the job was interrupted only at a clean break, since interrupting it in the middle of an I/O operation could be catastrophic. In order to prevent such problems, the job must have no outstanding requests to the operating system when it is checkpointed. All pertinent characteristics of the job must be saved. The best way of doing this is to just keep a copy of the memory allocated to that job, since that memory presumably has all necessary program values. It is also necessary to store the current status of the environment in which the job is executing, so that that environment can be recreated later.

Restarting the job then requires loading the copy back into memory and scheduling the job. Any other characteristics of the job, such as open files, for example, must be re-opened as they were when the job was previously running. Information such as this needs to be saved with the environmental information.

SUMMARY

Low-level schedulers control which processes are allocated time in the processor. One method for this is the round-robin system, where each process is allocated a fixed time slice in the processor. When each process exceeds the time allotted to it, it is placed at the end of the queue, and the process at the head of the queue is scheduled into the processor. This method can be varied by changing the time slices allocated to different types of processes.

A more sophisticated algorithm is to set up several process queues, and to allocate processes into the different queues via feedback mechanisms. Using such feedback mechanisms to dynamically modify the priorities and time slices allocated to each process allows the environment to be tailored specifically for processes that require different resources.

Intermediate-level schedulers are primarily concerned with optimizing the load on the computer. Different processes have different requirements for execution. The correct mix of these processes should be maintained in the queueing system at all times to allow for optimum usage of all resources.

High-level schedulers, also known as job schedulers, process jobs in the input job list and determine which job should next be sent to the intermediate-level scheduler. This is normally decided by the known characteristics of the job, such as estimated execution time and required resources.

EXERCISES

TRUE/FALSE

1. Low-level schedulers are concerned with jobs, not processes.
2. The round-robin system is the most efficient.
3. Dispatcher is another name for low-level schedulers.
4. The most sophisticated dispatching system is feedback queues.
5. The SJF algorithm dispatches the job that has been in the queue the longest.
6. Processor-intensive processes should not be queued with I/O-intensive processes.
7. The HRN algorithm favors short jobs or jobs that have been in the queue for a long time.
8. Implementing feedback queues requires tracking the performance characteristics of processes.
9. Not all systems require three different levels of schedulers.
10. Service levels refer to the amount of service a given process should receive at a given system load.

MULTIPLE CHOICE

1. The dispatcher:
   - **a)** Schedules the tasks into the processor
   - **b)** Is always very small and simple
   - **c)** Puts tasks in I/O wait
   - **d)** Never changes task priorities
2. The most complex dispatcher:
   - **a)** Should always be used
   - **b)** Should never be used
   - **c)** Is never used on large computers
   - **d)** Should only be used on large computers
3. Round-robin scheduling:
   - **a)** Is quite complex to implement
   - **b)** Allows interactive tasks quicker access to the processor
   - **c)** Allows processor-bound tasks more time in the processor
   - **d)** Gives each task the same chance at the processor

4. Processor-bound tasks:
   a) Use the processor more often
   b) Use more processor time
   c) Use less processor time
   d) Always take longer to execute
5. Feedback queues:
   a) Are very simple to implement
   b) Dispatch tasks according to execution characteristics
   c) Are used to favor real-time tasks
   d) Require manual intervention to implement properly
6. Complex scheduling algorithms:
   a) Use more resources than they gain
   b) Recover more resources than they use
   c) Always use many resources
   d) Are most appropriate for very large computers
7. I/O-intensive jobs:
   a) Use less processor time than most jobs
   b) Are constrained by their I/O requirements
   c) Run more quickly than processor-intensive jobs
   d) Should all be executed at the same time
8. The FIFO algorithm:
   a) First executes the job that last entered the queue
   b) First executes the job that first entered the queue
   c) First executes the job with the least processor needs
   d) First executes the job in the queue the longest
9. The SJF algorithm:
   a) First executes the job that last entered the queue
   b) First executes the job that first entered the queue
   c) First executes the job with the least processor needs
   d) First executes the job in the queue the longest
10. Checkpointing a job:
    a) Allows it to be completed successfully
    b) Allows it to continue executing later
    c) Prepares it for finishing
    d) Occurs only when there is an error in it

DISCUSSION QUESTIONS

1. Describe the three types of schedulers.
2. Describe round-robin scheduling.
3. Describe a simple feedback queue system.
4. List and describe process types.
5. Describe service levels.
6. Describe the FIFO algorithm for selecting jobs.
7. Describe the SJF algorithm for selecting jobs.
8. Describe the HRN algorithm for selecting jobs.
9. Briefly describe checkpointing.
10. Briefly describe the overall functions of a scheduler.

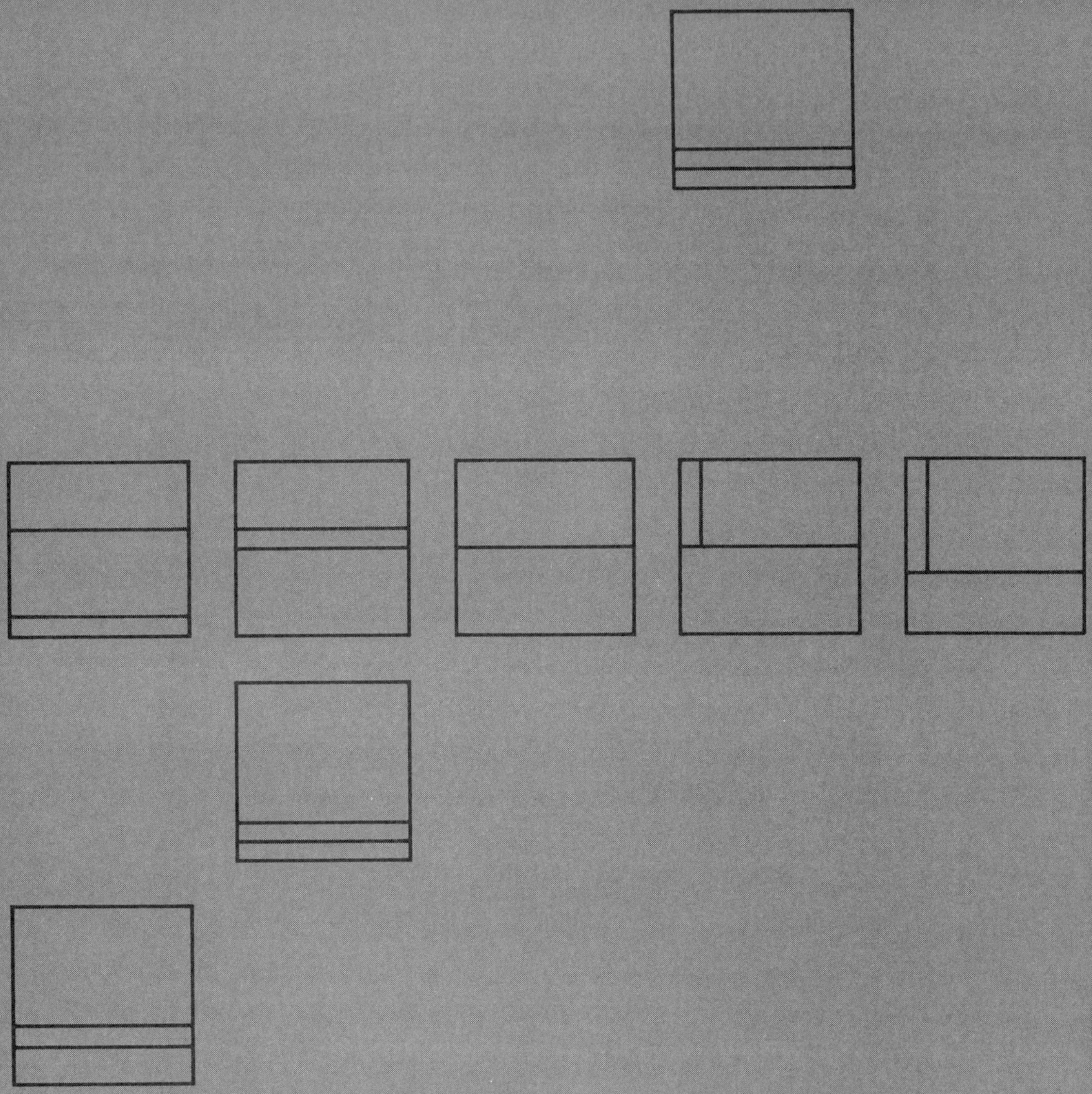

MEMORY MANAGEMENT

7

KEY TERMS

Relocatable	*Overlay segments*
Address	*Partitions*
Linkers	*Offset*
Fragmentation	*Loaders*
Garbage collector	*Compactor*
First-fit	*Best-fit*
Worst-fit	*Boundary registers*
SVC (Supervisor call)	*Swapping*
Overlaying	*Root segment*

INTRODUCTION

Multiprogramming causes great difficulties in the management of resources that must be shared between programs, and the most crucial of these resources is the internal memory on the computer. Very little memory management is needed as long as an operating system services only one program, but multiprogramming requires complex memory management.

Loading programs at a fixed memory location is extremely inefficient. Several improvements have been developed, but all of them require placing each program at different locations in memory. Much of the theory of memory management is an attempt to determine the best location to place programs.

Placing the programs at indeterminate locations requires the operating system to dynamically place the correct memory references in the programs when they are loaded into memory. This has the significant advantage that it allows the program to be written with no knowledge of where it is to be loaded. Allowing the memory locations to be inserted dynamically in programs is called making the program **relocatable,** which means that the program can be located wherever necessary within memory.

The location of an object (such as a variable, constant, etc.) in memory is known as the **address** of that object. The address of any object in memory specifies the exact byte where that object is located. Such addresses are specified as a number, usually in hexadecimal notation, that is the distance (or **offset**) of that location as measured from the beginning of memory.

FIXED MEMORY LOCATIONS

The simplest method of memory management is to load all programs at fixed locations, so that no relocation of programs is necessary. The most basic form of fixed memory management allows only one program in memory at any one time. That program begins at the beginning of memory, and continues through memory until the end of the program is reached. Each location in that program is relatively easy to calculate, since all that need be known is the offset of that variable from the beginning of the program. The actual location of the variables is the same as the offset of that variable from the beginning of the program, since all programs are loaded at the beginning of memory.

A better version of fixed memory management involves breaking memory up into small pieces, and loading programs into those smaller areas called **partitions.** The size of each partition is fixed, as is the beginning location of each partition. The partitions do not need to be the same size. This allows for programs of differing sizes to be loaded simultaneously.

A sample memory allocation is to divide memory into one partition containing one-half of available memory, one partition containing one-fourth of available memory, and four small partitions each containing one-sixteenth of available memory. This allows one large and one medium sized program to be run at any time, along with one small and four very small programs. This is an allocation suitable for most general applications.

Example 7-1:

PARTITION LAYOUT

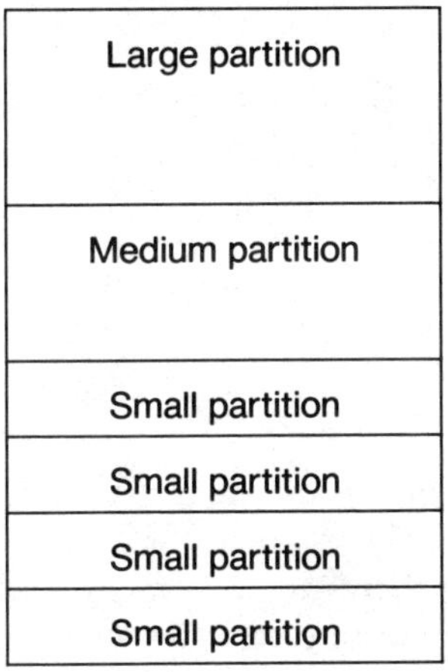

In a system such as this, programs are assigned to a specific partition when they are compiled. The location of the addresses in each program can be determined by adding the offset of the addresses within the program to the known beginning address of the partition in which that program is to run.

```
Actual address = (partition address) + (offset in program)
```

This calculation can be done either when the program is written or as part of the compilation process.

Setting up partitions in this way allows several programs to be in memory at the same time, but requires that the location and size of the partitions never be changed, since each such change requires re-compilation of every program that runs in that partition. Using this system also means that some very large programs cannot be run if those programs are larger than the largest partition, even though the total memory available may be large enough to run that program. It also means that a specific partition must be available when the program is to be run.

In the following example, programs 1 and 4 are compiled to run in partition C. If they are all trying to execute at the same time, only one is allowed into memory, while the other three partitions of the same size are unoccupied.

Example 7-2:

PROGRAMS WITH FIXED ADDRESSES

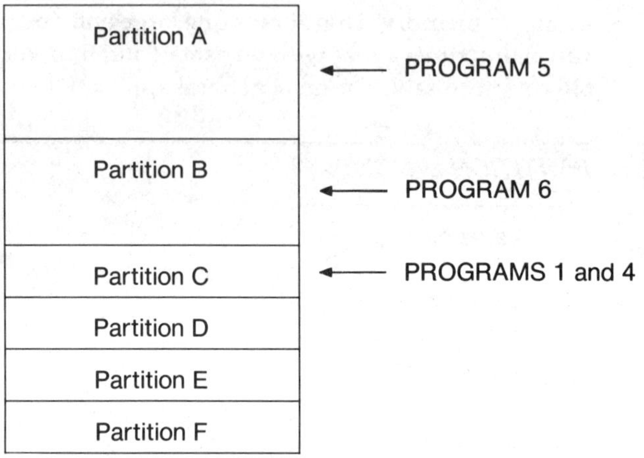

A slightly more flexible technique is to set up several possible partitions of varying sizes and origins. These partitions are divided into groups. Each group is a set of partitions that utilizes all of memory, and when the operating system is initially loaded, the operator selects which set of partitions is to be used at that time. Only programs that are compiled for the current set of partitions can be run while that set of partitions are loaded, but different sets of partitions allow different sets of programs to be executed. Some partitions may be identical across the different groups in order to allow certain generic programs to be run with each group of partitions.

RELOCATABLE PROGRAMS

Fixed partitions are a very simple solution to the problems of memory management, but they are not flexible enough for modern operating systems. Requiring programs to always execute at the same location in memory puts far too many restrictions on programs. A much better method of memory allocation is to allow programs to be loaded at any location. This requires that all the addresses in that program be modified to correctly match the location where the program is loaded.

The partitions may still have fixed sizes and fixed locations, but allowing the programs to be loaded at different areas allows those programs to be loaded into different partitions, which provides much more flexibility. Programs may still be required to wait until a partition of the correct size becomes available, but they are not tied to a particular partition.

In the following example, programs 1 through 4 are similar to those in the previous example, but here they are relocatable, and therefore can run in any available partition.

Example 7-3:

RELOCATABLE PROGRAMS

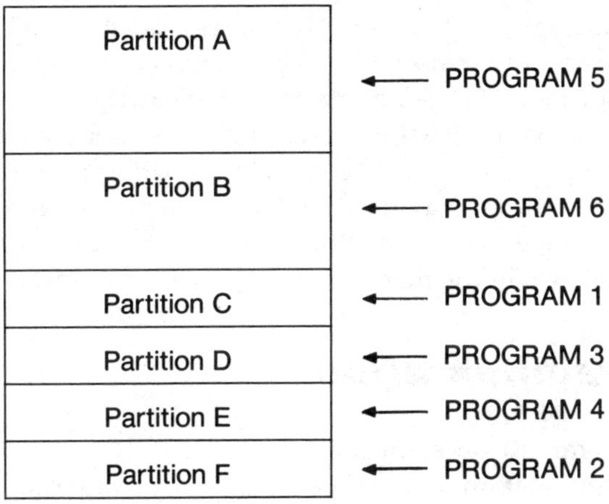

Making programs relocatable means that some process must modify all the addresses in each program when that program is loaded into partition. This is the function provided by the linkers or loaders that were covered in earlier chapters. The loader goes through each program, finds all the references to memory, and recalculates each of those addresses. This process must be repeated each time a program is to be loaded into a partition.

```
Actual address = (partition address) + (offset in program)
```

This calculation is exactly the same one that was performed for programs that were allowed to load into only one partition. The difference is that the earlier calculation was done during or before the program was compiled, while this calculation is done after the program is compiled, each time the program is loaded into memory. Doing these calculations at this point removes the requirement for re-compiling the programs in order to load them into different partitions.

Dynamic partition allocation

There is still a problem of inefficient memory utilization as long as partitions of fixed sizes are used, since programs come in all sizes, and only rarely will a program exactly fit a partition. A way to solve this problem is to have partitions that are not of a fixed size. There is no way of knowing in advance either the origin or length of partitions such as these, which complicates the memory management task, and greatly improves efficient utilization of memory.

Partitions are created when a new program needs to begin executing. The scheduling routines look at each of the waiting processes to determine their memory requirements. If there is an area of memory that is not currently in use, and it is large enough to satisfy the memory requirements of the highest priority waiting process, that process is scheduled. A partition is created in the free area of memory that is the correct size to contain the current process, and that process is loaded into that new partition.

Dynamic partition allocation has many advantages. Whenever there is enough memory free to contain a waiting process, that process can be scheduled without having to wait for a particular partition. The primary disadvantage of such an allocation method is the increased amount of complexity necessary in the memory management routines.

Fragmentation

A common problem that occurs with dynamic partition allocation is that of fragmentation of memory. This is very similar to the fragmentation in file system allocation. In this case, the fragmentation comes from partitions being allocated in a free area of memory and leaving only a very small amount of that area free. This free area of memory may not be large enough to be usable by any other programs.

Fragmentation conditions in memory should be handled similar to such conditions in the file system, that is, care should be taken when allocating memory to make the best use of the available area, and efforts should be made periodically to recover the fragmented areas of memory. One of the major design goals of the various memory allocation algorithms is preventing or reducing fragmentation.

A program can be run at intervals that collect all of the allocated and free memory areas into contiguous areas (this program is called a **garbage collecter**). It is also sometimes known as a **compactor,** since it compacts areas of memory usage. It should not be run very frequently, since it causes considerable system overhead, and if the memory allocation algorithms are designed well enough, it will not be needed often.

First-fit placement algorithm

There are several algorithms for determining where processes should be placed in memory. The three primary algorithms are: put the process in the first area in memory that is large enough to hold it, put the process in the memory that is the closest to the correct size, or place the process in the largest available area. Each of these algorithms has strengths and weaknesses.

The simplest algorithm, to place the process in the first memory area that is large enough, is known as the **first-fit** algorithm. It frequently leads to excessive fragmentation, since the first available memory area is usually somewhat larger than the process, but not necessarily very much larger. This frequently leads to small, free, unusable areas of memory. The biggest advantage of this algorithm is that it requires very little processing time in order to fit a process into memory.

Example 7-4:

FIRST-FIT ALGORITHM
(ALL PARTITIONS ARE EMPTY)

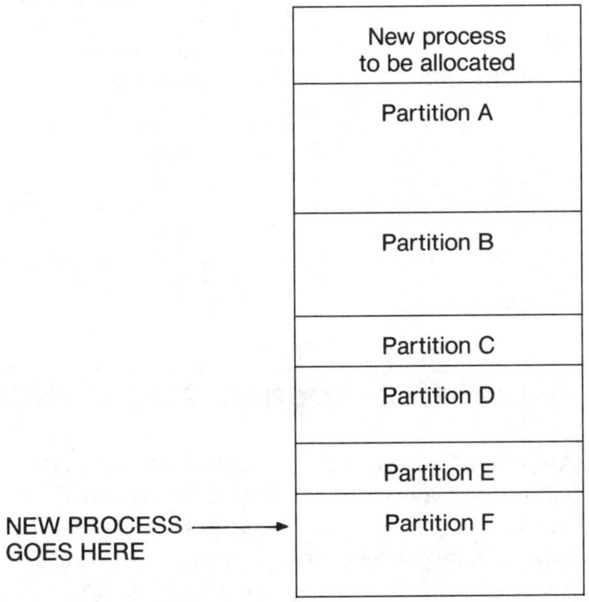

Best-fit placement algorithm

Another algorithm attempts to fit each process into the free memory area that is closest in size to the requirements of that process (the partition must be larger). It makes the best use of memory, since fewer fragmented areas of memory develop. The primary problem with this algorithm is the relatively large amount of processing time required to search all of memory to find the free area best suited in size.

Example 7-5:

BEST-FIT ALGORITHM (ALL PARTITIONS ARE EMPTY)

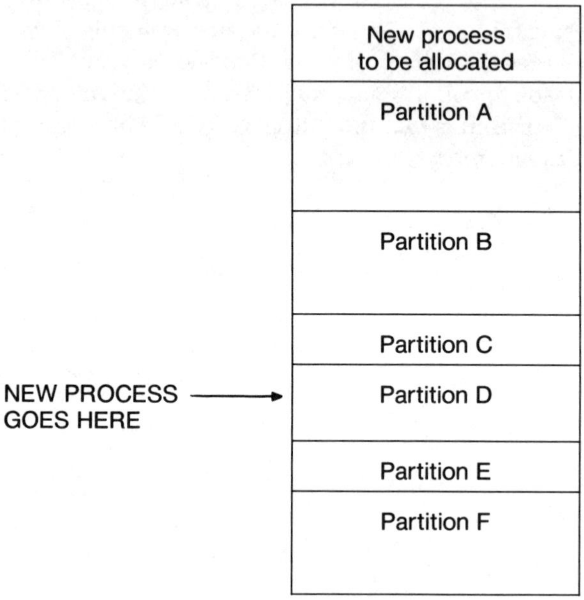

Worst-fit placement algorithm

An algorithm that at first seems ridiculous, but actually is quite reasonable, is sometimes known as the **worst-fit** algorithm. This algorithm attempts to always place processes in the largest available free memory area. This algorithm usually requires less processing time than finding the best fit, since it is much easier to find the largest free area than it is to find the best-fitting free area. Placing the process in the largest possible free area virtually guarantees that some part of that area will be unused. Because the process was placed in the largest available area, the unused part of that area tends to be quite large, and may be large enough to contain another entire process. Fragmentation is thus reduced, since the new free areas are large enough to be usable.

Example 7-6:

WORST-FIT ALGORITHM (ALL PARTITIONS ARE EMPTY)

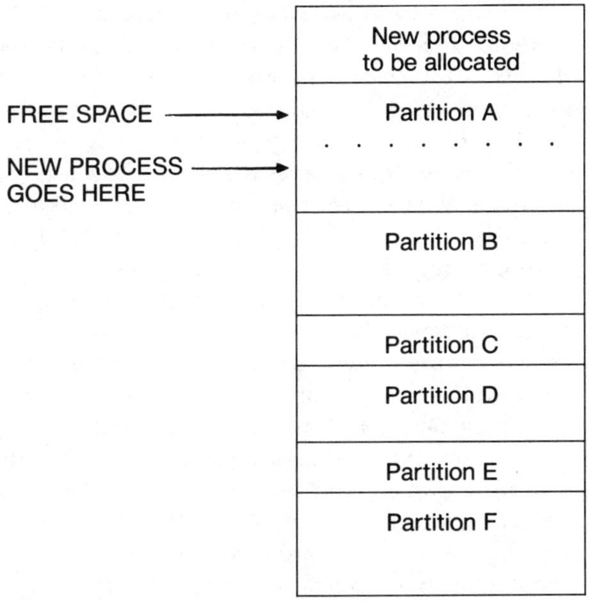

Loading a process into the smallest possible memory area usually results in very small areas of memory becoming completely unusable. The advantage is that the unusable areas are very small, but the disadvantage is that such small unusable areas are virtually certain. Loading processes into the largest possible area of memory makes unused parts of memory certain, but the likelihood that such areas may be large enough to be used by another process is quite high. The worst-fit algorithm is not common; the most common algorithms are either first-fit or best-fit. Determining the best algorithm largely depends upon the types of programs running on that system.

One solution to the problem of fragmentation is to use an allocation technique that does not require all memory allocations to be in contiguous groups. This is proven to work in file systems, but files are relatively stable compared to processes in memory. The overhead generated by the calculations necessary to do non-contiguous files allocations is quite small, but the overhead necessary to support non-contiguous memory allocations can become quite large. The necessity for such allocations has been essentially removed by the use of virtual memory systems, which break each process up into very small pieces, and require a contiguous memory allocation only for each of the pieces.

MEMORY PROTECTION

Any operating system that allows more than one process to reside in memory simultaneously must provide some facility to protect the memory belonging to each process from access by other processes. This is true even on single-user systems, since such systems almost invariably have both the user process and the operating system both in memory at the same time. Protection becomes even more crucial on multiprogramming systems, which allow multiple processes to reside in memory simultaneously.

For example, a process that is part of a user program cannot be allowed to modify any part of the operating system, or the system may fail. Even worse is the case where the system does not completely fail, but continues to execute with incorrect results, such as where the file writing routines in the operating system are accidentally modified to write files in different locations from where the operating system thinks they are being written. This type of change does not immediately lead to a system failure, but by the time the problem is detected the integrity of the file system is completely destroyed.

The usual protection method for single-user operating systems is to divide the memory into two logical partitions. One of these partitions is used by the operating system, and the other partition is used by the user programs. The operating system is normally loaded into memory starting at the lowest location, and extends upward through memory to some known location. The user program is then loaded into memory starting at the location where the operating system ends.

The address of the "boundary," where the operating system ends and the user programs begin, is loaded into a hardware register, and each memory access made by the user program is compared to the address in the boundary register. Such memory references are allowed only if the address is greater than that in the boundary register. This is a very easy check for memory violations, and since the boundary address is in a hardware register, such comparisons are very quick and efficient.

In operating systems supporting multiprogramming, the protection problem becomes more complex. Not only must the operating system be protected from access by each of the user processes, but those processes must be protected from each other. It is not sufficient to merely prevent user processes from modifying storage owned by another process, but those processes must also be prevented from even reading the storage owned by another process. This is important because some of the storage owned by other processes may be secret, such as financial data. If such protection mechanisms did not exist, user programs could be written that would simply snoop through all of the processes in memory until finding a process with critical data, then read that data and print it out.

One way of implementing protection in multiprogramming systems is to use many boundary registers. There must be a set of registers for each partition.

Systems with a fixed number of partitions require a fixed number of boundary registers (one set for each partition). Systems with a variable number of partitions must be set up so that whenever a new partition is created, a set of boundary registers is available for use with that partition. This is one reason why systems with a varying number of partitions usually have some maximum number of possible partitions that can be in use at any one time.

Each set of boundary registers contains the beginning and ending address of one partition, and is dedicated to the use of that partition. Each memory reference made by the program running in that partition is then checked against the boundary registers for that partition to ensure the memory reference is neither above nor below the limits of that partition.

Example 7-7:

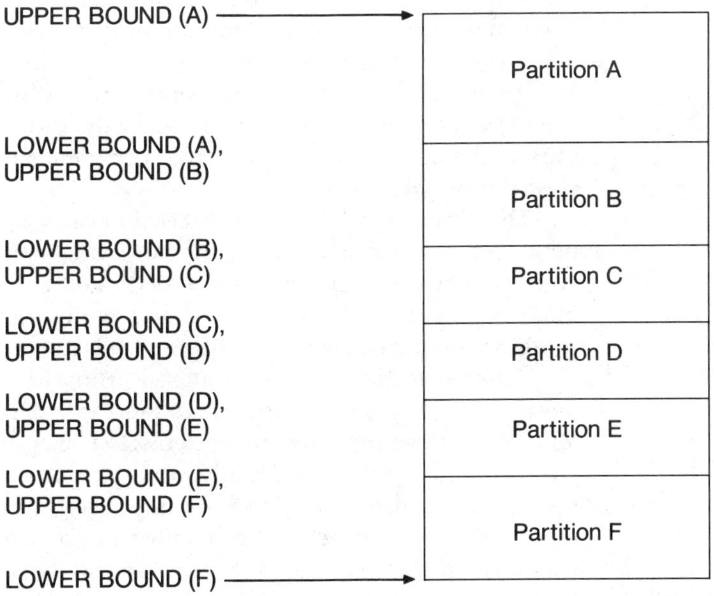

There are some cases where user programs may need to have access to memory that is part of the operating system. This is usually when using certain operating system facilities. The easiest way to provide this access is to allow the user programs to actually modify some area in the operating system. Allowing any user program to directly modify a location in the operating system is extremely dangerous, however, since it then becomes very difficult to determine whether that program is modifying areas beyond that allowed.

Some means must be available to provide access to those facilities without allowing user programs direct access to operating system memory. This access is usually provided via a technique called a **supervisor call,** or **SVC.** This is a facility available to user programs that allows them to request that the operating system, or supervisor, provide some system service to the user program. Such a supervisor call provides the operating systems service that the user program needs without actually allowing that program access to the operating system memory.

OTHER MEMORY MANAGEMENT ALGORITHMS

There are two other memory management algorithms that deserve mention. The first of these is known as **swapping.** This is a technique where partitions are not used; instead, all available memory except that which is allocated to the operating system is allocated to one specific program. That program executes for a period of time, until it is swapped out, and another program is given control of memory and the processor. When the program is swapped out, an exact copy of the memory allocated to that program is written out to a disk drive or special internal memory.

This technique was primarily used in early time-sharing systems, but it is now used occasionally in conjunction with virtual memory systems, where large portions of memory may be dedicated to one program, and the entire block is swapped out when another program is brought into memory. The combination of swapping and paging leads to very complex algorithms.

Another technique that was used primarily on early computers is called **overlaying** of programs. This was a precursor of modern virtual memory systems. As with virtual memory systems, the object of using overlaying is to provide more memory than actually exists to executing programs. Overlaying of programs is controlled by the program itself, unlike most memory management techniques which are controlled by the operating system. Overlaying was developed in response to computers with small physical memories, no virtual memory, and large memory requirements by user programs.

Overlaying is a process where the user program is divided up into several parts. One part is the **root segment,** which is the base of the program. This part must always remain in memory. There are other parts of the program, however, that do not execute at the same time, and can therefore take turns in memory. Examples of this might be different subroutines, both of which are called by the main program. Only one of these subroutines can execute at any one time, so therefore only one of these subroutines need be resident in memory at any one time.

A program written like this can be set up with overlays, where the two different subroutines take turns occupying the same part of memory. Because only the root segment and one of the subroutines need be in memory at any one time, the memory size necessary is only as large as the sum of the root segment size and the largest segment size. The user program is in control of which overlay segment is loaded at any time. Care must be taken to ensure that the overlay segment currently loaded is the one that is currently executing.

Overlaying is most useful when each overlay segment is approximately the same size. If there are only two overlay segments and one is very large while the other is very small, not much is achieved by setting up overlays.

The primary problem with overlaying is that it must be done by the user program instead of by the operating system. This requires much more effort by the programmer, plus a considerable knowledge of what overlays are and how to achieve optimum results. A better technique is to provide such services by the operating system, so that it is transparent to the programmer. Another problem with overlaying is that the process of doing the overlay is controlled by the user program, which is much less efficient than performing such functions in the computer hardware, such as is provided by paging systems.

Example 7-8:

OVERLAY STRATEGY IN ANY GIVEN PARTITION

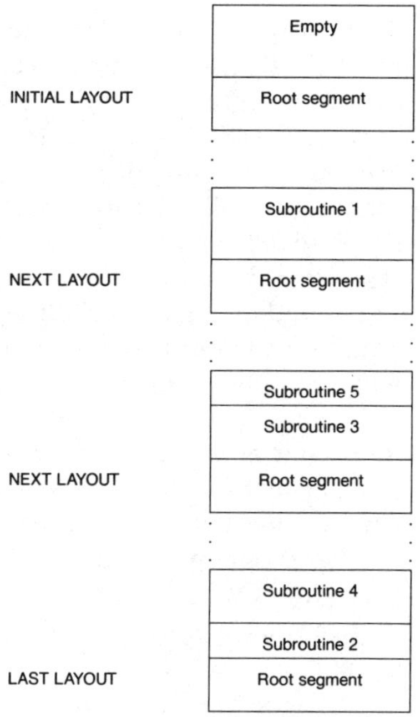

SUMMARY

Any program loaded into memory must have the correct values specified for any memory references made in that program. Programs can be loaded at a particular fixed location, which allows the values in memory references to be calculated when the program is compiled, but a more flexible approach is to set the program up so that it can be loaded at any location. The memory calculations are done by programs which load the programs into memory and prepare them for execution.

Memory can be allocated in a number of ways. The simplest way is to allow only one program into memory at any one time, and to load it at a specific fixed address. Multiprogramming systems require that several programs be in memory at any time, so memory is divided up into partitions. Simple partitioning involves dividing memory up into small areas, each of which starts at a specific fixed address. A slightly more advanced version of this idea allows different sets of partitions to be loaded in at different times.

The most flexible form of the partitioning system is to have the partitioning process be dynamic. In this type of system, each program has certain memory requirements, and when that program is loaded into memory, it is loaded into a partition that most nearly matches the size of that program. Such a system has a maximum number of partitions that can be in memory at any one time.

There are two primary algorithms for deciding which area of memory a program is loaded into. One algorithm, best-fit, checks each partition and the one that most nearly fits the program size is the one that receives the program. The first-fit algorithm checks partition sizes, and places the program in the first partition that is large enough to contain it.

When many programs are allowed to simultaneously occupy memory, some means must be provided for preventing any of those programs from accessing the memory owned by any of the other programs. This is usually implemented by sets of boundary registers. Each set of boundary registers contains the lowest and highest memory address owned by that program. Each memory reference made by that program is checked to ensure that it is between the low and high values. Any program that requires access to operating system functions is allowed to access those facilities via a supervisor call.

Other memory management techniques include swapping, where all of the available memory is allocated to one program, which is periodically swapped out to allow other programs into memory. A technique that was once quite common is overlaying. Overlaying requires a root segment, which is always in memory, and various overlay segments, which overlay one another in the same area of memory as needed.

EXERCISES

TRUE/FALSE

1. Single-user operating systems require no memory protection.
2. Fixed partitions are less efficient than variable partitions.
3. Linkers and Loaders are not needed with relocatable programs.
4. The worst-fit algorithm should never be used.
5. Garbage collecting refers to consolidating free memory areas.
6. SVC is a means of obtaining operating system functions.
7. Swapping is never used in modern operating systems.
8. Overlays are best with equal-sized subroutines.
9. Boundary registers are used for memory protection.
10. Programs designed to be loaded at a fixed location are inefficient.

MULTIPLE CHOICE

1. Relocatable programs:
   - **a)** Cannot be used with fixed partitions
   - **b)** Can be loaded almost anywhere in memory
   - **c)** Do not need a linker
   - **d)** Can only be loaded at one specific location
2. Fixed partitions:
   - **a)** Are very common in current operating systems
   - **b)** Are very efficient in memory utilization
   - **c)** Are very inefficient in memory utilization
   - **d)** Are most used on large mainframe operating systems
3. A linker:
   - **a)** Is not necessary with variable partitions
   - **b)** Must be run after the loader
   - **c)** Creates a load module
   - **d)** Is not needed with a good compiler
4. The garbage collector:
   - **a)** Is critical for efficient virtual memory systems
   - **b)** Prevents fragmentation from occurring
   - **c)** Is mostly used with fixed partitions
   - **d)** Collects fragmented areas of memory

5. The first-fit algorithm:
   a) Places a program in the first possible partition
   b) Places a program in the best possible partition
   c) Waits for the correct partition to become available
   d) Places the first program in the best partition
6. The worst-fit algorithm:
   a) Is only used when nothing better is available
   b) Places a program in largest available partition
   c) Should never be used
   d) Places a program in the smallest possible partition
7. Boundary registers:
   a) Are used for temporary program variable storage
   b) Are only necessary with fixed partitions
   c) Track the beginning and ending of programs
   d) Track page boundaries
8. Overlaying:
   a) Requires use of a loader
   b) Allows larger programs, but requires more effort
   c) Is most used on large computers
   d) Is transparent to the user
9. The root segment:
   a) Is the bottom-most partition in the system
   b) Is where the operating system is loaded
   c) Is the part of an overlay that is always in memory
   d) Is the part of an overlay that is replaced
10. Swapping:
   a) Works best with many small partitions
   b) Allows many programs to simultaneously use memory
   c) Allows each program in turn to use the memory
   d) Does not work with overlaying

DISCUSSION QUESTIONS

1. Describe fixed memory management.
2. Explain what is meant by "relocatable programs".
3. Discuss memory fragmentation.
4. Describe the first fit placement algorithm.
5. Describe the best fit placement algorithm.
6. Describe the worst fit placement algorithm.
7. Discuss the pros and cons of each of the above algorithms.
8. Briefly desribe how boundary registers are used with multiprogramming.
9. Describe how swapping works.
10. Describe how overlaying works.

VIRTUAL MEMORY

8

KEY TERMS

Pages	*Working set*
DAT (dynamic address translation)	*Thrashing*
Segmentation	*Page frames*
Direct mapping	*Map table*
Page fault	*Associative mapping*
Fetching pages	*Table lookaside buffer*
Anticipatory paging	*Demand paging*
LRU (least recently used)	*NUR (not used recently)*
Reference bit	*Page stealing*

INTRODUCTION

The traditional memory management techniques are not adequate for the memory requirements of modern programs. They do not utilize memory well enough, nor do they provide enough memory to satisfy many programs. The physical memory sizes on computers are simply too small for many programs to run efficiently. The solution to both problems is **virtual memory.**

All of real memory is divided into small pieces, normally two to four thousand bytes (2K - 4K) each, called **page frames.** Each page frame can hold a **page,** which is memory allocated to an executing process. Memory is copied onto **paging devices,** which are usually disk drives.

The primary limitation of the paging concept is the length of time it takes to write out and read in pages. Therefore, the speed of the paging device is very important. Disk drives are usually the fastest devices available, but in certain cases the efficiency of the paging system is so critical that the expense of a dedicated paging device is justified to obtain the extra speed in paging. Some manufacturers have developed devices for paging that have much higher data transfer speeds than disk drives. One example of such a device is memory similar to that contained in the computer but connected to the computer as a peripheral device.

An example of an implementation of virtual memory is the IBM MVS operating system. This system runs efficiently on computers with as little as four megabytes of internal memory, yet is able to provide a virtual memory allocation of sixteen megabytes to each of several users. Good throughput is achievable in such a system configuration with as many as ten to fifteen users, which represents a large improvement over simpler systems, which might allow only one such user at a time.

MEMORY ORGANIZATION

The basic concept of virtual memory is to extend real memory by the use of disk drives or other paging devices. Each page frame in the internal memory may contain a page of memory, while each page of memory in the system may be either on disk or resident in memory.

The correct size for page frames is a subject of some debate. Small page frames provide for efficient utilization of memory, but may lead to excessive processing of pages into and out of memory. Large page frames require much less processing of pages but may lead to inefficient utilization of memory if the programs being paged do not completely fill the pages. The best choice depends upon the programs running on that system, and the speed of the hardware that performs the paging. Recent IBM systems tend to use four thousand byte page frames, whereas the earlier systems used two thousand byte page frames. One reason for the change is that the disk drives used with the later systems are more efficient when transferring large blocks of data, therefore four thousand byte pages are better.

A less common system of virtual memory is similar to paging, except that the individual areas of memory are not necessarily all the same size. These areas of memory are called **segments,** and the process is called **segmentation.** Some segments are set up as groups of pages, with these groups handled separately from individual paging. At least one modern operating system implements a swapping algorithm for groups of pages, or segments. This allows individual pages to be moved in and out of memory as needed, but a complete program can be moved in and out of memory as one piece, thus reducing paging requirements.

One of the problems that must be overcome with paging is obtaining the correct addresses for each of the memory references in each page of memory. One of the reasons for not setting up partitions in memory similar to the way files are set up (small blocks and pointers between those blocks) is the overhead inherent in calculating addresses for each memory reference in each small area.

The memory reference overhead is overcome in virtual memory systems by designing the computer hardware so that the address calculations are done in the hardware instead of in the operating system. Since hardware calculations are much faster than software calculations, this makes the entire paging process much faster. Without such hardware, the process of paging could be so slow as to be unusable.

Programs are created in the same way with virtual memory as with non-virtual memory. Each memory address in that program is calculated, by a linker or loader, just as in non-virtual memory systems. These calculations assume that the program will be loaded into some contiguous area of memory. When the program is loaded, however, it is broken up into four thousand byte pages.

These pages may or may not actually be loaded contiguously into memory. Each of the memory addresses in each page of the program are re-calculated each time that page is loaded into a new page frame. The hardware that does the address re-calculations is called a "dynamic address translator," or "DAT."

There are several complex issues that must be handled in order to successfully set up and run a dynamic address translation system. The primary concern is keeping track of which memory address is on which page, and where that particular page is at any given time. This is normally done with a series of mappings. The two most common methods are **direct mapping** and **associative mapping.** Each of these techniques requires a **map table** which keeps a map of which pages are currently in memory, where those pages are in memory, which pages are currently on disk drives, and where those pages are on disk drives. Each process currently running may have a separate map table.

Example 8-1:

PROCESS PAGE ALLOCATION

This shows the way pages might be allocated for a small process using a total of twenty pages.

INTERNAL MEMORY

FRAME 83	Process page 0
FRAME 27	Process page 1
FRAME 98	Process page 5
FRAME 42	Process page 6
FRAME 71	Process page 20

PAGING DEVICE

SLOT 400	Process page 0
SLOT 401	Process page 1
SLOT 402	Process page 2
SLOT 403	Process page 3
. . .	. . .
SLOT 419	Process page 19

The address translation process breaks each memory reference down into two parts. The first part is the page on which that address is located, and the second part is the offset from the beginning of the page of that address. These two items are sufficient to find any address in a virtual storage system. Once the page of the memory reference is known, the address translation looks that page up in the page map table. If the page is currently located in memory, the page frame it occupies is specified in the map table. The address of that page frame is then added to the displacement within the page to form the correct address for that memory reference. If the required page is not currently in memory, then it must be read into memory and placed in a page frame. Once this is done, the above calculation can be done to find the address of that memory reference. The process of not finding a referenced page in memory is sometimes known as a **page fault.**

Direct mapping

The direct mapping process requires that the map table for each process contain an entry for every page belonging to that process. When some location in memory is referenced, the dynamic address translation hardware checks that reference against the map table. The map table tells the current location of that page. If it is in memory, then the address translation hardware takes the beginning address of that page from the map table and uses it to modify the memory reference so that it points to the correct location in memory. If that page is not currently in memory, it must be read in from a paging device. The location of that page on the paging device is determined from the map table, and that area is read into a selected page frame. After the page is read in, the memory reference can then be modified to point to the correct location in memory.

The direct mapping technique works quite well, but there is a serious problem with the speed of such an algorithm. Computers with large physical memory sizes have many pages, each of which must have an entry in the map table. This leads to a rather large memory overhead for the map table, and it must be kept in memory instead of in any special hardware. Keeping the map table in memory frequently causes an extra instruction to be performed to access that table each time a memory reference is made. Since the dynamic address translation hardware can usually do all necessary address resolution calculations with only one instruction, a program with many memory references may have to execute twice as many instructions just to resolve all memory references. This leads to unacceptable slowness, and other mapping algorithms are therefore more popular.

Example 8-2:

DIRECT MAPPING

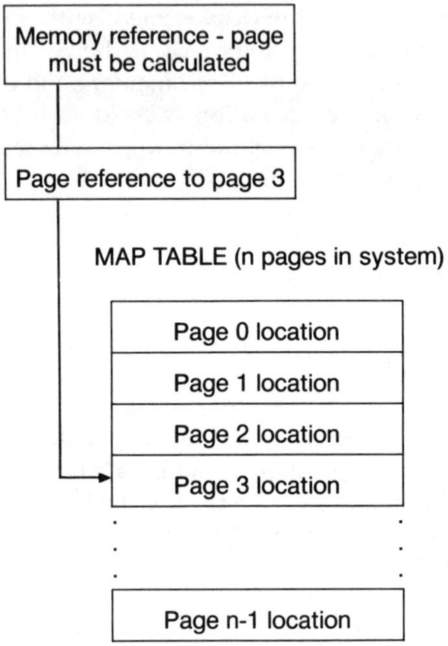

Associative mapping

An improvement on the direct mapping algorithm is known as **associative mapping.** Associative mapping still uses a page table like that used in direct mapping. However, the page table is kept in a special piece of hardware called an **associative array** that operates at a much faster speed than normal computer memory.

The associative array is designed specifically to contain the page map table. The name stems from the fact that the hardware is designed so that all page entries are searched simultaneously for the specified memory reference. Since the speed of this piece of hardware is much higher than that of normal memory, normal programs are not slowed in execution. The unfortunate part of associative mapping is that the special hardware involved is extremely expensive, so only a relatively small amount of such hardware can normally be included.

The expense of the associative array and the slowness of the direct mapping technique have led to many implementations that combine the best features of both. Probably the best compromise is one where some part of the mapping table is kept in a special associative array, and other parts are kept in normal memory. The part of the mapping table that is kept in the associative array is usually the part containing the most recently referenced pages. Most of the pages referenced in a program will be thus in the associative array, with only a relatively small percentage of page references coming from the pages mapped in normal memory. The algorithm keeps the recently referenced pages in the associative array assuming that pages that were recently referenced are much more likely to be referenced again in the near future than pages that have not been referenced recently.

Example 8-3:

ASSOCIATIVE MAPPING

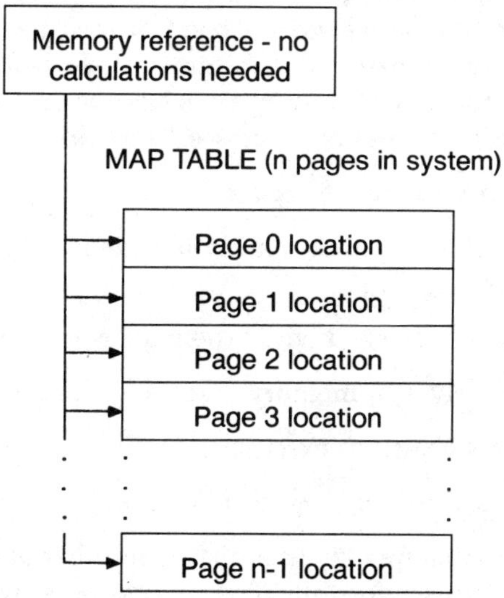

The implementation of a partial associative array is called a **table look-aside buffer** by IBM. If the algorithm for replacing page entries in the buffer is well chosen for the applications on that system, a buffer holding only fifteen to twenty percent of the total pages will trap eighty to ninety percent of the page requests. This allows processing almost as fast as with the full associative array but at a much smaller cost.

FETCH STRATEGIES

Two primary issues must be considered with virtual storage: when to read in a page, and where to put it in memory once it has been read in. Both of these issues have a variety of algorithms. Reading a page into memory is called **fetching** that page. The algorithms for determining when to read in a page are called **fetch strategies** and the algorithms for determining where in memory to place that page are called **replacement strategies.**

The simplest approach to fetching is to load all pages associated with a process when that process is initially loaded into memory. This tends to eliminate many of the benefits of paging, however, since it leads to large unused areas of memory, and prevents a process from being loaded until enough memory is free to contain the entire process. For these reasons, this approach is seldom used.

The most commonly used approach to fetching pages is called **demand paging.** This simply says that no page is fetched until a request is made for that page, that is, a memory address has been referenced that resides on that page. This approach has both good and bad features; it ensures that pages that are not needed are not fetched and it minimizes overhead from trying to determine which pages to fetch. However, it can lead to significant performance degradations with certain types of processes. The steps in demand paging are:

1. Memory reference occurs.
2. Map table is searched and the page is determined to be on the paging device.
3. Process is blocked while the page is fetched.
4. Page arrives in memory and the process is unblocked.
5. Process begins to execute again.
6. Memory reference is calculated for that page in memory.

A process that quickly uses a large number of sequential pages is severely hampered by this algorithm. The process must wait while a page is fetched, and then must wait again while the next page is fetched, etc. The net result is that most of the execution time of that process is spent waiting for pages to be fetched. One way to avoid this problem is to write each program so that it is modular. All memory references are close to one another, so that only a few pages are needed at any one time for that program to execute.

Another technique for fetching pages is called **anticipatory paging.** This is where the operating system attempts to guess which pages are more likely to be needed, and pre-fetches those pages, so that they are already in memory when needed. Such a system is very good when the guesses are successful, but very bad when the guesses are not as good. When most of the guesses are successful, each process is able to execute much faster, since the pages it next needs are already in memory, and no wait is needed.

Mistakes in anticipatory paging tend to feed on themselves if the algorithms are not developed very carefully. For example, a process requests a page, which is then fetched. The system anticipates that the next three pages will be needed, so it fetches them, which both uses up time for the paging as well as available page frames. The process then requests a totally different page, so the system then gets that page; the system guesses again at different pages it thinks will be needed and fetches those, with the attendant costs. It is not difficult to see that only a few processes that consistently confuse the system's anticipatory paging quickly lead to a situation where much of the system time is spent in doing wasted paging.

Anticipatory paging can be successful in some cases, primarily when the execution of the process owning the pages follows a sequential pattern. It is not possible, in general, to correctly predict which pages any given process may require in the future, which makes the technique of anticipatory paging a gamble. This gamble, however, may be successful for those processes which follow a simple pattern, such as moving sequentially through pages.

The cost of incorrect decisions is felt both in wasted memory and in lost time spent paging. The cost of wasted memory is becoming smaller and smaller as the overall cost of computer memories is reduced and as larger memories become available, but at the same time, system performance is becoming more important, so the penalty of lost time is becoming more serious. Anticipatory paging systems tend to be used more in computers with a large amount of memory where execution time is more critical than wasted memory. Even in these systems, however, the level of decision making by the paging system must be good enough to provide an overall gain in throughput instead of a loss.

REPLACEMENT STRATEGIES

When unused page frames exist in memory, the incoming page can be placed in any open page frame (pages need not be contiguous in a virtual storage system). The real problem arises when there are no open page frames. The correct algorithm for replacing pages in memory is very important since an incorrect algorithm will greatly reduce overall system throughput.

The ideal algorithm is one that replaces a page that will not be accessed until after every other page in memory. In simpler terms, it replaces the page in memory that will be idle for the longest time in the future. Since correctly predicting which page will be the last one accessed requires knowledge of the future, some algorithm is necessary that will come as close as possible to this ideal.

The simplest technique is to randomly select any page frame to contain the incoming page. This technique has very low overhead, but neither does it approach the ideal algorithm, since it is governed by chance. Operating systems with the sophistication to develop virtual memory systems also have enough sophistication to improve on random chance as a page replacement algorithm.

Practically all real page replacement algorithms mark each page frame with the time that the current page was placed in it. This allows calculations based on the length of time a particular page has been in storage. The simplest replacement algorithm is one based on the FIFO principle discussed in chapter 6. This algorithm says that the page that has been in storage the longest (the first in) is probably the page that is needed least, and therefore is the best candidate for replacement. The process that needed that particular page has probably finished with it and therefore it is no longer needed in memory.

The FIFO algorithm does not work well in practice. The usual reasons that a page has been in memory for a long time are that it is being heavily accessed by some process or that the process that is using it is blocked. Either way, it is a bad candidate for replacement. Using FIFO also requires that the time of paging in each page be stored somewhere, and that the table be searched every time a page is to be replaced.

Better algorithms have been developed that are not based on how long a page has been in memory, but instead on the recent activity level of that particular page. The basic algorithm, from which most other algorithms are derived, is called **least recently used** or **LRU.** This algorithm says that the page frame that is the best candidate for being replaced is the page frame whose contents have not been used for the longest time. This is based on the idea that if a page has not been used for a long time, it is not likely to be used in the near future.

Although LRU has intuitive appeal, it is not necessarily always best. In some cases, a particular page may not have been referenced for a long time because the process owning that page was waiting on some event such as another page being fetched. In this case, that is the worst possible page frame to use, since that page, having waited the longest, is now the most likely candidate to be used in the near future. Another problem with the LRU is that it requires that a record be kept of the time when each page was used. Considerable system overhead is incurred by: creating a time record of page usage, the storage necessary to keep that record, and searching all those records to determine which page to replace. Such overhead becomes very significant when it is incurred for every page replacement in the system.

The concept behind LRU, that of determining page frame availability by recent activity, is a good one. It is the method of determining activity that is ineffective. Merely checking the length of time since the last time a page was used is not sufficient, both because of the tremendous overhead that may be generated, and because of possible failures in the algorithm.

Example 8-4:

LRU ALGORITHM

REPLACEMENT ORDER	PAGES	TIME SINCE LAST USED
FIRST	Page frame 0	10.0 sec
	Page frame 1	.5 sec
SECOND	Page frame 2	8.2 sec
	Page frame 3	1.3 sec
	Page frame 4	0.1 sec
	Page frame 5	.3 sec
THIRD	Page frame 6	4.2 sec
	Page frame 7	1.6 sec
FOURTH	Page frame 8	3.1 sec
	Page frame 9	0.9 sec

A better variation of the LRU algorithm is sometimes called the **not used recently,** or **NUR,** algorithm. This algorithm merely tries to find a page frame that has not been used recently. The reasoning is that any page that has not been used recently is a good candidate for replacement, and the gains that can be achieved by finding the least active of this group do not warrant the overhead incurred.

This algorithm suffers from the same failing as the LRU; the page selected for replacement may just then be ready for use again. The chances of an inappropriate choice being made are greater here than with the basic LRU algorithm, but this is justified by the great reduction in overhead associated with this algorithm.

Unfortunately, better page replacement algorithms tend to balance better replacement strategies with extra overhead. It does no good to have a completely optimum replacement algorithm if the overhead generated by that algorithm is so great that the system cannot run more efficiently than with a worse algorithm. A better algorithm is one that may be less optimal and occasionally makes mistakes, but has less overhead. The NUR algorithm seems to be about the best compromise between accuracy and overhead.

The implementation of the NUR algorithm is quite simple. Each page frame has associated with it two bits which specify which of the four possible states there are for that page frame. The first bit is a **reference bit.** This bit is 0 when a page frame has not been referenced; it is set to 1 upon the first reference. Since pages are not fetched until a demand is made in demand paging systems, it would seem that the reference bits would be useless, since each page is referenced almost immediately after being placed in memory. Reference bits would also seem to be useless for determining whether a page has been referenced recently, since only one reference at any time sets the bit to 1. Both of these problems are circumvented by periodically resetting all the reference bits in the system to 0. This then makes all pages candidates for replacement, so for a very short period of time, many page replacement mistakes may be made. Any active page will be referenced within a very short time, however, so active pages quickly cease being candidates for replacements, and thus mistakes are quickly reduced.

This algorithm shows which pages have been referenced recently without any need for keeping time records, therefore the overhead of generating and storing these records is largely removed. The only record necessary is one bit that is set upon a reference, which requires much less time and memory than setting and storing a time. Any page without the reference bit on is a candidate for replacement, so very little overhead is generated in checking to find replacement candidates. The first page without the reference bit on is a candidate, and therefore the total checking is usually limited to a relatively small number of pages.

The reference bit accounts for only two of four possible states for each page frame. The remaining two states are specified by the state of the **modified bit.** This is a bit that is set whenever the contents of a page frame are modified. This bit exists for the sole purpose of reducing overhead in the paging system. The paging device normally contains an image copy of all virtual pages in the system. If a page that has been modified is selected for replacement, a copy of that page must be written out to the paging device. Of course, pages that have not been modified do not need to be written out to the paging device when they are replaced, since the copy of those pages on the paging device is exactly the same as the copy in memory. Therefore, only modified pages need be written out to a paging device upon replacement.

This means that replacing modified pages in memory incurs far greater system overhead than does replacing non-modified pages. The possible savings in overhead are great enough to justify the overhead generated by keeping a bit that specifies whether or not that particular page has been modified.

The combination of these two bits showing the status of a page implies that any page can be in one of four possible states:

- Not referenced and not modified
- Referenced and not modified
- Not referenced and modified
- Referenced and modified

The state of not referenced and modified is seemingly contradictory; obviously it is impossible for a page to be modified if it has not been referenced. This state exists only because the reference bits are periodically reset. A page that was modified before the last time the reference bits were reset, and that has not been referenced since the reference bits were reset, is in the condition of not referenced and modified.

The most desirable candidates for replacement are those that have been neither referenced or modified. These pages have not been active recently, and need not be written out to the paging device, so they are the best choice. The second best candidates are pages that have been modified but not referenced. These pages require additional overhead to write them to the paging device, but have not been referenced recently, so are less likely to be called back. The third best candidates are pages that have been referenced recently but have not been modified. These pages are probably not such a good choice since they have been active recently, but at least they do not require writing to a paging device. The worst candidates are pages that have been both referenced and modified since these pages are not only active, but also require writing to a paging device.

The NUR algorithm is implemented in many modern operating systems with the aid of the reference and modified bits. Those operating systems that do not use the exact NUR strategy usually use some slight modification of it.

Example 8-5:

NUR ALGORITHM

REPLACEMENT ORDER	PAGES	REFERENCE BIT	MODIFIED BIT
FIRST	Page frame 0	0	0
SEVENTH	Page frame 1	1	0
SECOND	Page frame 2	0	0
FIFTH	Page frame 3	0	1
NINTH	Page frame 4	1	1
EIGHTH	Page frame 5	1	0
THIRD	Page frame 6	0	0
SIXTH	Page frame 7	0	1
FOURTH	Page frame 8	0	0
TENTH	Page frame 9	1	1

OTHER STRATEGIES

Working sets

There are a number of additional techniques for enhancing the performance of a paging system. One of these uses the **working set** theory originally formulated by Peter Denning. This theory states that there is a minimum number of pages that each process uses frequently. All of these pages should be in memory when that process is executing, or excessive overhead will be generated in fetching and writing those pages. The size of the working set varies from one process to another and also varies during the life of a process. The specific pages contained in the working set also vary during the life of a process.

An efficient paging system identifies the pages in the working set of each executing process and attempts to keep those pages in memory at the same time. Only when it is absolutely necessary should the pages that are part of an active working set be paged out. The paging out of pages that are part of an active working set is sometimes known as **page stealing.**

Care should be taken not to invest a large amount of system overhead in calculating working sets, since the usual page replacement algorithms should be sufficient to prevent most cases of page stealing if those pages are truly active. Working sets can be quite useful for low-level schedulers, however, if all memory is occupied with active working sets, it is probably not a good idea to schedule another process into memory. Such a process would be forced to steal active pages from other working sets and thus would reduce overall system throughput.

Optimizing programs

Another technique that can be used to enhance the throughput of some programs is to write those programs so that execution is usually confined to any one local area in the program. It is acceptable for the program to occasionally branch to a remote area, such as a subroutine, but such branches should not be done often. The preferable technique is for the programs to execute in one section for as long as possible, then branch to another area and execute there as long as possible. This is in contrast to a program that executes a few instructions, branches to a remote location and executes a few instructions there, then branches to another remote location, etc. Such frequent branches are generally poor programming practice anyhow, since they make programs difficult to debug. They also make those programs inefficient in virtual storage systems.

Virtual storage systems tend to keep the pages that are most active in memory areas where instructions are actually being executed. A program that does a lot of branching to remote areas requires a large number of pages be available to it, whereas a program that executes in one area for a time requires only those pages containing the actual area that is being executed. The program requiring many pages may spend a large amount of time in page wait, while the different pages are fetched.

Example 8-6:

PROGRAMMING TECHNIQUES

TIME INTERVAL	PROCESS PAGES USED
	Good utilization of memory
1	0,1,8,9
2	0,1,8,9
3	0,1,8,9
4	0,1,8,9
5	0,1,5,7,8
6	0,1,5,7
7	0,5,7,8
8	0,5,7,8
9	0,5,7
10	0,5,7
	Poor utilization of memory
1	0,1,8,9
2	0,2,5,6
3	0,4,5,7
4	0,1,8,9
5	0,3,4,5
6	0,1,5,7
7	0,3,5,8
8	0,1,3,7
9	0,2,5,8
10	0,5,7

The movement to virtual storage systems has dramatically changed some perceptions of good programming techniques. An example of this is the usage of memory to store data. In the days before virtual storage systems were available, computer memory spaces were relatively small, so good programmers used many clever tricks to minimize memory usage. The basic idea was to maintain as much data as possible on disk drives or other storage devices, and to read that data into memory only when it was needed. The advent of virtual storage systems has completely changed this practice. On virtual storage systems, it is better to maintain as much data as possible in memory, since the paging process is far more efficient than any input or output generated by a program. This technique essentially uses the paging system as its input/output device.

PERFORMANCE ISSUES

Virtual storage systems have many wonderful features, but there are also some problems associated with them. The obvious problem, of course, is the overhead associated with the address calculations and with moving pages into and out of memory. Under normal circumstances, such overhead is minimal and is completely justified by the tremendous throughput gains that virtual storage provides. There are cases, however, when the overhead becomes unusually large. The address translation overhead is relatively constant, but the overhead from moving pages varies, depending on the amount of paging. When such overhead reaches an unacceptable size, the system is said to be **thrashing.**

Thrashing

A system that is thrashing has reached the point where most of the system resources are devoted to moving pages into and out of memory. Very little usable work is being accomplished by such a system. Thrashing can affect the entire system or an individual program. If several individual programs are thrashing, this will cause system thrashing.

Processes or programs thrash when most of their time in the queueing system is spent waiting for pages instead of actually executing. A process that repeats a cycle of entering the processor after being in page wait, and immediately requires a page fetch (which necessitates going into page wait again) is clearly thrashing. The programming techniques covered earlier help to avoid such conditions.

Avoiding paging

There are some cases where the speed of a particular process is so critical that the process cannot afford the extra time involved in doing paging. Modern operating systems offer several alternatives for such processes. The first level of performance improvement is to bias the paging system in favor of pages from that process so that these pages are only paged out under unusual circumstances. The next level is to actually lock those pages in memory and not allow them to be paged out at all. This is normally done only for critical systems processes that need to have the absolute best performance.

A more extreme case of avoiding the normal paging system is separating the memory into two sections, managing one with the normal paging system and the other with a non-virtual system. This has severe effects on the performance of the overall system and should be done only when absolutely necessary. One example where this is done is in the case of the IBM VM operating system, which allows other operating systems to be run as an application program. The other system can be allocated some portion of the total real memory as a non-paging memory. This provides the secondary system with vastly improved performance at the cost of a degradation in performance of the overall system.

There are cases where some process, or part of a process, must be retained in a particular location in memory for a known period of time. When this occurs, the critical pages must be temporarily locked into memory. Locking those pages tends to reduce the overall performance of the system, since some page frames are not available for paging, but since the locking is temporary, the reduction is not usually significant.

An example of page locking is the way certain types of I/O are done on IBM systems. The I/O system writes data out from a specific real memory location and reads data into a specific real memory location. The I/O commands actually contain the real memory address where the data is to be read from or to. Since I/O operations are quite slow compared to processor speeds, the chances are high that the pages containing those memory locations will be paged out by the time the I/O operation needs them. Even if those pages are fetched again, they will not be placed in the same physical locations in memory, which means that the I/O operations containing real memory addresses will be looking for areas in memory that are no longer correct. For this reason those pages must be locked into memory while the I/O operation is underway.

SUMMARY

Virtual storage systems use paging devices to emulate much larger amounts of memory than what actually exists on the computer. Such systems solve many of the common problems of memory management such as unused areas and incorrect partition sizes. Memory is divided up into small areas called page frames. Pages are written out to paging devices whenever they are not in use and pages on a paging device require a place in memory.

The real addresses of any memory reference in a page is calculated by hardware. It uses a map table to keep track of the location of each page in the system. A direct map contains information on each page in the system, but it occupies so much space that it must be kept in memory, which is rather slow for address translations. A faster method is to keep the map table in a special piece of very fast hardware called an associative array. This is extremely expensive, however, so the usual approach is to keep the information for the most active pages in the associative array, and to keep the rest of the map table in a direct map in memory.

There are two primary algorithms for fetching pages from a paging device. The normal algorithm is demand paging, where a page is fetched only when a process makes a reference to a memory location contained on that page. The other primary fetch algorithm is known as anticipatory paging, where the paging system attempts to anticipate which page or pages will be needed next in memory and to pre-fetch those pages so that they are already in memory when needed.

The simplest page replacement algorithm is random replacement, where the page to be replaced in memory is selected at random. A slightly better algorithm is first-in-first-out (FIFO), where the page that has been in memory the longest is the one that is to be replaced. This requires that the system maintain a record of the time each page was fetched, so the page that has been in the system the longest can be calculated. The most widely used page replacement algorithm is the least-recently-used (LRU) algorithm, which attempts to replace that page in memory that has not been used for the longest time.

The implementation of the LRU is frequently the not-used-recently (NUR) algorithm. The NUR uses two bits for each page; one bit is the reference bit, which is set when the page is referenced, and the other is the modified bit, which is set when the page is changed. Periodically, all the reference bits in the system are reset, so that only pages that are recently active have the reference bit set. The order for selecting replacement pages with neither the reference or modified bits set, are first; pages with the modified bit but not the reference bit are second; pages with the reference bit but not the modified bit are third, and pages with both the reference and modified bits set are last.

The working set theory states that each executing process has a certain number of pages associated with it that must be in memory at the same time in order to obtain efficient execution.

Paging systems occasionally lose control of the paging process to the extent that most of the activity in the system consists of paging instead of real work. Such a situation, called thrashing, is to be avoided at all costs.

EXERCISES

TRUE/FALSE

1. Virtual memory largely eliminates fragmentation problems.
2. Virtual memory uses hardware address translators.
3. Associative mapping is slower than direct mapping.
4. The table lookaside buffer is a form of associative mapping.
5. Segmentation involves virtual memory in pieces of non-fixed size.
6. FIFO is the best page replacement algorithm.
7. A modified LRU is the most widely used replacement algorithm.

8. The NUR uses a referenced and modified bit.

9. The NUR allows the modified bit to be set without the referenced bit.

10. Replacing pages in an active working set prevents thrashing.

MULTIPLE CHOICE

1. Dynamic address translation:
  a) Is part of the operating system paging algorithm
  b) Is useless when swapping is used
  c) Is the hardware necessary to implement paging
  d) Stores pages at a specific location on disk

2. The map table:
  a) Should be as large as possible
  b) Should be completely in the fastest hardware possible
  c) Is not necessary in the latest operating systems
  d) Allows pages to be located when referenced

3. A page fault:
  a) Occurs when a program accesses a page of memory
  b) Is an error in a specific page
  c) Is an access to a page not currently in memory
  d) Is a reference to a page belonging to another program

4. Demand paging:
  a) Fetches a page only when needed
  b) Fetches pages that are likely to be demanded
  c) Pages out pages when that page frame is needed
  d) Pages out pages in large groups

5. The LRU algorithm:
  a) Pages out pages that have not been used recently
  b) Pages out pages that have been used recently
  c) Pages out pages that have been least used recently
  d) Pages out the first page in a given area

6. The reference bit:
  a) Is set when the page is paged out
  b) Is reset when the page is accessed by a program
  c) Is set when the page is accessed by a program
  d) Is never reset

7. Thrashing:
   a) Always occurs on large computers
   b) Is a natural consequence of virtual memory systems
   c) Can always be avoided by swapping
   d) Can be caused by poor paging algorithms
8. The working set:
   a) Contains all pages referenced
   b) Contains all the pages that should be kept in memory
   c) Is the group of pages being used by all programs
   d) Is always resident in memory
9. Page stealing:
   a) Is a sign of an efficient system
   b) Is taking larger disk spaces for pages paged out
   c) Is taking page frames from other working sets
   d) Should be the tuning goal
10. Virtual system swapping:
    a) Allocates all of memory to one program
    b) Pages working set pages in and out as a group
    c) Is never as efficient as normal paging
    d) Is only used on systems that are thrashing

DISCUSSION QUESTIONS

1. Describe pages and page frames.
2. Discuss the proper size for pages.
3. Describe a dynamic address translator.
4. Describe direct mapping.
5. Describe associative mapping.
6. Discuss the pros and cons of demand paging vs. anticipatory paging.
7. Discuss the FIFO page replacement algorithm.
8. Discuss the LRU page replacement algorithm.
9. Briefly describe how the referenced and modified bits are used.
10. Describe working sets.

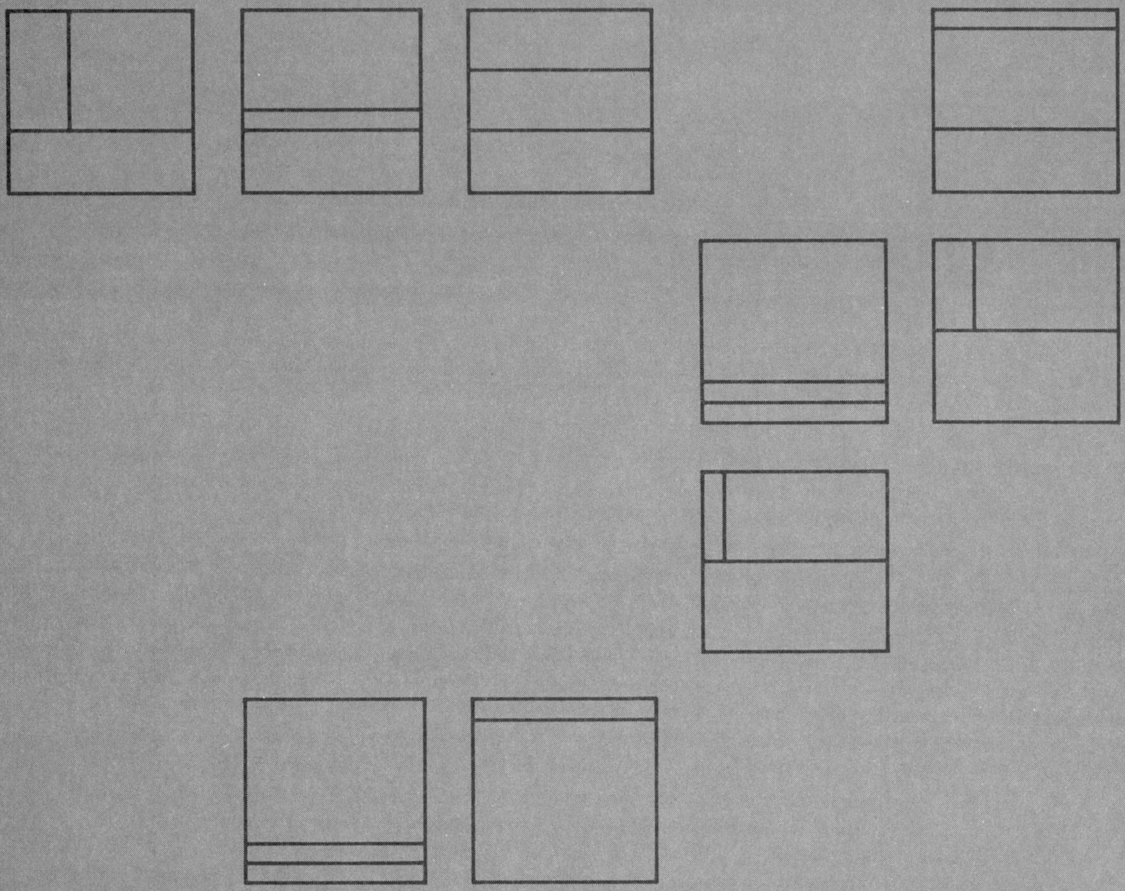

SYSTEMS PERFORMANCE

9

KEY TERMS

Control-unit busy
Seek
Channel
Paging rate
Device busy
I/O rate
Unit Record devices
Seek Analysis
Channel busy

INTRODUCTION

Systems performance consists of both monitoring and optimization. Optimizing the performance of the system is impossible without knowing its current performance characteristics.

Many modern computers have processors so powerful that the primary limiting factor on the overall computer performance is the system I/O. Getting data into and out of the processor becomes the most difficult problem to solve in optimizing overall system performance. Disk I/O represents the vast majority of the total I/O in the system. Optimizing disk I/O also has a tremendous effect on memory utilization, since paging activity requires a very high level of disk I/O. In some systems, in fact, the primary source of disk I/O is from the paging system.

The data gathered by monitors falls into two general classes. One class is measured data. Measured data is a value that has been counted by the monitor and is known to be accurate. The other class of data is sampled data, which is data that is extrapolated from samples gathered at time intervals. Such data is generally reasonably accurate if the monitor is set up to gather data at proper intervals and if the monitor itself is well designed. Any data gathered from samples, however, is inherently less accurate than data that is gathered and totaled completely. Before any dramatic system changes are made based on conclusions derived from sampled data, the sampling interval and technique should be carefully evaluated for accuracy.

One good method of validating monitor data is to use an independent system to look for a similar problem. For example, if the monitor samples indicate an overloaded processor, but actual jobs run on the system indicate no problem, then additional tests are necessary. If, however, the other tests indicate the same as the monitor, then that data is probably accurate.

PERFORMANCE TUNING WITH REAL-TIME MONITORS

Monitors are designed to supply the data necessary to improve system performance. This data must include information on processor, memory, and I/O performance. The data should also be divided into two general categories. Some data helps solve problems in real-time, while other data helps provide capacity planning information.

There are two basic types of performance monitors available that serve two different purposes. One type is a dynamic display that provides information in real-time as the information is collected and analyzed. This type of monitor is used to adjust system parameters as the system is running. The other type of monitor collects information about system performance over a longer time period, such as hours or days. This type of monitor is used primarily for long-term system tuning. The real-time monitor is discussed in this section, while the long-term monitor will be discussed in the section on tuning.

Real-time performance monitors should have two categories of displays. The primary display shows an overview or summary of the complete system performance. Additional displays provide more detailed views of specific aspects of systems performance. At least one detailed display should be available for each important component of system performance, such as disk drives, processor utilization, etc.

General displays

The overall display should provide enough information for the systems programmer to quickly determine if there is a performance problem in the system and, if so, in which detailed display he should look to obtain more information on that problem. The general display should contain a section showing the percentage of time the processor is spending processing programs, in page wait, in I/O wait, and idle. If the processor is spending most of the time processing programs, the optimum loading has probably been achieved. A significant percentage of time spent idle implies that there are not enough jobs available in the system. If jobs are waiting while the processor is idle, however, system parameters should be changed to allow more jobs to be scheduled.

A certain percentage of the total processor time is inevitably used by the operating system itself, but such overhead should be minimized. The general display on the real-time monitor should, if possible, show what percent of total processor time is being dedicated to operating system overhead. If this number becomes large, then some steps must be taken to optimize the performance of the system. Excessive I/O or page waits sometimes cause excessive overhead in the system, which can be reduced by reducing the I/O and page wait times. Other factors accounting for excessive overhead could be too much monitoring or tracking of systems activities or an inefficient setup of the system, such as not enough space allocated in memory for dynamic tables. Most systems programmers feel that no more than 10 to 20 percent of the operating system time should be devoted to overhead.

The percentage of time the processor spends in I/O and page wait varies from one system to another, but each one should normally be maintained at a relatively low amount. Ideally, the I/O and page wait percentages should be only 1 or 2 percent of the total processor time. This is frequently possible on smaller computers, but it is sometimes not achievable on large computers. Large computers require much greater amounts of paging and I/O in order to keep the processor fully utilized, and it may not be possible to optimize the I/O and paging systems enough to achieve this level of processor use. Experience has shown that such processors can sometimes not achieve more than approximately 70 percent utilization rates, with the remaining 30 percent divided up between paging and I/O wait.

If the processor is spending a large amount of time in either I/O or page wait, then the detailed displays should give more information about that particular aspect of the system. Detailed displays can also be used to determine the source of excessive system overhead, although the search is not as easy. A detailed display should cover each of the items summarized on the general display in depth.

The general display should include overall system paging information. This is expressed in terms of a system **paging rate,** which is often displayed in pages per second. The paging rate is the number of pages that are being read in or written out each second. Additional information pertaining to the paging rate can be determined by looking at the I/O display for I/O on the paging devices (which slows paging) and by looking at the detailed display showing information on each executing process in the system.

The paging rate that is reasonable varies widely between systems, depending on the size of the computer, the speed of the paging devices, and how well the paging is balanced between the paging devices. An excessive paging rate may be caused by only two or three processes that are paging excessively, and the overall rate can be reduced to reasonable levels by manually lowering the priorities of those processes.

There are a variety of ways of showing I/O information on the general display. One way is to summarize the overall system I/O performance, usually in terms of a single number showing the overall system I/O wait. Another way is to show a small portion of the I/O detailed display. This shows information about the most active devices, and the detailed display is only needed for the less active devices.

The detailed I/O information shows how the I/O is distributed among various interfaces and devices. The amount of time each device is spending waiting for I/O to complete is one of the most important parts of this information since this may be contributing significantly to the overall system I/O wait. If the I/O is unevenly distributed between devices, the device with the most I/O frequently is the one spending the most time in I/O wait. Depending on how well the overall system is tuned for I/O, one or several I/O devices may be causing problems. Once the device that is spending a large amount of time waiting for I/O is identified, the problems on that device can be alleviated.

A variety of other information may be shown in the general display. For instance, it might show the five processes using the most processor time and the five I/O devices with the most activity. This quickly allows the systems programmer to determine the source of major problems from the general display.

A useful feature of the monitor is to allow the systems programmer to dynamically alter the selection algorithm for the summaries shown on the general display. Normally the five processes using the most processor time should be shown, but if the system is having a problem with paging, the systems programmer might want to modify this so that the five processes shown on the general display are those using the most pages instead of those using the most processor time.

A brief summary of any areas where the system performance may be degraded may also appear on the general display. These areas vary from one system to another, but virtually every system has such an area. This information can be shown in the form of a brief warning message, so that any problem areas may be highlighted in this part of the display.

Other items may optionally appear on the general display. Examples of these items are the overall system I/O rate, total amount of memory in the system, total amount of memory available for use by non-system processes, total number of users or processes running, and total number of users or processes in the system.

Example 9-1:

GENERAL DISPLAY FOR THE IBM REAL-TIME MONITOR FOR THE VM SYSTEM

```
VM/370 CPU3081 16000K DATE 02/28/85 START 13:55:03 END 13:56:05

<-ACTUAL DATA  ->(IO SAMPLE) <-SAMPLED TRACE TABLE DATA ->

CH TYPE IOREQST SEC MXB MXW MXQ %DVB %CUB %CHB   %BMX %ERR %CNT

00 MPX     3708  60   0   0   0 .... .... ....   ....    6 ....
01 BMPX    2471  40   0   0   0 .... .... ....   .... .... ....
02 BMPX    2682  43   1   0   1 .... .... ....   .... .... ....
03 BMPX      13   0   0   0   0 .... .... ....   .... .... ....
04 BMPX    2342  38   1   0   4 .... .... ....   .... .... ....
05 BMPX     *** CHANNEL IDLE ***
06 BMPX     263   4   0   0   0 .... .... ....   .... .... ....
07 BMPX    2439  39   0   0   0 .... .... ....   .... .... ....
08 BMPX      14   0   0   0   0 .... .... ....   .... .... ....

USERID-> %CPU %CP %USR ISEC PSEC WSS RES PRI VMSIZE Q   STATUS

BATCH1K4  23   1   22   .0   40 950 448  99 16384K 3 ,PAGEWAIT
```

```
SYSTEM    7.0 7.0   .0   .0  1.3   0 826   0 16000K . ,SYSTEM

←IPL→←NIPL→       ←16 LOG ACTIONS INDICATED→

%USR %CP %USR  %CP %PAG %I/O %IDL %STO ISEC PSEC USR IQ WQ ACT
) 7  21   22   14  117   19    0   43   32  334 100 15  0  39
- 13 32   35   17   91   12    0   40   64  335 100 11  0  40
```

The meaning of each line is as follows:

```
VM/370 CPU3081 16000K DATE 02/28/85 START 13:55:03 END 13:56:05
```

This shows the operating system type (VM/370), the type of processor (3081), the size of real memory (16000K), and the time of the display.

```
← ACTUAL DATA →  (IO SAMPLE)  ← SAMPLED TRACE TABLE DATA →
```

This label helps differentiate between actual data and sampled data.

```
CH TYPE IOREQST SEC MXB MXW MXQ %DVB %CUB %CHB   %BMX %ERR %CNT
00 MPX     3708  60   0   0   0 .... .... ....   ....    6 ....
01 BMPX    2471  40   0   0   0 .... .... ....   .... .... ....
02 BMPX    2682  43   1   0   1 .... .... ....   .... .... ....
03 BMPX      13   0   0   0   0 .... .... ....   .... .... ....
04 BMPX    2342  38   1   0   4 .... .... ....   .... .... ....
05 BMPX     *** CHANNEL IDLE ***
06 BMPX     263   4   0   0   0 .... .... ....   .... .... ....
07 BMPX    2439  39   0   0   0 .... .... ....   .... .... ....
08 BMPX      14   0   0   0   0 .... .... ....   .... .... ....
```

This shows a summary of the I/O display, with the channel number, the type of channel, the total number of I/O interrupts (IOREQST), the percentage of time the device, control-unit and channel are busy, (%DVB, %CUB, %CHB), the error rate, (%ERR), and a few other pieces of information.

```
USERID→%CPU %CP %USR ISEC PSEC WSS RES PRI VMSIZE Q  STATUS
BATCH1K4   23   1   22   .0   40 950 448  99 16384K 3 ,PAGEWAIT
SYSTEM    7.0 7.0   .0   .0  1.3   0 826   0 16000K . ,SYSTEM
```

This shows a summary of the process display with the user name, the percentage of processor time that user is using (%CPU), the amount of that percentage that is system overhead (%CP), the amount of that percentage that is not system overhead (%USR), the I/O rate (ISEC), the paging rate (PSEC), the working set size (WSS), how many of those pages are currently in memory (RES), the overall priority of that user, the amount of virtual memory allocated to that user (VMSIZE), and the current status of that user.

```
←IPL→ ←NIPL→        ←16 LOG ACTIONS INDICATED→
%USR %CP %USR  %CP %PAG %I/O %IDL %STO ISEC PSEC USR IQ WQ ACT
)  7  21   22   14  117   19    0   43   32  334 100 15  0  39
- 13  32   35   17   91   12    0   40   64  335 100 11  0  40
```

This gives a snapshot of the overall system load. The top line shows the data from the last time slice, while the second line shows the data averaged over the period the monitor has been running. This average weighs recent data more heavily. The 3081 computer has two processors in it; the IPL columns refer to the first processor and the NIPL column refer to the second processor. The processor utilization is broken down into a system overhead column (%CP), and a non-system overhead column (%USR). The percent of system page wait is shown in the %PAG column, the I/O wait is shown in the %I/O column, the percent of processor idle time is shown in %IDL, the percentage of memory used is %STO, the I/O rate is ISEC, the paging rate is PSEC, the total number of users is USR, the number of users in queues is IQ, the number of users waiting to get in a queue is WQ, and the number of active users is ACT.

Detailed displays

A detailed display should support each of the areas that appear in summary form on the general display. Detailed displays should always be available to provide information on system I/O and process activity. Other detailed displays might show more specifics on various hardware and software resources, for example, how much processor time each specific major application program is using.

I/O displays

The I/O display is one of the most important in the system since performance problems tend to occur more often in balancing the I/O load than in any other area. This is primarily because the speed of the peripheral devices and connections does not differ greatly between the processors. The only way to provide more data to a larger processor is to provide more paths to the data, and sometimes such additional paths are just not sufficient to keep the processor fully utilized.

I/O problems are generally more amenable to improvement than are the problems in other areas because it is relatively easy to modify the configuration of the I/O system. Many such problems can be improved by just moving some critical system files or by changing the way certain devices are used.

The I/O display should show information on each I/O device in the system. If the system has a large number of I/O devices, this display may actually require several screens to cover all devices. Because of the number of devices involved, there should be several ways of sorting the display of I/O devices, so that the most important information is available on the first screen.

The most common way of sorting the I/O information is by the degree of activity on the devices. This is determined by the **I/O rate** which is a count of the number of communications attempts between that I/O device and the processor per second. The most active devices are the ones that are usually the most important devices for tuning purposes.

Another useful way of sorting is by the amount of I/O wait on devices. This is usually shown as a percentage of **device busy,** which is derived from the number of times the processor attempts to communicate with a device but cannot because that device is already busy. There are other ways of sorting the display that are sometimes useful, such as the error-rate per device, but the activity and wait time are the most common and useful.

Some systems allow the I/O wait to an I/O device to be broken down into different components. This processor may be waiting on the device itself or it may be waiting on the interface for that device. This interface is frequently known as a **control-unit,** sometimes in combination with a **channel.** Wait time spent waiting on the control unit is usually known as **control-unit busy.** The rate is the number of times the processor tried to communicate with an I/O device and could not because that device's control unit was busy. The distinction between device busy and control-unit busy is important, since one control unit handles several I/O devices, and if the wait time is on the controller, it may be possible to alleviate it by reducing the number of devices on that controller.

Other information may also be available on the I/O display. The percentage of the total system I/O each device is using is sometimes useful, since it simplifies the task of determining which device is using the most I/O. Some systems allow this to be further broken down into a percentage of I/O for a control unit. Error rates for devices are also useful, since this is a relatively quick way of finding devices that are having excessive error rates.

Example 9-2:

I/O DISPLAY FOR THE IBM REAL-TIME MONITOR FOR THE VM SYSTEM

```
VM/370 CPU3081 16000K DATE 02/28/85 START 13:36:26 END 14:00:14

←ACTUAL DEVICE DATA→←IO SAMPLE→(SAMPLED TRACE DATA)

DEV TYPE VOLSER IOREQ %CH %UT %WT MQ SW %DVB %CUB %CHB %ERR

2C0 3380 EDC2C0 61562  90  65   0  4  0    3 ....  ....  ....
C84 3380 EDC484 59578  88  60   0  4  0    0 ....  ....  ....
```

```
AC4 3380 EDC2C4 59434  87  47   0  1  0 .... .... .... ....
480 3380 EDC480 58828  95  52   0  4  0    0 .... .... ....
160 3380 EDC160 58423  94  69   0 12  0 .... .... .... ....
F44 3380 EDC744 58141  72  86   0  5  0 .... .... .... ....
964 3380 EDC164 58016  91  65   0  3  0 .... .... .... ....
740 3380 EDC740 56021  61  47   0  2  0    1 .... .... ....
741 3380 EDC741 27887  30  21   0  0  0 .... .... .... ....
F47 3380 VMRESG 18592  23  21   0  0  0    1 .... .... ....
E25 3380 EDC625  8951 100  17   0  0  0 .... .... .... ....
AC7 3380 EDC2C7  7269  10   8   0  0  0 .... .... .... ....
025 LINE         7259   7 .... .... ..  0 .... .... .... ....
743 3380 EDC743  5662   6  13   0  2  0 .... .... .... ....
03D LINE         5623   6 .... .... ..  0 .... .... .... ....
C87 3380 EDC487  5479   8  17   0  0  0 .... .... .... ....
```

The format is somewhat similar to the I/O summary in the general display. The first column DEV shows the actual address of each device. The second column shows the type of device, such as disk drive (3380) or communications line (LINE). The third column, VOLSER, shows the label attached to that device. The fourth column, IOREQ, shows the total number of I/O requests processed by that device. The fifth column, %CH, shows the percent of channel activity used by that device. This does not refer to total channel activity, but just to the channel on which that device is attached. Since there are many channels on the system, several devices may show very high percentages. The %DVB, %CUB, and %CHB columns show the amount of busy conditions on the device, control-unit, and channel. The last column, %ERR, shows the detected error rate for that device.

Process displays

Some of the important characteristics that should be displayed for each process are the percentage of total processor time that a process is using, the paging rate of that process, the number of pages that process has active in memory, how much I/O that process is using, and the priority of the process. The display should also present the information sorted by any of these characteristics.

Showing the percentage of total processor time that each process is using helps determine which process is using most of the processor. If one process is using too great a percentage of the processor, it may require a manual adjustment of the priorities in order to better equalize the usage. The operating system dynamically adjusts priorities constantly to best utilize all resources, but occasionally a process may require as much as several hours of processor time, and the systems programmer may wish to modify the system priorities in order to allow other processes to execute and finish while the large process continues at a low priority for several hours.

The paging rate of each process helps the systems programmer determine if any one or group of processes is using an abnormally high paging rate. The working set size, if such is used in that system, should also be shown. If the working set for a particular process is quite small, yet that process has a high paging rate, this may demonstrate a problem with that process. One step that might help is to change the paging algorithm so that pages belonging to that process remain in memory longer.

The process display should also show the overall priority associated with each process. Most operating systems attach at least two different priority levels to each process. One priority level is used by the various schedulers to schedule that process. Another priority level is assigned when the process enters the system as a job. Such priorities are frequently assigned by systems programmers to classes of processes.

For example, on a time-sharing system, interactive users would have a much higher priority than large processor-bound batch processes. When the job first enters the system, a determination is made as to the priority that job and all associated processes should have. The internal priorities may still be juggled by the schedulers as with any other process, but the overall priority is a factor in setting up the internal priorities. Such overall priorities can usually be changed dynamically by privileged users, such as systems programmers, in order to manage the throughput of the system.

The I/O rate for a process measures the times each second communication is attempted to an I/O device. Some systems display the I/O rate for different classes of devices, such as slow and fast devices.

Unit record devices are slow devices such as card-readers and line printers which transmit data in thousands of bytes every second. High speed devices, such as tape and disk drives, transmit data in millions of bytes per second. The difference between the two can be significant, since waiting on unit record I/O is nearly inevitable, but tape and disk drives are fast enough so that most processes should not spend very much time waiting on I/O on high speed devices. Any process that is consistently waiting on high speed I/O is a candidate for tuning.

There are two relatively common problems that may be highlighted by the process display. These problems involve processes with high paging rates with either a very large or a very small working set size. Either case can show a problem that is usually amenable to optimization, while other cases of processes with high paging rates may not be so amenable.

Example 9-3:

PROCESS DISPLAY FOR THE IBM REAL-TIME MONITOR FOR THE VM SYSTEM

VM/370 CPU3081 16000K DATE 02/28/85 START 13:55:03 END 13:56:05

USERID➤	%CPU	%CP	%USR	ISEC	PSEC	WSS	RES	PRI	VMSIZE	Q	STATUS
BATCH1K4	23	1	22	.0	40	950	448	99	16384K	3	,PAGEWAIT
SYSTEM	7.0	7.0	.0	.0	1.3	0	826	0	16000K	.	,SYSTEM
IPDRH	6.9	.6	6.3	5.8	2.6	3	0	64	960K	.	,IDLEWAIT
BATCHR	3.3	.7	2.6	11	3.8	163	216	40	4096K	3	,INSTWAIT
DIRECT	2.0	.4	1.6	6.4	5.3	290	0	64	3072K	.	,IDLEWAIT
BRMTWG	1.6	1.1	.5	1.5	4.5	3	1	64	960K	.	,IDLEWAIT
RSCS	.98	.68	.30	5.4	2.0	123	123	1	2048K	.	,IDLEWAIT
NVMJNG	.95	.40	.55	2.0	3.4	59	0	64	960K	.	,IDLEWAIT
UXMMP	.90	.66	.24	.7	10	15	42	70	4096K	1	,PAGEWAIT
UXPPA	.70	.53	.17	.5	8.2	3	10	70	4096K	2	,PAGEWAIT
UXMOSCAD	.69	.53	.16	.5	8.8	18	10	70	4096K	2	,PAGEWAIT
UXBDA	.62	.48	.14	.4	8.5	20	3	70	4096K	.	,IDLEWAIT
VMUTIL	.62	.30	.32	2.4	4.1	18	0	1	960K	.	,IDLEWAIT
UXCOMM	.61	.47	.14	.4	7.4	4	2	70	16384K	.	,IDLEWAIT
IPDJMW	.60	.22	.38	1.8	1.7	51	0	64	2048K	.	,IDLEWAIT

Processes with a small working set but a high paging rate are not uncommon. They are frequently processes that communicate constantly with other processes. Such a process issues a message, then goes into a wait state while waiting for a reply. The operating system pages that process out while it is waiting. If the number of messages and the timing of the messages is skewed, then the process may get paged just before a reply to the message is received, when it is paged back in. Such a process spends a large percentage of time being paged in and out, and overall system performance would be greatly improved by changing the paging algorithm to either lock those pages into memory permanently, or at least change the priorities so that those pages are not paged out as quickly.

A process with a large working set that also has a high paging rate does not usually indicate an inefficiency in the paging system, but instead usually means that the particular process simply needs a very large amount of memory. Such processes are much less amenable to the simple fixes such as that above, although in some cases locking pages or changing paging timing may help. The problem here is that since the working set is large, locking that many pages or changing the timing on them may have very significant adverse affects on the overall performance of the system. When the overall system load is not too high, such a process may be just left to run to completion. When the overall system load is high, the priority on that process can sometimes be reduced, so that it takes a smaller percentage of the overall system load. Such a change delays the execution of that process, but the system as a whole runs much better, thus getting a greater total amount of work accomplished.

PERFORMANCE TUNING WITH LONG-TERM MONITORS

Long-term monitors are used more often for performance tuning than are real-time monitors. Long-term monitors usually collect data over a period of several days, or weeks. Only when a problem has consistently shown up over such a period should significant system changes be made to avoid it.

Many of the pieces of information that the real-time monitor displays are the same pieces displayed by long-term monitors. Long-term monitors are customarily run for several hours each day, and conclusions are not drawn until several days or weeks of data has been collected and analyzed. Such monitors are used to resolve problems that are characteristic to the system instead of to a particular process. While real-time monitors usually display information on terminals, long-term monitor information usually is obtained from printed output.

General displays

The long-term monitor has a general information section similar to the general display in real-time monitors. The information shown is taken over a period of several hours, and should display the average, the maximum, and the minimum for each observation for that period. More extensive information, such as median and standard deviation, may also be supplied by some monitors. The information shown should provide a complete picture of the system performance during that time period.

Examples of the information contained in the general display are the percentage of processor utilization, the percentage of I/O wait, the percentage of page wait, and the percentage of processor idle time. The processes running during that period should be characterized by size and by resources consumed. The scheduling performance of the system should also be displayed, by showing the processes in each queue, how long they stayed in a particular queue, how many processes in each queue, etc.

Example 9-4:

GENERAL DISPLAY FOR THE IBM VMAP LONG-TERM MONITOR FOR THE VM SYSTEM

```
FIRST DATE 02/28/85  TIME 18:00:26 MONITOR STATISTICAL SUMMARY
LAST  DATE 02/28/85  TIME 23.00.06
```

VARIABLE	AVERAGE	MINIMUM	MAXIMUM	TIME OF MINIMUM	TIME OF MAXIMUM	STD DEV
LOGGED	42.35	38.00	79.00	26.56.26	18.02.25	6.12
ACTIVE	16.31	0.00	32.00	19.00.26	18.01.25	3.34
INQUEUE	7.08	2.00	16.00	27.00.26	18.01.25	2.62
DIALED	3.06	3.00	5.00	18.29.26	18.01.25	0.29
RAI	0.65	0.00	0.98	19.00.26	27.52.26	0.14
TOTCPU	61.03	15.80	98.90	19.34.56	21.27.26	23.32
IDLE	0.06	0.00	10.33	18.01.25	29.59.56	0.68
PAGEWAIT	26.03	0.02	82.54	20.00.56	19.34.56	20.32
IOWAIT	12.84	0.00	76.63	23.01.56	26.52.26	13.86

Each line on the general display shows the average, minimum, and maximum values for each of the items displayed. It also shows the time that the maximum and minimum occurred, along with the standard deviation for those observations. LOGGED shows the number of users logged onto the system, ACTIVE shows the number of active users, INQUEUE shows the number of users in the queues, and DIALED shows the number of users accessing the system via telephone lines.

RAI stands for resource availability index, a general measure of the availability of the system. This is a very useful, although not widely used, number. The RAI summarizes, as much as is possible, the overall system responsiveness in one number. It is the ratio of the number of times some resource is available over the number of times that resource is accessed. An RAI of 1 is perfect and implies that all resources are always available, which usually means the system is quite under-utilized. A ratio of 0.9 is quite good, while a ratio below 0.8 may indicate a problem. A ratio of 0.65, as here, shows a significant problem on resource availability.

TOTCPU is the percentage of processor utilization in the system. Some computers have more than one processor and TOTCPU is the average utilization between all the processors in the system. IDLE is the overall percentage of time that the processors are not in use. PAGEWAIT and IOWAIT are the overall percentage of time that the processors are in page and I/O wait.

Detailed displays

The long-term monitor also has detailed displays, similar to the real-time monitor, that usually focus on I/O and processes. Showing activity hourly for a period of a day may demonstrate that the activity level varies widely during the course of the day, and tuning for activity at one time of day would leave the system badly out of tune at a different time of day.

Such a display often will show one or two activity peaks at different times of the day. Each such peak will last for one to three hours. The activity at other times may be much less than at the peak times. Such peaks frequently occur between 9:00am and 12:00pm, and between 1:00pm and 4:00pm. The tuning must be designed, if possible, to ensure an acceptable level of performance during the peak period, even though such a high level of tuning may be completely unnecessary during the rest of the day.

I/O displays

The I/O section is very similar to that in the real-time monitor. One feature sometimes available in long-term monitors that is seldom available in real-time monitors is a **seek analysis.** This is used exclusively with disk drives. Each time information on a disk drive is accessed, that disk drive does a seek to actually find the information as described in chapter 4. This seek requires a physical movement of a part of the disk drive, and since physical movements are much slower than electronic movements, these seeks can sometimes take a relatively long time. The longest time for seeks is when they occur on widely separate areas of the disk. Seek analysis is an analysis of all the seeks performed during a specific time period on one or more disk drives. The analysis shows the frequency and location of the seeks, that is, what part of the disk received how many seeks.

Much of the cause of the device busy condition on disk drives is seeks. Therefore, decreasing the amount of time that device spends seeking will solve much of the device busy condition. The disk drive may actually be so busy that no amount of change in the seeks will improve the device busy condition, but usually it can be dramatically improved just by changing the seeks characteristics. If the device is constantly busy, some of the data on it should be moved to another device that is not so busy in order to reduce the amount of device busy on it.

The usual cause of excessive seek times is that the data on the disk drive is arranged so that the files with the greatest number of accesses are on widely separated locations on the disk. In such a case, much of the time is spent seeking between those two files, instead of in processing the data at either location. The solution is very simple; rearrange the files on that device so that both of the heavily accessed files are located in physically adjacent locations on the device.

Whenever a disk device has only one very busy file on it, that file should be placed as near as possible to the center tracks of that disk, so that any seek to or from that file will cover only one-half or less of the total disk surface. A file located at either edge of the disk can require a seek across the entire disk surface.

Device busy conditions can be handled by either rearranging the file locations on the devices, or by moving some files from active drives to less active drives. The basic principle is to balance the load evenly between all the disk drives in the system. Once such a balancing is completed, any remaining problems with device busy conditions may require adding new disk drives to the system.

Control-unit busy conditions, when the system supports such a condition, is a problem of too much activity on one particular control unit. This can usually only be alleviated by improving the balance between the devices on the control units. This is achieved by moving some of the devices on the most active control unit to another, less active, control unit. Another alternative is to move the most active files on the devices belonging to that control unit to the devices belonging to a less active control unit. If these solutions are not possible, then it may be necessary to add control units to the system.

Some systems, such as IBM mainframes, divide the I/O up into **channels.** These channels serve as the paths where data is transmitted between the processor and various I/O devices. Several control units may be attached to each channel, and several I/O devices attached to each control unit. A configuration such as this has the potential for "channel busy", where the path is not available for data transmission even though both the device and control unit may be available.

Channel busy conditions can be alleviated in a similar fashion to control unit busy conditions, by moving data to devices on less active channels, by moving devices to control units on less active channels, or by moving complete control units with attached devices to less active channels. If these steps are not sufficient, it may be necessary to install more channels.

Example 9-5:

I/O DISPLAY FOR THE IBM VMAP LONG-TERM MONITOR FOR THE VM SYSTEM

```
DATE 02/28/85 FROM 18:00:26 TO 23:00:06 DISK/TAPE I/O ACTIVITY
MONITOR HIGH FREQUENCY DEVICE SAMPLING RATE (SAMPLES/INTERVAL)
```

(Continued on page 180)

Example 9-5:
Continued from page 179

DEVICE ADDR	TYPE	VOLSER	← TOTAL I/O → ISSUED	RATE /SEC	MSEC/ I/O	ACTIVE I/O RATE	(PCT I/O) ON CH	OF SYS	%BUSY
160	3380	DSD160	1,203,250	28	16.2	28	81	9	45.0
161	3380	DSD161	85,117	2	12.2	3	6	1	4.0
162	3380	DSD162	29,083	1	3.0	5	2	0	1.6
163	3380	DSD163	7,714	0	10.3	0	1	0	0.5
168	3380	DSD168	7,469	0	0.2	25	1	0	0.4
169	3380	DSD169	158,399	4	6.4	11	11	1	6.9
2C0	3380	DSD2C0	1,259,616	29	16.4	29	58	9	48.0
2C1	3380	DSD2C1	317,929	7	13.2	10	15	2	13.7
2C2	3380	DSD2C2	564,452	13	10.8	23	26	4	24.9
2C3	3380	DSD2C3	17,145	0	10.2	1	1	0	1.1
3A0	3380	DSD3A0	24,954	1	1.1	10	32	0	1.1
3A1	3380	DSD3A1	20,874	1	0.5	17	27	0	0.8
3A2	3380	DSD3A2	32,255	1	0.7	19	41	0	1.4

The ADDR column shows the address of the I/O devices listed. The TYPE column shows the device type (in this case all devices are IBM 3380 disk drives). The next column shows the name, or label, on each of those devices. The ISSUED column shows the number of I/O requests issued by the processor during the monitored time period. The RATE/SEC column shows the average number of I/O requests issued each second during the monitored time period. The MSEC/I/O column shows the average number of milli seconds required for the I/O requests to be satisfied. The ACTIVE I/O RATE shows the average I/O per device for the samples taken. The PCT I/O ON CH column shows the percentage of the I/O on that channel. The PCT I/O OF SYS column shows the percentage of the total I/O that is to the listed device. The % BUSY column shows the percentage of time the listed device was busy when another I/O operation was requested.

Time displays

A common format for detailed displays is a breakdown, by time, of system activity during the monitored period. The individual time slices considered can be modified as desired. A frequent time selection is to make the monitor period approximate a normal working shift, such as day shift, swing shift, or graveyard shift. This can then be broken down into smaller time segments, such as every hour or quarter hour. Monitoring for an eight-hour period and breaking that period down into fifteen minute time slices allows the performance of the system to be studied closely without overhead from too-frequent time slices.

Detailed displays should be available to show the number of processes active, the total number of processes in the system, the system paging status, and the system I/O status. These numbers should be displayed for each time slice. This allows the daily performance of the system to be understood, since any performance characteristic that is transient and disappears within five to ten minutes will not be shown, while any characteristics that do show are significant enough for their effect on the system to be important.

Example 9-6:

TIME DISPLAY FOR THE IBM VMAP LONG-TERM MONITOR FOR THE VM SYSTEM

DATE 02/28/85 TIME 18:00:26 SUMMARY OF SYSTEM PERFORMANCE LOG

			← COMBINED PERCENT UTILIZATION →					
	USERS	USERS	← RUNNING →			← WAIT →		
TIME	LOGGED	ACTIVE	TOTAL	CP	PROB	IDLE	PAGE	I/O
18.15	73	27	112	46	66	0	59	29
18.30	61	22	107	43	64	0	78	15
18.45	54	21	121	48	73	0	62	17
19.00	52	21	140	40	100	0	48	12
19.15	48	21	119	39	79	0	59	22
19.30	43	18	59	28	32	0	114	26
19.45	43	17	103	35	69	0	83	14
20.00	44	17	135	41	94	0	49	16
20.15	44	17	156	42	114	0	33	10
20.30	43	17	168	40	127	0	27	6
20.45	43	17	148	35	113	0	40	12
21.00	43	16	183	29	155	0	14	3
21.15	43	18	181	41	140	0	15	4
21.30	43	18	168	51	117	0	23	9

This is a breakdown by time of system activity. The time intervals are fifteen minutes, and in this example start at 18:15 (6:15pm). The USERS LOGGED column shows the number of users logged onto the system for each time period. The USERS ACTIVE column shows the number of users actually using the processor during that time period. COMBINED PERCENT UTILIZATION is subdivided into the RUNNING column, which refers to percentages when the processor is active, and the WAIT column, which refers to percentages when the processor is waiting for something. The RUNNING columns include the TOTAL column, which shows the total percentage of processor utilization, and the CP and PROB columns, which refer to the processor utilization percentage in system overhead and in user programs. The WAIT columns show page wait, I/O wait, and idle time.

Process display

The user or process display shows all of the users or processes that were using the system during that time period. This display is also sorted by some characteristic, such as total processor time consumed. The display might show, for each process, the total processor time consumed, the percent of time in page wait, the percent of time in I/O wait, the average size working set it owned, its average paging rate, its average I/O rate, the total number of I/O interrupts it generated to unit record I/O, and the total number of I/O interrupts it generated to disk drives.

Example 9-7:

PROCESS DISPLAY FOR THE IBM VMAP LONG-TERM MONITOR FOR THE VM SYSTEM

DATE 02/28/85 FROM 18:00:26 TO 21:00:06 USER RESOURCE SUMMARY

		←	CPU			→	← STORAGE →			
		RELATIVE				TOT/	(WKSET)		(PAGE I/O)	
			CUM	← SECONDS →		VIRT	K BYTES		THOUSAND	
RANK	USERID	PCT	PCT	TOTAL	VIRT	RATIO	AVG	MAX	READ	WRI
1	BATCH1K4	33	33	17,145	16,493	1.0	8860	12324	954	6
2	BATCHM1	19	52	9,798	7,774	1.3	1242	11552	281	2
3	BATCHM3	14	65	7,233	6,262	1.2	699	8036	80	
4	BATCHM2	8	74	4,328	3,633	1.2	907	6064	133	1
5	BATCH1M6	6	80	3,369	2,612	1.3	681	4984	40	
6	VMBACKUP	6	86	3,221	1,956	1.6	519	1908	41	
7	SYSTEM	5	91	2,566	0	0.0	0	0	8	
8	BATCH	1	92	514	48	10.7	59	180	434	3
9	RSCS	1	93	513	177	2.9	466	692	51	
10	UXMOSCAD	1	94	359	73	4.9	58	1480	480	2
11	UTS	1	95	353	44	8.1	53	804	570	2
12	UXBDA	1	95	345	43	8.1	55	796	569	2
13	UXMPRTE	1	96	313	39	7.9	49	800	500	2

The RANK column orders the users by total processor time used. CPU characteristics and storage characteristics are grouped. The RELATIVE PCT columns show the percentage of processor time used by that user. The TOTAL and VIRT columns show the total amount of processor time and the time actually used by the user exclusive of overhead. The TOT/VIRT RATIO column shows the ratio of total to virtual processor time, which is a measure of system overhead for that user. The closer this value is to 1, the less the overhead involved. The next two columns show the average and maximum working set sizes for that user in thousands of bytes. The last two columns show the number of times that user has fetched a page into memory or written it out to a paging device.

Scheduler displays

At least one detailed display can be devoted to monitoring the performance of the system schedulers. The simpler display is one that shows a time breakdown, similar to that discussed above, for queue occupancy during the given time period. The display should show how many processes are in each queue, how long those processes have been in that queue, how many processes are waiting to get into each queue, and how long those processes have been waiting. Other features might show performance information on each of the processes in the queues, such as the average or total amount of the processor, paging, and I/O used. This information should be displayed for each queue, and for the waiting list for each queue.

The scheduling process is also subject to monitoring and displaying. Systems using spin locks should be closely monitored, since such techniques are particularly subject to scheduling problems. The display should also do a time breakdown. Each time period should show as much information as possible about the spin lock system, such as how many processes are spinning, the average length of time those processes have been spinning, how many processes are spinning from each queue, and how many processes are spinning for each major resource.

SUMMARY

Monitors are an indispensable part of operating systems. Without some means of determining the performance characteristics of the operating system, it is not possible to optimize the performance of that system, with possibly much of the processor power wasted. Improving the performance of the operating system can prevent the necessity of buying additional computing power.

Care must be used with monitoring of operating systems. A greater degree of monitoring also leads to a greater degree of overhead in the system. A general level of monitoring does not usually cause any performance problems, but some of the more involved monitoring options can cause significant system degradation, so such monitoring must be used with great care.

Sampled data is usually accurate, but an error is always possible with any sampling technique, so other sources of information should be used to corroborate the conclusions reached from the sampled data.

Monitors come in two general classes. Real-time monitors are used for immediate diagnosis of potential performance problems. The other class of monitors runs over a much longer time period and is used to determine long-term trends and problems. Much of system tuning comes from the long-term monitor data, while the real-time monitor is more frequently used for alleviating temporary bottlenecks.

Real-time monitors have a general display that provides a summary of the various features. Examples of these are percent of system processor utilization, percent of system page wait, and percent of system I/O wait. Other features in the general display can be a summary of the most active processes in the system and a summary of the most active I/O devices in the system.

The detailed displays on the real-time monitor provide information on the areas summarized in the general display. The most important of these are the I/O display and the process display. The I/O display shows the I/O devices in the system, sorted in various ways, with relevant information such as total number of I/O interrupts, percent of device busy, percent of control-unit busy, and error rate. The process display shows detailed information on the processes in the system, also sorted in various ways. Process information includes the priority of the process, the amount of processor time it has used, and the percentage of time it has spent in both I/O and page wait. Other parameters such as paging rate, working set size, and I/O rate, may optionally be included.

Long term monitors are used primarily to diagnose trends. They also have a general display, similar to the real-time monitors, which summarizes the overall information available. The detailed displays are also similar to those in the real-time monitors, except that here they sometimes have additional information. Such additional information can be reporting on the performance of the queueing system, or an analysis of the seek patterns on the disk drives. This allows the layout and structuring of the operating system to be optimized.

EXERCISES

TRUE/FALSE

1. Systems performance tuning requires systems monitors.
2. Only a real-time monitor is useful for performance tuning.
3. Real-time monitors should show page wait, I/O wait, and processor usage.
4. Page wait should not be greater than 10 percent, but I/O wait can be.
5. Most performance improvements come from tuning the I/O.
6. Seek analyses should be run constantly.
7. Scheduling performance should be reported on the long-term monitor.
8. Monitor data that is sampled should never be believed.
9. Disk drive seek time should be maximized.
10. Moving files usually solves device busy problems.

MULTIPLE CHOICE

1. The paging rate:
   - **a)** Should never be more than 100/second
   - **b)** Is greater for large programs
   - **c)** Is the number of I/O interrupts each second
   - **d)** Increases as the number of page faults increase
2. Device busy:
   - **a)** Is good, since that means the device is in use
   - **b)** Is bad, since that means the device is not available
   - **c)** Is bad only if the device busy rate is too high
   - **d)** Depends upon the system paging rate
3. Interrupts per second:
   - **a)** Is a good measure of the system I/O activity
   - **b)** Is a good measure of the system paging activity
   - **c)** Should never be greater than 1000/second
   - **d)** Is higher on smaller computers
4. Control-unit busy:
   - **a)** Is the same as device busy
   - **b)** Shows the availability of the path to devices
   - **c)** Can be prevented with more devices
   - **d)** Can be prevented by reducing the paging rate
5. Real-time displays:
   - **a)** Are used only for capacity planning
   - **b)** Are most useful for showing performance problems
   - **c)** Are useless for capacity planning
   - **d)** Cannot show the system paging rate
6. Seeks analysis:
   - **a)** Is used for analyzing paging problems
   - **b)** Is used for analyzing device busy problems
   - **c)** Is used for analyzing control-unit busy problems
   - **d)** Is only shown on real-time displays
7. A long-term monitor:
   - **a)** Should show any immediate performance problems
   - **b)** Should show I/O, paging, and processor activity
   - **c)** Need show only the I/O and processor activity
   - **d)** Usually reports only on terminal displays

8. A high paging rate:
   a) May also cause a high I/O rate
   b) Keeps the system running well
   c) Is a symptom of too much processor activity
   d) Always creates a slow system
9. Poor response times are caused by:
   a) Processor busy
   b) High I/O rates
   c) High paging rates
   d) Any of the above
10. A long-term process display should:
    a) Show which processes used the most processor time
    b) Show process activity by time interval
    c) Show resources used by the most active processes
    d) All of the above

DISCUSSION QUESTIONS

1. Briefly describe the purposes for which a real-time monitor is used.
2. Briefly describe the purposes for which a long-term monitor is used.
3. Describe a general monitor display.
4. Describe an I/O monitor display.
5. Describe a process monitor display.
6. Discuss why a seek analysis might be performed.
7. Describe a long-term monitor time display.
8. List some possible ways of solving a device busy condition.
9. Distinguish between device busy, control-unit busy, and channel busy.
10. Contrast the usage of general vs. detailed displays.

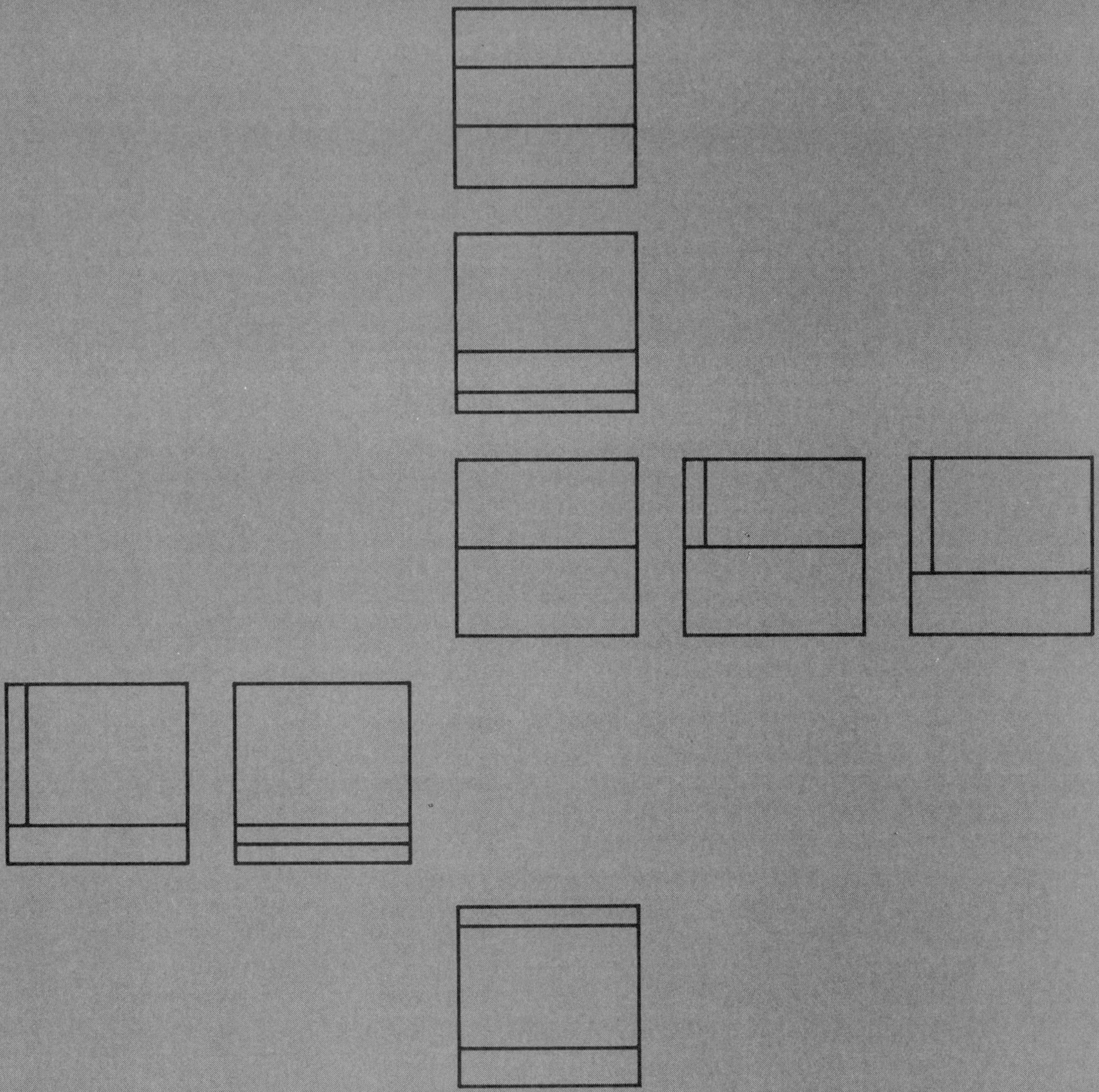

SYSTEMS SECURITY

10

KEY TERMS

Mantrap	*Halon*
Dial-in	*Dial-back*
Coder/decoder	*Passwords*
Hackers	*Problem state*
Supervisor state	*Trojan Horse programs*
Execute-only access	*Read-only access*
Copy access	*Write access*
DES (Data Encryption Standard)	*Encryption*
Public key	*Private key*
Link encryption	*End-to-end encryption*

INTRODUCTION

Security systems are usually a part of the operating system or another system added on top of the operating system. Most operating systems, particularly those designed for many users, have some level of security built in. Operating systems developed in recent years tend to have more security than those developed earlier. Very few operating systems, however, have a complete security system.

Security is necessary in three different areas of computer systems: access to the system, access to data or files, and access to memory while a program is executing. Only the first two areas are covered here since memory protection was covered in the sections on memory management. It should be noted, however, that memory management protection algorithms are necessary not only to prevent one program from accidentally destroying data belonging to another program, but also to prevent one program from deliberately reading data belonging to another program.

PHYSICAL SECURITY

Most people tend to think of security as being exclusively a software feature, but the first and most basic level of security is physical security. The level of protection placed on files is irrelevant if a violator can simply pick up a tape containing those files and carry it away. Physical security is a not an integral part of a systems programming text, however, so it will only be covered briefly.

Physical security becomes a much more difficult problem when dealing with microcomputers. Computer tapes tend to be relatively well monitored in most companies, but because floppy disks are so common, they usually are not monitored. Another problem is that microcomputers are small enough so that they can be physically removed, and they are often not located in a central area such as a computer room. The practical limits on security for microcomputers consist of fastening the unit to a large piece of furniture, putting a lock on it that prevents it from being used without the key, and securing the floppy disks in a locked cabinet.

Access control

Physical security is physical protection of the computer systems. This includes access to the computer systems and protection from hazards such as fires. Access protection is most usually achieved by instituting a guard system at the entrances to the computer facility. The first step is to have all the doors to the computer room locked, and only allow access by authorized individuals. This can be done by placing guards at the doors, but the most common way is to use an electronic guard system.

Electronic guard systems have electric locks on the doors. Each authorized person is issued a magnetically coded plastic card. This card is inserted into a special card reader just outside the door. If the code on the card authorizes the person to enter the computer room, the door is unlocked. More sophisticated systems leave the door unlocked for only a short period of time before relocking it, and allow only one person to enter the room each time the door is unlocked, thus preventing unauthorized persons from following an authorized person into the computer room. This card system can be set up for each room of the computer facility, so that each person's card is coded only for those rooms that he is authorized to enter.

Computer rooms that are heavily restricted carry this a step further with a system sometimes known as a **mantrap.** This is a double door, where the first door opens to anyone, but locks behind that person after entering. The card reader is between the doors, and must approve entrance before the next door unlocks to allow the person to continue on. A human guard at a distant location sometimes also scans the person with a video camera. This system not only prevents unauthorized entrance, but it also traps and holds any potential intruders. Unauthorized individuals require human intervention to free them once they have entered a mantrap.

Computer rooms usually have operations personnel in them at all times, but those rooms that have periods when no one is supposed to be in them can have various devices, such as motion detectors, placed in them to detect any unauthorized intrusions. Computer room operations personnel should also be alerted to be aware of and question anyone whom they do not know is authorized to be present.

Many computer facilities divide the various functions up into different rooms, and only allow personnel entry to those rooms where they actually work. This greatly reduces the overall security exposure. For example, the tape librarian may only be allowed into the room where the tapes are stored. Card readers designed for magnetically coded cards are able to determine whether a particular badge authorizes entry into a specific room, thus allowing specific room access to be granted on an individual basis.

Guards can be used at the doors to the building to prevent computer equipment or tapes from being moved out of the building without some authorization. This reduces the possibility of information or equipment being stolen. Similar systems should be used to prevent entry to the entire building by unauthorized personnel. The danger to computer installations comes more from attempted vandalism than from attempted theft, and much of the danger from vandalism can be prevented by not allowing authorized entrance to the building or to the computer facility.

A layout with separate access doors from the outside into each room allows personnel access only to that area where they have direct responsibility. Communications personnel, for example, should not have access to the main computer room or any of the other rooms. The doors between the rooms can be controlled with card readers to only allow authorized personnel access to more than one room.

Natural catastrophes

Natural catastrophes present a greater danger to computer rooms than human theft or vandalism. Many of the security systems in place in computer rooms are designed to prevent or control fires. Fire control in computer rooms is complicated by the fact that water tends to destroy computer equipment almost as effectively as fire, so fire control systems based on water are of questionable effectiveness. They also tend to be somewhat dangerous, since virtually all of the equipment in computer rooms is electrical, and water should not usually be used to control electrical fires.

Fire control is also complicated by most computer rooms having a raised floor, with large open spaces between the bottom floor level and the floor level used by people and equipment. These open spaces are used to run the cables connecting the computer equipment. The raised floor is usually from 12 to 18 inches above the actual floor, with the space in between frequently being completely filled by cables. Since many of the electrical connections and cables are in this area, it is quite subject to fires. Water is completely ineffective as a fire control agent in these areas because low height and piles of cables prevent it from spreading properly.

Most computer fire control systems use **halon** as a fire control agent. Halon is a chemical that extinguishes fire without damaging computer equipment. Two different fire control systems should be used: an automatic halon system between the floor levels that will go off if any fire is detected in that area, and another system for the computer room above the raised floor area. Computer rooms should have, at a minimum, an automatic sprinkler system designed to go off in case of any fires above the raised floor, and a better protection system is to have an automatic halon system above, as well as below, the raised floor. The primary reason for not using halon throughout the computer room is that halon systems are more expensive than plain water sprinkler systems.

ACCESS SECURITY

Once unauthorized physical access to the computer has been prevented, the next step is to prevent people from logging on or submitting a job without proper authorization. Three classes of unauthorized actions can be committed by a person achieving unauthorized access to computers. The best known is the destroying or changing of information. Stealing secret information is also a crime that can be vitally important. One other area that tends to be overlooked is the stealing of computer time. Mainframe computers tend to be rather expensive, and therefore the computing itself may be a valuable commodity. Some institutions give computer time freely to their employees or members, but many large businesses have been founded with the only product being the selling of computer time, and such time can be quite valuable.

Two distinct areas exist in which computer access security can be provided: establishing a link to the computer, and controlling access once the link has been established. The first area is a gray area between physical and software security, but the second area falls completely in software security.

Dial-in security

The prevalence of large nation-wide networks available to anyone has made many mainframe computers much more available. The physical link usually requires a **dial-in** connection by telephone to a computer. Security measures can be implemented on the receiving end of the dial-in link to ensure that only valid calls are connected. Such measures are virtually useless on computers belonging to a public network, however, so much planning should be spent before attaching a computer with sensitive data to a public network.

There are several different ways of screening incoming telephone links to a computer. The **dial-back** method uses a list of authorized telephone numbers in the computer, together with a telephone dialing system. When an incoming call is received, a calling telephone number must be entered, and that number is checked against a list of approved telephone numbers. If the number is not on the list the call is dropped. If the number is on the list, the call is disconnected and the computer dials that number to re-establish the link.

If the call was indeed made from the approved number, then the connection is made when the computer calls back and proceeds normally. If, however, the call was from some unauthorized source, then the call-back is to the wrong number, and therefore the unauthorized source is unable to complete the link. This, of course, has the limitation that it only allows links to be made from certain approved telephone numbers, which is not feasible if the users are moving from one location to another, and need access to the computer from each location. An example of this is a salesman, who may need to link with the company computer from different locations to input the orders for the day.

A system that can be used when the incoming calls are from unknown locations consists of a **coder/decoder** box in the physical link to the computer. Such a box might be attached to the telephone line between the terminal or microcomputer making the call and the wall telephone socket. This box puts a unique code signal into the call which can only be deciphered by a similar box

Example 10-1:

DIAL-BACK SYSTEMS

STEP ONE
Telephone call to computer

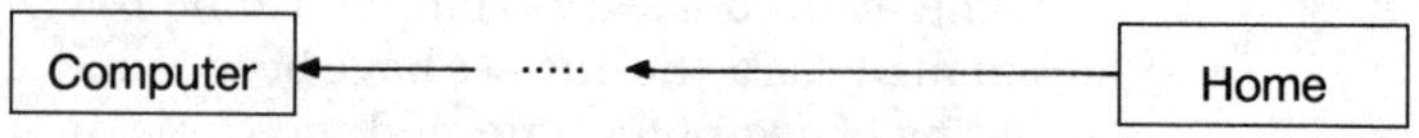

STEP TWO
Incoming user is checked for associated telephone number

STEP THREE
Telephone call to the user

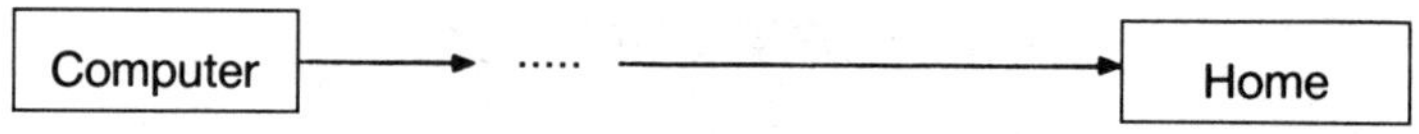

STEP FOUR
If the user called from the correct telephone number, the connection is made.

at the receiving computer. The state of the technology is such that boxes can be designed with millions of unique codes so that no two boxes have the same code. This system allows calls from any location as long as the appropriate code box is available. Such a system functions well as long as the distribution of the boxes is carefully controlled.

Password protection

When the physical link to the computer has been established, the next level of security is controlling the logical access to the operating system. This means controlling the logging on or submitting a job by the user, usually with **passwords.** A password is a special code word or series of letters and numbers that is associated with a particular user. The password must be entered before the user is allowed to access the system.

Password protection is probably the single most used security element in modern computer systems. Passwords can be quite effective if used carefully, but are almost useless if not. Password protection places the responsibility for system security into the hands of the users, which may be either good or bad, depending upon the users.

Microcomputer operating systems tend to vary widely in the degree of implementation of password protection, or any other protection for that matter. Some of them have password protection that is the equivalent of that offered on mainframe operating systems, but many have no protection at all. Many manufacturers feel that such protection is unnecessary on single-user systems. This is not always true, however, since even a single-user system can be used by different people at different times. Such a system is still accessed by many users (even though they are not using the system simultaneously) and consequently should have some type of access protection.

Passwords should not be long because long passwords are too difficult to remember. This usually leads to users writing down their passwords for reference. Writing passwords is one of the most common ways of allowing those passwords to become common knowledge. It is unbelievable how easy it is to find passwords by looking in the area around terminals, since many people leave their password near their terminal so that they can find it easily.

Passwords should also be longer than two characters, since short passwords are much easier to find by random trial. Short passwords are also quite easy to decipher by other users while it is being entered. One of the most common ways of allowing someone to find a password is to have that person standing near while the password is being entered. Even if the password does not appear on the screen, it is not too difficult to determine the password by watching the keys being struck, particularly if the password is very short, since only one or two keystrokes must be remembered or guessed at.

Example 10-2:

PASSWORDS

GOOD PASSWORDS	REASONS
TIMETORN	Mnemonic and easy to remember
GOHM5PM	"Go home at 5PM"—mnemonic
MY56CHEV	Numbers help increase security
WHY9AM	Mnemonic and includes a number

BAD PASSWORDS	REASONS
VI	Too short
EDKCIGIEKDI	Too long—not mnemonic
85948	Difficult to remember and should include at least one letter
MASSIE	My last name—too obvious

The operating system should mask or hide the password when it is typed in so that other people cannot read the password over someone's shoulder or on a discarded printout. Passwords entered on a video display should not be printed on the screen, and passwords entered on a hard-copy terminal should be masked by rapidly printing a series of characters over the top of the password so that it can not be deciphered.

Passwords should be changed at frequent intervals, such as every two to four weeks. If a password has been discovered by an unauthorized user, this may prevent that password from being used at all, or at least minimizes the damage. If any user thinks a password has been leaked to unauthorized users, that password should be changed immediately.

The most common causes of unauthorized users having a password are from maintaining the same password for too long (such as after employees have left a company) and from writing a password down. Whenever any employee possessing passwords leaves, all those passwords should be immediately changed. Some computer installations have arrangements with the personnel department at the company so that they are automatically notified when employees leave the company. This allows them to change passwords immediately. It may also be necessary to change passwords not directly connected with some employees, since they may have used other passwords while employed.

Many users, particularly casual users who do not access the computer regularly, have trouble remembering their passwords, so they write them down. These written passwords are usually located in some obvious place, such as on a terminal or a desk drawer. When it is necessary to write passwords, those passwords should always be located in some unlikely place, preferably at home, and passwords should only be written in unusual circumstances. Passwords should normally be memorized.

Access violators

The most publicized access violations occur by **hackers,** who are people who derive entertainment from using computers to perform difficult feats. Breaking into systems is one such feat on which some hackers tend to spend a large amount of time. These people seldom have malicious intent, but nevertheless sometimes do significant damage if they succeed in breaking into a system. Hackers frequently are very knowledgeable about computers and may succeed in breaking into a system where others would fail.

The other dangerous type of person is one who has malicious intent. This person may be trying to steal information to resell, or may be a disgruntled employee who is simply trying to get revenge by destroying data. This group is much smaller in number than hackers, but much more dangerous. They usually are not characterized by a great deal of computer knowledge, but tend to have specialized knowledge of a particular system. A hacker might try exotic decoding algorithms to break into a strange system, whereas people in this group are more likely to be familiar with the particular system they are attempting to access. They usually gain access from carelessness or inside knowledge, such as seeing a password written down, or from knowing passwords that have not been changed.

Monitoring violations

Any access control system must have a way to monitor and record all sucessful and failed access attempts. Many failed access attempts are legitimate mistakes, but some of them may be attempted violations. Many access violations are based upon finding passwords by trying different combinations of letters and numbers until the correct one is found. Monitoring such attempts may be the only way that an access violation, or attempted access violation, is detected.

Monitoring access attempts also allows a limit to be placed on the number of attempts allowed each user. The technique of trying different passwords to gain system access is impossible when the total number of access violations is limited. Many systems refuse further attempts after three or five attempts to access the system have failed. Intervention from systems personnel is required in order for that user to access the computer again.

Access violation techniques

One of the common methods used by access violators is to write a program that obtains operating system privileges for itself. Application programs normally run in what is known as **problem state,** while operating systems run in **supervisor state.** Supervisor state allows programs to access any facility of the computer, just like operating systems do, whereas problem state restricts the power of the programs. If an access violator's program can get into the system far enough to change the flag determining its state, then it can put itself into supervisor state and can then do almost anything in the system.

One trick that is sometimes used to obtain passwords from other users is to substitute a program for part of the normal operating system in the section that controls input job information. This is the program that the user talks with to submit a job or to logon to the system. Such a fake program functions identically to the operating system, as far as the victim can tell, but instead of just processing the access information, it records the passwords entered and then passes that user on to the normal operating system routines to process the access information. The victim cannot tell any difference between the operation of such a program and the normal operation of the system, but the access violator then need only look at the passwords stored by the fake program to get access to the account.

Another trick that is sometimes used is to hide special functions in a program that is used on the computer. The program is then unsuspectingly integrated into the normal operation of the system. It may or may not be a part of the operating system, but it is a part of the normal operation of business. The extra functions hidden in the program are designed to provide an entry into the system for the access violator. They may be as simple as trapping passwords and writing them out in another file where the violator can read them, or as complex as allowing a special, fully privileged, logon by the violator. Such programs are known as **Trojan Horse** programs, since they are taken into the system unsuspectingly.

Security system failures

One area of operating systems that sometime allows illegal access is the failure to properly handle cases where there is a problem with a communication line. Communications networks must commonly handle cases where a user is logged into a system via a network and the connection is lost in an abrupt, unintended manner. Examples of this are turning off the power on the user terminal, or the telephone company breaking the line connecting the user to the host. In such cases, the user is physically disconnected, but is not logically disconnected, since he did not log off from the computer. If the operating system does not logically disconnect that user immediately, then the next user to access the computer with that communications line may be reconnected on the previous users job, with complete access to all data and programs.

The communications network must also ensure that the user's job is stopped when the physical link is broken. Some networks maintain a logical link that requires an explicit command to remove even after the physical link has been removed. Such commands would normally be part of the procedure used when leaving the network, but the system must ensure that these commands are executed each time the link is physically disconnected. Connecting to another person's job does not allow the person complete access to the system, of course, since a logon process is still required, but it does negate any dial-back or coder/decoder schemes to prevent invalid links.

Controlling system data areas is also vital to systems security. Letting a user get access to system data areas may allow that user to modify critical parameters in the system controlling the privileges of his program, such as the supervisor/problem status. Such access is sometimes obtained by a user because system data areas pertaining to that user are either kept in the user's area, or are kept in an area accessible to that user. This is a major reason for using supervisor calls to access certain system services.

Parameters submitted to the operating system by users or programs should always be checked to ensure that nothing invalid has been attempted. Such parameters are a direct route to the heart of the operating system, and allowing them in without checking may allow a program to penetrate the system. A problem sometimes ensues if those parameters are not moved to an inaccessible area as soon as they have passed the validity check. Allowing the user access to parameters after the validity check, but before those parameters are actually used, allows the user to change the parameters, perhaps to something the violates the integrity of the system.

The most common reason for system access violations is simple human carelessness. Users write their passwords down and leave them inside a desk drawer or on the terminal itself, where they can subsequently be read by almost anyone. Another frequent source of information is the wastebaskets. Programs or papers containing sensitive information are frequently discarded carelessly in wastebaskets where anyone can read them. Passwords are frequently revealed by users when they give out their passwords to friends or acquaintances whom they do not know as well as they think they do. These friends may either intentionally or carelessly give them to someone who does use them to penetrate the system.

FILE SECURITY

The other major area of systems security, after system access, is protecting data on that system from access by users who are authorized to be on the system. Every computer system has dozens or hundreds of files on it. Some of these files may contain public knowledge, but others may be highly sensitive. Highly sensitive files should only be accessible by authorized users, not by all users on the system.

There are four basic levels of file access that can be granted to any user. The least access available is **execute-only access,** which is designed for programs. This allows other users to execute that program, but they cannot read or copy it. The next access level is **read-only access,** which allows other users to either read that file or execute it if it is a program. Some systems do not differentiate between the read-only and execute-only levels. The next access level is copy access, which allows a user to copy that file. Some systems allow files to be executed or read without being copied, although other systems do not differentiate between these options and allow any file that can be read to be copied. The highest level is **write access,** which is the ability to modify files. Any user with this ability can do anything with that file including erasing it or changing it in any way.

File access control depends upon the sophistication of the operating system. The simplest control is, of course, no control at all. This allows every user to access any file in the system, regardless of who owns the file. The least amount of control is to group all files belonging to a single user and to impose the same level of control over all those files as a group. The user owning those files specifies the level of access available to other users. More complex file security systems, however, allow access control for individual files.

File access is usually determined by passwords, just as is system access. The owner of the files sets passwords to control the access. One password is used for each type of access allowed, so if three different types of access are granted, three different passwords should be used. Not specifying a password for a particular type of access prevents that access from being allowed to anyone, while a special password, such as "ALL", can be used to allow everyone that access without requiring that they specify a password. This, in effect, provides public access at that level.

Example 10-3:

FILE ACCESS LEVELS

1. Execute only
2. Execute and read
3. Execute, read, and copy
4. Execute, read, copy, and write

POSSIBLE ADDITIONAL LEVELS

1. Update without adding to
2. Write without erasing

For example, all users may be allowed to read the files, so no password is used to control that access. Only selected users may be allowed to copy files, so a password is used for that. Users must specify that password before being allowed to copy files.

Some sophisticated security systems, by default, prevent any file access by any user except the owner. These systems allow the person owning the files to set the access privileges for files, and access is allowed to other users only if explicitly set by the file owner. File access privileges can also be set by a group administrator for several associated users. This allows higher levels of management to control the access levels of all the files in that group. Another option is to set different access privileges based not just on passwords, but on categories of users. For example, all users in Department B might be allowed to access the files of Department A without a password, while Department C might be allowed to access those files only with a password, and no other users are allowed any access.

File access systems should also monitor access violations just like system access violations. The monitoring can either be passive, so that violations are reported to an administrator, or active, where the user attempting the access is deactivated after a specified number of successive violations. The allowable number of access violations must be high enough so that legitimate mistakes do not cause users to be deactivated, but it must not be so high that violators can be successful with random password choices.

ENCRYPTION

One technique that is being increasingly used is that of coding, or **encrypting,** files so that they cannot be read even if access has been achieved. The most notable usage for encrypting files is in transmitting them between computers, but similar techniques can be used to encrypt individual files. Many techniques exist for encrypting files, and an encryption standard has been adopted by the National Bureau of Standards that is called the **Data Encryption Standard** or **DES.**

Encypting files is important whenever those files may be available to unauthorized users. This is particularly important when the data is in a form physically accessible, such as a tape that can be carried out of a building. It is also important when the file security system does not provide sufficient protection from access by unauthorized users. Data transmission lines, for example, are particularly subject to eavesdropping, so therefore data that is sensitive should always be encrypted before being transmitted over such lines.

All computer equipment can be monitored by sophisticated electronic gear that can decipher the data without any physical connection. Electrical and magnetic fields are set up around the equipment that can be decoded into the actual data being transmitted. For this reason, computers or data transmission lines that contain sensitive data should be physically shielded from eavesdropping. In the absence of physical shielding, all the data should be encrypted.

Encryption algorithms

Encryption algorithms use a key to modify the characters in a file so that the sequence of characters becomes unintelligible. Only the same key and algorithm can decode the characters so that the information again becomes legible. Most such encryption systems are good enough so that only an expert with a large computer can break the code without the key. Almost any encryption system can be broken, however, given enough expertise and computer time. The computer time is necessary because most such code-breaking schemes require that thousands or millions of combinations be tried until the key is found.

The most common method for encryption systems to be broken is by someone discovering the key. The key functions very similarly to a password, and so the weakest point in the system is usually protecting the key. Maintaining an encryption key to protect files on a computer system is not as difficult when those files are being transmitted, since the files and the key remain in one physical location. Some simple systems record the key as part of the encrypted file, which usually makes the code easier to break. Other systems record the key in a separate file, which is better, but still provides a way of obtaining the key, since that file cannot be encrypted. The best way is not to record the key anywhere, but this requires that the user remember the key or record it himself.

Files that are encrypted for data transmission have a more difficult problem, since the person decoding that file is physically distant from the person sending the file. This requires some means of transmitting the key to the receiver, as well as the file itself. This leads to the usual problem of trying to hide the encryption key. Another problem is the case where many locations may desire to transmit files to one central location. Sending a copy of the key to each of the distant locations is an obvious weak point in the security system.

One way to circumvent this problem is to use what is known as a **public key.** This type of system uses two different keys to encode and decode data. One key, the public key, is commonly available to everyone, but is used only for encrypting the data. It cannot be used to decode or decipher the data. Another key, the **private key,** must be used to decode the data. The private key is known only to the installation receiving the data. In such a system the public key is widely available, so that anyone can encrypt the data. The data is then transmitted to a central location, where the private key is used to decode the data. Such systems are quite common for functions where many locations must transmit coded data to one central location.

Encyption in data transmission networks is usually set up in one of two ways. Networks that encode the data at the sending computer and decode it at the receiving computer use **end-to-end encryption.** Networks that only encrypt the data between the links in the network use **link encryption.** Since most networks contain multiple links between the computers, these two methods are distinctly different.

SUMMARY

All security systems must start with physical security. This involves keeping the system physically inaccessible to unauthorized intruders. The doors of the buildings should be guarded, and the doors of the computer room should be protected either with human guards or with a magnetic card system. Such systems can be set up to allow access only to the specific rooms authorized for a particular person.

Physical security also involves protecting the computer installation against natural disasters, such as fires or earthquakes. Fire is the most common consideration. Automatic halon fire extinguishing systems are the best. The system should be set up to monitor and extinguish fires both under the raised floor area, and in the computer room itself. A minimal system has halon under the raised floor and sprinklers in the computer room.

Unauthorized access to computer systems is easiest on systems that are connected to public networks, or any system supporting terminals with dial telephone lines. Security systems here involve methods of verifying accesses. One method is to store a list of acceptable telephone numbers in the computer and have the computer call back when a user calls in. This verifies that the user has called from an approved telephone number. Another common method uses a coder/decoder box for each authorized user. When the user calls in, the box sends a special code to the computer verifying the transmission.

The most common method of controlling access to computers is with the use of passwords. Passwords should not be written down anywhere. Passwords should not be so long that they cannot be memorized, but should be at least four characters long in order to make it more difficult to randomly guess their characters. Most access violations involve either hackers who penetrate systems security simply for the challenge involved or people who have actual criminal intents. Most of these accesses are possible because passwords are either so obvious that they can easily be guessed or because some user has been careless and allowed the password to become available.

Many common tricks are used to obtain unauthorized access to systems. Among these are the Trojan Horse system, where a program that allows access is unknowingly loaded on the system. Many of the accesses are possible only because the operating system allows a program access to vital system data areas, or system parameters.

File security systems allow four different types of access to files. The lowest level is execute-only, where programs can only be executed. The next level is read-only, where files can be read or executed. The next level allows files to be executed, read, or copied. The highest level allows files to be modified as well as executed, read, or copied.

File access is also usually controlled by passwords. These passwords may be for a whole group of files or for single files, depending upon the sophistication of the security system. Such systems should also monitor and track any access failures in order to prevent anyone from finding a password by repeated guesses.

Any data that is in danger of being accessed by unauthorized persons can be encrypted so that that data cannot be deciphered even if it is read. This can be done to files so that an unauthorized access to that file still does not allow it to be read. The most common usage for data encryption is in data transmission, where the data may be physically available to many people.

Data encryption requires a key to code and decode the data. The security of the data, of course, is dependent upon the security of the key. Many installations which require that data be transmitted from various locations to one central location distribute a public key to the outlying locations. This public key is used to encrypt the files, but cannot be used to decode them. The decoding key is called a private key, and is only available at the central location.

EXERCISES

TRUE/FALSE

1. Security systems are needed in places such as banks.
2. No security system is completely unbreakable.
3. Physical security is not necessary with good software security systems.
4. The biggest physical danger to computers is fire.
5. Dial-back is only used for telephone computer access.
6. File access systems may allow execute-only access.
7. File security systems seldom use passwords.
8. Data encryption is primarily used in file systems.
9. Public keys allow anyone to read an encrypted file.
10. All security systems should monitor and log access failures.

MULTIPLE CHOICE

1. The best computer room fire suppression system is:
   - **a)** Sprinkler systems and wall fire extinguishers
   - **b)** Under-floor halon and wall fire extinguishers
   - **c)** Sprinkler systems over and under the floor
   - **d)** Sprinkler systems and under-floor halon
2. The most common systems security method is:
   - **a)** Passwords
   - **b)** Key-card systems
   - **c)** Mantrap
   - **d)** None
3. Dial-back systems:
   - **a)** Prevent hackers from calling the computer
   - **b)** Force the user to call the computer twice to get access
   - **c)** Requires no effort by systems personnel to implement
   - **d)** Receives calls, and calls back if user is authorized
4. Supervisor state is:
   - **a)** Entered by programs when they enter the processor
   - **b)** Required to perform any I/O
   - **c)** Only allowed to the operating system
   - **d)** Never used

5. Trojan Horse programs:
   a) Are legitimate programs that allow unauthorized access
   b) Are hacker programs that do not show on the system
   c) Really do not usually work
   d) Usually are immediately discovered
6. Files can have:
   a) Read access
   b) Copy access
   c) Write access
   d) All of the above
7. A public key encryption system:
   a) Allows anyone to decode the transmissions
   b) Only the correct sender can decode the data
   c) Only the correct receiver can decode the data
   d) The data is not encoded before being transmitted
8. Link encryption:
   a) Is more secure than end-to-end encryption
   b) Is less secure than end-to-end encryption
   c) Cannot be used in a large network
   d) Is used only to detect errors
9. Data encryption:
   a) Is most used by financial networks
   b) Is most used by public billboard networks
   c) Cannot be used by private installations
   d) Is not necessary, since data cannot be intercepted
10. The most common security failure is:
    a) Insufficient technology used to prevent breaches
    b) Too much emphasis on preventing physical access
    c) Depending on passwords
    d) Carelessness by users

DISCUSSION QUESTIONS

1. Describe a computer room card entry system.
2. Discuss the pros and cons of halon as a fire control agent.
3. Describe a good typical computer room fire control system.
4. Describe a dial-back system.
5. Briefly describe the characteristics of a good password.
6. List and describe the most common system access violators.
7. List and describe the four basic levels of file security.
8. Discuss why attempted access violations should be monitored.
9. Describe a public key encryption system.
10. Describe a Trojan Horse program.

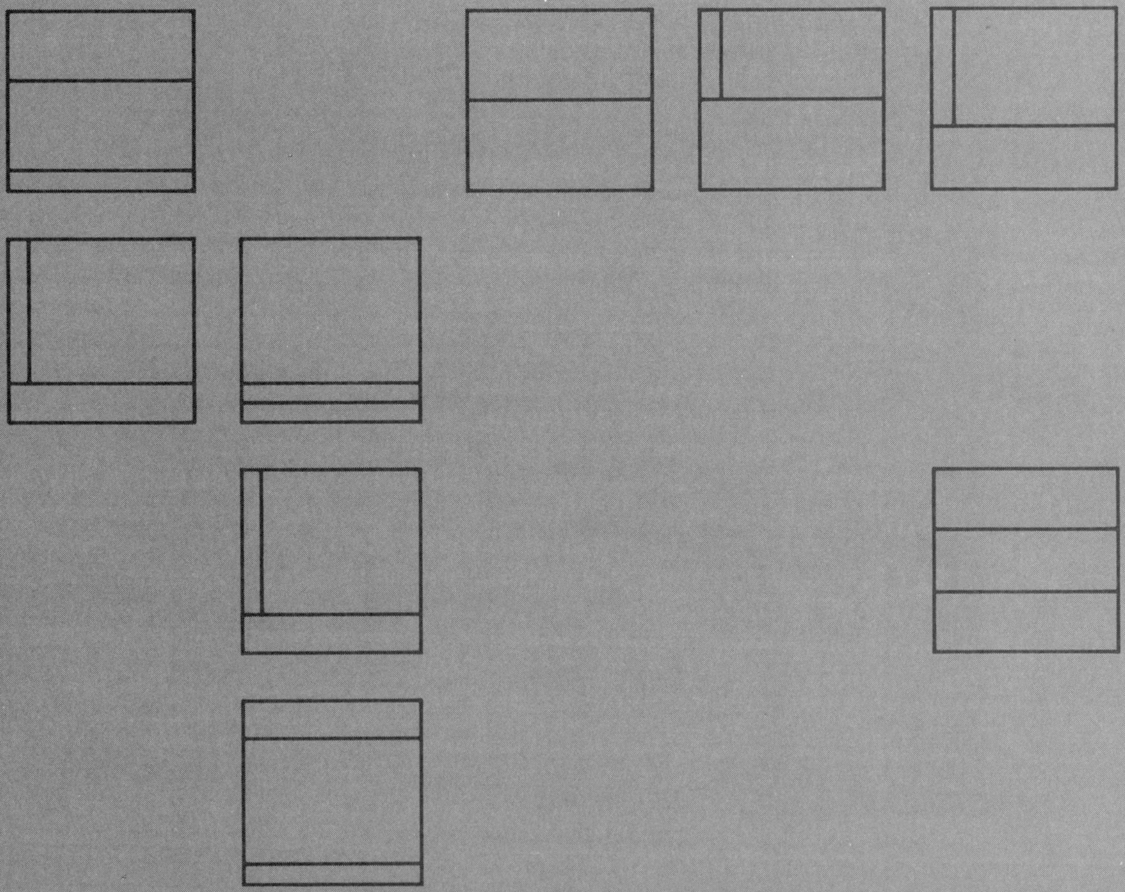

MULTI-PROCESSING

11

KEY TERMS

Parallel processing	*Vector processing*
Scalar processing	*COSTART*
COBEGIN	*never idle*
COEND	*Tightly coupled*
Loosely coupled	*Attached processor*
Master/slave	*Locking resources*
Co-processor	

INTRODUCTION

Multi-processing is the concept of putting more than one central processing unit in a computer. This is a common solution to the need for more computing power. This is important since many developing faster single processors are becoming increasingly difficult. Physical limitations such as the speed of light and heat buildup are causing much of the difficulty in increasing the speed of processors. New generations of processors are being developed constantly, with speeds much faster than the best available only three to five years ago, but this is still not enough to satisfy the demand. Most of the largest general purpose computers now use a multi-processor configuration to gain additional computing power.

The operating system must be able to efficiently manage all processors and allocate resources between them in the best possible way. This becomes an extremely difficult task for the operating system. The overhead associated with keeping track of which processor is using which resource or is running which process at any time is significant even when the management itself is done well.

The major management problem is handled by the algorithms managing resources. These algorithms use the same general principles as those used in single processor configurations, but the complexity of the task is increased considerably. As a consequence, the algorithms must also become more complex, with an attendant increase in overhead. The algorithms used in multi-processor configurations must be better developed than those used in single processor configurations if the overhead involved is not going to negate the additional power.

One common problem that must be faced with multi-processor systems is balancing the computing load between the different processors. It is so difficult to efficiently divide single tasks between processors that most implementations of multi-processor configurations do not even try. Each processor runs

Example 11-1:

SAMPLE DUAL PROCESSOR CONFIGURATION

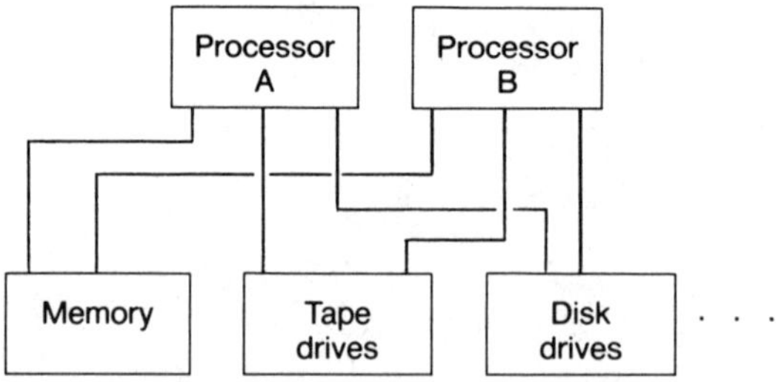

one discrete task at any one time. The additional processors only do work when two or more tasks are available. This is not a serious hindrance in most systems, where the workload consists of many relatively small jobs.

Configurations with more than two processors are vastly more complicated than even the two-processor configuration. The complexity of the system increases much faster than the number of processors added to the computer. Very few general purpose computers use more than two processors, although some very large ones have four processors. The trend, however, is to increase the number of processors, since it is much easier to handle the system complexity than it is to dramatically increase the speed of the processors themselves.

One would think that doubling the number of processors should double the job throughput speed, but this is not the case. In fact, the overall computer speed cannot be increased linearly by adding more individual processors. The major portion of the performance missing as each processor is added can be attributed to the increased overhead of managing that additional processor.

PARALLELISM

There are two basic methods to handle a multi-processor configuration. The simpler way is to treat each processor individually and schedule tasks separately for each processor. The more complex way is to treat all the processors as one virtual processor and schedule only one task to run on all processors simultaneously.

Running one task on several processors simultaneously is called **parallel processing,** because the processing is done together. This concept holds great promise for the future, since the ultimate computing power available in a parallel processing computer is almost unlimited. In practice, it is not quite so simple. Achieving a commercially successful parallel computer requires that vast obstacles be overcome. Parallel processing computers have had limited success with some smaller computer vendors, but the major vendors have not yet embraced the concept with their general purpose computers.

True parallel processing is not needed for most types of installations where general purpose computers are used. Such installations tend to run a large number of relatively small jobs, where the simpler approach to multi-processors (running them as separate processors) works quite well. Only in specialized areas, such as for some types of engineering or mathematical modelling, is the increased computing power needed for just one job. These jobs are so large that without true parallelism, the job may require days to finish. Probably one reason why true parallelism has not been developed more is that only recently has the market for such large computers been generally recognized.

Example 11-2:

MULTI-PROCESSORS WITH SEPARATE TASKS

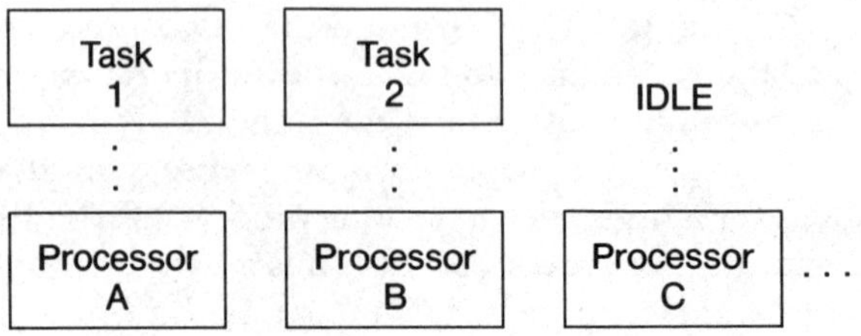

A recent example of the movement toward true parallelism is the support by IBM of a FORTRAN compiler that compiles jobs to run on as many as four processors simultaneously (the large IBM computers, models 3084 and 3090-400, have four processors). Even here, a fair amount is lost to overhead between the processors. The quoted increase in speed for a job running in four processors instead of just one is 3.3, which shows that 70% of one of processors is being used just for overhead.

True parallel processing is also sometimes called **vector processing,** because each operation is performed on a vector, or group, of numbers. Non-parallel processing is sometimes called **scalar processing** because each operation is performed on a single number. The process of converting an application program to function in parallel is sometimes called **vectorizing.** Most of the so-called supercomputers use some type of vector processing. These computers are mostly used for engineering and scientific applications. The market for such applications has been rather small in the past, but is rapidly expanding today, and most of the major computer vendors will soon be involved in that market.

Example 11-3:

MULTI-PROCESSORS WITH PARALLELISM

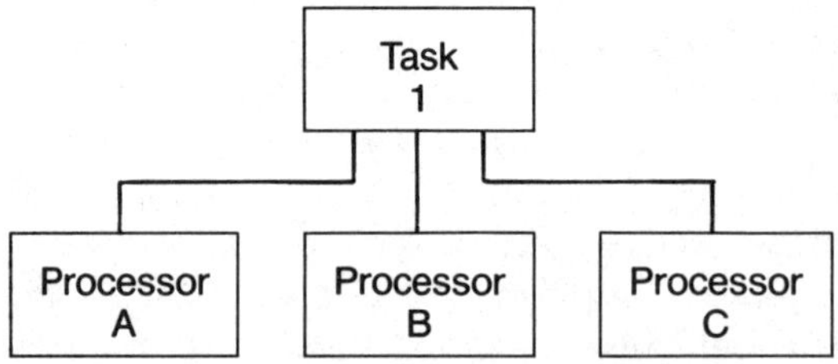

Vectorizing programs

There are many problems in implementing full parallel processing, not least of which is that humans tend to think sequentially instead of in parallel. Thus, much of the process of parallelism is alien. Computers, compilers, and applications programs are all designed to operate sequentially; in order to take full advantage of parallelism, all of them must be redesigned. Even after such a redesign, only certain types of problems are naturally suited for parallel processing. Many types of problems are naturally sequential problems and cannot be transformed into parallel problems.

An obvious example of program code that can be made parallel is:

```
DO I = 1 TO 10
X(I) = XOLD(I)
Y(I) = YOLD(I)
END
```

Here, the two assignment statements are not dependent on one another and can therefore be executed simultaneously by two different processors.

A less obvious example is:

```
DO I = 1 TO 10
X(I) = XOLD(I)
END
```

This can be rewritten as:

```
X(1) = XOLD(1)
X(2) = XOLD(2)
X(3) = XOLD(3)
X(4) = XOLD(4)
X(5) = XOLD(5)
X(6) = XOLD(6)
X(7) = XOLD(7)
X(8) = XOLD(8)
X(9) = XOLD(9)
X(10) = XOLD(10)
```

These ten assignment statements can then be set up to run on ten different processors simultaneously. If ten processors are not available, these statements can be divided into groups, with each group running on a single processor. In this way, a seemingly sequential iterative process is converted into a parallel process.

One way of vectorizing a program is to rewrite that program using special statements that designate which sections of the program can be executed in parallel. The compiler used must be able to understand the special statements necessary and to generate machine language code that properly utilizes the multi-processors. One way to specify such sections is with statements such as **COBEGIN** or **COSTART** and **COEND** to designate which sections of code are to be executed in parallel.

The COBEGIN statement is used to designate the beginning of the section to be executed in parallel and the COEND is used to designate the end of that section. The previous example could be rewritten as:

```
COBEGIN
X(1) = XOLD(1)
X(2) = XOLD(2)
X(3) = XOLD(3)
X(4) = XOLD(4)
X(5) = XOLD(5)
X(6) = XOLD(6)
X(7) = XOLD(7)
X(8) = XOLD(8)
X(9) = XOLD(9)
X(10) = XOLD(10)
COEND
```

Manually converting programs to run in a parallel mode is very difficult. Very few programmers really understand the concepts of parallel processing that are required to correctly set a program up to run efficiently in parallel mode. Incorrectly setting up the program may have no effect, it may cause the program to run inefficiently, or it could cause the program to fail to run. Even if the conversion is done correctly, it still may involve a large amount of work by the programmer, which is not desirable.

Because of the problems inherent in manually vectorizing programs, it is highly desirable to have that function done automatically. In cases where a program is very large, the only practical way to vectorize it may be to have it done automatically. The normal place where vectorizing is done is in the compiler. This requires that the programs be recompiled, but that is a relatively minor penalty in return for what may be a major decrease in job turnaround time. There are also vectorizers that read the source code of a program and write out a new source code.

There are obvious difficulties in writing a compiler that vectorizes programs. Compilers are not simple programs, and the additional analysis necessary to allow them to correctly vectorize programs tends to make them much more complex. Writing a compiler to detect the statements necessary to allow manual vectorizing of the programs is relatively simple. The more complex way is to automatically recognize areas of programs that can be vectorized, and to perform that vectorization. This can usually be done in two areas; one of these is the analysis of loops, similar to those already presented, and the other way is the analysis of arithmetic statements to allow those statements to be rewritten in a vectorized mode.

One of the reasons that only certain types of programs really gain anything through vectorization is that only certain types of statements can be vectorized successfully. In general, only arithmetic programs can usually obtain a significant performance gain from vectorization. Non-arithmetic statements are usually only subject to vectorization in loops, while arithmetic statements can be vectorized both in loops and in normal arithmetic statements.

Many arithmetic statements can be vectorized by utilizing some simple algebraic principles. For example:

```
X = Y + Z + A + B
```

is a simple, sequential statement, but it can be vectorized by rewriting it as:

```
X = (Y + Z) + (A + B)
```

which has the same meaning. This statement then consists of two independent sections which can be executed in parallel (the (Y + Z) and the (A + B) parts), although adding the two independent sums must still be done on a single processor. This final addition is one reason why vectorization seldom achieves the throughput speed gains one might expect.

The same principle can be used to divide up statements involving multiplications:

```
X = Y * Z * A * B
```

is equivalent to:

```
X = (Y * Z) * (A * B)
```

Arithmetic statements in general can frequently be rearranged in such a way that the statement consists of many small parts, each of which is independent of the other parts. These parts can then be processed in parallel, and the results of each of the individual calculations can then be processed together. This does not produce complete parallelism, since the last part of the calculation is done sequentially, but at least a large part of the overall calculation can be done in parallel.

The search for parallelism often leads to some portion of the available processors either not active or performing work that is subsequently not used. There are many cases where a piece of program code may be set up and performed in parallel only if a particular branch is taken in the program. If that branch is not taken, then that section of code may either not be executed at all, or it may require reexecution with new values. When this is the case, most systems execute that code anyhow, on the chance that it may be needed. The idea is that it is better to have processors performing work that may be wasted than it is to have them doing nothing. This is sometimes called the **never idle** rule.

An example of this is the statement:

```
IF (X=4) THEN Y=17
```

The calculation (Y=17) is needed only if the previous part of the statement (X=4) is true. Nevertheless, that calculation may be needed, so if a processor is idle, the calculation should be done whether or not it will be needed.

The degree of vectorization achieved by programs is dependent both upon the construction of the program and the sophistication of the compiler. Compilers that vectorize programs more thoroughly tend to require much more time and systems resources for the compilation, so an option that is sometimes available is to allow the programmer to determine the degree of vectorization to be used in the compilation. This allows quick compilations of programs in order to test the correctness of those programs for program debugging, but it also allows the code to be fully optimized when it is ready to be placed in production.

MULTI-PROCESSOR PHYSICAL ORGANIZATION

The physical organization of multi-processor computers is very similar to that of single-processor computers. Some multi-processor configurations are made up of two or more physically separate computers. These are each complete computers with main memory and a processor. They can either have separate peripheral I/O devices, or can share them through an I/O processor. This arrangement is called a **loosely coupled** organization. An example of such a setup is the VAXCLUSTER arrangement from Digital Equipment Corporation. Computers in a loosely coupled setup usually function relatively independently of one another without much true multi-processing.

Example 11-4:

SAMPLE CLUSTERED CONFIGURATION

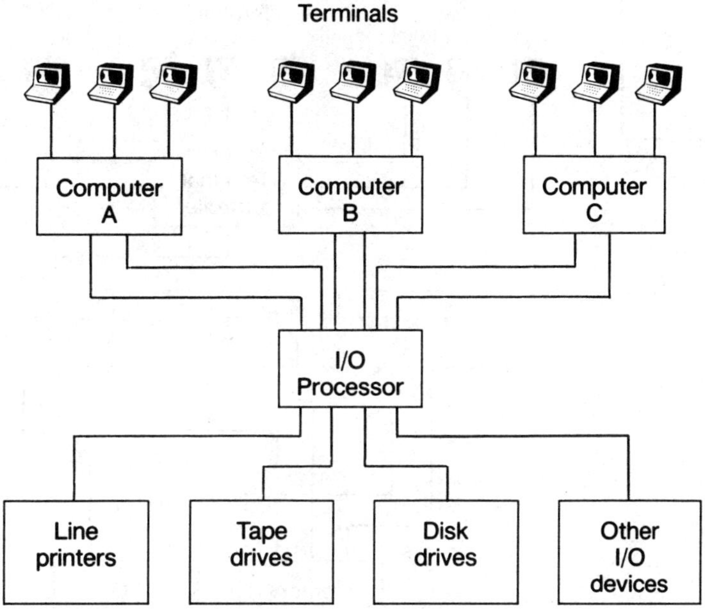

Each processing unit consists of a complete computer with both processor and memory, but most peripheral I/O devices are shared through the I/O processor. Access to computers is regulated by the I/O processor which serves as a gateway between the computers and peripherals. Terminals, however, are connected to individual computers instead of the I/O processor.

The true multi-processing environment has all the processors physically contained in one area; the memory, peripheral I/O devices, and the I/O processor are all shared by the processors. This setup is referred to as **tightly coupled.** A high degree of sophistication in the operating system is needed to optimize performance in such a system.

Example 11-5:

SAMPLE MULTI-PROCESSOR CONFIGURATION

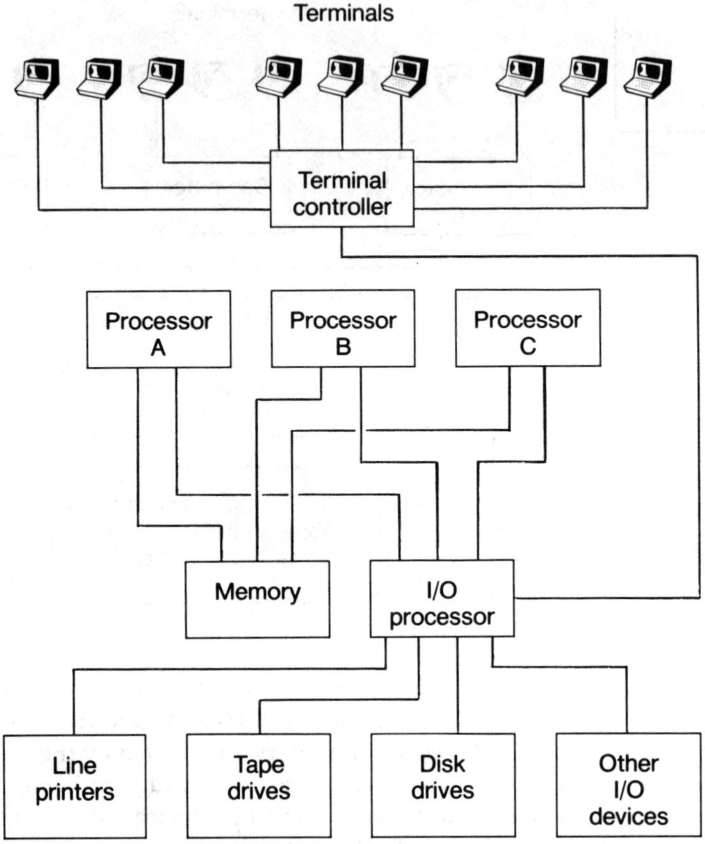

Multi-processor computers can be set up in two different ways. One method is for all the processors to have equal priority and tasks so that each part of the overall system load is divided up evenly between them. A simpler method is to use a **master/slave** relationship, where one processor functions as a master and the others as slaves.

The slave in the master/slave relationship is sometimes known as an **attached processor,** or **co-processor.** The master in the master/slave arrangement handles all I/O, memory accesses, etc. The attached slave processor is used only for simple computing on specified tasks. A common example of such an arrangement is an IBM PC with the optional 8087 chip installed. The primary processor is the Intel 8088, and the attached co-processor is the Intel 8087. The co-processor is used only for specific computing on certain numeric applications.

Attached processor configurations are very useful in cases where the attached processor is specialized and performs only one function, but is much less useful when the processors are equivalent. Such systems, if properly handled, are more efficient when each of the processors have an equal role to play.

Example 11-6:

SAMPLE ATTACHED PROCESSOR CONFIGURATION

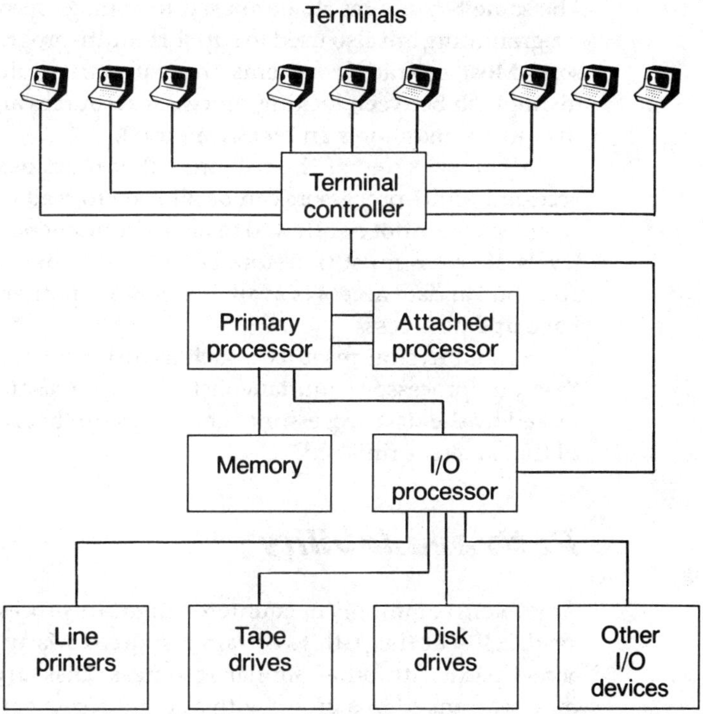

True multi-processor configurations have a significant advantage in system availability as compared to single processor or attached processor configurations. Single processor computers become completely unavailable whenever the processor fails or is unavailable for any reason. Attached processor computers become completely unavailable only when the master processor fails; they will usually continue running if the attached processor fails. True multi-processor configuration computers, however, can usually continue running when any of the processors fail. The computer becomes completely unavailable only when all, or most of the processors fail.

A true multi-processor configuration allows each processor equal access to all system resources such as memory and I/O devices. The operating system itself can run on any one of the different processors. It may run on one particular processor by default, but should be set up to run on any processor if the default processor becomes unavailable for any reason.

Managing resources

The same techniques that are used to manage resources in supporting multi-programming are also used to support multi-programming with multi-processors. Most operating systems that support multi-processing do not really distinguish between locking processor resources and program resources, since the same semaphores and locks are used.

Memory is one of the resources that must be locked in order to serialize accesses. Multi-processors can be allowed to read from memory simultaneously, but they cannot be allowed to have simultaneous write operations. Different levels of access must therefore be defined, where read access is always available, but update access is available only if another processor does not already have update access.

Some physical resources, such as disk drives, cannot be available to more than one processor simultaneously for any reason, so such resources must be locked by the first processor to gain access to that resource and not released until that access is finished.

Path availability

A problem commonly encountered in multi-processor computers is that of unavailability of the path to certain resources. Many systems resources share an access path with other similar resources. Disk drives, for example, are commonly arranged in a group with a single access path to the group. Whenever a data transfer is in progress to a single disk drive in the group, that path is not available to any other disk drive or processor. This is less critical in single processor configurations, since the processor is usually already busy handling the data transfer operation. Multi-processor configurations, however, may have more than one processor attempting to perform I/O at the same time, so the unavailability of the single data path means that one or more processors may be delayed while waiting for the data path to become available.

The usual method of alleviating this problem is to provide additional paths from the processors to the resources. There are usually not as many paths as there are elements in the resource group, nor as many as there are processors, but adding one extra path greatly reduces the resource contention problems inherent in multi-processor configurations.

The number of paths that should be used is dependent upon the total number of processors, the amount of access expected to that particular resource, and the number of elements in the resource group. It is also heavily dependent upon limiting the complexity of the overall system to a manageable level. Most resources are adequately served by two paths. Configurations using more than four processors may require more than two paths, and certain highly accessed resources may also require more than two paths. The most common example of such a resource is memory, which may be divided into small physical partitions (not related to the partitioning done by the operating system), each of which has one or two paths.

Tables that specify the current status of the resource must be maintained for every system resource. Those tables are used to show whether it is currently being used by another processor. Resources that should be included in this list are I/O devices, memory, and operating systems tables. The components of the operating system itself, such as system tables, should be kept rather small, and maintained in widely separated areas in order to maximize the probability that such components will be available to processors.

SUMMARY

Computers are becoming more and more powerful, and one way of implementing such power is by adding additional processors into the computer. Many computers now have two processors, some have four, and a few have more than four. Such a configuration greatly increases the available computing power in that computer, although at a considerable cost in additional overhead and management problems.

Multi-processor computers can be set up in two different ways. One way is to use those processors to run independent tasks. This reduces the management problems, but requires that at least as many tasks always be running as there are processors in the system, since otherwise one or more processors will be idle.

The other method is to run many processes of one program simultaneously on all available processors, called vector or parallel processing.

Converting programs to run in parallel, called vectorizing, can be done manually using special programming constructs that notify the compiler that certain blocks of statements can be executed simultaneously, or automatically by the compiler. The better way, of course, is to have the vectorizing done automatically. Such automatic vectorizing is normally done by rearranging certain groups of statements so that they are independent of one another, and can therefore be executed simultaneously.

Processors can be set up in a master/slave relationship. One processor is the master and controls allocation of all system resources. In a true multi-processing configuration, each processor shares equally in all system tasks and resources.

All systems resources must be shared among the processors, which causes significant overhead problems. The sharing requires extensive management, which is usually implemented by setting up tables for each resource. These tables control the allocation of that resource. The tables allow the locking of the resources so that the various processors are allowed to control the resource only when no other processor has prior control.

EXERCISES

TRUE/FALSE

1. Not all multi-processor computers use parallel processing.
2. Any program can be vectorized with significant performance gains.
3. No major vendor offers computers with more than one processor.
4. The best way to vectorize programs is manually.
5. Parallel processing provides an increase with computing power with no significant problems.
6. Loosely-coupled systems are easier to manage.
7. Multi-processing provides increased reliability.
8. Attached processors are always better than true multi-processors.
9. Managing system resources is much more difficult with multi-processor configurations.
10. Parallel processing can provide huge gains in performance for certain types of programs.

MULTIPLE CHOICE

1. Parallel processing:
   a) Is quite easy to implement
   b) Is always faster than scalar processing
   c) Allows many operations to be performed simultaneously
   d) Is much more expensive than scalar processing
2. The "never idle" rule:
   a) Causes maximum efficiency for each processor
   b) Improves overall throughput by wasting some resources

- **c)** Only works when all processors are fully utilized
- **d)** Is only used on processes that are completely parallel

3. A loosely coupled organization:
- **a)** Has more than four processors
- **b)** Places all the processors in a separate physical box
- **c)** Links actual computers instead of just processors
- **d)** Is more difficult to implement than tightly coupled

4. An attached processor:
- **a)** Is used on only a few computers
- **b)** Causes all processors to function equally
- **c)** Is more difficult to implement than a co-processor
- **d)** Is used only for limited functions

5. A co-processor:
- **a)** Is relatively easy to support in software
- **b)** Causes all processors to function equally
- **c)** Works with any application
- **d)** Is quite common in modern computers

6. The most difficult problem with co-processors is:
- **a)** Finding suitable applications
- **b)** Keeping all processors busy
- **c)** Managing shared resources
- **d)** The cost

7. Applications:
- **a)** Cannot run on multi-processors
- **b)** Immediately run on multi-processors
- **c)** Must usually be recompiled to use multi-processors
- **d)** Can always be made efficient on multi-processors

8. Multi-processor configurations:
- **a)** Are more efficient than scalar configurations
- **b)** Are less efficient than scalar configurations
- **c)** Work equally well on all applications
- **d)** Are very efficient, but only on some applications

9. Resources are managed:
- **a)** With each processor equally
- **b)** By only one processor

   c) By sophisticated locking mechanisms
   d) More easily with multi-processors

10. Attached processor configurations:
   a) Are available on only a few large mainframes
   b) Are available on all computers
   c) Are available on many computers, even microcomputers
   d) Require very sophisticated hardware and software

DISCUSSION QUESTIONS

1. Describe true parallel processing.
2. Compare and contrast vector and scalar processing.
3. Describe the function of the COSTART and COEND statements.
4. Describe the "never idle" rule.
5. Describe a loosely coupled multi-processor organization.
6. Describe a tightly coupled multi-processor organization.
7. Describe an attached processor multi-processor organization.
8. Discuss resource management locks used with multi-processors.
9. Discuss path availability with multi-processors.
10. Briefly discuss how compilers can vectorize programs.

NETWORKING SYSTEMS

12

KEY TERMS

Local Area Networks (LANs)	*Long lines*
Analog lines	*Digital lines*
Bandwidth	*Twisted pair*
Fiber optic cable	*Node*
Coaxial cable	*Network topology*
Link	*Multi-drop link*
Point-to-point link	*Star network*
Bus network	*Hierarchical network*
Ring network	*Unconstrained network*
Polling	*Token passing*
Packet	*Slotted ring*
ISO Network Standard	*Data link layer*
Physical link layer	*Network layer*

CSMA/CD (Carrier Sense Multiple Access/Collision Detection)

KEY TERMS

Session control layer	*Presentation control layer*
Application/user layer	*Baseband*
Transport layer	*Broadband*
PBX (Private branch exchange)	

INTRODUCTION

One of the most important areas in the computer world today is setting up and maintaining telecommunications networks between computers. One special case of computer communication that is becoming very well known is **Local Area Networks,** or **LANs.** A LAN is a network set up between various computers which are relatively close physically to one another.

Current data communications developments are focused on linking mainframes or minicomputers to one another, linking personal computers to one another, and linking personal computers or terminals with mainframes or minicomputers. The technology used to link different sized computers tends to vary since smaller computers usually require much less sophisticated and expensive technology than do the larger computers.

There are many ways of setting up data communications networks. Since the whole field is relatively new, no single standard exists to allow the various vendors to use the same type of technology in setting up networks. Many different systems were developed, but these have gradually been reduced to only a few major designs. Standards have now been adopted for setting up networks, but because of the proliferation of network designs, no single design has been adopted. Three different standards have been widely adopted for LANs, and many more designs are used for large computer networks.

There are two major users of networks. One group needs remote access to computers. This group demands immediate access and fast response at all times, but seldom transfers very much data. A network serving such a group should emphasize reliability and availability. The other group of users are computers which frequently transfer massive amounts of data. A network serving this group must provide very high speed data transfer, but need not always be available, since such transfers may only occur occasionally.

BASIC CONCEPTS

Network systems can be divided into long-distance and local. There are networks that combine both local and long-distance, and there are networks that do not fit clearly into either, but the majority of networks fit clearly into one group or the other.

Long-distance networks use a connection system sometimes called **long lines.** These are usually telephone lines, although they can be satellite connections, infrared links, or other technologies. Telephone lines are divided up into two general groups. **Analog lines** are used to transmit analog signals such as voice communications. These signals use continuous frequencies, similar to a sine wave. **Digital lines** are used to transmit digital data, such as computer communications. Digital data are discrete signals, usually consisting of a few distinct frequencies. Digital lines usually have a higher data transmission speed and a lower error rate than analog lines, but are also currently more expensive.

The amount of data that can be transmitted over a line during a given time interval is dependent on the speed of that line and the error rate. This data amount is also sometimes called the **bandwidth** of the line. Line speeds are normally quoted in "bits per second" or "bps," which is the number of digital bits transmitted every second. Common line speeds are 300, 600, 1200, 4800, 9600, 19200, and 56000 bits per second. Line speeds above one thousand bps are usually quoted in "Kbps," which is "Kilo bits per second," or thousands of bits transmitted per second. A line speed of 9600 bps is thus quoted as 9.6Kbps.

Local area networks use many types of wiring to connect the elements of the network. The connection can be made quite cheaply where only low-speed lines are desired. The most frequent type of connection is similar to the connection used by the telephone company. It uses two wires in a configuration known as a **twisted pair.** Higher speed local connections use a cable similar to that in television broadcast transmissions, known as **coaxial cable.** A more recent development which holds great promise for the future is **fiber optics.** Fiber optic links can transmit more data faster than virtually any other type of link. They also usually have a much lower error rate. Unfortunately, fiber optic cable is still rather expensive, but this will change in the near future.

NETWORK DESIGN

There are several ways to set up networks. The particular design chosen for a network is dependent upon the types of equipment on the network, the data transmission requirements for the network, and the intended purpose of the network. Each of the pieces of equipment on the network that can transmit or receive data is called a **node.** The path between nodes is called a **link.** The design of the network (the way the links and nodes are connected) is called the **network topology.**

Links can be of two different types. The **point-to-point** link connects only two nodes. The **multi-drop** link connects many nodes. Point-to-point links are most common in connecting a small number of nodes, normally ones that require very high speed or long-distance data transmissions. Multi-drop links are used to set up networks that cover only a relatively short distance and usually do not require such high speed data transmission rates. Multi-drop links are necessary in any network containing a large number of nodes where any node must be able to communicate with any other node, since the number of links required to implement point-to-point links with a large number of nodes is astronomical. Point-to-point links are quite feasible even with a large number of nodes, however, if each node need communicate with only a few other nodes.

An example of the two links is a network containing two mainframe computers in different cities with a group of personal computers in each city connected to the mainframe computer. The personal computers in each city might be connected to each other and to the mainframe with a multi-drop link, whereas the two mainframe computers would be connected with a long line point-to-point link.

Example 12-1:

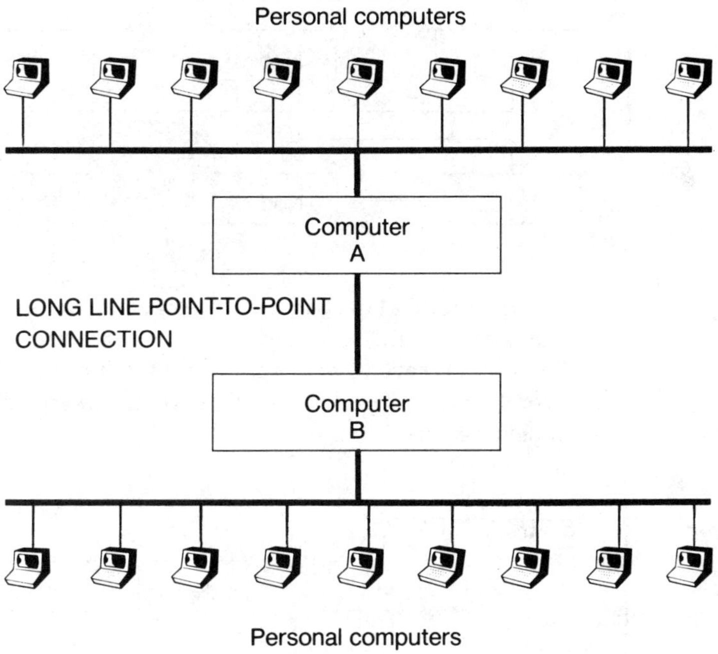

Network topologies

The simplest architecture for a network is to connect only those nodes that need to communicate with one another. The links between nodes in this scheme exist only where a specific link is needed. This architecture is sometimes called a **mesh** or **unconstrained** network.

Another architecture is the **star** configuration, where one node is central, and all other nodes are connected to that central node. This configuration is probably most useful for cases where the central node is a mainframe or minicomputer used to collect and store data, and all the other nodes are terminals or personal computers used for viewing the data. The star configuration is not appropriate when a large amount of the network communications is between nodes other than the central node.

Bus networks are a central link, or bus, that has each node connected to it. This layout is appropriate for networks where each individual node may frequently need to communicate with any other node. The popular Ethernet LAN is an example of a bus network. Bus networks are very reliable, since, unlike other configurations, any node or group of nodes can fail without affecting the rest of the network. This is because the only nodes involved in transmitting messages are the sending and receiving nodes. No node is necessary for retransmitting the data or for keeping the network intact.

Example 12-2:

UNCONSTRAINED NETWORK

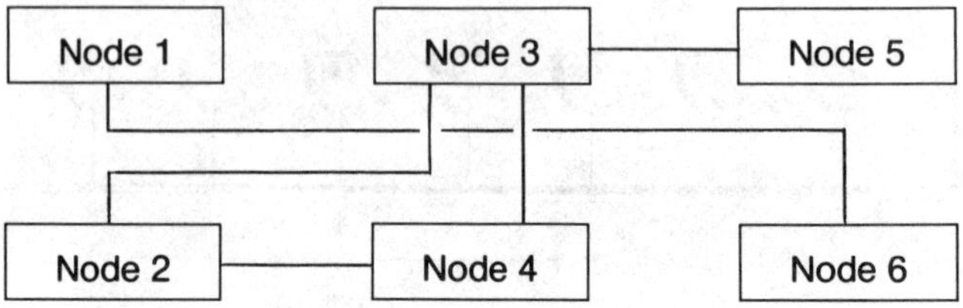

Hierarchical networks are designed in a form similar to a tree, where one node serves as the root, and all other nodes branch eventually from that root. The root has several nodes connected to it directly, and those nodes may have several nodes connected directly to them, and so on. This structure continues as far as necessary.

Example 12-3:

STAR NETWORK

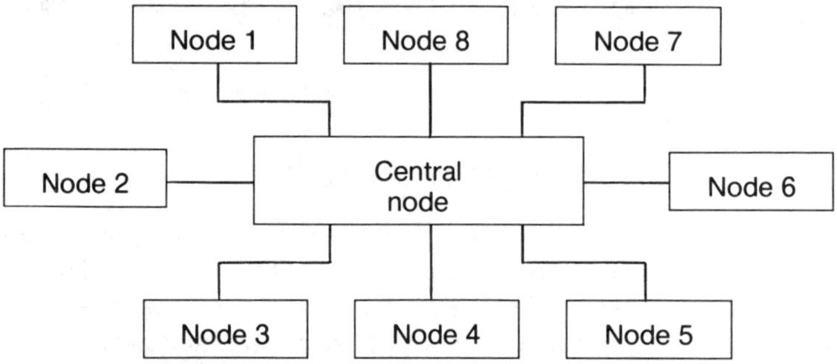

The hierarchical network is very good if certain individual nodes communicate frequently with a controlling node, which in turn communicates to a higher level node. An example of a simple arrangement like this is to set up a corporate mainframe computer, which communicates to a group of departmental minicomputers. Each minicomputer then communicates with several personal computers. This design is not good when nodes at the bottom level of one branch need to communicate with nodes at the bottom level of another branch, since such a communication requires going through all the links up to the point in the hierarchy where the two branches meet.

Example 12-4:

BUS NETWORK

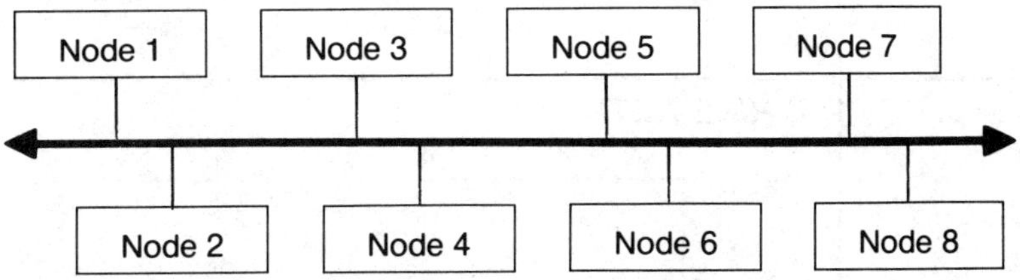

The final network configuration is the **ring network.** This is set up so that each node is linked to the next node, and the whole network forms a ring, so that the last node in the ring is linked to the first node. Data is transmitted from any node to the next node on the ring, which either retransmits the data or receives it. Rings are not as reliable as buses, since the failure of any one node in the ring causes the whole network to become unavailable. Rings may also be slower, since each piece of data must be retransmitted by each node in its path until it reaches its destination. Since the path of each piece of data is predetermined, however, much less overhead may be involved in routing the messages. Rings also serve very well when a very high volume of data must be transmitted, since managing the transmissions is relatively easy.

Example 12-5:

HIERARCHICAL NETWORK

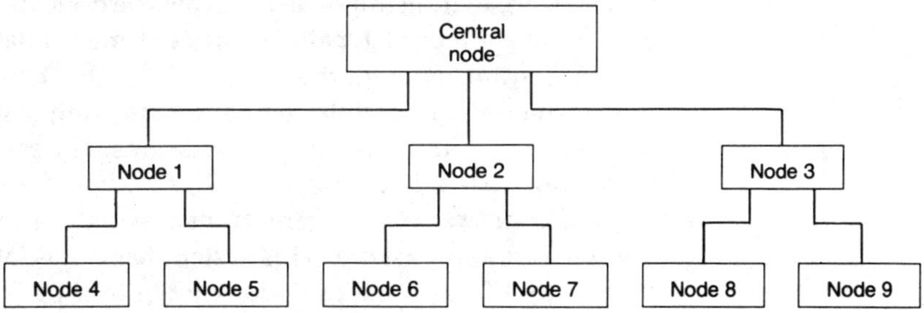

NETWORK ACCESS-POLLING

Much of the complexity in designing networks lies in determining how the nodes will be attached, and how they will gain access in order to transmit or receive data. The design of the network architecture is usually closely tied to the method chosen for controlling the way the nodes access the network. Access to the network by the nodes must be controlled, since each node might choose to transmit data at the same time, resulting in very little information being successfully transmitted. The biggest problem in controlling network access is preventing or managing simultaneous transmissions by more than one node.

Example 12-6:

RING NETWORK

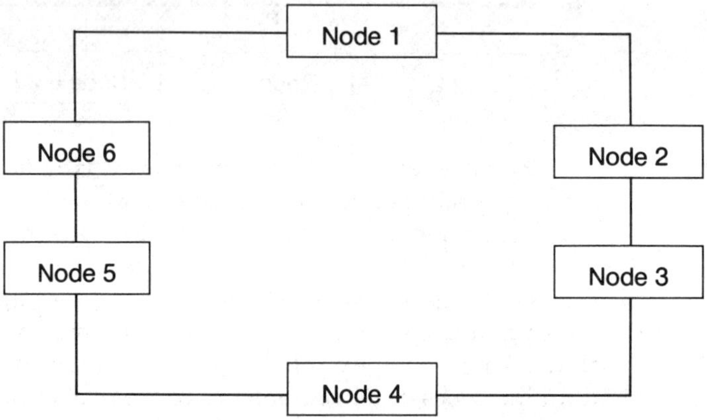

One way of controlling access to the network is through a **polling** technique. This gives each node on the network the ability to transmit only at a specified time. The polling can be done from a central location, where some master node periodically queries each of the other nodes to determine if that node wishes to transmit data. It can also be done in a decentralized basis, where each node has a predetermined slice of time available to transmit data. Setting up the central node so that it queries each of the other nodes sequentially means that only one node can be transmitting at any one time, so there is no problem with simultaneous transmissions. The same objective can be achieved by setting up the decentralized nodes so that no two time slices are the same.

Another way to prevent transmission contention is with a technique known as **token passing.** This system has a specially coded bit package that is transmitted from node to node, known as a **packet.** When a node wishes to transmit, it must wait until the next time it receives a packet. It can then hold the packet and transmit its message in place of the packet. That message goes to the next node, which retransmits it. The message is continually retransmitted until it reaches the node it was intended for. That node then reads the message, modifies it to indicate that it was read successfully, then transmits it to the next node. The message then continues until it returns to the original sending node. That node determines that the message was read successfully, and then transmits the packet to the next node to indicate that the network is again free.

The token passing algorithm only works on ring networks since each node sends messages only to the next node, and each message must eventually return to the original sending node. The packet is passed around the ring, with any node not wishing to transmit simply sending the packet on to the next node. This network design is known as a **token ring.** The token ring has been adopted as a standard for many types of LANs; IBM has been the primary backer of the token ring design.

The simple form of the token ring is not very efficient for many applications, since no other data can be transmitted until the first message returns to the transmitting node. If the ring is large, the overall data throughput may not be very high.

One way to partially overcome this problem is to have many packets on the system. This form is sometimes called a **slotted ring,** because each individual packet can be thought of as a slot that has data inserted in it. The network is designed as a ring, and the packet circles the ring just as in the token ring, but there are many packets simultaneously on the ring. Each packet contains an indication of whether it contains valid data or is empty. If the packet contains data, then part of the packet indicates the node that transmitted the data and the intended receiver of the data. The major problem with such a setup is that if the individual messages transmitted are small, the control information contained in each packet may actually be larger than the data in that packet. In this case, much more information is being transmitted than is actually needed, which is inefficient.

NETWORK ACCESS-CONTENTION

Some networks allow any node to transmit at virtually any time. This inevitably leads to cases where transmissions are made simultaneously, causing garbled information. This problem is handled by retransmitting the garbled information.

The most common algorithm for managing such a network is called **Carrier Sense Multiple Access/Collision Detection** or **CSMA/CD.** "Carrier Sense" means that each node monitors the network before transmitting. If any transmission is currently in progress, it waits before transmitting. Only when no transmission is in progress does that node transmit. "Multiple Access" means that the node is free to transmit data when it thinks that the network is free; it does not have to wait for any specified time or signal before transmitting.

This system prevents most cases of multiple transmissions, but it is possible that two different nodes can begin transmitting at the same time, since each of them will have checked the network at the same time and found it clear. Each transmitting node continues to monitor the network during transmission, and can detect transmissions by other nodes. This is the "Collision Detection" part of the name. If another transmission is detected, each transmitting node immediately stops transmitting, waits for a random amount of time, and then begins the transmission process again. If another node has already begun transmitting, the network will be busy, so the first node will not transmit. If the network is not busy, the first node restarts the previous transmission. It is possible that both nodes may begin retransmitting at the same time, causing the same problem again, but if each node waits a random amount of time, this will not happen often. If it does, another wait virtually eliminates the possibility of it happening a third time.

CSMA/CD networks tend to be very efficient for smaller networks and for networks that do not require many frequent data transmissions, since each node can usually get quick access to the network for transmission. This network is very efficient when the number of collisions is kept low. It becomes inefficient when the number of collisions is high, since each collision results in lost and retransmitted data. The system becomes less efficient in large networks, since the presence of a large number of nodes increases the possibility of collisions. This algorithm also works much better when the packets transmitted are large, since collisions are less likely. The packets must have a certain minimum size in order to guarantee that any collisions can be detected. Some networks have been developed using "collision avoidance" instead of "collision detection", but have not achieved the success of the CSMA/CD networks.

NETWORK STANDARDS

Networks are so important, and becoming so common, that some standard is necessary for developing networks. Such a standard has been developed at the theoretical level. It was developed by a group called the "International Standards Organization," and is called the **ISO Network Standard.** It defines the way nodes in a network should communicate with one another, and has divided the process of communications into seven distinct levels or layers.

The bottom-most layer is the **Physical link layer.** This defines the way the mechanical and electrical parts of the link are designed. It may also include any software necessary to make the physical connection work properly.

The next higher layer is the **Data link layer.** This layer controls the way the data is transmitted over the physical link. It performs error checking on the transmitted data, addresses the message packets properly, and decodes the addresses on incoming packets.

The next layer is the **Network layer.** This layer controls the way the messages are set up to move from one node to another. It ensures that a path is available to the receiving node, and that not too many messages are being transmitted at once. This layer sets up and maintains the path between nodes.

The **Transport layer** ensures that the data is being transmitted correctly once the path has been established. It is not concerned with the establishment of the path, but controls the transmission once the path is established. It ensures that messages are actually transmitted and is not concerned with the mechanics of the transmission.

The **Session Control layer** is a bridge between the services provided by the Transport layer and any functions provided by the computer at the node. The Transport layer is independent of operating systems, but the Session Control layer varies depending upon the operating system at each node.

The **Presentation Control** layer translates the transmitted data into a form that can be used in the receiver. It performs any necessary encoding or decoding of data necessary for display or processing.

The highest layer is the **Application/user layer.** This layer provides the services that are seen and used by users. Examples of such services are file transfers or database management systems.

Most contemporary network designs follow this standard to some extent. Not every layer in the standard is implemented in every network, but the functions that are present are layered in a manner similar to that given in the standard. Examples of such networks are IBM's SNA and Digital Equipment Corporation's DNA.

PRIVATE BRANCH EXCHANGES

One of the ways that communication networks are frequently implemented is through the use of **private branch exchanges** or **PBXs.** PBXs are extremely common today. In fact, most business telephones are run through a PBX. PBXs were developed for use with telephones but are seeing increased use for data communications.

At one time, all telephone calls from a location required a line to a central exchange, usually one or a few per city, which then routed that call forward toward its destination. This is quite inefficient in the case of many business calls which may be to another location within the same building. Some means was needed to allow local calls to be handled without requiring a central exchange. This freed the central exchange to handle calls where it was actually needed, such as those calls to a physically distant location.

The PBX is a local exchange, similar in function to the central exchange, that receives incoming calls and routes them on toward their destination. If those calls are to a distant location, then the next step in the linking is usually a central exchange, but if the calls are local, such as within the same building, then the PBX handles the call itself, and the central exchange is not involved. The PBX is also sometimes known as a PABX (Private Automated Branch Exchange), CBX (Computerized Branch Exchange), or DBX (Digital Branch Exchange).

Example 12-7:

ISO NETWORK STANDARD

Application/user
Presentation control
Session control
Transport
Network
Data link
Physical

LANs can be implemented with the use of a PBX. Large PBXs are very complex computers that are quite capable of handling data communications as well as voice communications. Less expense is usually involved in implementing a PBX-based LAN, since the PBX itself is frequently already in place, and usually only requires an upgrade to function as a LAN controller. Wiring, which can sometimes be used for data communications as well as telephones, is already in place from offices to the PBX, although new wiring is sometimes required. One potential problem with the PBX network is that, since it is controlled from a single point, if that point fails, the whole network is unusable. This is not usually a major concern, since the technology is quite reliable and can be repaired quickly.

OTHER TYPES OF LOCAL AREA NETWORKS

There are two other types of LANs that should be considered; **baseband** LANs and **broadband** LANs. Both refer to a technique for encoding the signal to be transmitted. Broadband networks use the same techniques as cable TV and require that the signals be transformed into analog form for transmission.

Baseband communication technology places the signal directly on the physical link, whereas most other techniques use a carrier signal, with the real signal modulated on top of the carrier signal. A carrier signal is a constant signal that is transmitted across the link. Slight changes in that signal are used to transmit data. Baseband signals are called that because they are at the "base", or lower part, of the bandwidth on the link. Baseband networks are used primarily for data communications, and the complete bandwidth of the channel is devoted to that signal. An example of such a network is the popular Ethernet.

Example 12-8:

PRIVATE BRANCH EXCHANGE

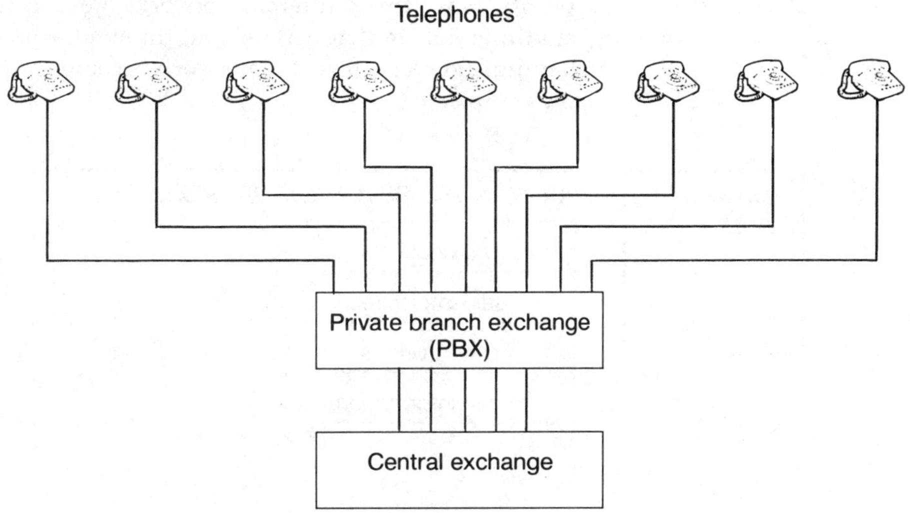

Broadband networks run on the same type of coaxial cable as cable TV, and use that cable in a similar fashion to television transmissions. They are called broadband because the bandwidth of the cable is quite wide (it allows a large amount of information to be transmitted simultaneously). Digital data must be transformed to analog form before being placed on a broadband cable.

Example 12-9:

A CHANNEL OF A BASEBAND LAN

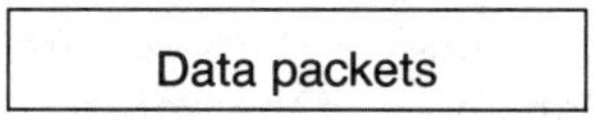

The primary advantage of broadband networks is its flexibility. Unlike baseband, the link is not exclusively devoted to data communications. The same link can share transmissions of data, audio, and video. One link can be used to integrate virtually all communications needs. The bandwidth on the cable is sufficient so that the data part of the transmission is not penalized by sharing the cable with other channels containing audio and video signals.

Broadband networks theoretically offer a complete integration of communications needs into one network. In practice, this complete integration has seldom been achieved. Three different logical networks end up coexisting on one physical network, since the three different types of communications are seldom presented in an integrated form.

The primary problems associated with broadband networks are their complexity. Since three different networks are effectively integrated into one, if anything fails in that network, all three networks will be unavailable. Maintaining and controlling the network becomes much more difficult because of the complexity.

Example 12-10:

A CHANNEL OF A BROADBAND LAN

Data packets
Audio information
Data packets
Video information
. . .
Video information

SUMMARY

The primary divisions of networks are long-distance and local. Long-distance networks are usually telephone lines or satellite links spanning a long distance. Local networks provide service to physically adjacent users.

Networks consist of nodes, which are the points that actually send and receive data, and links, which are the connections between the nodes. The amount of data that can be transferred between the nodes is determined by the bandwidth or transmission speed of the link.

The configuration of networks is called network topology. The simplest design is the mesh or unconstrained network where nodes are connected only to nodes with which communication is desired. This presumes that most nodes do not need to communicate with most other nodes. The star design has a central node controlling the network, with all other nodes connected to that central node. The bus design has a central bus which has all nodes connected to it; no one node controls the network. The ring design has all nodes connected in a circle. The hierarchical design is a tree-structured setup where one node forms the root, with several nodes connected to it. Each of these nodes may then have several other nodes connected, each of which may have other nodes connected, etc.

There are several algorithms for controlling network access. Polling techniques are best for large networks. This allows a node to transmit a message only when given permission. The permission may be granted by a controlling node, or it may be predetermined to be available at certain times. This insures that no two nodes will ever transmit at the same time.

An example of a polling network is the token-ring, which is a ring network with tokens that are passed from one node to the next. This token is actually a small message or packet. A node that wishes to transmit data pulls the token off the ring, and sends the message in its place. The message circles the ring, is read and flagged by the intended receiver, then returns to the sender, who then returns the token to the ring.

Some networks allow nodes to transmit at any time, which tends to be more efficient for smaller networks. This leads to collisions, but if the network is not very busy, then the collisions do not degrade performance significantly. A common way of implementing this is the CSMA/CD method. This requires each node to monitor the link before transmitting, and to only transmit if the link does not contain another message. The transmitting node must monitor the link during the transmission to detect such a collision. If a collision is detected, the node waits a random amount of time, then tries to transmit again. This guarantees that the transmission is eventually completed successfully.

Standards have been developed to control the way networks are designed. The best known of these is from the International Standards Organization.

Most common networks today implement many or all of the features listed in this standard. The standard calls for each network to have seven different layers, each serving a different type of function.

The Physical layer handles the physical connection. The Data Link layer checks for packet addresses and errors. The Network layer controls the flow of messages. The Transport layer controls the messages once the path has been established. The Session Control layer is a bridge between the network features and the node features. The Presentation Control layer sets the messages up to be read by the computer. The Application/user layer provides services such as file transfer to the user directly.

Local Area Networks can be set up using telephone systems such as PBXs to control the network. PBXs are used by the telephone company to control and route telephone calls within a small local area, such as one company building, without requiring those calls to go to a central exchange. Such PBXs can relatively easily be upgraded to provide similar services to LANs.

Most LANs are designed using either baseband or broadband technology. Baseband dedicates a channel to the network, and is very good for local, high-speed communications. It is relatively simple, fast, and reliable. Broadband technology integrates voice, data, and video transmissions on the same channel. It is more complex, and thus it is more difficult to design and maintain networks on it, but it also provides greatly enhanced flexibility.

EXERCISES

TRUE/FALSE

1. Multi-drop links are better than point-to-point for networks with many nodes.
2. Network topology refers to type of nodes on a network.
3. Bus networks are usually quite reliable.
4. Ring networks are the most efficient.
5. Token passing requires collision detection algorithms.
6. CSMA/CD is an example of a polling network.
7. Baseband LANs are always better than broadband LANs.
8. The networking standard calls for seven layers in networks.
9. Many networks pass messages in packets.
10. The star network is best for mainframe/terminal networks.

MULTIPLE CHOICE

1. LANs:
   - **a)** Use long-lines
   - **b)** Use twisted-pair or coaxial cables
   - **c)** Have no standards available
   - **d)** Are not used when large computers are available
2. Network topology:
   - **a)** Is independent of the usage of the network
   - **b)** Must be one of three possible configurations
   - **c)** Depends upon the equipment and usage desired
   - **d)** Depends upon the type of mainframe available
3. Polling networks:
   - **a)** Wait for a node to indicate a communication
   - **b)** Are most useful for small networks
   - **c)** Use the CSMA/CD protocol
   - **d)** Are most useful for large networks

4. A token-passing network:
 a) Uses the CSMA/CD protocol
 b) Is useless on large networks
 c) Transmits information in packets
 d) Is sometimes called Ethernet

5. Possible network configurations are:
 a) Ring network
 b) Mesh network
 c) Hierarchical network
 d) All of the above

6. Network standards:
 a) Call for a five-layer set of protocols
 b) Exist only for individual manufacturers
 c) Define a seven-layer standard
 d) Use the seven-layer Ethernet standard

7. Baseband LANs:
 a) Allow multiple types of transmissions on one cable
 b) Are more complex than broadband LANs
 c) Have a higher bandwidth than broadband LANs
 d) Are dedicated to data transmissions

8. The token-ring network:
 a) Is an example of a CSMA/CD network
 b) Is most suitable for small networks
 c) Is a polling network suitable for large networks
 d) Should not be used without a mainframe computer

9. The CSMA/CD network:
 a) Uses polling to prevent multiple transmissions
 b) Allows multiple transmissions and retransmits
 c) Works best on large networks
 d) Is able to correctly interpret multiple transmissions

10. The PBX:
 a) Is obsolete communications technology
 b) Routes all calls through a central exchange
 c) Allows voice and data transmissions to be kept separate
 d) Integrates voice and data transmissions

DISCUSSION QUESTIONS

1. Contrast LANs with long-lines.
2. Contrast multipoint links with point-to-point links.
3. Describe a ring network.
4. Describe a bus network.
5. Describe a polling access technique.
6. Describe a token-passing network.
7. Describe a CSMA/CD network.
8. List the parts of the ISO network standard.
9. Describe a PBX.
10. Describe a slotted ring network.

TWO

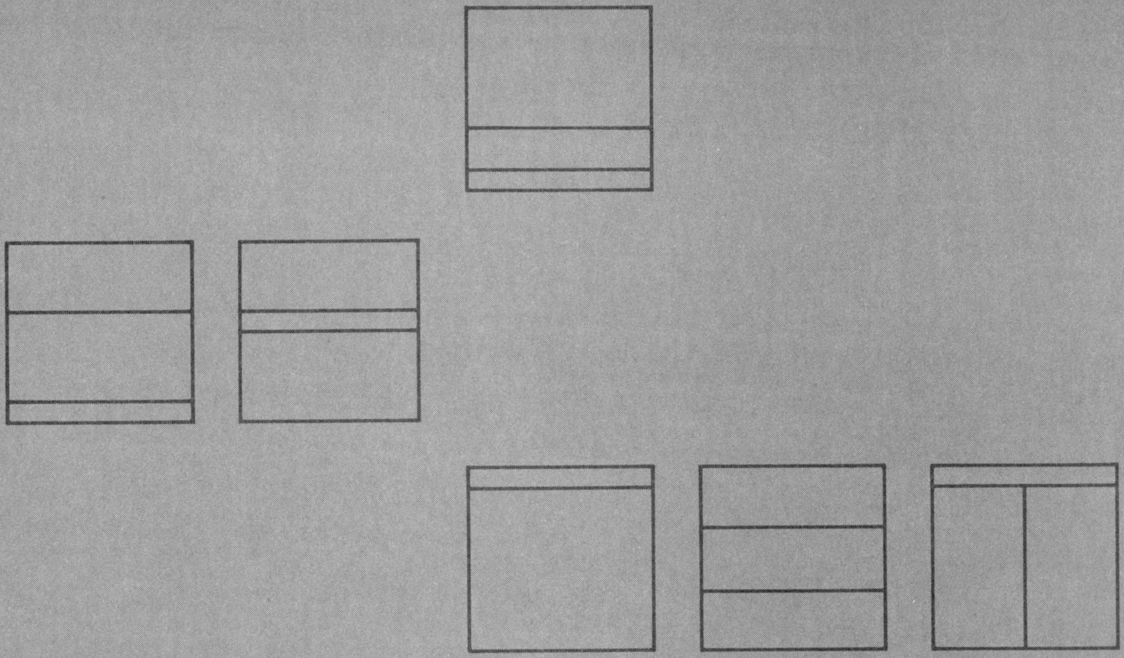

PC-DOS

13

KEY TERMS

EDLIN	*COPY*
DEBUG	*FORMAT*
FDISK	*Root directory*
Path	*Hidden file*
Write-protect tab	*Piping*
PC Network	*Server node*
Redirector node	

INTRODUCTION

Personal computer operating systems are very useful for developing a good understanding of operating systems, since they reflect an earlier point in the evolution of mainframe operating systems.

PC-DOS is an operating system that provides most of the functions of any normal operating system. It does not yet contain some of the features considered necessary for mainframe operating systems such as multiprogramming and multi-user capabilities. Other features missing are memory management techniques such as virtual memory.

OPERATING SYSTEMS SERVICES

The set of operating systems services provided by PC-DOS is somewhat smaller than that provided by most mainframe operating systems, but most of the important features are provided.

The most important feature of PC-DOS is not a characteristic of the operating system itself, but is the vast number of software tools available to run under it. These tools are not supplied with the operating system, but are sold by a wide variety of vendors.

The primary tools available from vendors fall into five general categories. There are word processors, spreadsheets, data base managers, utilities (such as compilers), and assorted productivity aids (such as calendar management).

Example 13-1:

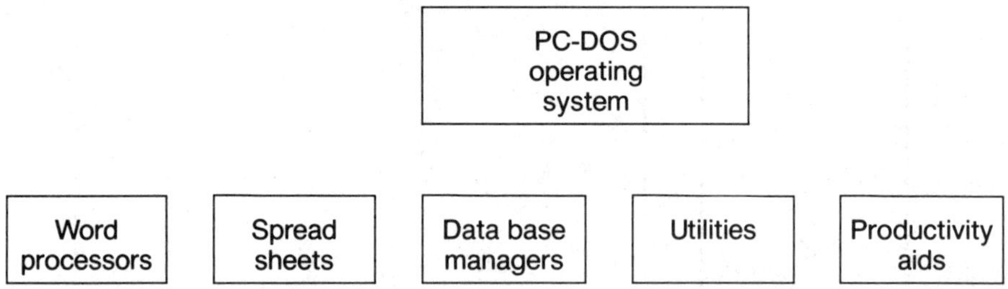

The editor provided with PC-DOS is not a full-screen editor, but it does incorporate most of the other features needed by users. Only a minimal editor is needed, since anyone desiring a more complete, full-featured editor can find a tremendous variety of packages that provide this service.

The editor is called **EDLIN.** It is a line editor. It allows lines to be added, deleted, moved, copied, inserted, and listed on the screen. Other features available allow searches for specific strings, with or without those strings being replaced with another string.

PC-DOS does not include any assembler or compilers. They are separate, extra-cost options. The assembler that is available is a relatively complete assembler that has most of the advanced features available with mainframe assemblers. This is also true of the wide variety of compilers can be acquired to run on PC-DOS. COBOL, FORTRAN, C, and Pascal are the most common. More than one version of most of these compilers are available. The primary distinction is that, because personal computer compilers are designed to be usable with floppy diskettes, some of the steps in the compilation process are separated. This makes the compilers somewhat more difficult to use, since the user must initiate each of the individual steps.

The PC-DOS **LINK** program supplies the features of a link editor. A loader is not supplied with the system. The LINK program operates on previously compiled or assembled programs. It takes the input object code file, finds any additional object code files needed, combines those files, and creates a relocatable load module. It can also produce a listing which shows which object modules were combined, and any errors produced by the linking.

The **DEBUG** program aids the development of programs. It allows programs to be run in a controlled environment where their actions can be monitored and altered as desired. Any programming errors can be detected and fixed as they occur. The DEBUG program is used to display and change the contents of a file and then to execute that file.

The PC-DOS operating system has a very useful feature, called **piping,** which is derived from the UNIX operating system. This allows the output from one program to be directed to a second program for use as input. This is quite useful when setting up a stream of jobs to run, since many such streams require that a sequence of jobs execute, with each job using the output of the previous job as input. Other operating systems require that an output file be defined as output from the first program, and then as input to the second program. This accomplishes the same purpose as piping, but is considerably more clumsy.

Example 13-2:

PIPING

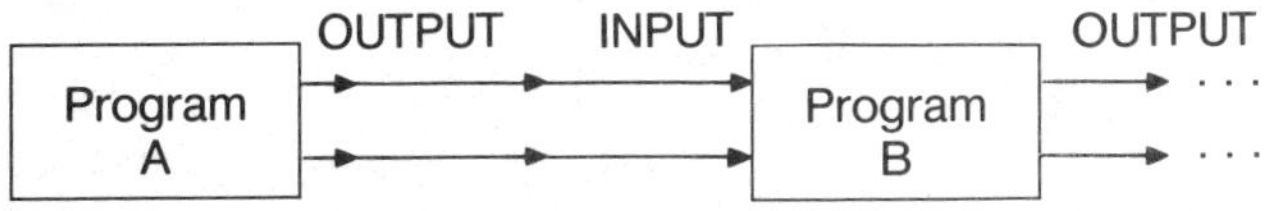

Systems generation

The PC-DOS systems generation process is quite simple for a variety of reasons. The system itself is relatively simple and does not have many of the parameters that complicate systems generation on mainframe systems. It is also designed to be set up and installed by the average person who knows nothing about computers.

A file on the system disk has all the setup parameters necessary. This file is called CONFIG.SYS. The user uses EDLIN to enter the startup options into this file.

The first option is:

```
BREAK=xx
```

where "xx" is the word ON or OFF. This instructs the operating system to check for the keystrokes Ctrl-Break during all functions, instead of just during particular functions.

The next option is:

```
BUFFERS=x
```

where "x" is the number of I/O buffers to be used. I/O performance to a fixed disk is improved with an increased number of buffers. However, each buffer takes part of RAM memory, so systems with small memories do not use large numbers of buffers. From 1 to 99 buffers are allowed.

Unusual devices can be supported by PC-DOS, but the program necessary to control those devices must be written by the user or vendor of that device, and explicitly included in the CONFIG.SYS file. The inclusion is done by specifying:

```
DEVICE=filename.ext
```

where "filename.ext" is the file name of a program that performs the actual device control.

Other options available in the CONFIG.SYS file include a virtual disk drive, control over the maximum number of file control blocks that can be open at any one time, control over the maximum number of files that can be open at any one time, specification of which country's date and time format is to be used, and control of the maximum number of disk drives that can be used.

All that is really necessary to prepare a floppy diskette for use within PC-DOS is one command. The **FORMAT** command prepares the media. Placing the operating system on that media is accomplished with one option on the FORMAT command.

The FORMAT command is not used when setting up a fixed disk. Fixed disks are similar to floppies, in that they must be initialized before being used. A special command called **FDISK** must be used to properly initialize a fixed disk.

One feature available when the system is set up is the ability to partition a fixed disk into several different areas. Each of these areas can be used for a different operating system. This allows the same fixed disk to support more than just PC-DOS. This is very useful in cases where both PC-DOS and some other operating system are needed. Most PC users, however, use only the PC-DOS operating system, so they do not partition the disk. The FDISK service then presents a series of menus that guide the partitioning of the fixed disk.

FILE SYSTEM

The file system used in PC-DOS incorporates many of the features of the UNIX file system, such as tree-structured directories. The basic file available in PC-DOS is a sequential file with varying length records. The end of each record is marked with an end-of-line character. The format of varying length records is typical of a file created by a terminal, and the end-of-line character usually used is also that generated by a terminal.

File names in PC-DOS consist of two primary parts: the file name and the file name extension. The file name consists of from one to eight alphabetic or numeric characters. It may optionally be followed with a one to three character extension, which is used to specify the use of the file. Common file names are:

- ACCT.DAT for a data file
- MYPROG.BAS for a BASIC file
- HISPROG.ASM for an assembler source code file

The PC-DOS file system was originally designed to run only on floppy diskettes, and frequently required several floppies be present in order to do useful work. It now runs on both floppy and fixed disks, and the requirement for accessing multiple disk drives is still present. Because of this requirement, the disk drive may be specified as an integral part of each file name.

All disk drives, whether fixed or floppy, are named with an alphabetic character. This character is assigned to that drive when it is installed into the system. A file on that disk drive should have the correct drive letter specified as part of the file name. Since many files may be referenced on one particular drive, PC-DOS uses the concept of a **default drive**. Any file names with no drive specified are assumed to be on the default drive. Sample file names are:

- A:PROJ.DAT — A data file on drive A:
- C:PROJ.DAT — A data file on drive C:
- B:SAMPLE.BAS — A BASIC file on drive B:
- SAMPLE.BAS — A BASIC file on the default drive

One nice feature of the PC-DOS file system is the use of tree-structured directories. A directory table contains the names and pertinent information on all files associated with the directory. One or more of the entries listed in that table may be other directories, each of which contains it's own set of files. This allows sets of files that are logically related to be in one group, while others files are segregated from them, and available only when specifically required.

The directory that is available by default when the system is first started is known as the **root directory.** All other directories are attached to the root or to other directories. Directories attached to a higher-level directory are known as **subdirectories.** Directories may be nested several levels. The list of directories needed to access that file starting from the root is known as the **path** to that file.

It is not necessary to always specify the path to a file as part of the file name. The default directory may be changed from the root to any subdirectory at any time. Any file name specified without a path specified is implied to be in the default directory. The name:

```
A:\DIR1\DIR2\FILENAME.EXT
```

specifies a file with a file name of FILENAME, an extension of .EXT, a drive designator of A:, and two sub-directories, DIR1 and DIR2, following the root directory.

Example 13-3:

SAMPLE DIRECTORY TREE

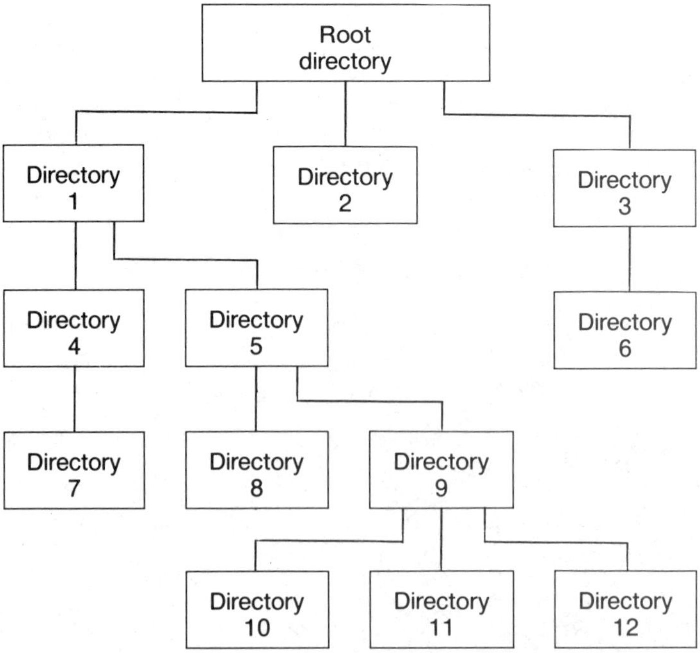

New sub-directories can be created with the MD (make directory) command.

The new subdirectory may be specified as a path, in which case the new sub-directory is created at the end of the path, or it can be just the new sub-directory name, when it is created as a sub-directory of the current directory.

The default directory can be changed with the CD (change directory) command.

Sub-directories can be removed with the RM (remove directory) command.

Sub-directories can only be removed after all files in them have been erased.

The file structure in PC-DOS is designed to make maximum usage of disk space. Because of the need to conserve disk space, the files have variable record length format, so that little space is wasted (fixed record lengths tend to waste space). There are cases, usually in load modules, where the format is fixed, and some space is wasted, but most of the files are of variable length.

PC-DOS allows wide use of wild-card specifications in file names; virtually every command allows such wild-cards. The symbol "?" is used to replace one character in a file name, and the symbol "*" is used to replace many characters. These wild-cards can be used anywhere in the file name or the extension, but not in the device specification or the directory path.

Example 13-4:

WILD-CARD FILE SPECIFICATIONS

The following is a list of the files contained on the disk:

TEMPOR.DAT

TEMPORAR.DAT

TEMP4.DAT

TEMP1.DAT

TALLY.DAT

SPECIFICATION	FILES FOUND
T*.DAT	TEMPOR.DAT
	TEMPORAR.DAT
	TEMP4.DAT
	TEMP1.DAT

(Continued on page 256)

Example 13-4: *Continued from page 255*

	TALLY.DAT
TEMP?.DAT	TEMP4.DAT
	TEMP1.DAT
TEMP*.DAT	TEMPOR.DAT
	TEMPORAR.DAT
	TEMP4.DAT
	TEMP1.DAT

PC-DOS has a very good backup system. It is easily accessed and uses simple commands. There is no backup available for floppy diskettes, since they can be backed up by copying them onto another diskette, or by copying individual files. The total capacity of the fixed disks used with PC-DOS is much larger, and fixed disks are not removable, so they require a backup system.

The only problem with the PC-DOS backup system is that it backs up the fixed disk only to floppy diskettes, instead of to some faster, higher-capacity media such as tapes. The backups are quite usable, but the capacity of floppy diskettes is so small that a large number of them is required to do a complete backup. A complete backup on a fixed disk may require dozens of diskettes.

The PC-DOS backup system allows either full or incremental backups. The incremental backups can either back up all files created or modified after a particular date or all files that have been created or modified after the last backup. This allows the usual operating system backup algorithms to work correctly, with a full backup at one or two (or more), week intervals, and incremental backups in between.

Virtually all common file system commands exist in PC-DOS, and are usually quite easy to learn and use. Wild-card specifications may be used anywhere a file name is valid in the command. The commands emphasize simplicity and ease of use.

A list of the file names and other pertinent information about the files can be obtained with the DIR command.

It frequently uses wild-card specifiers, such as "*.*" to list many files. Individual file names can be used as well. The DIR command can be used to list files on any available disk drive and in any accessible directory.

Files can be erased with the ERASE command.

If all files in a directory are specified (by specifying *.*), the operating system asks "Are you sure (Y/N)?" and requires an affirmative response before the files are actually erased.

Files can be renamed with the RENAME command. This command takes two arguments: the old file name and the new name.

Files can be copied with the COPY command. It also takes two arguments.

The file specified by the first name is copied and given the new name. The copying can be across directories or devices.

Other commands can be used to compare the contents of two floppy diskettes, to copy one diskette to another, to compare the contents of two files, and for several other, less common, functions.

Multiprogramming

One of the most significant areas where PC-DOS is lacking in capabilities is in multiprogramming. PC-DOS does not explicitly allow more than one task. This causes serious problems when an application is running, since the entire computer is dedicated to that application. When PC-DOS was first introduced, multiprogramming was not as great a requirement. The computing power in the PC was not really sufficient to support more than one task, but as the PCs become more powerful, the users become more sophisticated. Future releases are expected to have such capabilities.

One of the most important areas to provide multiprogramming capabilities on the PC is for printing files. This is a task that any PC can easily handle while doing other tasks, and it is also a task that tends to take much time. Both of these reasons lead to a large amount of frustration when an entire PC is devoted to printing a large file. PC-DOS has a multiprogramming print capability so that files can be printed while other activities are going on.

JOB AND TASK SCHEDULING

PC-DOS is not a multiprogramming operating system, so the problems of scheduling tasks do not really arise. As a single tasking operating system, the next task to be executed is always the next task requested by either the user or a command stream of some sort. That task cannot begin until the current task finishes, since all tasks are single-threaded through the processing unit.

The only time PC-DOS runs multiple tasks is with the print spooler. The task of printing the file from its location in memory is interleaved with the current executing task. Most print spoolers use a very simple algorithm for their multi-tasking. The spooler program just takes a small, but constant part of the overall processor time. Since only one other task is running, and that task usually takes input from the user, this algorithm works satisfactorily.

Several other applications have been written that are designed to run under PC-DOS to provide the multi-tasking support that is lacking in PC-DOS. To

PC-DOS, these applications appear as a single task that is always in control of the processor. The multi-tasking applications have the real applications running under them, and provide the multi-tasking support to allow several user applications to run simultaneously. The primary flaw in this technique is that it requires another layer of software (the multi-tasking application) between the processor and the real applications, thus adding to the overall overhead and decreasing performance. It also uses up more of the total available memory.

The scheduling algorithms used by the multi-tasking applications vary from one application to another. Many of them use a simple round-robin scheduling algorithm, modified by priorities so that one task is always favored over any others. This is because there is usually one task that is being run and monitored by the user, while the other tasks are running in the background. The task that is interacting with the user should have a very high priority, so that the user does not perceive delays, while the background tasks are not usually damaged by delays, since the user is not interacting closely with them.

MEMORY MANAGEMENT

Memory management under PC-DOS is quite simple. It is also quite limited in the capabilities provided to the user. The most pressing current problem with memory management under PC-DOS is the limitation in the maximum amount of memory supported. PC-DOS does not support any memory above 640K. This is a serious problem, since many PC-DOS applications currently in use need more memory. This is only the theoretical maximum amount of memory available; the actual limit is either that value or less. Regardless of the amount of memory installed, however, more than 640K are never available.

PC-DOS requires at least 36K bytes of memory. It is normally loaded at the low end of physical memory, so that a theoretical maximum of the 604K bytes are available for applications. Large amounts of additional memory are used to maintain information on the computer monitor and to provide many of the primitive operating system functions, but this memory is not taken from the total available, since each of these items has a special section of memory devoted to it.

Application programs are loaded into memory above the operating system, and have the use of memory up to the limit. These applications normally place the program first, and use any remaining memory for user data. If the program is quite large, or the computer does not have the full 640K of memory installed, the amount of memory available for the user may be quite small.

In this example, the application program uses 320K memory, and only 512K is installed on that computer.

Example 13-5:

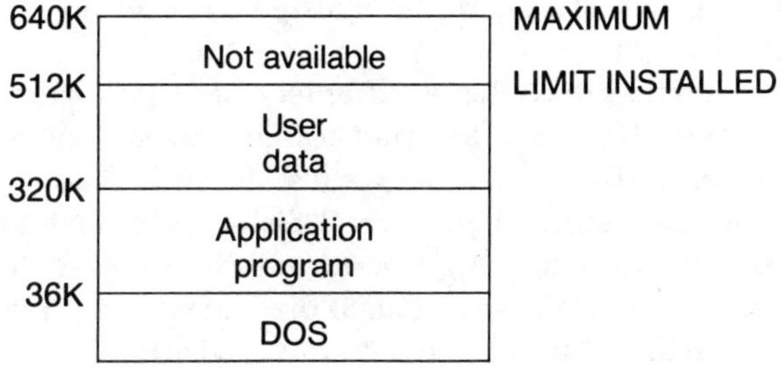

Virtual Memory

PC-DOS does not support virtual memory at all.

PERFORMANCE MEASUREMENT AND TUNING

The performance of PC-DOS is not usually subject to improvement by any of the normal systems tuning techniques. The basic areas of improvement lie in increasing the amount of memory available on the system and from changing from floppy diskettes to fixed disks.

The single most limiting factor in personal computers is usually the speed of the floppy diskettes used for storing data. This problem can be alleviated by placing some of the data on fixed disks, which have a much higher performance level. If a fixed disk is not available, or does not provide sufficient performance, then a virtual disk may be created in memory. Such a virtual disk is another benefit of increasing the memory on the system.

The virtual disk software allows a section of memory to be reserved from normal usage, and treated exactly like a floppy diskette drive. This reduces the amount of memory available for program usage, of course, so it requires either small programs or a large amount of memory in the system.

One advantage of most virtual disk setups is that they can use the memory above the normal PC-DOS limitation of 640K, so that if the computer has a very large amount of memory installed, a virtual disk can be used without encroaching on the usable memory. PCs actually allow more memory to be installed than is usable by PC-DOS, although the virtual disk setup is about the only application that can use the additional memory.

Virtual disks are assigned a drive letter, and are accessed by that letter just as are physical disk drives. This drive letter must be different from the drive letters already in the system. Once the drive letter has been assigned to the virtual disk, that disk can be accessed by applications just as though it were a real physical disk.

Virtual disks have extremely high performance since all I/O is done to memory instead of to a physical disk drive. The major drawback is that, if the power is shut off, all data is lost. For this reason, virtual disks are somewhat more dangerous than normal disk drives. Virtual disks can always be safely used to provide a high-performance media for read-only data. They can be used to receive written data if that data is copied to a physical disk drive before the virtual disk is removed or over-written, or power is shut off. If the data is not copied to a physical disk before the power is shut off, then the data that was written to the virtual disk is lost.

The following two examples show virtual disk use with a PC-AT (which supports memory over one million bytes, but not between 640K and 1M bytes) and with a normal PC (which does not support the higher memory). Both setups have two disk drives already, which are addressed as drives "A", and "B". The virtual disk drive then becomes drive "C".

Example 13-6:

VIRTUAL DISK USAGE WITH LARGE MEMORY (PC-AT)
ONE 360K VIRTUAL DISK

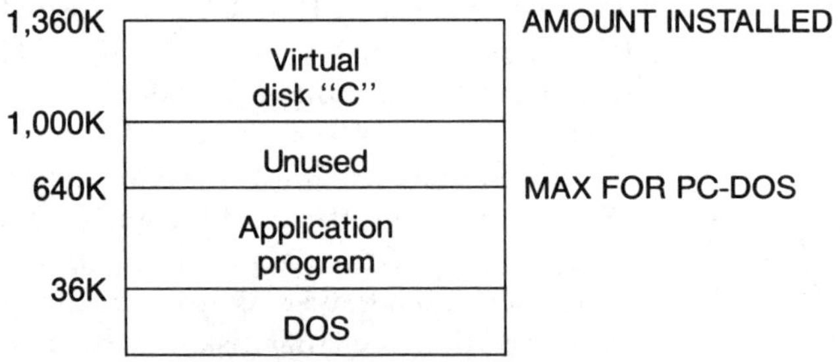

VIRTUAL DISK USAGE WITH NORMAL MEMORY (PC)
ONE 180K VIRTUAL DISK

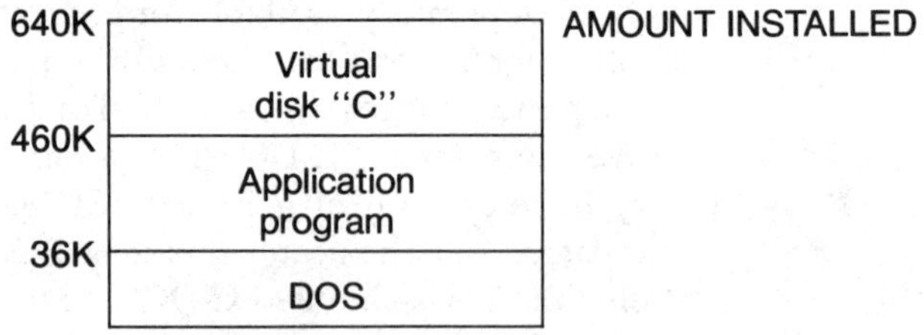

This statement to set up a virtual drive is put in the CONFIG.SYS file. An example is to have the CONFIG.SYS file contain a statement such as:

```
DEVICE=VDISK.SYS 180 256 64
```

which sets up a virtual disk containing 180K of storage, with each sector of data 256 bytes long, and with a maximum of 64 files.

SYSTEMS SECURITY

Systems security is an area which is both absent and often unnecessary in PC-DOS. All files are normally available to the user of the system, and no logon is required. Some rudimentary security does exist, but usually only in specific areas.

The operating system files themselves are available to the user, so some steps should be taken to safeguard them. The operating system is in two parts, one of which is the kernel, and the other which contains many of the commands in the user interface. The command portion of the system is a file that may be modified or erased like any other file. The kernel of the system, however, is stored on disk as **hidden files.** The user is not able to access these files except when initially loading the system into the computer. Hidden files do not appear in directory listings, and cannot be altered by normal commands.

The other, limited security feature is the ability to specify diskettes that cannot be written on. Each diskette has a notch cut near the upper right corner. If this notch is covered over (such as with tape), write access to that diskette is prohibited. Diskettes containing distribution software usually do not have such a notch, so they can never be written on. Other diskettes may have the notch covered with a **write protect tab,** which prohibits write access to the diskette until that tab is removed.

A relatively recent security feature that is available on some models of the PC requires a key to access the system. This, of course, is only useful if the PC is also physically fastened down, so that it cannot just be picked up and carried away.

One subject relating somewhat to PC security is the issue of distributing copy-protected software. This has received a tremendous amount of discussion in the industry, and is a very controversial subject. The basic idea is that some means of preventing copying of distributed programs is necessary. PC software is very difficult to monitor, since it is so easy to transport and use on different PCs, so the possibility for rampant, illegal copying exists.

Many vendors use sophisticated locking mechanisms to prevent the software from being copied. There are many copy programs that break that locking mechanism, so this policy has had only limited success. Placing such locking mechanisms on software also tends to limit its usefulness, since it must usually be copied to place it on a fixed disk or to make backup copies. Many vendors do not use copy-protection at all. This is particularly appropriate for corporate software, where it is very difficult to conceal cases of widespread copying.

MULTIPROCESSING

PC-DOS contains only a limited form of multi-processing. A co-processor can be used for numeric calculations, and must be a specific model (the Intel 8087 or 80287). The presence of the numeric co-processor is specified by a hardware switch set in the computer.

The operating system does not contain complicated algorithms for determining which operations should be routed to the numeric co-processor. Routing must be explicitly requested by the executing program. Such programs check the correct bit in the operating system to determine if the co-processor is present and subsequent numeric calculations are directed to the co-processor.

The purpose of this co-processor is not to supplement the operation of the primary processor, but rather to replace certain aspects of that operation.

Example 13-7:

INSTRUCTION FLOW WITH A CO-PROCESSOR

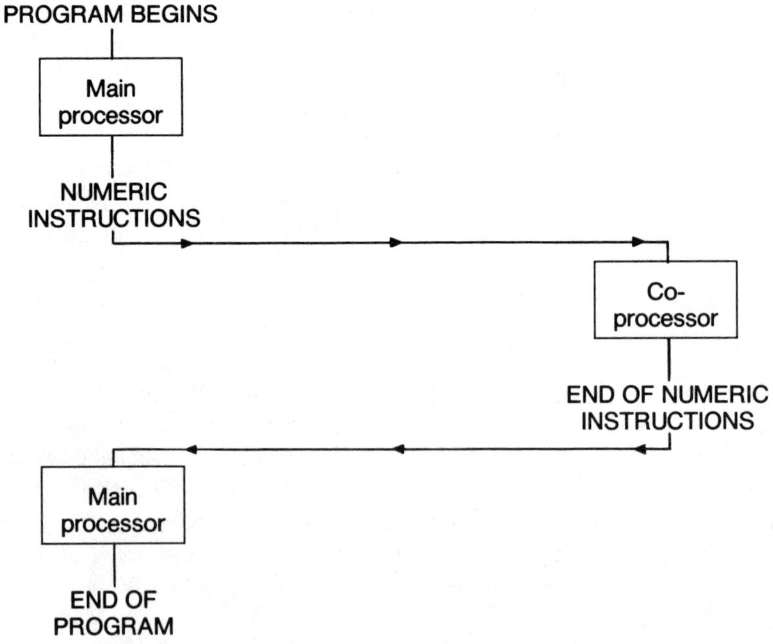

Numeric operations are handled on the co-processor instead of on the primary processor in order to make those operations much faster. The primary processor, however, is not able to continue running independently of the co-processor. Thus, there is a performance gain from doing numeric operations faster, but not from overlapping processing.

NETWORKING SYSTEMS

Release 3.1 of PC-DOS is the first release to contain any networking features. Earlier releases did not support any form of networking although other manufacturers added this capability. The networking system provides resource sharing, particularly for disk drives and printers. In contrast to this, most mainframe networks emphasize transferring data and supporting terminals. Mainframe network nodes tend to be either terminals or fully configured mainframes, while PC networks tend to consist of a few nodes which maintain resources and many nodes which then share those resources.

The network support is in two different parts. The part that performs most of the network functions is not a part of PC-DOS. It is called the "PC Network Program" and is an extra-cost option. The PC Network Program requires certain functions from the operating system, however, so PC-DOS does become integral to the network.

A network can attach to various models of IBM PCs. IBM's PC Network can connect up to seventy-two computers, and can span a radius of up to 1000 feet. The data is transmitted over the network at two million bits per second. The cable used is a broadband cable with normal broadband connectors, and the protocol used on the network is CSMA/CD. This is the same protocol as is used by Ethernet networks, which are quite common with PCs, but the two networks are not interconnectable.

Each PC on the IBM PC Network must have a "PC Network Adaptor" board installed in it, and the network itself is controlled from a "PC Network Translator Unit". One Network Translator must be installed in each network. The total length of the network cable, is measured as a radius from the Translator Unit. If more than eight computers are to be installed on the network, then an additional unit, called a "PC Network Base Expander", must be added to the network. The Base Expander is also required if the network grows to a radius of more than two hundred feet.

The network supports three different functions:

- Sharing disks
- Sharing printers
- Sending and receiving messages

The interface to the network varies depending upon the type of service desired. Some of the services are handled transparently to the application. For example, an application uses the network to access data in exactly the same fashion as if that data were resident on a local disk. Other services, such as sending and receiving messages, may require the execution of certain operating system commands. The most complex aspects of the network, such as configuration, are handled primarily from full-screen menus, which provide a very easy, user-friendly environment for accessing the network.

The disk and printer sharing are handled similarly. Each node in the network can be either a **redirector** or a **server** node. Redirector nodes do not have shareable disk or printer resources; those are maintained by the server nodes. Redirector nodes trap application requests for printer or disk service, and send those requests to the server node which maintains the disk or printer. The server node then satisfies the request from its disk or printer, and ships the response back to the redirector node. The redirector node receives the response, sets it up to look as though it just came from a local disk or printer, and transfers it back to the application that requested the service.

The disk or printer that belongs to the server node is defined on each of the redirector nodes, so that the applications running on each of those nodes can access that disk or printer as though it were attached locally. This allows one central disk or printer to serve multiple nodes. Such an arrangement is much cheaper than providing disks or printers at each node. As long as the resource requirements are relatively low, such an arrangement works quite well. If the requirements for a specific resource become very high, then sharing that resource may cause significant delays.

Sharing a printer is a comparatively uncomplicated task, but sharing a disk drive becomes somewhat more complex, since operations from various nodes may be interleaved on that disk drive. The most serious problem is multiple access to shared files. PC-DOS has a relatively simple locking mechanism for shared files. Various levels of access to the data can be specified, and different locking levels may apply to different access levels. The locking mechanisms allow individual records to be locked in shared files. This locking must be specifically requested by an application that is accessing the data. Reading data normally does not require locking the records, but if that data is to be changed in any way, the records must be locked.

Several different nodes in the network may try to print files at the same time, so the network also provides some management support for printing files. The network software maintains a queue of print requests, and services the request at the top of the queue whenever the printer becomes available. Each node on the network can then submit print requests and continue processing without having to wait until those requests have been satisfied.

Messages can be sent among the nodes on the network. Any node can send a message to any other node; or one node can broadcast a message that is received by all other nodes on the network. Files can also be transferred between nodes if desired. Some of the more complex message sending facilities have a menu-driven access, in order to simplify the operation of the facility.

Example 13-8:

SAMPLE NETWORK CONFIGURATION

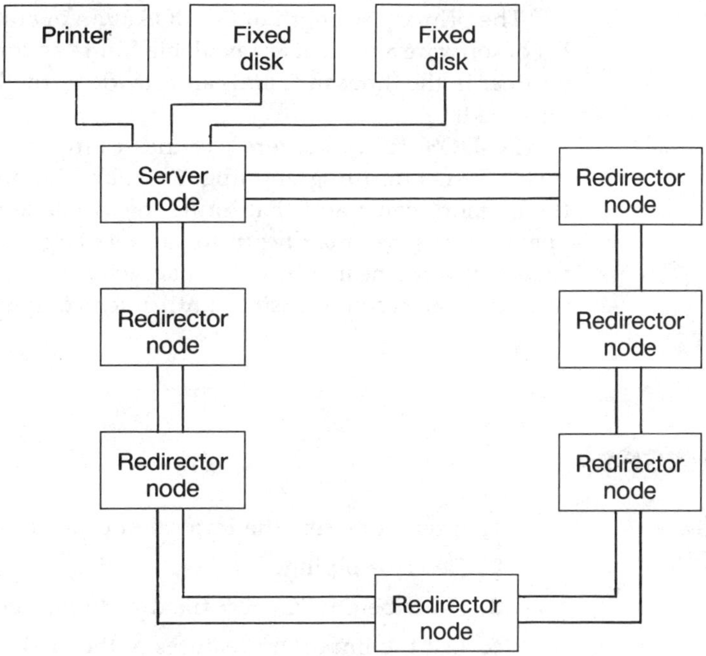

One location on the network must be used to set up and administer the network. Such tasks are relatively minimal on this network, however, when compared to similar tasks on mainframe networks. The network must be configured when it is set up to specify which nodes are to be servers and which are to be redirectors. The setup may also specify which resources are to be shared and names for some or all of the nodes.

Managing the network primarily consists of checking periodically to ensure that all components are functioning properly. Sometimes the queue of files to be printed may become unusually large, at which time part of the queue may have to be directed to another printer or otherwise redirected. Whenever nodes are added to or deleted from the network their names must also be added or deleted.

SUMMARY

The PC-DOS operating system has become the dominant microcomputer operating system during the last few years. The operating system is a strange combination of some quite advanced features, such as the file system, with other features completely lacking.

The primary strength of PC-DOS as an operating system is the vast number of software tools that are available from vendors to run under it. These tools number in the thousands and can provide virtually every function that can be imagined.

PC-DOS still has severe weaknesses in several areas. The most pressing such area is multiprogramming. Probably the next most serious weakness is the memory constraint that limits the available memory to 640K bytes. The operating system must begin to support larger memory sizes, which is also expected in the near future. Virtual memory is a necessity for the future, but this will not become feasible until microcomputers all have very fast fixed disks.

EXERCISES

DISCUSSION QUESTIONS

1. Briefly describe the important characteristics of PC-DOS.
2. Describe piping.
3. Describe the PC-DOS file directory structure.
4. List the important features of the PC-DOS file backup system.
5. Describe the multiprogramming provided by PC-DOS.
6. Describe the memory layout with PC-DOS.
7. Describe a virtual disk.
8. Discuss the PC-DOS multiprocessor support.
9. List and briefly describe the primary functions of the PC-DOS network.
10. Provide a sample network configuration.

UNIX ULTRIX-32 Implementation

14

KEY TERMS

Case-sensitive input	tar
Shell	C-Shell
Bourne shell	Miniroot file system
History variable	vi editor
grep	awk
make	lex
troff	yacc
Bootstrap	nroff
format	acctdusg
config	newfs
newsys	Pseudodevices
IVP (installation verification program)	sync
Super-user	fsdb
fsck	dump
dd	find
restor	Address space

KEY TERMS

Child process	*uustat*
Fork	*Parent process*
Filter	*at*
Foreground process	*Background process*
Daemons	*Cron daemon*
df	*Event-wait code*
Process priority	*Data area*
Text area	*Process image*
Stack area	*First-fit algorithm*
Process table	*cu*
uucp	*uuname*
uux	*Backup catalog*

INTRODUCTION

UNIX is the only operating system that is currently supported on microcomputers, minicomputers, and mainframes from different vendors. The major problem area in UNIX is incompatibility between the various versions; even though it runs on virtually all computers, not all implementations are the same. There are two different major UNIX standards available, plus countless versions that either do not follow any standard, or that follow an older standard.

One standard is "UNIX System V", which is the current AT&T supported standard. The other major standard is "UNIX Berkeley 4.2bsd", which includes enhancements made by the University of California at Berkeley to earlier AT&T versions of UNIX. There are also many versions of UNIX available that follow one of the many older standards. AT&T has only recently become seriously interested in supporting UNIX as a commercial product. The version that they are now supporting is System V, so future AT&T enhancements will be to System V.

UNIX systems traditionally have not been well supported or easy to use. UNIX commands tend to be rather cryptic and difficult for the unskilled user. This problem can usually be overcome by placing user interface overlays on the system. The previous support for UNIX (documentation, bug fixes, and problem resolution) has not been at the level required of a successful commercial system.

The version of UNIX that Digital Equipment Corporation supports for their VAX computers is called Ultrix, and is primarily compatible with the Berkeley 4.2bsd version of UNIX. It is one of the best documented and supported versions of UNIX in existence, so it is the subject of this chapter. It also seems to be evolving faster than most major UNIX products.

The major strength in UNIX is that it runs on a wide variety of computers. A user can theoretically migrate from a personal computer to a very large mainframe without changing the features of the operating system. This is a tremendously useful feature for any installation that requires people to use several different types of computers. For example, instead of requiring engineers to learn three different operating systems in order to use a PC, a workstation, and a mainframe, it is only necessary that they learn one operating system. Removing the time and frustration of learning two additional operating systems allows each engineer to do much more engineering.

UNIX is a very powerful system; it allows experienced users to quickly and easily do things that are difficult or impossible on other systems. One of the primary strengths of the system is that it was designed for the express purpose of aiding program development. It is one of the most popular systems available for program development.

UNIX is perhaps the most flexible of all the major operating systems and has more potential than many of the other major operating systems since its structure is not as tightly locked into one form. The challenge for UNIX is to gain the things it now lacks while not losing any current strengths. This will not be easy, since some deliberate trade-offs have been made to gain some of those strengths. The recently increased support AT&T is giving UNIX may be the impetus needed to give it the features it is lacking.

OPERATING SYSTEMS SERVICES

One of the strongest overall features of the UNIX operating system is the number of services it offers. Very few other operating systems offer the number that UNIX does. Those operating systems that do offer a large number of tools usually have them as extra-cost options, while UNIX systems include these services and tools with the operating system.

The orientation of the UNIX system is to facilitate software development, so there are many tools offered that are designed for this purpose. There are not many services that are designed to provide a production environment for large applications, so that is an area that UNIX does not support as well. UNIX tends to support interactive users quite well, since software development is usually an interactive process.

User interface

The user interface in UNIX has a normal complement of both good and bad features. It is directed toward the experienced programmer. Unfortunately, user friendliness has been sacrificed to obtain efficiency for programmers. The usability of the UNIX interface seems largely determined by the degree of familiarity the user has with it.

One of the somewhat unusual aspects of UNIX is that all input is **case-sensitive.** Many systems make no distinction between input entered in upper or lower case, but UNIX does. All input must be entered in the proper case to be valid, unless the particular application running deliberately ignores the difference between upper and lower case.

Example 14-1:

CASE-SENSITIVE INPUT

"vi" is a valid command, but "VI" is not
"vI" is not
"Vi" is not

"cat" is a valid command, but "CAT" is not
"Cat" is not
"CaT" is not
"CAt" is not

Virtually all of the UNIX system commands consist of short, cryptic mnemonics. This is very nice for the experienced user, since it allows many functions to be performed with a minimum of keystrokes, but it is a nightmare for the novice user. UNIX systems for general users frequently have an additional user-interface placed between the users and the system, since otherwise the combination of case-sensitive and cryptic commands makes the system very difficult to learn.

One of the nicest features that an operating system can provide is full-screen interfaces between the users and the programs. These interfaces have traditionally been lacking in UNIX. However, many of the more recent implementations of UNIX have been incorporating full-screen interfaces. Some implementations, particularly on microcomputers such as engineering CAD-/CAM workstations, have gone so far in improving the user interface that it actually becomes one of the strongest features of the system.

Shells

A **shell** is a user interface that replaces the operating system's native interface. The UNIX system offers two shells, the **C-Shell** and the **Bourne Shell** which allow programmers to easily set up new commands or new mnemonics for the old commands. Clever use of the shells allows the system interface to be vastly improved, since more descriptive mnemonics can be provided for many system commands.

One problem with the UNIX shells, however, is that they were developed at different times and places, so some functions exist in only one shell. This is complicated by the fact that some duplicated functions are accessed differently between the two shells. Even worse, some of those functions operate identically, while others operate in slightly different ways.

One other nice characteristic of the UNIX C-Shell is its ability to recall and use the last few commands entered. This is done with the **history variable,** which can be set to remember the last few commands entered. These commands can then be called back and reentered by using the **history** command. A recall feature like this is very useful when long commands must be entered repetitively with only minor variations. The previous command can be called back, modified with only two or three keystrokes, then reentered; typing a whole new command might require thirty or forty keystrokes. This is particularly valuable on UNIX, since many of the commands tend to have rather long and complex parameters which are difficult to enter accurately.

Editors

UNIX provides a wide variety of editors, some of which support full-screen use. One of the most common of these is the **vi editor** which has been included with many versions of UNIX. Vi performs all the usual functions of full-screen editors and people who are familiar with it tend to believe that it is unbeatable.

An important characteristic of vi is that, when any character on a screen is changed, only that one character need be transmitted to the computer, instead of the whole screen, as with other full-screen editors. This allows a significant amount of systems I/O to be avoided.

Piping

Piping under UNIX allows the output from one program or utility to be directed to the input of another program or utility. This is similar to the piping described in Chapter 13 for PC-DOS.

Software tools

UNIX has a vast array of software tools available. Probably no other system has as many tools included with the system. Most of the tools are included so that UNIX can be the best possible system for program development.

The primary compiler available is for the C language. UNIX systems are usually written in C, so that compiler is almost always included with the system. The Pascal compiler is usually available, a FORTRAN compiler is sometimes included, and other compilers or assemblers may be included.

A brief list of the most common UNIX software tools follows:

▪ adb	A symbolic debugger
▪ awk	A pattern scanner
▪ calendar	A personal log file
▪ crypt	Encrypts files
▪ cref	A cross reference generator
▪ dc	A simple calculator
▪ graph	Draws graphs
▪ grep	Searches files for matching patterns
▪ lex	A lexical analyzer for expression analysis
▪ make	Maintains groups of programs
▪ regcmp	An expression compiler
▪ sed	A text stream editor
▪ sno	A SNOBOL interpreter
▪ sort	A sorting program
▪ spell	A spelling checker
▪ yacc	An input analyzer

The pattern scanning program, **awk,** can be used to scan lines of text to search for a particular pattern of characters. When a specified pattern is found, an editing operation may be performed on that pattern. Such a tool is always part of editors, but is seldom available on other operating systems as a program that can be called and used without requiring an editor.

The program called **grep** is somewhat similar to awk; instead of processing input lines, it searches through many different files. This is a very useful way of determining which files contain a certain character pattern. Many computer users, particularly programmers, tend to create a large number of text files with descriptive names and then later have trouble remembering just which file contains which information. The grep program searches those files to find which one has the specified information.

The lexical analysis program, **lex,** is used to analyze input lines to break parts of those lines into expressions. Such an analysis is normally required as part of any compiler or language processor, but may also be useful for any program that must perform syntax analysis on input lines. The rules that governed the specified instructions must be input to lex, which then produces output which is a general purpose language that recognizes expressions of the proper type.

The **make** program is one of the most useful tools in UNIX for program development. This program is designed for environments where a finished program may consist of many pieces. Each part may require a different procedure to update and may be updated at different times. It automates the process of ensuring that all requisite programs are updated in the proper fashion.

A file must be set up that contains all necessary information on how to update each module in the program, and which modules are dependent on which other modules. When the **make** command is issued, it reads this file and uses the information in it to ensure that all modules are at the current level. This involves automatically recompiling all modules that have been changed and any prerequisite modules, if necessary. It also automatically relinks all necessary modules.

The input analyzer program, **yacc,** is used to analyze the input given to a program. It can be used for relatively simple input, just to return specific words or numbers, but it is most used for programs that have extremely complex inputs.

The input to yacc consists of the input data, a routine to process the simple input, certain language rules to be applied to the input data, and sections of program to handle each case where an input rule is found to apply. This function is known as **parsing,** and the input rules are known as **grammar rules.** The output from yacc consists of parsed input data, or input data that has been analyzed and broken down into component parts. This data can then be easily processed by another program without any further analysis.

UNIX has two text formatting tools called **nroff** and **troff.** These provide many of the word processing needs that require extra software packages on most systems. Nroff is designed for quick, draft-quality copies, while troff provides high-quality features suitable for many advanced word-processing tasks. Nroff produces output for simple terminals and printers, while troff produces output for high-quality printed output devices such as typesetting machines.

Software development tends to be much faster on UNIX than on most systems, particularly when major applications are being developed. Many of the tools in UNIX can be included as part of the application, with no further programming necessary. For example, if the application must receive and analyze command string input, most systems require that the programs perform these functions. UNIX systems, however, provide the lex and yacc functions, so accessing these tools at the appropriate location in the application performs the necessary analysis with no further programming required.

Systems generation

The systems generation process for UNIX systems is much simpler than for most commercial mainframe operating systems. This is both good and bad, since some of the simplicity is achieved by eliminating options which might allow the system to be better tuned for performance purposes. The examples used here are taken from Ultrix-32. Set-up features tend to vary considerably between the different implementations of UNIX systems although the principles remain the same.

The first step with a new ULTRIX system is to load the contents of the distribution tape onto a disk drive. A very small UNIX file system (called a **miniroot** file system) is included on the tape specifically for this purpose. This miniroot file system is copied from the tape to the disk by a stand-alone copy utility on the tape. When the miniroot file system is on the disk, it is loaded into the computer and a minimal UNIX system started. This minimal system is then used to load the full root file system from the tape to the disk. Once the full system is on disk, that system is loaded into the computer and started. This system is then used to load the remaining system files from the tape into the proper file system.

When new or additional disks are required by the ULTRIX system, those disks first must be formatted specifically for ULTRIX with the **format** command. The disk is set up with standard block size and format at every available location on the disk.

New file systems must usually be set up in order to make the new system fully usable. The **newfs** command builds a new file system. The newfs command is a user-friendly version of the UNIX **mkfs** command which can also be invoked directly on ULTRIX. There are various options available that can be specified for the new file system, most of which tailor the file system to best fit the type of disk drive available. These options can be largely pre-configured by copying a manufacturer-supplied file that corresponds to the disk type into the reference directory.

The system itself must be configured by using the **config** command. The config program uses a configuration file which contains parameters specifying the exact configuration desired. Sample set-up files are supplied with the system.

The configuration file contains the following parameters:

- Computer model
- Computer identification
- Location of the root file system
- Device specifications (location and type)
- List of special devices
- System image name
- Location to store system dumps
- Description of paging areas
- Miscellaneous other options

When the configuration file is complete, the system image is created by running the config program.

The new kernel is built using the make program. This is used to produce a new system image, which should have the same name as that specified in the configuration file. This new kernel is copied to the root directory, so that it is accessed whenever the system is started.

The IPL (or boot) can be performed from the computer hardware or from UNIX itself. The programs that perform the IPL read certain records on the system disk and use the information contained in those records to read other records. This process is continued until the entire system kernel is in memory and the system is running. Programs that do this are also sometimes known as **bootstrap programs,** because they pull more and more of themselves into memory, similarly to the old phrase "lift oneself by one's bootstraps."

The new kernel that has been installed on the system does not become active until the next time the system is booted. This is a safety feature. If a problem has been discovered, it will usually be possible to fix the problem and reload a corrected kernel. If this reload process did not exist, any problems discovered during the kernel build might cause the system to crash, making it very difficult to correct the problem and rebuild the kernel.

If there are serious problems with the new kernel, they will frequently cause the system to crash when it is booted; consequently, there is no system available to build a new kernel. In cases such as this, the old kernel must usually be restored from a backup tape, and the whole process begun again. This is the reason that the old kernel should always be available, usually on tape, whenever a new kernel is placed in use.

There are several special devices that must be listed in the configuration file. These devices do not represent real physical devices but instead represent a necessary function, and specify the physical location of that function. This physical location is usually a disk drive, and may be either the same or different disk drives for most of the functions.

One such special device is the root device. This is the disk drive that is to contain the file system root, and the disk drive that is accessed when the system is initially loaded. The swap device is the device to hold swap files. The dump device is the disk that is to contain any dumps generated by the system.

The ULTRIX system has another series of devices that must be included that have no actual reference to physical devices. These are referred to as **pseudodevices.** Such devices must be specified in order to ensure that their function is supported by the operating system, even though no actual hardware is present.

The minimum pseudodevices necessary are:

- pty
- loop
- inet
- ether

These pseudodevices are used for various system functions such as certain networking functions. There are a variety of other special and pseudodevices available that are not required.

FILE SYSTEMS

The UNIX file system is somewhat similar to that discussed earlier for PC-DOS, since many of the concepts of the PC-DOS file system were taken from UNIX. UNIX also has a hierarchical file structure that is designed for interactive use. One of the major strengths of the UNIX file system is that it is designed so that virtually all I/O is device independent. A programmer usually need not be concerned with the type of device when programming I/O.

UNIX file names consist of from one to fourteen alphanumeric characters. It may have many of the special characters (*, ?, -, etc.), included in it, but since many of these characters have special meanings, using these characters can lead to unexpected results.

Directories

The tree-structured directories in UNIX are set up very similarly to the directories used in PC-DOS. Each directory contains the names and pertinent information on all files considered to be in that directory. One or more of the files listed may be other directories, each of which contains its own set of files.

There is no pre-allocation of disk space for the UNIX file system. Instead, space is allocated individually to each file as it is required. There is no way of preventing a single user from allocating and using all of the space available, leaving nothing for the other users. Some systems attempt to prevent this by placing a maximum limit on the amount of space any single user can own, but those same systems usually let that user remove the limit.

The usual method of controlling file allocations on UNIX systems is to manually monitor the amount of free disk space available. Whenever the available space begins to fill up, more space can be made available or some users convinced to delete some files. The **acctdusg** command displays the amount of disk space currently allocated.

File access control

One of the primary strengths of the UNIX file system is the very high level of file access control. Each file has nine flags associated with it in the file directory. These flags are grouped in three sets of three. Access to files is divided up into three different levels: "execute-only", "read-only", and "write". Each of these three levels is available to three different groups of users: the "file owner", the "group", and everyone else.

The file system was originally set up this way to facilitate program development. The idea is that a programmer has a set of files that he alone should have access to, another group of files that anyone in his department or group should have access to, and a final set that anyone may have access to. The execute-only mode is also very useful, since it allows programs to be available for execution without any fear that those files may be copied or read.

The default access level for UNIX files is to provide complete access to everyone, and a specific action must be taken in order to apply a higher level of access control to files. Some systems have the option that this default can be changed when the system is being installed, since providing every user with complete access to all files by default is frequently not desirable for commercial systems.

UNIX also has a particular class of user called a **super-user,** who has complete access to every file on the system, regardless of the level of access control existing for that file. Most systems have such a class of user, since it is necessary for many of the privileged systems functions, but most systems tend to segregate the privileged functions among several different users, so that any one particular privileged user may only perform specific privileged commands. In contrast to this, there is only one class of super-user on UNIX, and anyone knowing the password to the super-user account can also perform all of the other privileged functions.

Since some of the functions necessary to keep the system running from day-to-day require knowledge of a super-user password, such passwords are often known by several different people. Allowing several people to have access to all the privileged functions in the system is a serious potential security gap, since some of these people may not possess the high level of knowledge to match the complete privileges available.

File system reliability

Probably the most serious shortcoming of the UNIX file system is the relatively poor level of reliability that it possesses. Perhaps because UNIX was designed for, and has primarily been used by, skilled users, the lack of reliability in the file system has not been as much of a problem as it is when that same system is made available to the average commercial user.

The primary source of the unreliability in the UNIX file is the way the directory information is maintained. Each change to a file must be stored in several different locations, and if the system crashes between the time the first change is recorded and the time the last change is recorded, an error in the file system will appear. Probably the worst feature for reliability is that UNIX keeps many of the directory blocks in memory. These are the blocks that have been most recently accessed, and they are maintained in memory in order to enhance the system performance. If the system goes down after a file has been written but before these blocks have been written, an error will occur in the file system.

These blocks are written to disk whenever the **sync** command is issued. This command is issued at regular intervals by the system. The length of the intervals is determined at each installation. Longer intervals may improve performance, but they increase the probability of file system errors occurring. The intervals should probably be no longer than five seconds for commercial systems. The sync command should always be issued just before the system is shut down. The recommended procedure is to issue it twice, after all other system activity has ceased, and before shutting down the system. This reduces the chance of file system errors occurring because the memory blocks were not written to disk.

Many system utilities are included with the system to help maintain the accuracy of the file system. The **fsck** utility interactively checks and repairs any inconsistencies in the UNIX file system. Another, more flexible utility called **fsdb** allows experienced UNIX systems programmers to actually change the file system at the lowest level. This is used when the file system damage is complex for the fsck utility. In many cases, the damage to the file system may be too bad to repair before any problem is detected. File system errors are an extremely serious problem since they may lead to major losses of critical data.

The occurrence of file system errors in UNIX systems cannot be ignored, but neither should they be over-emphasized. When errors occur, the file system patching utilities are usually sufficient to recover from the problem.

Device independence

The UNIX file system achieves device independence by arbitrarily designating all I/O in the system to emulate reading or writing a file in the file system. Even when I/O is being done to a terminal, that terminal is treated like a file in the file system. This sometimes leads to a slight loss of performance because additional overhead is frequently involved to achieve such a virtual file system. The gain is that all I/O is very simple to handle. Programs can do I/O to a file without being concerned whether it is a real file or not. The system I/O interface to programs can also be very simple, since only one type of I/O is handled.

I/O is sent to a specific device by re-directing output to the actual destination before running the program. The operating system contains a **device driver** for each device supported by the system. Device drivers are small programs that contain the device-dependent programming necessary to do I/O to that particular device. When the I/O is redirected to a specific device, the device driver in the operating system controls how that I/O is performed.

File backup and restore

UNIX systems do not have a file backup and restore system that easily allows both full and incremental backups, but it does have most of the necessary individual pieces of such a system, so only a relatively small amount of tailoring is necessary in order to build a complete backup system from these pieces.

The **dd** command is used to do a full dump or restore. This command is designed to copy individual files, but an entire file system can be copied with it if that file system is specified in the command. Files can be copied to either disks or tapes, so a full backup can be done by specifying an entire file system be copied, and then directing that copy to a tape drive. A full restore can be done just by specifying the tape drive as the input and a disk drive as the output.

There are two ways incremental dumps and restores can be done. The **dump** and **restor** commands dump and restore individual files, but are not really designed for incremental backups. A backup system must still be written, although it can make use of the dump and restore commands to perform the actual file transfers.

Setting up the backup system is made easier by the **find** command which searches all directories for files meeting certain criteria. The criterion that can be used to set up an incremental backup system is to find all files that have been modified since a particular date. These files can then be the ones dumped.

Probably the best way to dump the files to tape is with the **tar** command instead of the dump command. The tar command allows both files and entire directories to be reloaded by name, instead of by a code number required by the dump command.

Setting up an incremental backup and restore system then requires that programs be written to use the find command to search all applicable directories for files that have been modified since the date of the last dump. The program must then dump those files, probably with the tar command. Care must be taken to save the list of files that were dumped to each tape, and the date of those files being dumped. This catalog file must be updated each time a new backup is done. Managing catalog files is frequently one of the most difficult tasks that backup systems must perform.

Programs must also be written to perform the restore function. Such programs must be able to read all the catalogs created by the dump program to determine which files, from which date, are backed up on which tape. Once this has been determined, the program must have the proper tape mounted, and the file restored from that tape to the appropriate directory.

MULTIPROGRAMMING

UNIX has some rather interesting and unusual features in the way multiprogramming is handled. Many of these are features that other operating systems would do well to adopt, and others are simply cleaner implementations of features already a part of other operating systems. There are also a few items, considered an integral part of most operating systems, that are not included in UNIX.

Programs are started executing in UNIX by first setting up a memory area (called an **address space**) to contain the program, and then loading the program into that area. This address space is usually a copy of the area from where the program was called. This may lead to some unnecessary overhead in duplicating memory areas, but it also provides a high level of independence between the programs without requiring that data be copied by the program from the original memory area.

All tasks executing in a UNIX system are called **processes.** A process that has been created by another process is called a **child** of that process. The program that has created child processes is known as the **parent process.** The parent processes may execute at the same time as its children or it may wait until those processes have finished executing. A program started by the user from a terminal is considered to be a child process of shell, and consequently the shell may either wait on that program to finish, or it can continue running at the same time as that program.

Example 14-2:

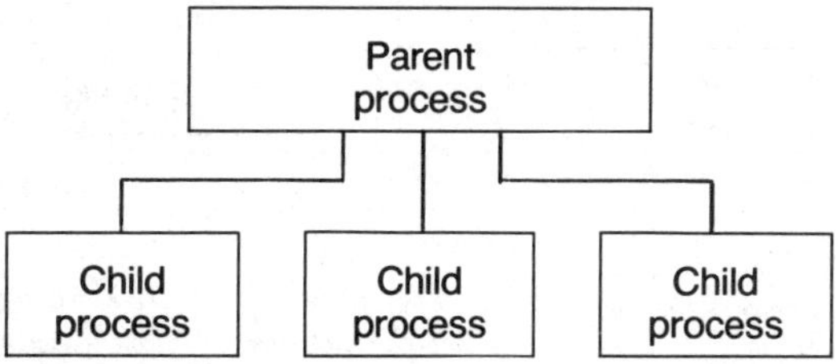

The task of creating a child process is done with a **fork.** A fork is a request to the operating system to create a child process. This system call requests that a new address space be created which is identical to the current one. The new address space is only distinguished from the address space belonging to the parent process by the system name applied to each address space.

In the following example, the original process (labelled "Parent process") forks and creates a new process, the "(1) child process". The parent forks again and creates another new process, the "(2) child process". The "(1) child process" forks itself to create a new process, called "(3) child process". At this point, the (1) child process is now both a child and a parent process.

Example 14-3:

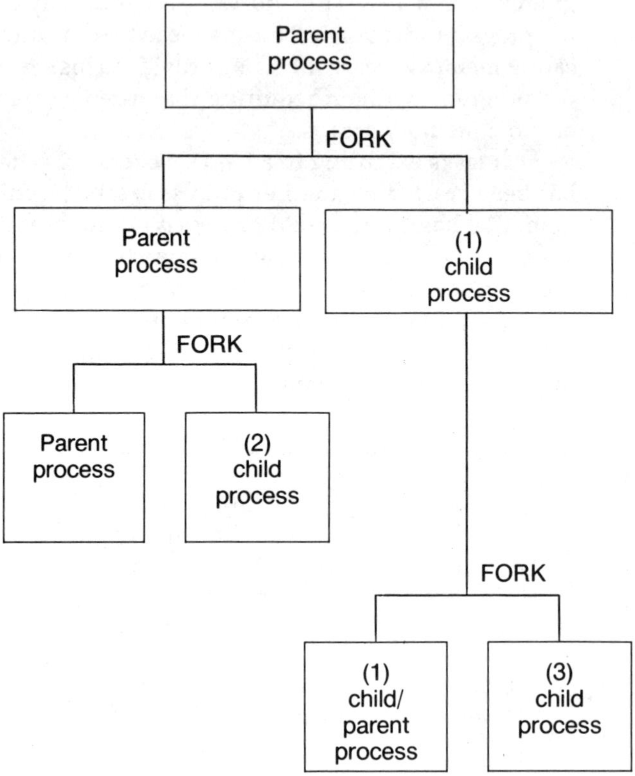

Setting up child processes in this fashion greatly enhances the ease of communication between a parent process and any children. A pipe can be set up by the parent before the child appears which takes output from the parent and directs it as input to the child process. This pipe is very useful for jobs that consist of a series of programs, since the earlier programs have a direct route for communication with programs started later.

Another useful feature of UNIX systems is the concept of a **filter** program. This is a program that takes a single file as input, produces a single file as output, and has as its sole function the processing of the input to produce the output file. This usually involves modifying the format of the input. Filters become particularly useful in combination with pipes.

Most operating systems do have facilities that allow output from one program to be channeled to another program, but it is not done in nearly so nice a way. It is usually required that the first program create a disk file, write the data into it, then close the file. The second program can then access the file and read it to get the information. This is a rather clumsy procedure that requires a high degree of synchronization between the two programs to prevent failures. Such synchronization is usually obtained by requiring the first program to finish executing before allowing the second program to begin executing. The UNIX pipe system is a vast improvement over this, since it provides a clean and simple means of communication between the programs.

Almost all processes in the UNIX system are eventually descended from the shell, since any processes started by a user are children of the shell, and any processes started by those processes are therefore descended from the shell. This becomes important when the user who started the initial process logs off the system. Some versions of the shell automatically kill all child processes when the user logs off, while others let them continue running. The user always has the option of specifying that child processes not be killed when he logs off.

UNIX uses the concept of **foreground** and **background** processes to distinguish between interactive and batch processes. A foreground process is one that is running at the same level as any other process started by a user; only one such process can be running for each user. A background process usually runs at a lower priority, and is independent of the user.

UNIX also allows background processes to be scheduled to run at a particular day and time with the **at** command. Any individual process can be scheduled in a batch-like mode with the at command, but there is no facility for providing automatic scheduling of background processes.

Many of the normal service functions of an operating system are implemented in UNIX with **daemons,** which are processes that are always executing in the system. These processes are used to provide functions such as controlling printers. For instance, the **cron daemon** is used by the systems administrator to perform certain functions automatically at specific dates and times.

JOB AND TASK SCHEDULING

The scheduling algorithms in UNIX systems tend to be rather simplistic. The emphasis is on keeping all the algorithms simple, instead of on optimizing throughput or efficiency. The algorithms are not necessarily inefficient; no attempt has been made to design them to achieve maximum throughput.

Processes are scheduled by forcing them to wait on events. These events may be almost anything, from I/O waiting to complete to processor unavailability. Each process has an **event-wait code** in the kernel. The process that is currently executing does not have the event-wait code set, but all other processes do.

The event-wait for processes is roughly equivalent to the I/O wait, page wait, and so on for other operating systems. Event wait encompasses all possible wait states. Processes may be freed from a particular event-wait condition by receiving a signal from whatever condition caused the event-wait. When that event-wait condition has been cleared, the process is then eligible to gain access to the processor, and will gain that access in due course.

Each process in the system is given a priority that is used to determine how that process is to be scheduled. All system processes have higher priorities than all user processes, so that system processes are always given control of the processor before user processes.

Process priority can be modified by a number of different conditions. A process priority is most usually modified by the length of processor time utilized by that process. Processes that use a large amount of processor time have their priority lowered, while processes that have not been allowed access to the processor get higher priorities. This is accomplished by maintaining a ratio of processor time to clock time. This ratio is recalculated each second, and the priority is modified in inverse relationship to the ratio.

The basic scheduling mechanism is round-robin, with each process allocated a one-second slice of processor time. This is modified, of course, by various events, such as the running process becoming blocked. The running process can also be forced out of the processor if another, higher-priority process that has been waiting suddenly becomes available.

The feedback mechanisms in the scheduling system that change the priorities based on the amount of processor time consumed are a simple, yet effective, way of modifying priorities. Processes cannot lock the processor away from lower priority processes, since the longer that process spends in the processor, the lower its priority.

The process scheduling algorithms are not particularly sophisticated, but nevertheless manage to incorporate many desirable features. They achieve a very good compromise between complexity and performance, although they fall short of optimum usage of computer time.

MEMORY MANAGEMENT

UNIX memory management design varies widely depending upon the hardware on which it is running. The memory management part of the UNIX kernel is in the machine-dependent section. Those concepts of memory management that are at a high enough level to be independent of the computer architecture are somewhat more consistent between different UNIX implementations.

The most common way of implementing memory allocation is to reserve a small area for critical information, and to divide the rest of memory between user and system processes. This tends to be very dependent upon the specific architecture of the computer on which that system is running.

Every process in the system has a block of memory allocated to it. This block, called the **process image,** is divided into three areas called the **text area,** the **data area,** and the **stack area.**

The text area is shared by many processes, but cannot be modified by any other process under normal circumstances. This is a good area to place system information that must be available to almost all processes, but that need not be modified by those processes. The stack and data areas may be modified only by the process that owns them since they are not shared with other processes. The size of these areas is dynamic, and depends upon the requirements of the process. The data area contains the major portion of most processes.

The data area is divided into two different parts, one of which is owned by the process, and the other is owned by the system. This allows the data to be divided so that critical system data relating to that process is not modified. Only non-system data is contained in the process part of the data area.

The stack area is available to the process for temporary data storage. This area automatically changes size as needed, whereas the data area only becomes larger when an explicit request is made.

The system maintains a **process table** to keep track of processes that are not currently active. Enough information is kept about each process to allow the system to recover that process when needed, and change it back to an active status.

VIRTUAL MEMORY

UNIX systems frequently do not have virtual memory as it is normally defined, but they do usually use a swapping algorithm. This keeps all the memory necessary for a process in one contiguous block, and swaps it into and back out of memory in that block. This block of memory includes both the data area and the stack area but does not include the read-only shared segment, which remains in memory to be shared by all processes. The data area includes both the process data area, and the system data area.

The basic algorithm for UNIX swapping is the first-fit algorithm which places a process in the first physical location which is large enough to fully contain it. This same basic algorithm is used both for memory and for the disk drives that are used for swapping devices. This algorithm has the advantage of simplicity, but it lacks the sophistication necessary to efficiently manage memory on a large, heavily loaded mainframe.

One of the primary reasons for a process to be swapped out is growth of memory requirements. When the memory requirements for a process increase, a new, larger block of memory is allocated to that process. If such a larger block of contiguous memory is not available, then the larger process is swapped out until such a block of memory is available.

The swapping algorithm determines which process is to be swapped back into memory from the swapping device by an equally simple algorithm. The process to be swapped in is the one which has been swapped out for the longest time. If that process requires a large amount of memory, then another, smaller process, may be swapped in first, but the larger process will not be allowed to remain swapped out for very long after it qualifies for swapping back in.

Whenever processes are swapped in, some space must be available for them to occupy. On lightly loaded systems, plenty of unused space is available. On more heavily loaded systems, some other processes must be swapped out to make room. The success of the swap-out selection algorithm is one of the most critical areas in the system as regards overall system performance.

The first candidate processes to be swapped out are those processes currently waiting for slow events, such as I/O to a line printer. These candidates are ranked by age, with the oldest being the most likely to be swapped out. The algorithm is weighted slightly to favor swap-out for large processes, as opposed to small processes, but this is not a major factor. No process may be swapped out if it has just been swapped in. This reduces the potential for thrashing in the swapping system.

The swapping algorithms are like most of the algorithms in the UNIX kernel: elegant, but not very complex. These algorithms were deliberately chosen in order to maintain the simplicity and small size of the kernel, and the performance loss was considered a reasonable trade-off. This is certainly true for cases where the UNIX system is used for program development. Such algorithms, however, must clearly be made more efficient if UNIX is to be used as a major production system on large mainframes.

PERFORMANCE MEASUREMENT AND TUNING

There are very few facilities available in UNIX for performance measurement and tuning. Since the orientation of the system is as a software development system instead of a commercial time-sharing system, such tools were deemed less important. Some vendors have implemented such tools on their versions of UNIX, but as yet, none have gained widespread acceptance. Tuning a UNIX system is done more by general principles and seat-of-the-pants estimates than is true of most commercial operating systems. Most UNIX systems do not require much tuning, especially since not a large number of tuning parameters are available.

The ULTRIX system does have a set of performance monitoring tools that are adequate. These can be used to report various I/O, system process, virtual memory, and user statistics.

The most crucial element of performance tuning is to monitor the file systems to prevent them from filling up. This can be done with the **df** command, which is used to display the amount of free space left in the file system. The file systems have an option that reserves a certain amount of space for emergencies and overflows, so that the total amount of free space reported can sometimes be greater than 100%. The free space display should be used to identify file systems that are becoming full and file systems which have a rapidly changing amount of free space. Either of these cases may require individual attention.

If it is determined that there is a disk space problem, then other commands can be used to display more detailed information about the usage of the space, such as the number of blocks each sub-directory is using. Since each sub-directory is normally allocated to one user, this is a good way of determining who is using most of the space.

SYSTEMS SECURITY

Systems security is not a high-priority item on UNIX systems. The security available in the file system is quite good with nine different levels of access control for each file. The overall system security is about the same as most other major operating systems. Each user requires a password to log onto the system, but no other security is customarily implemented. Specific installations may, of course, add their own modifications to enhance security.

MULTIPROCESSING

UNIX is not, in general, a multi-processing operating system. There are specific implementations of it that various vendors have used on computers with multiple processors, but even here the usual technique is to run UNIX as a subset of some other operating system. This approach allows UNIX to run on multiple processors without requiring any internal modifications to UNIX to make it support such multiple processors, but it also eliminates many of the normal advantages of multiple processor configurations.

NETWORKING SYSTEMS

UNIX has some capabilities for communications between systems, but it does not have full networking features. There are several different commands available under UNIX to provide communications features between UNIX systems. UNIX systems also frequently use other networks, such as the Ethernet network, or, in the case of ULTRIX, Digital Equipment Corporation's DECnet. The normal DECnet implementation is discussed in chapter 17 and therefore will not be covered here.

The **uucp** command is used to copy files between a directory on one UNIX system and a directory on another UNIX system. It requires that a link be previously established between the two systems, but once the link has been established, the copy operation is quite simple.

The **cu** command allows a user to access another system, either UNIX or some other operating system, and log on to that system as a terminal. This, in effect, means that the current UNIX system provides the software necessary to control the communications with another system. It is also necessary that a modem be attached to the current UNIX system, in order to establish the physical communications link.

The **uux** command is used to execute commands that may require input from several different systems. It determines the files necessary for the correct execution of the specified command, searches all available systems for those files, then executes the command on the system specified. The output can then be sent to any required system.

Other commands are also available that facilitate establishing and maintaining the communications links. The **uuname** command lists all known network nodes that are linked to the current system. The **uustate** command is used to monitor the status of the communications links and of cross-system requests.

SUMMARY

The UNIX operating system is very good for its intended purpose. It was originally designed as a system for software development, and it works very well as such a system. Many of the features that make it a superior software development system, however, also make it a questionable environment for running large production applications.

UNIX provides an incredibly wide range of tools to support software development. Many of these tools are not available on other operating systems. The file system is designed for interactive use, especially for software development. Many of the features of the UNIX file system have been picked up and are now being used by other operating systems.

The bulk of the operating system is contained in the service programs, instead of the kernel. The idea is to provide the minimal features needed in the kernel, and to concentrate the system in the service programs. This approach works well for software development, since the primary need is for the services, but it does not work as well for production applications, which require greater performance.

A long-standing problem area in the UNIX systems is the level of documentation and maintainability of the system. The design and early releases of the system pre-supposed a high degree of sophistication on the part of the users. Perhaps because of this assumption, the documentation and maintenance of the system required a high level of knowledge.

EXERCISES

DISCUSSION QUESTIONS

1. Briefly discuss the weaknesses of the UNIX operating system.
2. Briefly discuss the strengths of the UNIX operating system.
3. Briefly discuss the UNIX shell.
4. Briefly describe the functions of lex, yacc, and make.
5. Briefly describe the UNIX file directory structure.
6. Describe the file access levels provided with UNIX.
7. Discuss UNIX file system reliability.
8. Discuss parent and child processes.
9. Briefly discuss the basic UNIX scheduling algorithms.
10. Show how memory is allocated with UNIX.

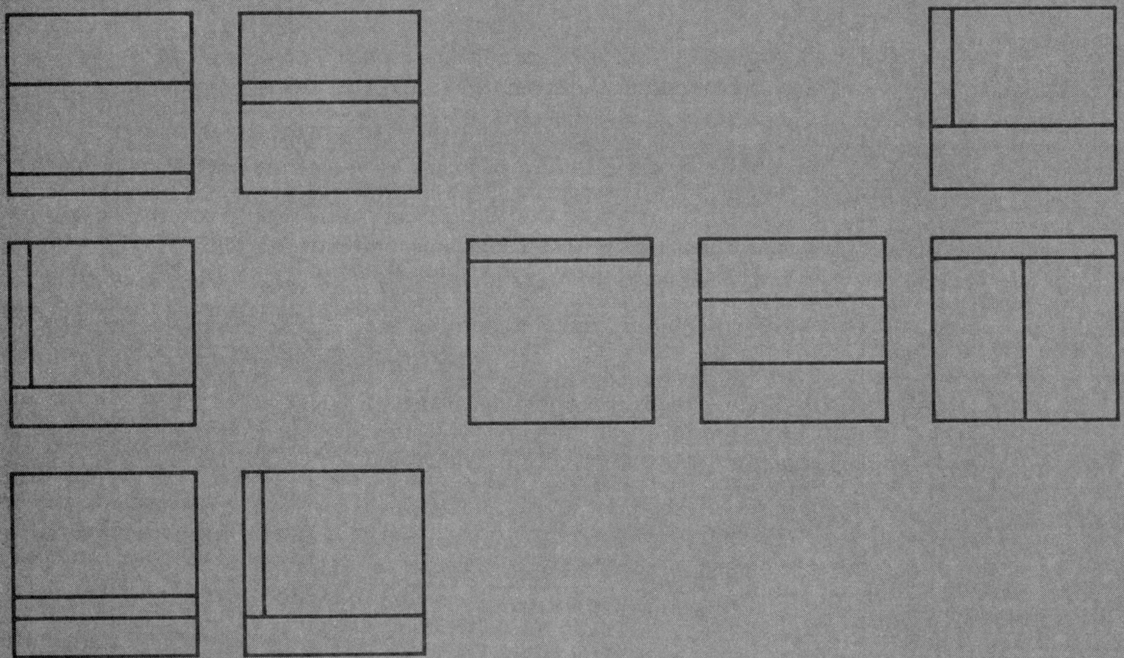

VIRTUAL MACHINE (VM) High Performance Option 3.4

15

KEY TERMS

EXEC2	*RUN*
Starter system	*REXX*
DMKSYS	*PREP*
Saved segments	*DMKRIO*
File mode	*DMKSNT*
Single processor mode	*Minidisks*
External interrupts	*Device address*
Q1, Q2, and Q3	*Machine-check interrupts*
Run list	*Eligible lists*
Deadline priority	*True run list*
Resident nucleus	*Average queue delay*
Guest operating system	*Transient nucleus*
Scrolling	*Paging manager*

KEY TERMS

Free list	*VM handshaking*
Swap list	*Flush list*
Pre-paging	*Swap faults*
Disposable page collector	*Trimming*
Reserved page frames	*Virtual = real*
Page zero	*Storage keys*
Indicate (IND)	*Moving cursor algorithm*
Preferred paging space	*Page migration*
Alternate path	*Byte multiplexer channel*
Selector channel	*Block multiplexer channel*

KEY TERMS

Prefix storage area	*RSCS directory*
Direct signals	*Prefix registers*
Emergency signals	*External call signals*
Setting affinity	*Defer locks*
Critical section	*Global system lock*
Real Storage Management lock	*VMBLOK lock*
PVM (Pass-through Virtual Machine)	*RSCS routing table*
RSCS link table	*RSCS profile*

RACF (Resource Access Control Facility)

RSCS (Remote Spooling Communications Subsystem)

Binary Synchronous Communications Protocol (Bisynch)

INTRODUCTION

This section focuses on the VM operating system from IBM. Each of the physical features of a regular computer (such as disk drives, tape drives, card readers, etc.) are simulated by VM, so that the user is able to use each of those devices as though they were real.

VM is very good as an interactive system, and it is the only major IBM operating system that was designed to be interactive. The major problem with VM is the lack of software tools available on it. The normal complement of compilers and editors is available, but there is not, as yet, the large number of application programs available for it.

History of VM

There have been several different generations of VM. It began in the 1960's as a system called "CP-67," which did not achieve, and was not planned for, wide commercial success. It then became known as VM/370, because it ran on the IBM 370 series of computers. This system went through six different releases, culminating in VM/370 Release 6, which was the last released version of VM/370. There were two short-lived enhancements to VM/370, called VM/SEPP and VM/BSEPP. Neither of these enhancement levels was continued.

The next major step was the release of VM/SP, or Virtual Machine/System Product, which is the current VM release. The current release is known as VM/SP Release 3. Future enhancements are planned for at least two more releases.

A modification of the basic VM/SP system is the VM/SP High Performance Option system, or VM/SP HPO, which is based on VM/SP, but contains enhancements and modifications to support very large mainframe computers with the highest possible performance level. The information in this chapter is relevant to VM/SP HPO Release 3.4, which is based on VM/SP Release 3.

VM Structure

VM consists of two major components: the Control Program (CP), and the Conversational Monitor System (CMS). CP is the basic operating system which manages all the computer hardware, and presents each user with a fully-configured virtual machine.

The virtual machine provides virtual devices, such as disk drives, printers, etc., that appear to function just like real devices. The data that is transmitted to or from those virtual devices can be mapped into a real device or simply remain in the virtual device. Any data transmitted to or from virtual disk drives or tape drives is always mapped into real devices, however.

The unit-record devices (card readers, card punches, and line printers) do not map directly into physical devices. Data sent to one of these devices passes into the data spooling system maintained by CP. If the requested destination of the data is a real device, it is routed to a real device. The requested destination can be another virtual device, in which case the data never leaves the spooling system. One of the primary methods for transferring data between users is to send it to another user's virtual card reader. That user can then read the data just as though it were coming from a real card reader. In this case, the data is never actually sent to a real device, but instead is always maintained in the CP spooling area.

Example 15-1:

THE VIRTUAL MACHINE

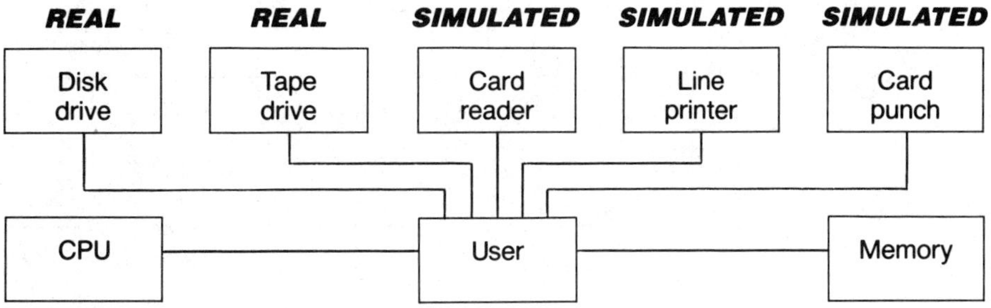

The CMS component of VM provides the file system, the user interface, and the operating system services. CMS is a single-user operating system that runs only as part of VM. It cannot run on a real computer, but must be run in a virtual machine under VM.

Virtual machines can also be used without the CMS component by running another operating system in each virtual machine. When a complete operating system is run in a virtual machine, it is unable to distinguish the virtual machine from a real computer. This other operating system executes just as it would on a real computer, although somewhat more slowly because of the additional overhead from having CP running on the real computer. Such an operating system is known as a **guest** operating system.

Guest operating systems can be set up so that users actually log on to them instead of VM. This facility allows many copies of the same operating system to run at the same time on one computer, such as when testing a new release of an operating system before putting it into production. It also allows different operating systems to run at the same time, so that the same computer may be simultaneously servicing some users with MVS, some with DOS, and some with VS1.

Certain applications programs can be run in a virtual machine in the same fashion as a guest operating system. Any program to be run in this fashion must be able to manage the physical resources of a computer, just as an operating system does, because the virtual resources provided require such management. The advantage of running such programs under VM, instead of on a real computer, is that virtual machine environments can be quickly and easily set up, while physical computers are much more difficult and expensive to set up. This is particularly true for programs that require special physical hardware since such hardware can be easily simulated under VM.

Example 15-2:

VM STRUCTURE

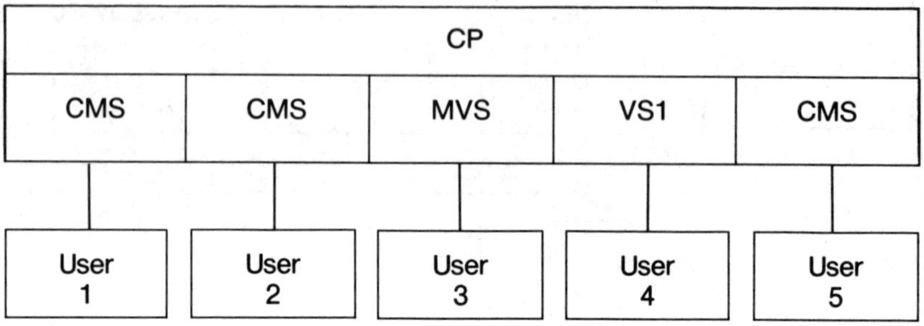

OPERATING SYSTEMS SERVICES

Most of the operating systems services provided by VM are provided by the CMS component. The CP commands that are available to the general user manage the virtual resources instead of functions such as program or file maintenance.

The services provided by VM are usually user-friendly, with easy-to-use interfaces. The list of services provided is much shorter than most other operating systems.

User interface

The user interface between CMS and the user is quite good. Much thought has been given to providing an environment that is useful to both the novice and the experienced user. The interface between CMS and the user is a compromise between the needs of each of these, with the experienced user probably favored slightly in the end result.

VM was designed to be used for time-sharing instead of batch, so the command structure is appropriate for interactive use. The command structure is designed quite similarly to the command structure of other time-sharing systems such as PC-DOS.

VM is not a system that can be used effectively by a person who is inexperienced with computers. Software packages are available that add another layer of interface designed for the complete novice. These packages provide a system where virtually all commands can be executed from a menu, with explanations of the functions of each command. They also add somewhat to the system overhead, however, and are quite time-consuming and clumsy for experienced users, so the basic VM system does not include these packages.

There are two ways to enter most commands. The command can be written out completely or it can be abbreviated to just two or three letters. The less experienced user will tend to more readily remember the full mnemonic for the command, while the more experienced user will use the abbreviations in order to reduce keystrokes.

A full-screen editor is provided that has a large list of features. The following is a brief list of some of those features:

- Simultaneous access to multiple files
- Multiple windows
- Setup features modifiable by the user
- Simultaneous access to multiple locations in the same file
- Macro capability (a series of executable commands in a file)
- A normal complement of search, replace, copy, and move commands

One common feature that the editor does not have is the ability to scroll the screen. Many computers track the cursor position on the screen, and when that cursor moves off the screen, either above, below, or to the side, the information on the screen is adjusted to display what is under the cursor. This is called **scrolling.** Such a facility is not available under VM because the terminal communications protocols do not support the feature.

The file directory can be displayed in a full-screen format with the display sorted in a variety of ways. This display shows the file names, the file sizes, the physical organization of the files, and the last time each file was modified. Most normal CMS commands can be performed on files directly from the display without requiring the name of the file to be entered separately.

Error messages usually display both a code number, and a terse summary of the error in English. More information about the error can be obtained by looking up the code in a reference manual, but some errors can be solved with the short summary provided with the error.

CMS has a HELP system that is quite extensive, so that complete information is available on all commands. One shortcoming of this HELP system, however, is that it is not context-sensitive.

The VM HELP system requires that the user go through a series of full-screen menus in order to obtain information about any particular feature. This provides the necessary information, but not as easily as the context-sensitive help systems. If users are in the middle of some application, they may have to exit that application in order to obtain the needed HELP information.

Software tools

VM has essentially no software tools supplied with it. A fair number of tools are available that run under VM, but almost all of them must be ordered separately. This is an area where the UNIX system has a definite advantage over VM, since almost as many tools are included with UNIX as are even available under VM.

One reason for the scarcity of tools under VM is that, until relatively recently, many people viewed VM solely as a means of running other operating systems, and thus placed many of the tools on the guest operating systems, instead of on VM. This trend has since reversed, and many installations are now running VM as a system by itself, but the large number of tools that are available on some systems have not yet appeared on VM.

Virtually all of the common programming languages are supported on CMS. IBM offers compilers for BASIC, COBOL, FORTRAN, Pascal, and PL/1. There is also a C language compiler available. IBM also supplies an assembler for IBM 370 assembler language. Other compilers are being made available regularly, both by IBM and by independent vendors.

Object code files produced by the languages and linker may be executed directly with the RUN command. This loads the files into memory and begins executing them. This is most useful when debugging programs since running programs this way causes the message "EXECUTION BEGINS" to appear on the screen when the program begins executing. Programs that have been saved on disk as load modules do not generate this message.

After the program has been fully debugged, it is more efficient to create a load module on disk, since that load module may be executed directly without requiring that the linking process be repeated. The method for executing a load module is simply by giving its filename.

The job control language on CMS is very good; in fact, it is among the best available on any system. There are two different versions available. The simpler version is **EXEC2** and the more complex version is **REXX.**

EXEC2 is an interpretive command processor. Its basic function is to stack a series of commands in a file, and execute them as a group with no intervention necessary from the user. This function is expanded by several facilities in the processor that allow parameters to be passed into the batch file, so that commands can be modified by inserting different parameters. It also has a simple I/O system that allows I/O to and from disks and terminals. Rather complex applications can actually be written using the EXEC2 processor, but they tend to run slowly and be difficult to understand, so EXEC2 programs probably should be limited to simpler applications.

REXX is a superset of the EXEC2 command processor. It is a complete programming language. REXX maintains many of the features of EXEC2 but also contains far more features than EXEC2. Complex applications written using

REXX tend to be more efficient and easier to understand than similar applications in EXEC2.

REXX also has the advantage over EXEC2 of being compilable, whereas EXEC2 can only be interpreted. This allows applications to be developed in REXX in an interpretive fashion, then compiled for optimal execution speed during production use.

Systems generation

The systems generation process for VM can vary widely in complexity. A simple running system can be installed very quickly and easily without much knowledge of VM. A system that is tuned and optimized for a large number of users, and that is installed on a large mainframe, requires a large amount of knowledge of systems programming and of VM.

The VM for microcomputers can be installed by anyone who is reasonably familiar with VM and the microcomputer, and does not require a systems programmer. Installing VM on a small mainframe is somewhat more complex, but can be done by an average systems programmer. IBM distributes the system already set up, and this setup is suitable for use on a small mainframe where the number of users and the amount of hardware available are both rather small. This setup is not usually suitable for large mainframes, however.

A VM system of some type must be running in order to generate the new VM system. A **starter system** is supplied with the new VM system for those installations that do not currently have a VM system. This is a very simple VM system that is set up to run on virtually any computer and contains just enough VM components to allow a new system to be generated.

New VM systems are supplied on magnetic tapes. The first file on the tape is a stand-alone format program, so that a disk drive can be formatted to receive the VM system. This program is accessed by booting the computer using that tape as a source. When all the disk drives are formatted, the starter system can be loaded onto them by the second file on the tape. Booting the computer again from the tape loads the transfer program, which then reads the rest of the tape and transfers the starter system on to the formatted disk drives.

If a VM system is already being used, the entire system generation process can be done in a virtual machine on that VM system. This allows that virtual machine to easily be configured to match the starter system. If no VM system exists, care must be taken to ensure that the real computer configuration matches that in the starter system closely enough for it to run. For example, there are several ranges of disk and tape drive addresses configured in the starter system. Not all of these addresses must have a real device present, but any devices that are present must be connected at addresses matching those in the starter system.

After the starter system has been successfully placed on disk drives, the computer should be booted again from those disk drives in order to load the starter system into the computer and start it running. When this has been accomplished, a minimal VM system is running on the computer.

The starter system is now used to load the components of the production VM system to be generated. Much of this is done automatically. A program (written in EXEC2) called **PREP** is used to automatically perform much of the loading process. This program is loaded onto the system from another tape. It is then executed to format the disk drives that are to receive the new VM system, and to load in the CP and CMS components. These are the components that are used to build a working copy of VM.

PREP can also be used to perform other functions: loading the source code to CP and CMS, printing out some of the sample installation files, creating tapes with stand-alone bootable utilities on them, and modifying the new system's HELP files.

The same PREP program can be used to load the HPO modifications to CP and CMS. It can also be used to load the source for the HPO modifications, similarly to the normal CP and CMS source.

After all the CP and CMS components are loaded into the new system, the next step is to generate a new "nucleus", or kernel, for both CP and CMS. Before the CP nucleus is generated, the new system must be configured to match the physical configuration of the computer on which it is to run. There are four primary files to be modified to change the configuration.

The file that controls all virtual machines in the system is the **directory.** This is a file that specifies all details of any virtual machine that can be used in that system. Details include such things as the userid, the password, the amount of virtual memory to be available, the number, size, type, and physical location of virtual disks, and any privilege levels available. The privilege level determines whether users can execute only general commands or if they can use commands that affect the functioning of the system itself.

Any virtual machines that are to be used by the operating system must be set up in the directory. A minimum of at least one is necessary for the system to boot, and the normal minimum for a functioning system is from five to twenty.

The **DMKRIO** file contains the layout of the physical I/O devices attached to the system. Every peripheral device that is to be accessed by the system must be defined in this file. The entry for each device must have an address which specifies the channel, control unit, and device. All control units and channels must also be defined in this file. Any features that are available on the physical devices, such as alternate paths, must be defined here. Each device and control unit must also specify type and model, so that the system is able to use them correctly.

The DMKSYS file contains mostly information about the processors and various operating system features. This file specifies the physical characteristics of the processors in the system. It also specifies how the paging and spool systems are to function. This is where preferred paging or swapping areas are set up. Many other features are also specified here.

- How the accounting system functions
- How the operating system clock is to be set
- Where to place system dumps
- The device containing the CP nucleus
- The userid for the system operator
- How often to check for lost I/O interrupts

The **DMKSNT** file contains all necessary information about the location and size of systems **saved segments,** which are subsystems used with VM. Systems that are specially designed and used frequently may become saved segments. This is a process where an image copy is made of the program after it is loaded into memory, and that image is available on a read-only basis to many users.

After the configuration files have been set up properly, the new CP nucleus can be built with the **GENERATE** program. This program can be used to reassemble any of the four primary configuration files or to build a new CP nucleus. The new directory must be loaded in a machine-readable format. The other three files must be assembled before the new nucleus so it will contain the most recent updates to those files. After this, the nucleus can be built and loaded onto its proper location on disk.

The system continues running as before; if the new nucleus contains any errors, they can be corrected before doing any harm. The new nucleus does not take effect until the computer is booted again, so this is a good opportunity to find and correct errors. If no errors are found in the CP nucleus, the CMS nucleus can then be generated by the GENERATE program. The CMS nucleus is loaded onto the beginning of the CMS system disk. This nucleus is accessed by everyone who uses CMS.

The system should now be booted to start the new CP nucleus. If there are errors when the system starts or runs, it may be necessary to restore the starter system, correct the source of the error, and rebuild the CP nucleus. The new system should immediately be backed up on tape, so that a copy exists in case of emergencies.

CMS is usually kept as a saved segment, since it is explicitly designed for such, and CMS's performance is more critical than almost any other component of VM. If CMS is to be made a saved segment, then the new nucleus should contain the proper information about it from DMKSNT, and it should be saved into the location reserved for it.

The systems generation is essentially complete at this point, even though several hours of work may yet be required in order to set up all the necessary disk areas for the various applications and users. Each of the applications, such as the compilers, has its own installation procedure, and must be installed separately.

Each user must also have an entry placed in the directory for the virtual machine that is to be allocated to that user. That virtual machine must be tailored to fit the user's requirements, although this usually requires very little work. All the disk space allocated to the users must be formatted in preparation for their files. If a VM system was previously in use at that installation, the user entries can usually be taken from the old directory and copied into the new directory, but if this is the first VM system, then the directory must be set up from scratch. Setting up the directory is a relatively simple task.

Example 15-3:

VM HPO SYSTEMS GENERATION

1. Format disk drives
2. Load starter system
3. IPL starter system
4. Load VM components with PREP
5. Load HPO with PREP
6. Set up directory, DMKRIO, DMKSNT, and DMKSYS
7. Build new CP nucleus
8. Load new CP nucleus
9. Build and load new CMS nucleus
10. IPL new CP nucleus
11. Build additional components as necessary

FILE SYSTEMS

The VM file system is completely contained within CMS; CP has no file system. A guest operating system that is running under VM is given an area of disk of its own, and may set up any type of file system it chooses.

A unique characteristic of VM is the concept of **minidisks.** A minidisk is a virtual disk. It is the way disk storage is made available to virtual machines. A minidisk can be any part of a real disk. It cannot be more than one physical disk. This area is available to the virtual machine as though it were a real disk. Guest operating systems commonly have complete physical disks dedicated to them, but CMS users usually have only a very small part of a real disk devoted to each user.

Example 15-4:

MINIDISK STRUCTURE

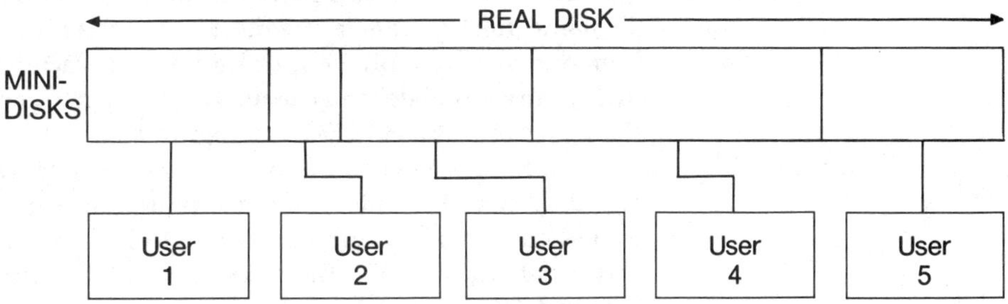

Before CMS is able to use a minidisk to store files, it must be formatted. The disk was already formatted by CP when the system was generated, but each minidisk must be formatted again by CMS. This not only provides a format that CMS expects, it also allows CMS to set up a file directory that keeps track of files and blocks on the minidisk.

The system directory controls the piece of the disk each minidisk occupies. The minidisk is allocated by a system administrator who decides how large the minidisk should be, and where it should be located on the disk drive. Much care must be taken when allocating minidisks to ensure that all minidisks are self-contained (two minidisks cannot overlap into the same area).

A virtual machine can use as much or as little of the minidisk space allocated as desired. Any space not used is left vacant; it cannot be used by other virtual machines. One of the primary shortcomings of the minidisk concept is that, since disk space is not shared, a large amount of the available disk space is allocated but not used. This leads to a significant waste of disk space.

When more space is required, it is not possible to increase the size of the minidisk. The allocation can only be increased if the space adjoining the old allocation is not used by another minidisk. Even if it is possible to increase the allocation in a contiguous area, the CMS file system cannot make use of the increased space without reformatting the entire minidisk. When the available space is filled, the only way to increase the size of the minidisk is to have the system administrator allocate a larger minidisk in another area and copy all files from the current minidisk to the new one.

Fixed length blocks are used for the CMS file system. The individual files may have either fixed or variable length blocks and records, but the allocation of the minidisk is done in fixed length blocks. All files are mapped into those blocks by CMS. The block size can be either 800, 1024, 2048, or 4096 bytes. The larger block sizes allow more efficient disk I/O on the newer IBM disk drives which are most efficient when transferring large blocks of data. A smaller block size might be used if most of the files are smaller than the block size, since each file uses at least one block. If all the files are very small, much of the disk space might be wasted with large block sizes.

CMS does not have a hierarchical file structure. Each file is identified by a file name, file type, and a **file mode.** Both the file name and the file type can be from one to eight alphabetic or numeric characters. The file name is a descriptive name for the file, and the file type is used to specify what the file is, such as "FORTRAN" for a FORTRAN program.

The file mode is a one- or two-character symbol that specifies on which minidisk that file resides. The first digit is an alphabetic character, the optional second character is a number from 0 to 9. If the second character is not specified, it defaults to 1. The file mode allows files with the same file name and file type to exist on different minidisks.

Each CMS user may have files on many minidisks, and some means must be available that distinguishes between the files on the different minidisks. This is accomplished by the file mode. All minidisks are designated by a one-letter name, and this name becomes the alphabetic part of the file mode for any files on that minidisk. The default minidisk that almost all users have is the "A" minidisk.

Since the same file name and file type may exist simultaneously on many minidisks, a search order must be set up to determine the order in which the minidisks are searched (if the file mode is specified, no search is necessary). The search order is strictly alphabetic; the first minidisk searched is the "A" minidisk, the second is the "B" minidisk, etc. If a new minidisk is accessed as a letter that already exists, the access to the previous minidisk accessed by that letter is dropped, and the new minidisk is accessed in its place.

The CMS system disks are normally accessed as the "S" and "Y" minidisks. This places them far enough down in the search order so that user minidisks are normally searched before the system minidisks. This allows the user to create a file with the same name as a disk-based system command, place that file on the "A" minidisk, and have that file accessed instead of the system command by the same name. This allows users to redefine system commands as desired.

The number following the letter in the file mode is optional. If it is not specified, it defaults to "1". Other numbers have special meanings. A number of "0" prevents other users from reading that file, even if they have access to the minidisk on which the file is maintained. This allows users to give other users access to their minidisks while having some files that those users cannot access.

There are three general levels of disk access granted within VM. The lowest level is read access, the next level is write access, and the highest level is multi-write access. Multi-write access allows more than one user to have write access to the same minidisk at the same time.

CMS is designed as a single-user system, so the file system has no locking mechanism to control updates to files. A file and block directory is maintained both in memory and on the disk, but they are maintained separately. The copy in memory considered the master copy. The copy on disk is loaded into memory only when the disk is first accessed. In cases where many users have write access to the same minidisk at the same time, both users may read in the old directory from disk, write files to disk while updating the copy of the directory in memory, and then write the updated directories back to disk. Since neither user knew the other was updating the directory, there is a very high probability that the two write operations will destroy the integrity of the directories. For this reason, multi-write access to minidisks should be allowed only in special cases and then with careful supervision.

The directory entries for each user's minidisk specify passwords for read, write, and multi-write access. If a particular level of access is not allowed, such as multi-write access, then no password is specified for that access. If anyone is permitted a particular level of access, then the password for that access can be replaced with the keyword "ALL," which allows anyone access with no password required.

There is no mechanism (other than the file mode of 0) of granting or restricting access to individual files. Other special levels of access control are available, such as allowing read or write access only if no other access is already in place. This makes it possible to prevent write access from being granted if some user already has read access.

MULTIPROGRAMMING

VM has been a commercial operating system supporting large numbers of users for several years, and is designed to run efficiently on a wide range of mainframes. As a consequence, it has a very sophisticated level of multiprogramming support. The algorithms and techniques used in HPO 3.4 of VM are better than usual, since one of the explicit objectives of this release is to provide very efficient performance on IBM's largest computers.

VM assigns each user a virtual machine when that user logs on to the system. The total number of virtual machines on the system at any one time is the total number of different programs executing. VM forces each virtual machine to execute only one program at a time, so the total number of programs is limited by the total number of virtual machines on the system.

This rule can be violated when a virtual machine contains another operating system (such as MVS) which runs many programs. There are two different ways this is handled. One way, which is used in special cases, allows the virtual machine to control one of the real processors. This is only possible on computers with more than one processor. VM can control one processor, and the program controls the other processor. This is called **single processor mode** and currently only works with MVS.

The other method is to force that virtual machine to only run one program at a time. This is achieved by having the virtual machine do its own scheduling among the time slices allocated to it, and VM then schedules the entire virtual machine as one program, regardless of what that program is doing. This leads to a problem of slow turnaround time, since several programs are trying to run in a time allotment sized (by VM) for only one program. This can be alleviated by tuning VM to give that virtual machine a larger than usual allotment of processor time.

The batch system creates a virtual machine for every program. This ensures that each program has associated with it a normal complement of control blocks and data areas, and is treated fairly by the scheduling algorithms.

Interrupts

VM is an interrupt-driven system with several different types of interrupts possible. The most common interrupts are **I/O interrupts,** and others are **SVC interrupts, external interrupts, program interrupts,** and **machine-check interrupts.**

Many interrupts are not processed directly by VM, but are passed almost unchanged into a specific virtual machine. Since real computers get interrupts, so should virtual computers. I/O interrupts are almost always passed to a virtual machine since almost all I/O is initiated by a virtual machine. Exceptions to this rule are made in the case of system-initiated I/O, such as paging and spooling. SVC interrupts are not passed to the virtual machine if the real computer is running in supervisor state, but if it is in problem state, these interrupts are also passed.

Machine-check interrupts usually signify a failure somewhere in the computer hardware. These take priority over anything else. The interrupt handler tries to determine the severity of the error. Some errors merely need be recorded and do not affect the functioning of the computer, but other errors require that either part or all of the computer be shut down. The machine-check interrupt handler takes the appropriate action once the severity of the error has been determined.

Program interrupts can come from a variety of causes. If the computer is in supervisor state, such an interrupt is a serious problem which results in system failure. If the computer is in problem state, the interrupt must have been generated by a virtual machine. Many of these interrupts are passed directly to the virtual machine to be handled there. Most of the others indicate a need to do some type of simulation.

Virtual machines are not allowed to execute in supervisor state, yet they frequently contain programs (such as operating systems) that execute privileged instructions. These instructions cannot be executed by the virtual machine, so VM simulates the execution of those instructions for the virtual machine. The results presented to the virtual machine are identical to the expected results. In some cases, the simulation requires that VM actually execute the same privileged instructions itself, then report the results back to the virtual machine. Such privileged instruction operations in a virtual machine can generate a program interrupt. Other program interrupts can be a result of the virtual machine referencing a memory area that is not in memory, requiring VM to do a paging operation.

Priorities

Each virtual machine has a priority level associated with it. The position that virtual machine maintains in the system queues is, of course, a factor of how much it is waiting on resources, but this priority is used to position the virtual machine in the queues when it is eligible. The default priority value is 64; the range is from 1 to 100. The lower the numeric value of the priority, the higher the priority.

There are two ways to obtain a different priority for a virtual machine. The logon characteristics of that virtual machine can be modified so that the priority is assigned a different value when the user logs on. This is useful for cases where it is known that that virtual machine always needs either a higher or lower priority. Priorities can also be changed by a privileged user at any time while that virtual machine is logged on the system.

Resource Management

VM uses techniques for managing resources to prevent problems with deadlock and inefficient handling of tasks. These algorithms are intimately intertwined with similar techniques for handling multiple processors, so they are handled in the section on multiprocessing.

JOB AND TASK SCHEDULING

VM has three primary divisions of tasks, and each of these divisions has further subdivisions. It also makes use of the feedback principle in moving tasks from one queue to another.

Tasks in the highest two divisions are regarded by the system as being **in queue,** while tasks in the lowest division are not considered to be eligible to be placed in queue. The lower division has three separate queues (called Q1, Q2, and Q3) that are used to hold tasks. These are not officially called queues because the tasks at this point are not allowed into the processors. They are called **eligible lists** because the tasks in them are eligible to be run. The next level up is the **run list** which contains tasks that are either ready to run or waiting only briefly. The highest level division is the **dispatch list** which is sometimes known as the **true run list.** Tasks that are to be placed in control of a processor are selected only from the dispatch list.

Any task not in the dispatch list cannot be executed and must first be moved into the dispatch list. Any priority calculations that are performed are based on the time check when a task is dropped from the run list, not when the task is removed from the dispatch list or the lower queues.

The feedback mechanism in VM queues is called **deadline priority.** This is a number that is a composite of all the characteristics of a task. There are many different factors that are considered in calculating the deadline priority.

Tasks are categorized into either Q1, Q2, or Q3 on the basis of how much processor time they consume. Q1 is designated for tasks that require only a small amount of processor time but require it often. These are usually tasks that involve a large amount of terminal interaction. Q2 tasks are more CPU-intensive and are only allowed access to the processor 1/8 as often as Q1 tasks, but are allowed to remain in the processor 8 times as long. Q3 tasks are the most processor intensive. They are only allowed access to the processor 1/64 as often as Q1 tasks, but then remain in the processor 64 times as long. Categorizing the tasks in this fashion greatly reduces the system overhead generated by the scheduling process.

All tasks start out in Q1, and are either left there or moved to Q2 or Q3 based on their performance. The critical item is I/O done to a terminal. When a task performs I/O to a terminal, VM assumes that that task is time-sharing, and therefore moves it into Q1. Any task in Q1 that completes its turn in the processor without doing any terminal I/O is moved to Q2. Any task in Q2 that completes six turns in the processor without doing any terminal I/O is moved to Q3.

Example 15-5:

QUEUE ALLOCATION

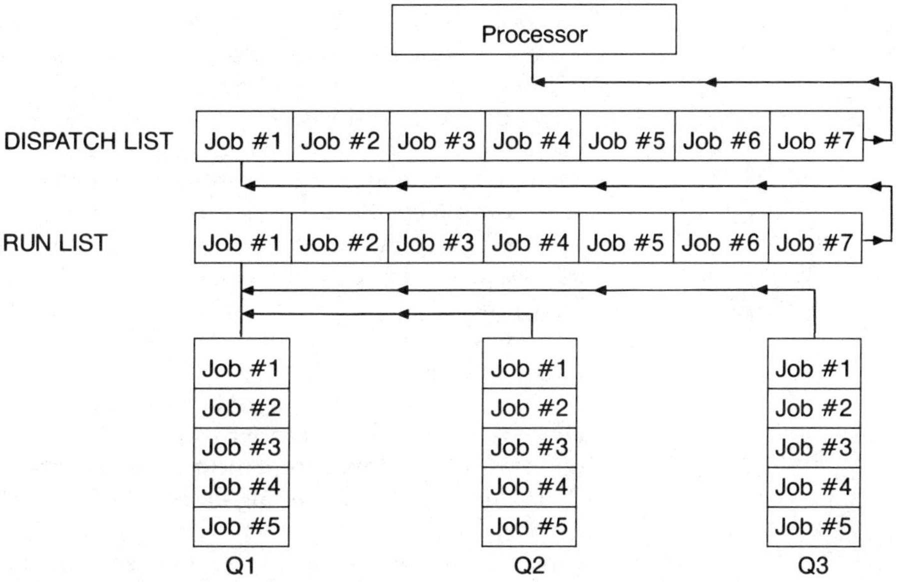

The difference between Q1, Q2, and Q3 is that the deadline priority is calculated differently for tasks in each of the different queues. Another factor in calculating deadline priorities is the amount of time that a task spends making one cycle through all the queues to get access to the processor. This is the **average queue delay;** when this value increases, the deadline priorities are changed correspondingly.

The average queue delay is designed to affect the queueing algorithms on heavily loaded systems to ensure that terminal tasks get access to the processor frequently, even if more processor intensive tasks are correspondingly penalized. This is accomplished by the average queue delay. Since Q2 and Q3 tasks spend more time in the queue, their average queue delay values are much higher than that of Q1 tasks, thus favoring Q1 tasks in allocating processor resources.

The priority value that each task has associated with it is also used to affect the deadline priority value. Making the task priority higher ensures that it gets more access to processor resources. It is sometimes possible to significantly degrade overall performance by changing this value, since the normal algorithms are designed to provide maximum performance to each virtual machine, and if a processor Q2 or Q3 task is given a very high user priority, then that task can be scheduled into the processor as though it were a Q1 task. Each time it gets the processor, it gets a Q2-sized time slice, thus making much less time available to the rest of the tasks. This can easily lead to an overall slowdown on the system.

Tasks in the eligible lists are all ready to execute. Each of these tasks has associated with it an estimate of the working set size. The tasks remain in the eligible lists until a sufficient number of page frames is available in memory to contain the expected working set of that task. The deadline priority controls the order of the tasks within each of the queues, so new tasks just entering the queue may or may not be placed at the end. When sufficient page frames become available the next task is moved into the run list.

The task at the head of any of the eligible queues may or may not be the next task moved into the run list, even though it has the highest deadline priority. The task that is moved is the task with the highest deadline priority which also has an estimated working set size small enough to fit into the available page frames.

Not all tasks in the run list are actually runnable. Some tasks can become temporarily not runnable after using the processor for a short time. Some of these tasks are dropped from the queues, but others remain in the run list for a short time. If a task is waiting on certain functions, such as VM simulating a privileged instruction, the wait is not long enough to justify the overhead involved in moving that task out of the queue and then later back into the queue, especially since it will need another piece of processor time as soon as the simulation is finished.

Those tasks in the queue that are actually runnable are in the highest list, the dispatch list. Tasks are placed in both the run list and the dispatch list in order of deadline priorities. Separating the runnable tasks into another queue prevents the overhead necessary in determining which tasks are runnable each time a new task is to be placed in the processor.

Tasks that are waiting on some types of I/O can remain in the run list for a short time before either the I/O completes or they are dropped from the queue. The length of time such tasks remain in the queue is a parameter that can be modified by systems programmers. Lengthening such times causes tasks to wait much longer before being queued, but it also reduces the overhead involved in moving tasks between queues. There can be additional overhead involved, since tasks that are in queue are treated differently than are tasks not in queue.

One case where it is sometimes useful to extend the length of time a task remains in the queue before being dropped is a task that is continually communicating with other virtual machines. Such a task spends most of its time waiting for a response, so it is subject to being dropped from the queues regularly. If many messages are being received, and the timing is such that most of the messages are received just after the virtual machine has been dropped from the queue, then considerable overhead is generated from continually moving that task between queues. It is therefore useful to extend the queue time for that virtual machine, since doing so removes most of the overhead it generates.

Tasks that are dropped from the queue give up ownership of page frames, so systems with high memory utilization immediately allocate those frames to other tasks. If that task is quickly ready to run again, it can be delayed significantly by having to wait for a new set of page frames. Such delays can dramatically degrade the performance of certain tasks, and the additional paging load of writing those pages out and immediately reading them back in also adds to the system overhead and to the delays for that task. The system can perform much better if such tasks are allowed to remain in the queue for longer time periods before being dropped.

The deadline priority calculations include the time, so tasks that have been in that queue for a long period of time are more likely to be removed from it than tasks that have been there only a short time. Other factors can cause some tasks to remain in a particular queue much longer than others, but all tasks should eventually be removed.

MEMORY MANAGEMENT

Both CP and CMS manage memory. CP manages the real memory, and CMS manages virtual memory, but they both have memory management algorithms. The real memory management uses complex paging algorithms, but CMS, which manages only virtual memory, uses more traditional memory management techniques. Since it is a single-user system running under the control of CP, it does not use paging.

CMS uses a relatively simple memory management algorithm. All of the memory space allocated to a CMS virtual machine is divided up into partitions. These partitions are located in memory in a sequence at locations that seldom change.

The low sections of memory are used by CMS itself, and cannot be directly accessed by the user. These memory areas perform many different functions. The amount of usable memory available to programs depends upon the amount of virtual memory allocated to that virtual machine, minus that memory used by CMS. The areas reserved for the operating system are unavoidable overhead and are approximately the same size regardless of the total amount of virtual memory available.

CMS is divided into two general pieces: one piece is always in memory (the **resident nucleus**), and the other piece consists of many smaller parts that are normally left on disk storage and only moved into memory when that function is requested (the **transient nucleus**). Functions that are requested frequently are usually part of the resident nucleus, particularly if such functions do not require a large amount of memory. Functions that are requested less frequently or that require a large amount of memory are usually made transient.

Resident functions execute much faster than do transient functions since transient functions must be loaded into memory before they can execute. The problem with making functions resident, of course, is that each function uses memory; therefore a trade-off must be made between performance and memory usage. Later releases of CMS have made more functions resident than did previous releases, primarily because VM is now designed to run on very large mainframes, where plenty of memory exists and speed is very important. Versions of VM that are designed to run on small computers have fewer resident functions since memory utilization is more critical on them.

The lowest area of memory is used by CMS to maintain pointers and flags that are used by the system. Many of these are addresses of system routines. This area usually occupies approximately 20K bytes of storage.

The next area of storage is called **user free storage area** which provides storage to user programs. This area is approximately 35K bytes of storage. Just above the free area is the **transient program area,** which is where the transient parts of the nucleus are loaded. This area is approximately 10K bytes.

The next area is the **nucleus free storage area** which is very similar to the user free storage area except that this area provides storage to the nucleus. This area is quite large, occupying approximately 65K bytes.

All of these areas together occupy 128K of memory. These areas occupy all of storage below the user programs. All user programs are loaded into CMS at this location.

Example 15-6:

CMS MEMORY ALLOCATION

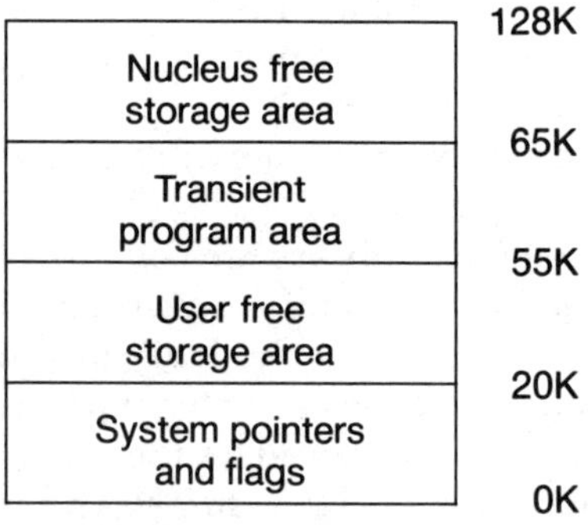

User programs are loaded into the area called **user program area.** The size of this area is variable and depends upon the total amount of virtual memory allocated to that virtual machine. This area is usually at least one megabyte and can be as large as several megabytes.

The user programs are loaded at the low address of the area, and can expand upward as needed, to the upper limit of the area. If the user program requests more free storage than is available in the user free storage area in low memory, then additional free storage is allocated to the program from the top of the user program area. This effectively lowers the high limit of the area, and the user program can then expand only to the new, lowered limit.

The upper limit of the user program area is determined by the beginning of the CMS Nucleus Area which is loaded into memory above the user programs. This is the resident part of the CMS nucleus, and must always be loaded into memory. The CMS nucleus starts at some pre-defined location, which effectively limits the possible storages sizes available to user programs. The usual way to circumvent this problem is to set up two separate CMS nuclei, where one nucleus is designed for virtual machines with small memory allocations, and the other nucleus is designed for virtual machines with large memory allocations. The nucleus for small virtual machines is loaded at a relatively low address, while the nucleus for the large virtual machines is loaded at a high address. The actual size of the CMS nucleus can vary, but it is commonly about 250K bytes.

The last area of memory is reserved for the **system loader table** which is the area containing information on any programs loaded into the user program area. This table is always loaded into the highest possible area of memory (unless the memory size of the virtual machine is too small to allow this area above the resident nucleus, in which case it is loaded below the nucleus, and takes space away from the user program area).

Example 15-7:

SAMPLE CMS MEMORY ALLOCATION

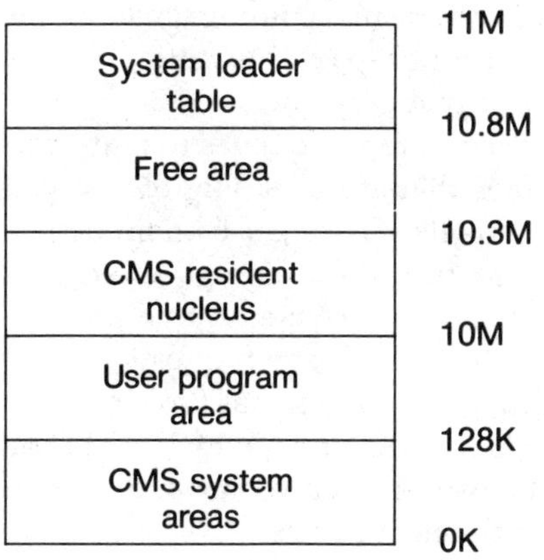

VIRTUAL MEMORY

All releases of the VM operating system have used virtual memory, but High Performance Option 3.4 is the first release of VM to implement page swapping as well as a normal paging system. Far more attention has been paid to improving performance in this particular system than is usually the case.

The paging manager manages memory to optimize job throughput, while using a minimum of systems resources itself. All storage is divided up into page frames of 4096 bytes. A page can be either "pageable" or "non-pageable" depending on whether it can be written out or not.

Pages in memory can be non-pageable for many reasons. The most common reason is that I/O is being performed to or from that page. Physical I/O requires a specific, unchanging, memory address as a location to read the data from or write it to. This address is placed in the I/O command when the I/O starts, and cannot be changed later, so the correct page must still be at that location when the I/O completes. The only way of guaranteeing that the correct page is still in that location is to not allow that page to be paged out. Such a condition is temporary; as soon as the I/O completes that page is again eligible for paging out.

The CP nucleus is similar to the CMS nucleus in that it is divided up into two parts. One part is resident and is always in memory, while the other part is transient, and each part of it is loaded into memory only when it is required. Any page that contains an active part of the transient nucleus is considered non-pageable until that part of the nucleus ceases to be active. These pages are also temporarily non-pageable. Any page that contains a part of the resident nucleus is considered permanently non-pageable.

Pages can also become non-pageable if they are locked in memory. A privileged command is available in VM that allows a systems programmer to pick certain pages that can be made non-pageable, usually for performance reasons. These pages remain non-pageable until another command is issued to allow them to become pageable again.

There are three different queues that are used in paging. The **free list** is a list of page frames that are most eligible to have new pages placed in them. Page frames in this list no longer contain active pages, and are thus the best candidates for new pages, since no page writes are necessary. Page frames are added to the free list from several sources.

The primary source of page frames for the free list is the **swap list.** Page frames belonging to programs that have been swapped out become free. The next best source is the **flush List,** which is a list of page frames belonging to the programs that have been removed from the active queue, so they are less likely to need pages in the near future.

Example 15-8:

PAGE FRAME SOURCES

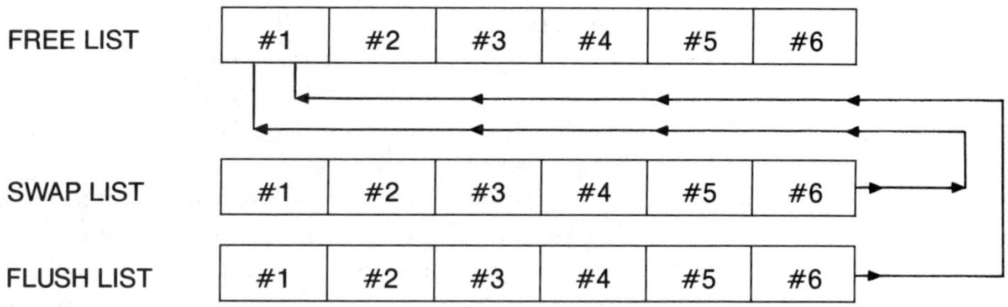

Swapping

This release of VM has added swapping to the normal paging algorithms. Swapping tends to keep the working set of a program together, so that less time is wasted by a program in waiting on paging. It also allows more efficient usage of the latest generation of disk drives, since I/O operations to them are much more efficient when large amounts of data are read or written.

Normal paging calls for the entire working set of a program to be contained in memory at the same time in order to facilitate execution of that program, but this sometimes becomes impossible on heavily loaded systems. The overall efficiency of the system goes down when too many programs are running to allow the complete working set of any program to be contained completely in memory. The overall paging rate goes up unacceptably, and each program spends too much time waiting for pages. Swapping is an attempt to solve this problem by keeping the entire working set of a program together. The program is not allowed in the processor as often, but it can do more real work while it is in the processor. A much smaller amount of system time is spent on paging, even though the number of pages read in or written out may be the same.

The swap queues consist of lists of programs that are no longer in the active dispatch queues. Dropping a task from the active queues does not guarantee that that program is swapped out, but it does place it on the swap queues. If the system is not heavily loaded, and that task becomes active again quickly, then its pages are still resident in memory, and therefore paging overhead is saved by not having to page that task back into memory.

The swap queues are divided up into two categories: one queue is for interactive programs, and the other is for non-interactive programs. Programs in the non-interactive swap queue are swapped out first, since they probably will not require processor time as quickly as interactive programs. It is not good to swap out a program that may have to be swapped back in quickly. Interactive programs tend to need processor time at irregular but frequent intervals, and are more likely to need to be swapped back in quickly.

Tasks are initially placed in the interactive swap list. If a particular task does not become active within a certain amount of time, that task is then moved to the non-interactive swap list. At that point, the task is either really non-interactive or it is interactive but not active at the moment. The default for this time interval is twenty seconds (this can be changed by systems programmers).

Tasks that have been on the non-interactive swap list for longer than a certain amount of time are moved to the flush list. The default for this is one hundred seconds, and can also be changed by the systems programmers. Systems that are heavily loaded can have tasks on the swap lists being swapped out before the time limit expires, but if the system is less heavily loaded, the time limit can run out and the task ends up on the flush list.

All pages that are swapped out at any one time are grouped into swap sets. The number of pages in a swap set is a parameter that can be set by systems programmers. All of the pages in any one swap set must belong to only one virtual machine. After a task has been swapped out, any page frames in memory belonging to that task are placed on the free list. If that task has any pages in the normal paging area and in the swap area, those pages in the normal paging area are deallocated without being read back in. This is to prevent the same page from existing simultaneously at two locations on the disk drive.

VM uses some pre-paging in an attempt to improve the performance of tasks by reading in pages before they are needed. When a task is placed in the active queues, but before that task has actually been placed in the processor, certain swap sets belonging to that task are swapped in and made ready for execution. This effectively gives up some extra I/O in an attempt to reduce the number of page or swap faults encountered by that task when it begins executing. The default number of swap sets to be pre-paged is two for interactive tasks and none for other tasks.

When a task is dropped from the active dispatch queues, it undergoes a process known as **trimming.** This is designed to determine which pages of its working set it was actually using. Any pages that that task did not reference while it was in the active queue are considered to be unnecessary and are placed in the **trim set.** These pages are no longer part of the working set, and the size of the working set is reduced accordingly. When the trimming process is complete, the trimmed pages are added to the flush list, and the task has a new, smaller, working set size.

The utilization of memory is regularly monitored for pages that are in memory that are not necessary. This is done by the **disposable page collector,** which scans a table of the pages to find any that are not being referenced. Whenever the disposable page collector scans the table, it resets any reference bits that are set. Any pages that do not have the reference bit set have not been referenced since the last time the disposable page collector was run, so such pages are not currently active. They are added to the flush list for potential paging out.

Many of the computers that run VM are quite large. VM will only directly address sixteen megabytes of real memory, which has become a serious constraint for many installations. Consequently, support exists in VM to handle memory sizes greater than sixteen megabytes, even though such memory cannot be directly used. The memory above sixteen megabytes is used as a paging area.

Any page that VM is processing must be in the part of memory below sixteen megabytes. If such a page exists in the upper part of memory, it must be moved to the lower part of memory before it can be used. This is clearly not as efficient as being able to directly address all of memory, but it is much more efficient than using a disk drive to page onto.

VM is very closely tied to the sixteen megabyte limit, and modifying the system to allow the upper part of memory to be directly addressed requires a very major rewrite of the entire system. This is not something even IBM is prepared to do casually or quickly. Such changes will probably occur in the future, in fact, there is already a specialized version of VM (VM/XA) that has vastly improved handling of the larger memories. This is not yet a complete system, however, since it is primarily designed to run guest operating systems. Systems with more than sixteen megabytes of memory under the current implementation of VM have significantly higher performance for memory-intensive applications than do systems without the extra memory.

Paging performance options

There are several options available for tuning the paging system for increased performance. Some of these options involve giving increased performance to one virtual machine at the expense of decreased performance to the other virtual machines. This can sometimes be desirable, particularly in the case where that one virtual machine is running a complete operating system. That operating system can have several users logged onto it, and it is clearly not fair to allow all of those users the same level of performance that is given to each single user on VM. In this case, the guest virtual machine should be set up so that each of its users receives approximately the same level of performance as each other user on VM.

One way of giving one or more virtual machines better performance is to set up reserved page frames for that virtual machine. This causes a certain number of page frames to be always available for that particular virtual machine. This is most useful on heavily loaded systems where certain virtual machines require quick access to memory.

Page frames are not reserved for any virtual machine when it is not logged on. As soon as it does log on, VM allocates a minimum number of page frames to it so that it can begin execution. If this number is less than the number requested to be reserved, then the number is gradually increased as the page frames become available until the requested number of page frames are reserved. These page frames remain available to that virtual machine until it logs off.

Since reserving page frames for one particular virtual machine removes that number of page frames from the pool available to all users, the option should be used very carefully. More than one virtual machine can have page frames reserved, but if the total number of reserved page frames becomes very large, the overall system performance can degrade significantly.

A more extreme option is to allocate large sections of memory to one virtual machine for its exclusive use, and to not share memory between that virtual machine and the other virtual machines. This significantly enhances the performance of the one virtual machine, since VM does no paging in that area, but it also completely removes that memory from the pool of available page frames, so the other virtual machines suffer significantly. This option is called **virtual equals real** or **V=R** because the virtual memory is as good as real memory.

The virtual machine that runs in V=R memory is restricted to just that block of memory. It cannot share in the normal paging pool. That virtual machine is usually an operating system that has a paging system and does its own paging in the block of memory allocated to it.

When a V=R virtual machine references memory addresses, those are real memory addresses, not virtual memory addresses. The only exception to this is the bottom-most page in memory called **page zero** which contains many pointers critical to the performance of the system, and consequently cannot normally be made available to a virtual machine.

Another option, called **preferred machine assist** or **PMA,** allows a V=R virtual machine periodic access to page zero of real memory. This access must be managed very carefully in order to prevent VM's pointers from being changed. PMA is designed for cases where MVS is run in a virtual machine under VM, usually on computers with two processors.

By using V=R memory, PMA, and another option called **single processor mode,** the MVS virtual machine runs under VM with virtually no degradation as compared to running MVS by itself. The single processor mode allows the virtual machine to have complete control over one processor on a two-processor computer. These options allow both VM and MVS to be run on a large two-processor computer, with both operating systems achieving performance levels comparable to running alone on a single-processor system. This is achieved by effectively dividing the physical resources between the two operating systems. Each system is given control over one processor, one part of real memory, and shared control of page zero.

Memory access protection

VM has mechanisms to guard against memory access violations. These restraints exist only to protect real memory, so programs running in a virtual machine have complete access to all virtual memory given to that virtual machine. For example, such programs can write data in page zero of memory; this is a virtual page zero, and has no relationship to the real page zero.

Memory access protection is implemented with hardware mechanisms called **storage keys.** These keys are assigned to small blocks of memory, either 2K or 4K. The more recent IBM mainframes use 4K storage keys, but the older ones used 2K keys. The operating system, which must run on both, supports both the 2K and 4K storage keys. Since virtual memory pages are 4K in size, the 4K keys tend to be more efficient. Computers that are using more than sixteen megabytes of memory must use the 4K keys.

When any access is requested to a location in memory, the key associated with that access request is compared to the storage key associated with the requested location in memory. Only when the access is validated by the key is that access allowed. This applies to reading data from memory as well as to writing data in memory. If the access is not valid, a program interrupt is generated and passed to the requesting program.

Paging devices

Paging devices normally are just disk drives, but there are special cases where paging performance is a problem of sufficient magnitude to justify special hardware. These devices usually involve memory, similar to that in the computer's main memory, but accessed by a channel similarly to disk drives. Some devices, usually manufactured by companies other than IBM, emulate disk drives and require no modifications to the operating systems. IBM sells a paging device that requires changes in the operating system, but this in turn allows higher performance levels.

The paging device sold by IBM is a normal IBM disk controller that has been modified to contain a **cache memory** that is used to temporarily store pages, and sophisticated programs to manage the cache memory. Since the cache memory is used only for paging, it is possible to analyze the normal paging requirements, and to optimize the cache memory management for those paging requirements.

The goal is to have as many page accesses as possible come from the cache memory instead of from disk drives. The more active pages are kept in the cache memory and only the less active pages need be written to disk drives. Such a paging device can reduce the page access time to a fraction of its normal value on systems that are able to fully utilize the paging device.

PERFORMANCE MEASUREMENT AND TUNING

The degree of performance measurement and tuning available on any operating system is largely a factor of the number of different options that are available for displaying or changing system characteristics. VM High Performance Option 3.4 has performance as a primary goal, so there are a large number of different features that allow performance tuning. Understanding each of these features is necessary, since otherwise tuning may lead to a system that runs less well.

Performance measurement

There are three different levels at which data can be collected to measure the performance of VM systems. The simplest level is through several commands which display high-level summaries of the current system performance. Some of these commands can be executed by general users, while others can only be executed by systems programmers. The next level is through an on-line monitor, usually IBM's Real Time Monitor (RTM), sometimes called SMART. This monitor provides more extensive and detailed information than is available through the VM commands. The highest level is with the MONITOR facility in VM, which collects data over a period of hours or days. The information collected with the MONITOR facility is quite extensive, and another program, such as VMMAP, is used to analyze it.

The IND Command

The primary VM command to display performance data is the **INDICATE** command, which is commonly abbreviated to **IND.** The simplest version of this command is available to all users of the system. It displays, in three lines, a general overview of system performance. This overview shows the percent processor utilization, the paging rate, the swapping rate, the percent of time spent in paging wait, the percent of time spent in I/O wait, and some general indicators of the system load.

Other versions of the IND command that are available only to systems programmers can be used to display a variety of things. One version shows the specific usage of each user, such as processor time consumed, number of pages in memory, size of the working set, and number of swaps performed. Another version is used to display a list of all tasks that are in I/O wait, and for which device each is waiting. A commonly used version of the IND command is used to display all tasks that are either in the run queues, or the eligible queues. This shows all the tasks in each queue, and the current status of each of those tasks.

The Real Time Monitor

The VM Real Time Monitor allows a more in-depth look at the system resources. Many of the displays from that monitor were presented in the chapter on performance tuning.

The MONITOR command generates a very large amount of raw data. This data is normally kept in the system spool area until it is analyzed by another program. Such analysis and reduction of the data should be done often, usually once a day, to avoid unnecessarily clogging the spooling system with large files. Specific types of monitoring may generate much larger than usual amounts of data. In such cases, it may not be possible to keep this data in the spooling system for even a short period of time. Such large amounts of data can only be collected by attaching a tape drive to the system, and collecting the data directly on the tape. The VMAP program is set up to use input data from either the spool system or from a tape.

Data may also be collected on tapes when there is some need for it to be archived. Such archived data is useful for evaluating the value of changes. The usual course is to collect and analyze the data, make changes based on that data, then collect and analyze more data to compare with the previous data. Collecting the data on tape may also be useful in cases where some analysis program at a different location is used to analyze the data. For example, the vendor might want to run capacity planning programs to determine when the customer should buy more computers. Such programs might not be available to the customer, so the data must be collected at the customer's site, placed on tape, and taken to the vendor's site for analysis.

One feature of MONITOR and VMAP is analyzing seeks on disk drives. Probably the most common problem in large VM systems is I/O wait on disk drives caused from data placed in less than optimal locations on those disk drives. Unfortunately, there is a tremendous amount of overhead associated with doing a seek analysis, so it should not be run casually. It also generates thousands of records of data. A good way to do a seeks analysis is to run it only on selected devices for only a few seconds of each minute.

Performance tuning

Performance measurement, of course, is only useful if the system is to be tuned based on the measured data. There are many different parameters in VM that can be varied to improve systems performance, and only the most important of these areas will be covered here. In most cases, the default values are sufficient for most parameters, and only a relatively few need be changed. The areas most subject to tuning are the paging and I/O systems.

Inefficient performance in the paging system is one of the most common problem areas in large VM systems. The impact of an inefficient paging system may not be significant if the system if lightly loaded, but if the system is heavily loaded, the impact may be very serious.

Reducing paging

Several methods are available to reduce the total paging in the system. If the bulk of the paging activity is coming from a single virtual machine, the solution might be easy. The most extreme course is to put that virtual machine in V=R area so that it does not have to page at all. This may be somewhat deceptive, however, since if that virtual machine is another operating system, it may be doing its own paging. That paging does not show up on VM as paging, but it nevertheless degrades the system.

A less dramatic route is to lock pages into memory. This means that certain pages are always in memory, and are not subject to being paged out. Locking pages can be useful for a particular virtual machine, but since it removes page frames from those eligible for paging, the rest of the system suffers somewhat. In some cases, however, the gain is sufficient to compensate for the penalty. This option is usually done more for the purpose of favoring a particular virtual machine than for improving overall performance. The best page to lock on a virtual machine is page zero since that is the one that tends to be referenced the most.

A more general approach is to reserve page frames for a specific virtual machine. This does not keep any specific pages in memory; instead it guarantees that a certain number of page frames are always available for that virtual machine. Locking pages in memory requires prior knowledge of which pages to lock, whereas reserving page frames does not require this knowledge. The most referenced pages are always the ones in the reserved page frames. This option can sometimes improve overall system performance, but it is used more often to improve performance on a selected virtual machine.

One of the most useful features for improving overall system performance, as well as performance on a selected virtual machine, is to set that virtual machine so that it is not dropped from the run queues when it becomes inactive. In some cases, particularly with virtual machines that communicate with other virtual machines, a virtual machine may become active shortly after being paged out. Preventing such a virtual machine from being dropped from the run queues not only improves its performance, it also improves overall system performance since the paging rate goes down somewhat.

There are several commands that set system parameters that can reduce the amount of paging in the system. Some of these parameters are: the minimum working set size, the default number of swap sets swapped in, the size of the swap sets, and the length of time a virtual machine remains in a swap queue.

Unnecessary paging may occur if the size of the minimum working set is not appropriate, since pages are made available to fill the working set, whether or not those pages are actually used. The number of swap sets swapped in when the virtual machine is placed in the run queues is of similar importance, since if this value is too large, unnecessary pages are swapped in, while if it is too small, later paging is necessary to bring in more pages. The size of the swap sets determines their usefulness. The amount of time on the swap queues also may cause unnecessary paging, since too short a time results in virtual machines being dropped from the queues even though they may have to be swapped back in almost immediately.

Improving paging performance

Many things can be done to improve performance on the paging system. One of the first ways is to place all paging activity on the fastest available paging devices. Some of these devices, such as dedicated memory devices, cache memory disk controllers, and high memory, have already been discussed. If none of these devices are available, then paging activity must be on disk drives.

Different types of disk drives have vastly different performance specifications, so the paging activity on disk drives should be placed on the fastest ones available. In the VM world, this is currently the 3380 disk drives. A parameter in the system configuration files (DMKSYS) specifies which devices are to be used for paging and the order in which they are to be used. This allows the faster devices to be used first, with the slower devices used only after the faster devices are filled. Paging areas specified on faster devices are called **preferred paging space.**

Only a relatively small part of any one disk drive is usually allocated to paging, in order to minimize the overall activity on that disk drive. The rest of the disk drive should be allocated to very low activity functions.

The most critical factor in optimizing disk response for paging is to minimize seek distance on the device. This can best be accomplished by defining only one high-activity area on that disk drive. VM has an internal algorithm, called the **moving cursor algorithm,** which attempts to place the pages on the paging disk device in such a way as to minimize seek distance on the disk drive. This algorithm works relatively well when allowed to work unhindered.

The most active pages should be maintained on the faster paging devices. There is no way of knowing in advance which pages are the more active, so some of the inactive pages end up on the faster paging devices. This is not a problem as long as plenty of paging space exists on those devices, but when that paging space begins to fill, a condition arises where a significant part of the fast paging area is filled with inactive pages, while some of the active pages are relegated to slower devices.

Inactive pages can be periodically moved from the fast paging devices to the slower devices. Such a movement is called **page migration.** This maintains only the more active pages on the faster paging devices. Such a migration adds somewhat to the overhead on the paging system since it makes the paging devices active, but the gain in paging speed usually more than compensates for this.

Page migration can be forced at any time by a privileged system command, or it is invoked automatically at certain times. Whenever a certain portion of the preferred paging space is filled, page migration occurs automatically.

An unusual feature available on some operating systems running as a guest in one virtual machine under VM is the ability to change the way that operating system functions in order to take advantage of VM facilities to enhance throughput. This feature requires that the guest operating system be designed for that function.

One such operating system is IBM's OS/VS1, which is a batch-oriented operating system that originally was designed to run stand-alone, but now is frequently run as a guest to VM. Its **VM handshaking mode** makes use of VM facilities for various system functions.

A significant cause of paging overhead in the system is when a guest operating system tries to use a paging system itself, in addition to the normal VM paging system. Such a setup tends to cause paging problems, since the two systems may operate at cross purposes. The VM handshaking in OS/VS1 stops OS/VS1 from paging. Because of this, the additional overhead from two systems both doing paging is eliminated, and thus overall performance is enhanced.

Improving disk I/O performance

Probably the area most subject to improvement, other than the paging system, is the disk I/O. A number of methods are available for improving disk I/O performance, many of which were discussed earlier in the chapter on performance tuning, but some of which are unique to VM.

One common area, where all operating systems have problems with the I/O system, is obtaining access to disk drives. If one disk drive in a group is involved in an I/O transfer, the channel between the computer and the entire group of disk drives is unavailable until that transfer finishes. This leads to cases where a particular disk drive required by some program is idle, but unavailable, because another disk drive in the same group is using the path.

VM allows more than one channel to be defined between disk drives and the computer. This feature requires that the hardware in the disk controllers support more than one path. When the disk controllers are fully configured, a maximum of eight paths can be available between the computer and any one disk drive. This greatly reduces the time it takes to establish a connection between the disk drive and the computer, which may greatly reduce the total time involved in performing I/O operations. This is particularly valuable in installations that are having excessively high channel busy or controller busy conditions.

Each I/O device has a primary path specified in the DMKRIO system configuration file. Whenever an I/O request is received for that device, an attempt is made to use the primary path. If that path is busy, VM then looks at the first alternate path. If that path is busy, the next alternate is checked. This process continues until either a free path is found, or all alternates have been checked. If all paths are busy, the I/O request is placed in queue, and subsequently runs on the first available free path.

VM has particular sensitivity to the location of certain minidisks that contain system files. Many of the components of the CMS system are disk-resident files that the users access on a single central location. The "S" and the "Y" minidisks contain major portions of the CMS operating system, such as all the disk-resident commands. Each user accesses these two minidisks to execute those commands. If there are a large number of users on the system, the disks containing those two minidisks may develop serious problems with busy conditions.

These two minidisks should never be placed on the same disk drive, and neither should share a disk with any other active minidisk. Some systems have such problems with access to these minidisks that multiple copies of them are kept. This requires building multiple copies of the CMS operating system, but is one way of guaranteeing quick access to the CMS system disks. A general rule is that one set of CMS system disks is adequate for up to approximately fifty users.

Another approach that works very well is to purchase special hardware that contains cache memory, similar to the devices available for paging. These cache devices work extremely well on the CMS system disks, since the disks are both read-only and heavily accessed.

Installing a cache device can have a dramatic effect on CMS system performance if accesses to the "S" and "Y" minidisks were frequently blocked by device busy conditions. The number of device busy blocks after installing a cache device may be one-third the previous level. The cache device may also alleviate the need for more than one CMS system disk, since each set of CMS system disks supports several hundred users.

There are three types of channels that are used in IBM mainframes. The **byte multiplexer channel** is often used for low-speed data transfers such as to card readers or line printers. Each device sends a byte of information per transfer on the channel, with transfers from different devices interleaved, so that devices may transmit simultaneously.

The **selector channel** allows only one device to transmit at a time, but that device transmits large quantities of information. Such a channel is best used with tape drives, which may require a long time before being ready to transmit a block of data, but transmit large amounts of data very quickly when ready.

The most common type of channel, the **block multiplexer channel,** is used with disk drives. It is essentially a combination of a byte multiplexer and a selector channel. It interleaves data from various devices similarly to the byte multiplexer channel, but each individual data transmission consists of a block of data, similar to the selector channel. While a selector channel is devoted to a particular device until it finishes, the block multiplexer channel is only devoted to one device for the duration of that block of data, and may be used by other devices between blocks of data from that device.

There are very few options in configuring the channels on a computer, since certain devices such as disk drives must be placed on block multiplexer channels, but each individual virtual machine can be set up differently. VM simulates a real computer for each virtual machine, so each virtual machine also has simulated channels. These channels default in ways that may be less than optimum for certain virtual machines. In particular, minidisks belonging to a virtual machine may be adversely affected by being configured incorrectly. This does not usually affect the performance of the overall system, but it does affect that individual user.

Virtual channel zero in a virtual machine is a byte multiplexer channel, so any virtual card readers or line printers should be placed on that channel. It is not usually a good idea to place minidisks on channel zero, since they will not perform well. Other virtual channels default to selector channels, which is not a problem as long as only one minidisk is defined on that virtual channel. If multiple minidisks are defined on the same channel, however, that channel should usually be defined as a virtual block multiplexer channel. If the virtual machine is running a guest operating system, it may be necessary to define certain channels as block multiplexer channels in order to have the guest operating system run correctly.

SYSTEMS SECURITY

The VM operating system has a level of security that is approximately the same as many other commercial operating systems. Virtually all areas have some security, but in no area is that security very complex. Almost all security features in VM are implemented with passwords.

Access to the system requires knowledge of both a logon name and a password. Either of these can be from one to eight characters in length, and can consist of either alphabetic or numeric characters. Attempts to log onto the system are controlled, and after a certain number of attempts the user is disconnected. The number of attempts allowed is a parameter that can be set by a systems programmer. Each time the logon limit is exceeded, a record of the event is made, and that record is available to systems programmers monitoring the system. The primary shortcoming of the technique is that, after the logon attempt limit is exceeded and the user disconnected, the same user can then reconnect to the system, and begin trying to logon once more. The same number of attempts to logon are allowed as before.

File security is determined by the passwords assigned to the user's minidisks. If a password does not exist for a particular level of access, then that access is denied. If a password does exist, then it must be known before that level of access is granted. A password of "ALL" specified in the directory for any particular access type allows anyone that access to the minidisk with no password required. Only the read access password is normally specified as "ALL," since write access to a minidisk should usually be carefully controlled.

The only security available on individual files is to specify a file mode of 0 which prevents that file from being accessed by other users. Any file that can be accessed for reading can also be copied or executed.

Software products are available, both from IBM and from independent software vendors, to enhance the security available on the VM system. These products are suitable for increasing the level of security available to the point of satisfying most installations. These products are add-on software packages that control access to both files and the computer, although the emphasis is on file access control.

The IBM security product is called the **resource access control facility** or **RACF.** It improves the computer access control by having facilities that can require the user change his password at certain time intervals, prevent the new password from being any recently-used password, require that the password conform to certain rules, and to record each time a logon access fails. The most important improvement to the normal VM access security is the feature that allows a userid to be suspended after a specified number of logon attempts fail. This prevents passwords from being determined by random combinations of letters.

RACF file access control mechanisms greatly extend the normal VM levels of file access. One feature that is added is departmental control of certain files. Most files have access privileges determined by their individual owner. Some files, however, are used more by a department than by any one individual. RACF allows some files to be departmental files, and to have their access privileges determined by a departmental representative as well as by the actual owner.

Minidisk access is also extended beyond the level normally available in VM. Whereas VM normally allows three different levels of minidisk access, RACF extends those access levels to apply to individual userids or to userids contained within specific departments. For example, this allows a minidisk to be set up that allows write access to the owner, multi-write access to one other userid, read access to all users in the same department, and no access to other users.

Some other security packages extend this same concept even further to apply it to individual files, so that each file may have access determined for certain userids or departments. All worthwhile security packages maintain extensive records, (called **audit trails**), of all accesses to protected facilities and of all failed attempts to access those facilities.

MULTI-PROCESSING

VM is designed to run on either a single- or dual-processor computer. High Performance Option 3.4 has been enhanced specifically to optimize performance on dual processor configurations. VM does not support computers with more than two processors. It can be run on IBM's quad-processor computer, the 3084, but that requires two different copies of VM be run simultaneously. This, in effect, treats the quad-processor computer as two different dual-processor computers.

VM supports dual-processor configurations in both attached processor (AP) and multi-processor (MP) modes. Both processors share the same main memory in both modes, but in AP mode only the primary processor performs I/O operations, whereas in MP mode both processors perform I/O operations separately.

Prefix storage access

Both processors require some area of memory to keep certain critical information such as pointers to systems areas. This area is normally page zero of main memory, but, of course, both processors cannot use the same page zero. This problem has been solved by allocating a **prefix storage area** or **PSA** separately in memory for each processor to use for storing critical information. This area is usually at the top of physical memory, although under certain circumstances it may be located elsewhere.

Each processor uses a separate **prefix register** to resolve memory addresses in the prefix storage area. These prefix registers are used as an offset to the prefix storage area. Whenever a program that is executing on a particular processor references a memory address on page zero, the value in that processor's prefix register is added to the specified memory address, and the new value points into that processor's prefix storage area. The program then accesses the value in the prefix storage area just as though that value were stored in real page zero in a single-processor computer. The prefix registers and prefix storage areas provide what is effectively a virtual page zero for each processor.

Processor communication

There are certain times when one processor must be aware of the status of the other processor, such as when one processor fails. There are three types of signaling mechanisms available in VM to allow the processors to communicate with each other. **Direct signals** are generated when a button is pressed on the computer's physical console, **External call signals** are communications telling the other processor to become aware of something, and **Emergency signals** require an immediate action from the other processor.

System clock

Most computers have internal clocks that are used for various functions. This clock is critical on IBM mainframes because it is used to time and synchronize many critical system functions. Multi-processor configurations frequently provide a separate clock to each processor (these clocks are sometimes called **time-of-day,** or **TOD,** clocks). They maintain the current date and time accurate to a small fraction of a second. When two such TOD clocks exist, they must both have exactly the same value; otherwise, the separate processors may become confused and make errors.

The TOD clocks are checked by VM when the system is first started. If the values differ at the higher levels (such as hours or days), the system halts and requests the operator to enter the correct date and time. If the values differ by fractions of a second, the system automatically synchronizes the two different clocks.

Processor affinity

An option exists in VM to request that any particular program be run on a specific processor. This is called setting **affinity,** because the program can be thought of as having a liking for one particular processor. This is a rarely used option for most installations, since using it without a strong reason may significantly degrade performance. The usual reasons for using this option are an attempt to balance systems performance, such as setting a CPU-intensive program to run in a processor that is doing mostly I/O. The only other reason is if one processor has a special hardware feature that the other processor does not have, but that is required by a particular program.

Memory access

An ongoing problem in any computer with two or more processors sharing the same memory is that of synchronizing memory changes, so that one update to a particular area of memory is completed before another is allowed to begin. A classic case of the problem is where both processors are incrementing a counter. Both processors read the current value, then one processor increments and stores the new value, immediately followed by the other processor incrementing and storing another new value. Since the second processor had read the old value (not the value newly updated by the first processor), that value is wiped out.

Some means of locking memory is necessary to prevent this problem. VM utilizes locking mechanisms that prevent the one processor from updating a value that the other processor is currently updating. This sometimes leads to one processor having to wait while a value is being updated, but the wait time is kept to a minimum by careful programming and the implementation of certain instructions, such as the "test and set" which check the status of the location before changing its value.

Processor scheduling

The most complex issue in implementing multi-processors is the scheduling of tasks and resources. This is an ongoing problem and the efficiency with which it is handled largely determines the success of the operating system. Care must be taken to avoid any deadlock problems, but at the same time, anything that degrades performance must be eliminated. Many of the features implemented in VM for this purpose are those that were discussed earlier in the text.

VM uses **defer locks** and spin locks for scheduling. These locks are set up and maintained by the lock manager. When a defer lock is not available, the lock manager tells the requesting program, thus deferring the request. A spin lock causes the lock manager to continually loop until that resource is available. Spin locks tend to create systems overhead and should be used carefully.

One of the most frequent resources to be locked is the operating system itself. Virtually any operation that updates operating system data, such as queues, must use locks, since that information must not be updated at the same time by more than one section of the operating system, or by more than one processor. Any section of the operating system that uses a lockable resource is called a **critical section.** Such sections should be kept as small as possible, since the resource will be locked while that section is executing.

The operating system must always be careful to avoid the case where both processors try to lock the same resource at the same time. This is relatively easy in the case of peripheral devices, since such devices have a hardware manager that schedules requests. Operating system queues and data areas are kept in memory and must also be lockable.

VM uses many different locks to control resources. One of these locks is an overall system lock called a **global system lock,** while the others are locks designed to lock only one resource. The smaller locks are usually spin locks, while the overall lock is usually a defer lock.

Most parts of CP require a lock since they are manipulating critical information. Because the global system lock is used so often on so many resources, if spinning is required on each of those resources, a significant percentage of the system time will be spent spinning. There are some CP functions that simply cannot wait, and these functions require spinning, but they are kept to a minimum.

The most important of the smaller locks is the **VMBLOK lock.** The VMBLOK is the system control data block that is created and maintained for each virtual machine on the system. It is the primary data area for storing control information about that virtual machine, and so is critical to the functioning of that virtual machine. The VMBLOK lock is a defer lock; if the VMBLOK is not available, the request is deferred until it is available. This lock is required before a virtual machine starts executing in order to prevent the operating system from modifying the VMBLOK while the program is running.

The smaller spin locks have a hierarchy where each lock has priority over the next locks on the list. The top lock is the **real storage management lock.** It forces the accesses to the free list, the flush list, and the paging queue to be serial. In the absence of such a lock, both processors might update these lists simultaneously. It is a spin lock both because the anticipated wait time is short and because access to the paging system information is not usually something that can be deferred.

I/O devices are at the same general level in the locking hierarchy as real storage. Each I/O device has a group of data blocks that allow the system to control that device. By controlling access to these blocks, the locking mechanism controls access to the I/O devices themselves. This lock is also a spin lock and forces all accesses to the I/O control blocks to be done in a serial fashion.

In a multi-processor environment, each processor has its own separate dispatch list. These lists are also lockable, since each processor can access both dispatch lists. Preventing processors from accessing the dispatch list belonging to the other processor would reduce the need for locking the list, but would also reduce the ability of the system to balance the load between the processors. Allowing the processors to access both dispatch lists allows an idle processor to pull a job from the dispatch list of a busy processor, thus improving overall throughput on the system.

There are several other locks which are used to manage various system functions, such as timer interrupts, the run list, and the dispatcher request queue. The hierarchy of the locks is very important since that is how the deadlock condition is prevented from occurring. No processor is allowed to obtain another lock at the same or higher level as a lock it already holds. It can only get a new lock at a lower level in the hierarchy. The locks have been arranged so that no two locks at the same level are necessary at the same time. This effectively prevents the deadlock situation. Since no processor is allowed to obtain a new lock at the same or a higher level, both processors cannot be trying to get the other's lock, since at least one of those locks must be at a higher level than that currently held.

Example 15-9:

THE LOCKING HIERARCHY

Global system lock

Real storage management lock   I/O lock

Dispatch list lock   Run list lock

Timer request lock

Dispatcher request queue lock (2)

Private locks

Free storage lock

Multi-processor performance improvements

The performance of multi-processor computers is much more difficult to maintain than single-processor computers. Consequently, there is a much larger list of items that can potentially improve or degrade the performance of a multi-processor computer.

VM is designed to run on IBM mainframe computers and is therefore designed for optimum performance on those computers. One of the characteristics of some of the large IBM mainframe computers is a special piece of hardware called a **store-in cache.** This is a special type of memory which is much faster than normal memory. It is used for temporary storage of information that has been fetched from the regular main memory. When that information is needed by the processor, it need only go the the fast cache to obtain it, instead of to main memory.

Such a cache is quite small is size when compared to main memory, and is filled with certain special instructions. These instructions are designed so that they operate much faster if only one section of cache need be filled with each fetch from main memory. For this reason, it is desirable that control blocks that are used frequently by the system be able to fit into one section of the cache. There is also less contention between the processors when each processor need access only one section of the cache. For these reasons, each of the most frequently used control blocks in VM has been set up to optimize the usage of the cache.

Providing separate queues for each of the processors also helps their performance. Both the free storage list and the dispatch list are very frequently accessed and modified by running processors. If only one copy of each list exists, then a large amount of overhead is generated in accessing those lists, since each list must be lockable. One of the nice features of separate lists is that each list tends to be accessed by only one processor when the system becomes heavily loaded, since the only time one processor usually needs to access the lists belonging to the other processor is when that processor is idle. As the system becomes more heavily loaded, neither processor will be idle, and therefore no access to the other processor's list is needed. Since such access by the other processor tends to degrade performance because of possibly waiting on a lock, it is most important that such accesses not occur when the system is heavily loaded, while some loss in performance is less important when the system is lightly loaded.

Allowing each processor to look at the dispatch list for the other processor, and to move tasks from that list to its own dispatch list under certain circumstances, also enhances performance. Sometimes the best possible scheduler may not be able to correctly balance the load between the two processors, since it has no accurate way of predicting how long individual tasks may require to either complete or go into a wait-state. In cases such as this, one processor may be busy and have a list of tasks waiting in its queue, while the other processor is idle, and has no tasks left in its queue. It is desirable in such cases that the idle processor be able to inspect the queue of the other processor, and to move tasks from that queue to its own.

NETWORKING SYSTEMS

VM is not noted for extensive networking capabilities. It does have components that provide communications functions, but these features are generally not as advanced as are offered in many other operating systems. Upcoming releases of VM are planned to expand these facilities. VM communications are currently handled almost completely by two different software packages: **Remote Spooling Communications Subsystem** or **RSCS,** and **VM Passthrough Facility** or **PVM.**

Example 15-10:

VM COMMUNICATIONS

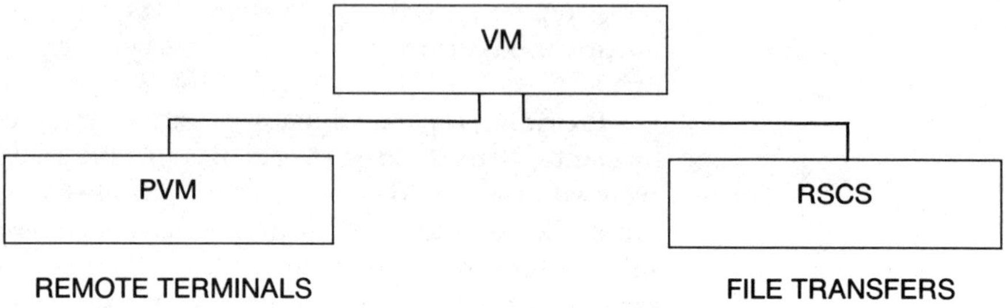

RSCS

The RSCS program is used to perform file transfers from one location to another. A location can be another computer, another user, or a peripheral device. It works relatively well but has several limitations. The basic purpose is to allow remote job submission and output retrieval and it works quite well for these purposes. Jobs can easily be submitted to run on another computer on the network and then have the output sent back to the original node. It does not work as well for generic file transfers, however, since it imposes restrictions that are sometimes a problem.

RSCS runs in a virtual machine under VM. It takes the place of the normal CMS system in that virtual machine. It is actually a small operating system which must be configured in the same way as other systems. It has a nucleus that resides on a minidisk and is invoked by booting that minidisk. A variety of RSCS commands are available, some to general users, and some only to systems programmers.

RSCS is used by identifying files and then sending them with the VM spooling system to the RSCS virtual machine. The identification on the file determines whether it is to be sent to another virtual machine in the same computer, to another computer, or to some peripheral device. RSCS decodes the identification, and forwards the file to the correct destination.

In the case of a large network involving many sites, a file may have to be handled by several different RSCS virtual machines before reaching its ultimate destination. The path the file takes to reach its destination depends upon the physical connections available. RSCS sends the file over the best path available, but sometimes that path may involve several intermediary nodes in the network.

Normal RSCS transmissions use the **binary synchronous communications protocol** or **bisynch.** This is sufficient for transmitting files between strictly IBM equipment, but does not connect well with many of the computer products such as workstations from other vendors. It also does not follow the current IBM SNA standard protocol. SNA support is scheduled for availability in VM in the fall of 1985, after which time the older bisynch protocol will probably tend to fade away.

RSCS operates in an almost completely automatic manner. It can be automatically started shortly after the system is booted and will continue to operate with no intervention required. It is only necessary to manually monitor RSCS if a problem develops somewhere in the network, normally because of the failure of a piece of hardware.

Each element of the network, such as computers or workstations, is regarded as a node in that network. The nodes are divided into two general groups. Nodes that are computers which appear as a peer to the computer on which RSCS is running are called **system nodes,** while nodes that are terminals or workstations which regard the computer on which RSCS is running as a host are called **station nodes.** Station nodes cannot be connected to one another, but must be connected directly to a system node.

RSCS consists of three primary parts: a supervisor, system services, and line drivers. The supervisor monitors and schedules the different functions required of RSCS. It supports many tasks, and is very similar to the scheduler in a normal operating system. The system services section of RSCS provides functions required by the line drivers and the operator. The line drivers provide the communications to each specific node of the network. There is a separate line driver task for each node, although there are only a few common types of line drivers.

RSCS uses the VM spooling system for file transfers when communicating with a virtual machine or with another system node. Sending a file from a virtual machine on one computer to a virtual machine on another computer, especially when the two computers are not directly linked, requires several steps. The virtual card punch in the sending virtual machine is first directed to the RSCS virtual machine on that computer. Then a special tag is set up that is automatically placed on all files punched by that virtual machine. This tag contains both the name of the destination computer, and the destination virtual machine. The virtual machine then virtually punches the file to be transferred. The sending virtual machine is finished at this point, since all succeeding steps are automatic. Care should be taken, however, to ensure that the virtual punch is redirected from the RSCS virtual machine after the last file is sent, since all files punched will go there until the redirection occurs.

The RSCS virtual machine receives that file in its virtual card reader, which is also just another part of the spooling system. As soon as the RSCS machine is not busy it looks at the file in its reader. It deciphers the tag on the file to determine the file's eventual destination. It then searches an internal table to find an available route to that destination. After a route has been determined, it sends the file to the next stop in the route.

If the destination is another virtual machine in the same computer, then the spooling system is used again to transfer the file to that destination. If the destination is a peripheral device attached to RSCS, then RSCS sends the file over the link to that device. If the destination is a directly connected system node, then RSCS sends the file over a communications link to that node. If the destination is an indirectly connected system node, then RSCS determines the best path for the file to travel, and sends it to the next system node on that path. This process continues until the file arrives at its eventual destination.

RSCS uses two different tables, the **link table** and the **routing table,** to determine the path a file should take to arrive at a specified destination. The link table lists all nodes in the network that are directly attached, and specifies which link should be used to reach each of those nodes. The routing table lists the nodes that are not directly attached to this computer, and specifies which directly attached node should be used as the first link in the path to get to the specified node. This table also allows alternate paths to be defined to nodes so that if the primary path is not available, another can be tried.

RSCS is configured for a specific installation by setting up the directory file and the profile files. These files are used to specify the exact configuration of the network, and the way transmissions and nodes are to be handled. The RSCS directory is the primary file for defining the network.

There are several different options available in the RSCS directory. These options are used to specify the name of the local node in the network, which is the node created by this RSCS virtual machine, and to define the characteristics of all the links connected to this node, together with the proper line driver to be used with each of those links. Other RSCS directory features include defining the alternative routes that can be used for accessing other nodes, and defining the userids of users privileged to control the functioning of RSCS.

The RSCS profile is used to automatically start the RSCS virtual machine. Each link in the network must be individually activated before it is usable, although activation usually just requires starting the line driver for that link. Any other RSCS commands can also be placed in the RSCS profile, and will be automatically executed every time RSCS is started.

The various RSCS commands are designed to manage network nodes and files in the network. They allow functions such as activating or deactivating a link, stopping or restarting transmission of a file, changing the characteristics of a file, changing the order in which files are being transmitted, or removing a file from the network.

RSCS commands also allow privileged users to modify the network configuration while RSCS is running. Nodes, links, and routes can be added, changed, or deleted, without requiring that RSCS be shut down. When the physical configuration is changed permanently, the actual configuration files should be changed, so that the new configuration is automatically loaded each time RSCS is started.

Another frequent usage of the dynamic configuration commands is to allow a failing node or link to be bypassed. Sometimes a single link or node may fail, which means that no further communication is possible to that link or node. This is not too important if only one node is lost, but if that node was used as part of a route to several other nodes, then all of those nodes become unavailable. In such cases, it is desirable to be able to set up a new route to those distant nodes, and this route must then be temporarily defined to RSCS.

PVM

The PVM communications system is designed to allow users to interactively access remote computer systems through a local system, as though those users were directly connected to the remote systems. The actual connection is only between the user and the local computer, and that computer then has the connection to the other computers.

There is almost no difference between accessing a remote computer with PVM and actually being connected to that computer. The only detectable differences are that an additional step is necessary at the beginning of the logon process, and the response time is often somewhat slower.

Computer systems that can be connected via PVM include any systems that support a particular type of IBM terminal control units. The system may be running either VM or other IBM operating systems such as MVS, and the connection works equally well with each. Two VM systems may communicate via a PVM system on each VM system, but PVM also communicates with non-VM systems by emulating a remote terminal control unit.

Two different PVM systems communicate with one another using the same communications protocols as used by RSCS. The normal protocol is the bisynch protocol, although a special link, called a **channel-to-channel adaptor,** may be used to link computers that are physically close. All of this is invisible to the user, since all of the user's interactions are with the target system, instead of the local system. Once the remote system is accessed, no further interaction with the local system is necessary.

The PVM system, similarly to the RSCS system, also runs in a dedicated virtual machine under VM. It can be accessed by CMS users whether or not they have logged on. This allows users to access another computer system without requiring a userid on the local computer system.

A PVM network is somewhat similar to an RSCS network in that there two different categories of nodes on the network. PVM nodes are similar to the RSCS system nodes in that links can be made through a PVM node to another node further down the network.

The PVM network is set up by defining the possible links and nodes in the network. The first step in setting up a given link is to determine if the requested node is directly connected. If so, the link can be made immediately. If not, then the tables are searched to see if the requested node exists anywhere in the network. If that node is not defined somewhere in the network, then the connection cannot be made. If the node is available anywhere in the network, then possible routes are searched for links that lead to that node. This search may require checking several different routes in order to determine if any directly connected active links exist that provide a route to the requested node.

Most of the necessary information needed to run the PVM virtual machine is contained in the profile and the configuration file. The profile file is executed when the PVM virtual machine is started. It contains a series of commands, usually commands to start the links that are to be activated automatically. This allows PVM to be started automatically when the system is booted. Manual intervention is only necessary to handle the exceptional cases such as starting a new link or diagnosing and fixing a failing link.

The configuration file is used to specify the configuration of the local PVM virtual machine and the network to which it is linked. It contains essentially the same information as the RSCS configuration file. It defines the node name for this PVM virtual machine, gives a description of the directly connected links, contains possible routes to other nodes, specifies the locations of nodes that require terminal controller emulation, and has a list of the userids that are authorized to use privileged PVM commands.

Both the PVM and RSCS virtual machines can be tuned. These are the two most common virtual machines that suffer from the problem of being communication systems that tend to get paged out just as they need to be in memory.

There are two common steps that are usually sufficient to alleviate these problems. The first is to prevent those virtual machines' pages from being placed on the flush list when that machine begins waiting for an interrupt. The other step is to prevent those virtual machines' from being dropped from the queue when it goes into a wait state. The combination of the two steps keeps the virtual machines in the run queues and their pages in memory, so that it can immediately become active again when the next interrupt is received. These steps reduce the overall system overhead and paging rates and also dramatically improve performance on the virtual machines themselves.

In cases where the virtual machines may still get paged out before the next interrupt is received, it may be necessary to take further steps such as reserving page frames for those virtual machines (perhaps in conjunction with locking certain pages permanently in memory). If pages are to be locked, then page zero of the virtual machine is the best candidate, since it is the most frequently accessed and it has much of the data necessary for the functioning of the RSCS and PVM virtual machines.

SUMMARY

The VM operating system is unique in that it is the only major commercial operating system that allows other operating systems to be run under its control. It can be used both for running one or more other guest operating systems or as an interactive environment with the use of the included CMS single-user operating system.

There are several different implementations of VM, primarily depending upon the computer hardware. These range from VM/PC at the lower end, to VM HPO at the higher end. The user interface to all these different versions, however, is virtually identical, so that the system always appears the same to the user.

The versions of VM that are designed to run on the larger mainframe computers are carefully designed to make optimum use of the features available on those systems to improve performance. One of the primary design goals of the current implementations of this version is optimizing performance on large IBM mainframes.

Some of the performance features include implementing very sophisticated scheduling algorithms and using both paging and swapping to make optimum use of paging devices. Many changes have also been made to the system to improve performance on computers with two processors. One aspect of the improved performance goals is the ability to run the MVS operating system as a guest under VM without any significant performance loss. This has been so successful that it is possible currently to run MVS as a guest under VM with 95% of the efficiency of running that system stand-alone.

There are two primary areas where VM can be developed further. One area is increasing the number of applications and tools available to run under it. There are many such applications available now, but this is an area where VM is eclipsed by many other systems.

The other are where VM should improve is in further support for the new hardware architectures developed. IBM's highest performance computer architecture provides significant growth opportunities, and is clearly the direction IBM is taking for their highest-performance computers and systems. VM, as a full system, does not yet support the XA architecture. There is a version of VM that does support it, but that version does not yet contain full end-user features. This is clearly a direction that IBM will take in the future.

EXERCISES

DISCUSSION QUESTIONS

1. Briefly describe the Virtual Machine concept.
2. Describe the CMS HELP system.
3. Describe EXEC2.
4. Briefly discuss the concept of using an existing VM system to generate a new VM system in one virtual machine.
5. List and provide a short description of the four files that are primarily used to configure VM.
6. Describe the minidisk concept.
7. Discuss how multiprogramming works with virtual machines.
8. Briefly summarize the VM HPO queue system.
9. Compare and contrast paging and swapping.
10. Compare locking page frames, locking pages, and allocating V=R space.
11. List, with a brief description, the three usual VM performance monitoring tools.
12. List four types of data that can be gathered with MONITOR.
13. Describe ways of reducing paging.
14. Describe ways of increasing paging speed.
15. Discuss how to place the CMS system disks for best performance.
16. List and describe IBM channel types.
17. Briefly describe some of the features of RACF.
18. Describe how the prefix storage area is used.
19. Discuss the value of separate queues for each processor.
20. List and briefly discuss the common VM networking products.

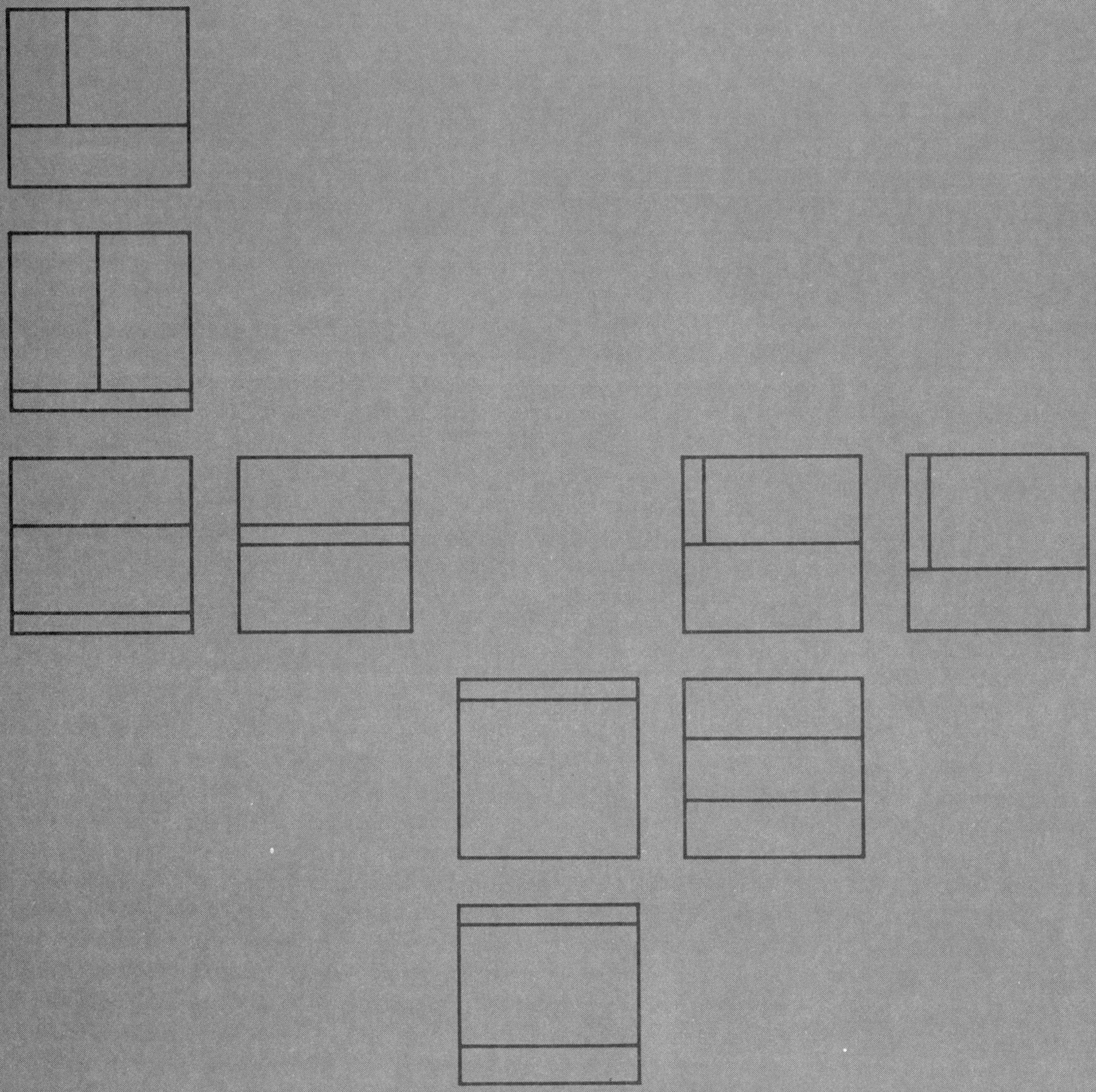

MVS XA Version 2 Release 1.1

16

KEY TERMS

Extended Architecture	*Iogen*
Foreground	*Partition*
Time Sharing Option (TSO)	*Background*
Broadcast messages	*TSO prompt*
Positional operands	*CLIST*
Data Facility Product (DFP)	*PTF*
Distribution libraries (DLIBs)	*Sysgen macros*
APAR	*Data sets*

TSO Structured Programming Facility (TSO/SPF)

Customer Information Control System (CICS)

System Modification Program Extended (SMP/E)

Eligible device table gen (edtgen)

Input/Output Configuration Program (IOCP)

Installation Verification Program (IVP)

KEY TERMS

Partitioned Data Set (PDS)	*Cataloged files*
LIST	*ALLOCATE*
PROTECT	*PDS member*
Address space	*I/O interrupts*
Supervisor	*SVC interrupts*
Restart interrupts	*Dispatching priorities*
System Resource Manager	*Mean-time-to-wait algorithm*
Rotate priority	*Fixed priority*
Dispatcher	*Wait task*
Real Storage Manager (RSM)	*Page backing*
Data Facility Data Set Services (DFDSS)	

KEY TERMS

MultiProgramming Level (MPL)	*Application layer*
Higher page table	*Domain*
Page fix count	*Lower page table*
Monitor I, II, and III	*Top page table*
Common page data set	*Working set*
Local page data set	*Exception reports*
Discrete profile	*PLPA page data set*
Cross memory services	*Generic profile*
Systems Network Architecture (SNA)	*Function management layer*

System Management Facilities (SMF)

Resource Measurement Facility (RMF)

Resource Access Control Facility (RACF)

KEY TERMS

Transmission subsystem layer

Synchronous Data Link Control (SDLC)

Network Control Program (NCP)

ACF/VTAM

INTRODUCTION

The IBM MVS operating system is the operating system of choice for many of the installations using large IBM or IBM-compatible mainframes. IBM concentrated much of their systems development effort on MVS for several years at the end of the 1970's, apparently in an effort to encourage a complete migration to MVS as the only major IBM operating system.

History

MVS is the logical successor to earlier IBM operating systems that were designed primarily for batch processing. The MFT system was one of the earliest of the so-called OS family of operating systems from IBM. It supported many programs but with only a fixed number of tasks, thus the name (Multiple programming with a Fixed number of Tasks). The next member of the family was MVT (Multiple programming with a Variable number of Tasks).

The MFT and MVT systems were followed by the virtual memory systems designed to utilize the virtual memory hardware on the then-new 370 family of computers. The first of these was OS/VS1. This system is actually still in use by many installations, although IBM has stopped enhancing it. It allowed a potential of up to sixteen megabytes of virtual memory to be divided up among all users of the system.

A fixed number of partitions were set up to allow jobs to run in the system. A partition has the memory allocation and operating system facilities necessary to execute a job. Each job must be run in a partition, so the number of simultaneous jobs is limited by the number of partitions available. Each partition has a predefined amount of memory available, and the total amount of virtual memory available on the system is divided up among the partitions. This amount is fixed, and as larger amounts of memory are defined for each partition, the total number of partitions must be reduced.

The more popular member of the VS family of operating systems was OS/VS2, which was a significant improvement over OS/VS1. The first version of OS/VS2 was also called SVS, but this was a rather short-lived precursor to MVS. The primary distinction, at least at the simplest level, between VS1 and MVS is that MVS allows each partition in the system to have up to sixteen megabytes of virtual memory. The total virtual memory available is not sixteen megabytes, but the total of the number of partitions multiplied by sixteen megabytes for each partition.

The MVS operating system has evolved tremendously from its first beginnings as a primarily batch-oriented system, to the current implementation, called MVS/XA. It still has a very highly developed batch system, and many of the jobs run are batch jobs, but it also supports many interactive users through a variety of subsystems. MVS is only used on relatively large computers since the system is so large and complex that there is a significant amount of overhead involved in running it.

This chapter covers the MVS/XA release of MVS, which is clearly the version of MVS that IBM will be primarily supporting in the future. It is also the most major change in the MVS operating system since it was first released, with hundreds of man-years of development effort invested in it. The primary impetus for the XA release of MVS was the fact that the old IBM computer and system architecture was becoming inadequate for current and future needs.

All new computers from IBM that are of sufficient size to allow MVS to run have the necessary hardware support for XA. Both the operating systems and the computer hardware make frequent usage of addresses, so both must be heavily modified in order to change the address size. XA operating systems will not run on computers that do not have the XA hardware support.

Another major change for MVS/XA is greatly increased performance in the I/O system. Many changes have been made in both the hardware and software to improve I/O performance. Much of the processing necessary to handle I/O was previously done only in the central processor, but many of these functions have now been off-loaded to subsidiary processors dedicated just to I/O. Other changes improve the way I/O is handled on computers with multiple central processors, so that an I/O operation started on one processor may sometimes complete on the other processor. This reduces the wait time necessary to complete the operation.

OPERATING SYSTEMS SERVICES

MVS has a tremendous number of features and services available. These services and features are not like those available in the UNIX operating system, for example, but tend to be designed more for applications users instead of software developers.

MVS tends to be the operating system of choice where the primary usage is large applications, such as finance or manufacturing. Many of the services available either help such applications, or are designed to allow such services to be offered. Few, if any, such aids are included with the operating system. They must all be purchased separately, either from IBM or from a third-party vendor.

User interface

The user interface in MVS systems has not traditionally been a strong point. In fact, users have been known to curse the interface. Much of the reason for this is that MVS was an evolutionary step from systems that were primarily intended for batch processing, so the user interface seemed to be added as more of an afterthought. This situation has improved tremendously in recent years, although some might say that more improvement is still needed.

The terminal interface environment and the batch environment tend to overlap considerably in MVS, since jobs can be submitted from the terminal to run in batch mode. The terminal environment is called the **foreground** and the batch environment is called the **background.**

TSO

The user has two ways of interfacing with the MVS operating system: either through the batch system or interactively. The interactive interface uses a part of the operating system called **Time Sharing Option** or **TSO.** TSO serves as the interface between the terminal user and the operating system. It allows the user to enter programs, data, or commands from the terminal.

TSO is not a full-screen system, although many of the applications running under it are full-screen applications. An extension to it, which provides a full-screen interface, is available. This extension is discussed in the next section.

TSO users can send messages to one another or to the system operator. Messages sent between users require that the sending user know the location and userid of the intended receiver. Messages sent to the system operator need only specify the userid of the operator. The operator, or systems programmers, can also send special messages to all users on the system. Such a message need not specify the userid of each user, but can be sent to all users by specifying "ALL" as the destination.

Example 16-1:

TERMINAL COMMUNICATION

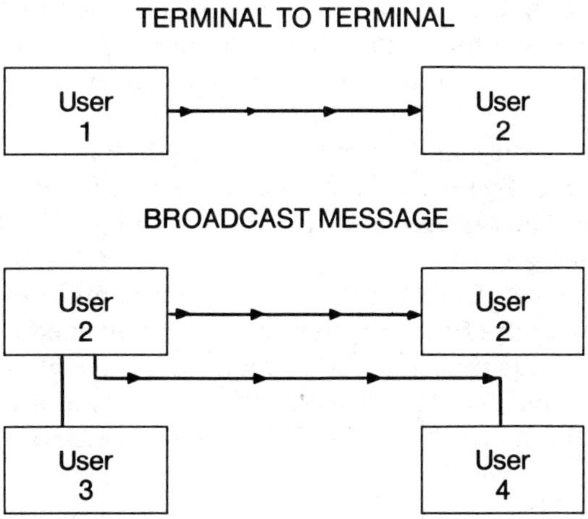

The characteristics of the TSO user interface can be tailored to match the requirements of each user by modifying several parameters. These parameters can have new values assigned for one individual session or for all future sessions. The user can change these parameters by changing a **user profile** which contains the parameter values.

The TSO commands are set up to handle both the novice and experienced user. The commands can be typed in full, which provides a useful mnemonic for the novice user or they can be abbreviated to satisfy the experienced user. The vast majority of commands can be abbreviated. Those commands require that only enough characters be entered to make the command unique. This sometimes requires only one letter, and sometimes four or five letters.

Many of the TSO commands require additional parameters or operands. There are two types of operands used with TSO commands. The **keyword** operand requires that a key word be entered, followed by a value enclosed in parentheses. The key word is some word known to the operating system, and the value in parentheses following it is the value the system assigns to that key word.

The other type of operand is known as a **positional** operand. The value of these operands is determined solely by position. The first value typed in following the command is assigned to the first operand, the second value is assigned to the second operand, etc. Positional operands are best for operands that are entered frequently, since they require fewer keystrokes. Keyword operands are best for operands that are entered infrequently, since tying that key word to its value tends to reduce the number of errors made while entering the values.

A TSO HELP facility is available to provide information about the TSO commands. It provides extensive information about the commands available, including the syntax, the operands, and the function of that command. All of the above information can be provided for a command, or any one of the three categories of information (syntax, operands, and function) about that command.

If a command is not known the HELP facility can still be used, since entering "HELP HELP" gives a list of commands and the syntax used with each of them. The primary disadvantage of the TSO HELP facility is that it is not context sensitive.

The **CLIST** facility is used to store and execute commands from a file. Many of the functions that must be performed regularly consist of a series of commands that must be entered each time, although perhaps with different operands. The CLIST facility allows files to be set up with commands in them, and the complete group of commands is executed by just executing the CLIST file.

CLIST files can have variables defined, so that areas of the file can be changed each time it is executed. Input to the variables can be obtained interactively from the terminal, from another file on disk, or when the CLIST execution is first requested. Some variables are pre-defined by the operating system to provide certain pieces of information, such as the time and date. These variables can be read, but cannot be modified.

TSO/SPF

One of the best parts of the MVS user interface is the extension to TSO, called **Structured Programming Facility** or **SPF.** This is a menu-driven system that is designed to optimize program development time. It has many features to make the user interface much simpler.

Virtually every aspect of the SPF interface is menu-driven, which reduces the amount of knowledge necessary in order to make effective use of the system. Menus provide the interface to the usual compilers, the assembler, the linker and loader, and for the maintenance of libraries, files, and disk volumes. There is also a menu-driven interface to the SCRIPT text processor, which facilitates preparation of documentation.

SPF also has tutorials available on-line for the person who is not able to use even the menus. The tutorial can be studied sequentially in order to provide a complete overview of SPF, or selected portions of it can be displayed as information on a specific subject. The tutorial can be accessed either by a menu selection from the initial menu, or from virtually anywhere within SPF via a special key. The tutorial is context sensitive if selected with the special key.

The primary type of terminal used with IBM systems is the IBM 3270 terminal family. SPF utilizes many of the features of the 3270 to improve the user interface. One such feature is **programmable function keys** or **PF keys** on the 3270. These are single keys that can be assigned a value by the user. Whenever the key is subsequently pressed, it is as if that value is entered. Such values are usually character strings which form commonly used commands.

SPF allows the user to set up the PF keys to perform many of the normal commands in SPF. Most of the commands commonly used in SPF can be set up on PF keys, so that only one keystroke is necessary in order to issue a specific command. The PF keys default settings are a generic set of definitions that are useful for most people.

The editor used with SPF, called **Edit,** is a full-screen editor. It has a group of simple commands that allow the user to perform most common tasks. Many of the commands can be set up on PF keys. The commands in the editor perform all the usual functions, such as searching, copying, moving, and replacing text. There are also several less usual features, such as displaying the text in hexadecimal, or specifying that certain lines in the text should not be displayed even though they are in the file.

One somewhat unusual feature of SPF is the ability to use a **split screen,** which is the same feature that is called windowing on most computers. It splits the physical terminal screen into two different logical terminal screens.

The windows are created by moving the cursor to the line where the division between the windows is desired and entering an EDIT command. The area above the cursor becomes the top window, and the area below the cursor becomes the bottom window. The user can interact with the system from either window by moving from one window to the other.

Most SPF applications can be used in the split screen mode, although only one screen is active at a time. Some applications, such as TSO commands, do not allow the screen to be split while they are active, but they can still be executed after the screen has been split.

There are four basic types of screen formats presented to the user by SPF. The most common display is the **option selection menu** which allows the user to choose one from a number of possible actions. Each option displayed has a number associated with it. The choice is made by typing in the number associated with the desired option and pressing the **ENTER** key. That option may lead to either some action being performed, or to another option selection menu, with another set of possible options.

The **data display** screen format is used to display the contents of a file such as a program listing. The **member selection list** is somewhat similar in appearance to the option selection menu. It displays a list, each item with an associated number, of the members of a library. A member may be viewed by entering the appropriate code on the line that displays that member name.

The **parameter entry menu** allows the user to enter input data to some program or function. The parameters are displayed as labelled fields, and the user must enter information to fill those fields. SPF attempts to predict the values necessary for some parameters, and enters the data accordingly. The user can either leave that default information, or enter corrected information. This prediction is based on the last parameter information entered.

Software tools

The MVS operating system has a very wide range of software tools available. The system and its direct predecessors have been in existence for so long that an incredible number of tools have been developed for them. None of these tools are included with the purchase of MVS, however. The primary emphasis for applications running under MVS is toward those areas which have traditionally required large amounts of processor power or high volumes of data storage, such as financial management and manufacturing packages.

Program development

MVS supports a very complete selection of compilers. These include COBOL, FORTRAN, Pascal, and PL/1. Some of these languages also have more than one compiler; for example, there have been as many as three different FORTRAN compilers supported at the same time. There are also other compilers available, but the above list includes the most used compilers. The assembler for IBM assembly language is included with the operating system, but all of the compilers are extra-cost options.

The source programs can be kept in either normal files or in libraries of files. The compiler or assembler can be invoked from either TSO commands or from batch commands. After the program has been compiled, the object code can also be stored either in normal files or in object code libraries. MVS has both a linker and loader that can be used to actually run the programs. Both the linkage editor and the loader can also be invoked from either TSO or from batch commands.

The linkage editor creates a load module which is stored either as an individual file or as a member of a library. This load module is immediately executable. The linkage editor is available on TSO with the LINK command. The loader, which is available on TSO with the LOADGO command, does not create a load module, but it does perform most other functions of the linkage editor, such as resolving memory references and loading the program into memory to be executed.

Many of the tools available under the MVS operating system are large databases, or other subsystems of similar size and complexity. IBM sells a number of databases, and other vendors supply several more. There are also several offerings that are designed to allow non-sophisticated users to interface with the system to use major applications.

CICS

One of the primary applications available to run under MVS is the **Customer Information Control System** or **CICS.** CICS is designed to provide an interface between the user applications and the operating system for data base and data communications functions. This is a major system which provides many functions that are sometimes included in the operating system itself on other operating systems.

CICS has three major parts. The first, and primary, part is **real-time management functions,** which are very similar to operating system functions. The second part is **real-time system service functions,** which are usually simple and small, but important, functions. These are also very similar to functions performed by operating systems. The final category is **functions that are not real-time,** which is a catch-all for those parts of CICS that are not real-time.

The real-time management functions include such things as task management, storage management, program management, and time management. The resource management done by CICS is on top of any resource management done by MVS. CICS is not managing real hardware. It is managing various items of work in the system, and in this area it serves as a type of front-end processor to the work done by MVS.

Example 16-2: *CICS*

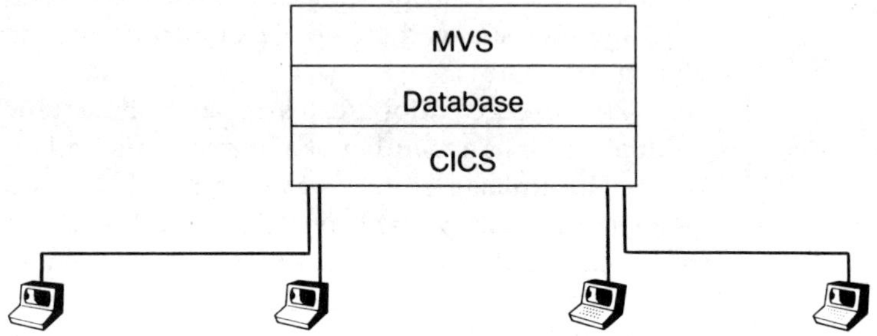

CICS is a transaction-oriented processing system. A transaction is defined as a function with an input and an output. Many of the transactions handled by CICS are from or to the terminal. This is part of the reason for the emphasis on real-time features in CICS. The tasks, storage, program, and time management features provide additional operating system features to application programs. CICS has a large number of macros that can be used by application programs to request and use system functions that would normally either not be available at all or would be much more difficult to use.

The real-time system service functions provided by CICS are used for maintaining the CICS system. They include such things as setting up CICS master or operator terminals, gathering system statistics, and shutting down the CICS system.

The functions of CICS that are not real-time are such things as CICS initialization, which is used to bring the CICS system into operation. Another function is the DUMP feature which formats and prints dumps from CICS.

DFP

One of the newer tools available on MVS is called **Data Facility Product,** or **DFP.** This product is now a major portion of the MVS/XA operating system and encompasses many of the features that were previously offered by a variety of products. It is designed to provide a comprehensive approach to managing data for an installation which is using the XA features of MVS/XA.

DFP has an entirely new method of handling data called **ICF catalogs** which provides an easy and efficient access to the file system. It also provides enhancements in resource locking so that data resource contention is not as high. Additional support is included for the latest versions of cache memory disk controllers which allow such controllers to be used more effectively. Many of the system tools considered in this chapter, such as the backup system, are included as part of DFP.

Systems generation

The systems generation process for MVS is seldom a simple task. A minimal reconfiguration is relatively quick and easy, but any major change or the initial set up of the system is often hard. The basic process consists of setting up the proper modules in the proper libraries.

The system is distributed from IBM on magnetic tapes which contain a basic system, some stand-alone utilities for formatting the disk drives and loading the basic system, and the components of the production system. These components are distribution libraries, or **DLIBs.** The system generation process involves selecting and tailoring modules from the distribution libraries and placing those modules in the proper run-time libraries.

SMP/E

A tool that is critical for either generating or maintaining the MVS operating system is the **System Modification Program/Extended** or **SMP/E.** Any modification that must be done to a major component of the operating system is done with SMP/E. Some systems programmers complain that some modifications are made "in spite of SMP/E" instead of "with the help of SMP/E", but many of the control features that they complain about were designed to provide more reliability in the operating system.

SMP/E requires that the operating system be updated in a controlled fashion. The primary goal is to maintain the reliability of the operating system while it is being changed. SMP/E performs three different types of functions. It chooses which modifications should be applied to the system from a larger group available, it actually does the installation by running the appropriate utility programs, and it keeps a record of every change made.

There are four types of system modifications that are possible. The **APAR** modification is distributed by IBM (usually to only a few customers) to immediately fix some critical problem in the operating system. APARs are designed to be temporary, and are soon superseded by **PTFs.** PTFs are also distributed by IBM, but they are distributed to all installations using that operating system, and are designed to remain in place for a much longer period of time than APARs, usually until the next major release of the operating system.

PTFs tend to be more carefully researched than APARs, and are therefore likely to fix the problem better, and less likely to cause other problems. They are distributed at regular intervals, usually about once each month. The PTF distribution tape is configured so that it only contains modifications for those software components that exist at a particular installation.

Installations with skilled systems programmers sometimes design and install their own modifications to the operating system. This can be either to correct some error or to add an enhancement. This is a process that should be viewed rather critically, since putting such a modification in the system requires a significant amount of knowledge if the system is to be reliable afterward. It also requires that that installation maintain the modification through all future releases of the operating system.

The final type of system modification is a functional modification, which is not designed to fix a problem, but to add some function that did not previously exist in the system. Such modifications may be either in the form of another program to be added to the system, changes to the system itself, or both. Such functional modifications do not happen often (perhaps two to three times each year).

One of the most useful features of SMP/E is the tracking of modification levels. A common problem encountered in modifying an operating system is a modification that is installed may actually pre-date another modification that was already installed on the system. If this happens, then the last modification installed may partially or completely destroy the previous modification, which can cause severe problems. This tends to be a rather difficult problem to solve, since reviewing the documentation shows that both modifications were installed on the system. Even if the documentation does show the date of the modifications, as well as the date they were applied, it is very easy to not notice that the modification with the latest date was not the last one installed. SMP/E tracks modification dates, along with modification installation dates, and generates a warning if an attempt is made to install a modification that was created earlier than a previously installed modification.

The modification record maintained by SMP/E is very useful in cases where a modification is installed, and the system or some functions fail. Frequently the problem is not due to the last modification, but to the combination of modifications installed. The record allows the systems programmer to determine just which modifications were installed, and thus to determine the cause of the problem. The record is also necessary in case modifications need to be removed from the system. Few things are more difficult and frustrating than trying to determine which modifications have been applied to the system, especially if the reason for the search is to determine which modifications must be removed in order to get the system to run.

Many of the components of the operating system that are not installed by the SYSGEN program require individual attention by the systems programmer to install. Much of this process can be automated by SMP/E. Using SMP/E to install these products improves both the efficiency of the installation, and the simplicity.

There are three types of systems generations normally performed on MVS/XA systems. The complete sysgen is done whenever major changes are required to the system libraries. The iogen is used to make changes to the I/O device configuration; it cannot be used to make changes in any area not directly connected with the I/O device configuration. The third type of systems generation is to the **eligible device table** or **edtgen.** This is used to specify the way devices are allocated on the system. An edtgen, similarly to the iogen, cannot be used to make any other changes at the same time. It is not possible, for example, to change the I/O configuration while doing an edtgen, or to change the eligible device table while doing an iogen.

Example 16-3:

SYSGEN TYPES

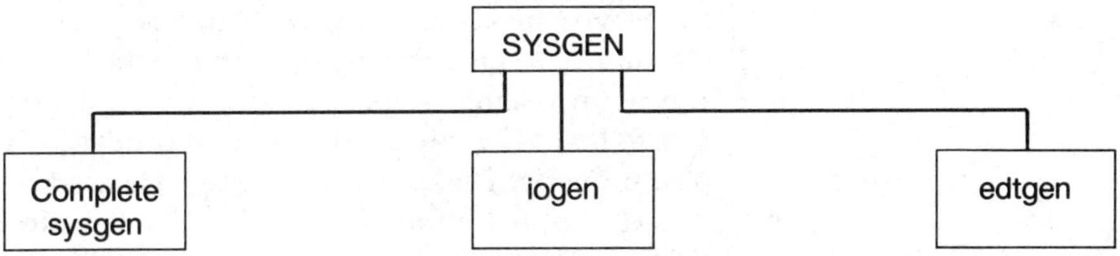

There is a separate part of the iogen process that must also be performed whenever a new I/O configuration is to be installed called the Input/Output configuration program or **IOCP.** The IOCP is required to define the I/O configuration. The normal iogen defines the I/O configuration to the operating system, and the IOCP is necessary to define the configuration to the computer hardware.

IBM computers (as well as many other vendor's computers) are designed with both hardware and microcode necessary to run the computer. The microcode is used to take many functions that were previously locked into the hardware, and make functions into software. That software is loaded into the computer when it is turned on, and is necessary for physical functions.

Most of the recent large computers from IBM have had the configuration process placed more in the firmware than in the hardware. The IOCP sets up the firmware to correctly recognize the physical configuration. It is not necessary on all IBM computers, but it is necessary on the models on which MVS/XA is usually running. The IOCP program is provided in order to make the firmware configuration process easier.

All three types of system generations are done in basically the same way. The distinction between the types is that many of the steps used in the complete sysgen are not needed for the iogen or edtgen. Two distinct stages (I and II) are necessary for all three types of sysgens.

Before either Stage I or Stage II of the sysgen can be started, the systems programmer must carefully study the current system status and determine what steps are necessary to get to the desired system status. Most sysgen options are in the form of **sysgen macros** which must have different values assigned in order to change system parameters. The macros that are to be changed must be selected, along with the new values to be assigned to each macro. These selections must be complete before the first step of the actual sysgen process.

The Stage I sysgen takes as input the sysgen macros that have been previously set up by the systems programmer. These macros are carefully checked for errors. Syntactical errors and some semantic errors are located. If there are no errors found, then those macros are expanded into a series of jobs. These jobs include all necessary job control statements.

Stage I processing is actually one large assembler language program. The sysgen macro instructions are input to the assembler and assembled the same way as an assembler application program. The system libraries must be available to that assembly process, so that the sysgen macro instructions are assembled properly. The output from Stage I is used as input for Stage II.

Most of the effort in Stage I is in determining the exact way to code the sysgen macro instructions. Errors are rather frequent, since any slight mistakes in coding the macros causes an error, but those errors are also usually quite easy to fix. The diagnostic message often points directly to the error, and usually all that is necessary to fix it is to correct a simple error in the way the macro was coded.

The output from Stage I is the list of job control commands, and is used as input to Stage II. Stage II builds the new system. The necessary modules are copied from the distribution libraries into the correct run-time libraries. If necessary, some of those modules may be re-assembled and link-edited to form new modules.

Stage II consists of a linked series of jobs that must be run to create the correct libraries. The number of jobs necessary varies depending upon whether a complete, or partial, sysgen is being done. A complete sysgen requires seven different jobs, while an iogen requires only five jobs, although the sequence is the same for both sysgens.

The jobs in Stage II create all the necessary files and libraries to allow the system to run normally. Each job in the sequence creates or updates a particular file or library, so if an error occurs on one job it is usually possible to re-run just that job, or at least just that job and the jobs following it in the sequence. The last job in the sequence is the one that activates the new system, so it should be run only if all other jobs in the sequence have run correctly.

Stage II errors are frequently not readily apparent; in fact, some of them may not show up until the system is tested. When the error is determined the resolution is still sometimes quite complex, since Stage II errors tend to be more conceptual mistakes than just coding mistakes.

The final step in any systems generation process must be testing to ensure that the final product works as planned. The MVS system includes an installation verification program or **IVP** which checks out the functions of the products in the system. This is not, of course, an all-inclusive test, but it does ensure that the major functions of all the products work as planned.

The IVP programs should be run after either a complete sysgen, an iogen, or an edtgen. Separate parts of the IVP are available to test just the I/O configuration or the eligible device table without requiring the entire IVP to be run. The final test of any system, of course, is running the programs that are normally run at that installation, so a selected group of application programs should be run in addition to the IVP after any major change.

FILE SYSTEMS

The file system in MVS provides a wide variety of different file types. There are probably more different types of files in MVS than in almost any other system. Many of the file types are designed to optimize performance for large applications. One reason for the wide number of file types is that MVS includes support for many of the file types used with earlier OS operating systems as well as support for the newer file types.

Files in MVS are almost always called **data sets.** Specifying a file for use by an application usually requires the name of the file, and the name and type of the volume on which the file resides. Files that are referenced frequently can bypass the requirement for specifying the volume by being **cataloged.** Cataloged files have an entry in a catalog set up, so that when the file is referenced by name, the system can automatically locate the associated volume information.

The same files, and file conventions, are supported under both TSO and the batch system, although there are some areas where the TSO conventions are somewhat more strict than the batch conventions. The same files are accessible both through TSO and the batch system, since all files are placed in what is, effectively, a large pool of disk area.

File names can be a maximum of 44 characters long. Each file name is divided up into sections called **qualifiers.** The qualifiers are joined into a file name by periods. Each qualifier can be from one to eight characters in length, and can contain either alphabetic or numeric characters, although the first character of each must be alphabetic.

Example 16-4:

SAMPLE MVS FILE NAMES

JONES.TEMP.DATA
USER1.MYPROG.FORTRAN
SMITH.APPL.WEEKLY.DATA
KERI.TEMP

TSO supports wild-card specifiers in the file names. The asterisk is used to specify any number of characters at that location in the file name. Wild-card specifiers can be used in each qualifier in a file name. They can also be used in conjunction with specified characters as part of one qualifier. For instance, "*TEMP.DATA" specifies all files with a type of "DATA", a name qualifier ending in "TEMP", and starting with any characters.

Files used with TSO should follow certain naming conventions, although they are not always forced. TSO files normally have three qualifiers. The first qualifier is the userid of the TSO user, the second is the name of the file, and the third shows the type of file. Thus, all files for a given user should begin with the same qualifier. This allows easy identification of the files belonging to that user and also prevents a file being accidentally named the same as another file belonging to someone else.

The userid qualifier is not needed when specifying the file name on many TSO commands, since the assumption is made that the userid qualifier is the same as the logon userid. In fact, if access to a file which has a different first qualifier is required, then the file name must be specified with quote marks to indicate a non-standard file access. The file name qualifier is completely free, and can be anything. The file type qualifier should usually reflect the type of the file, such as PASCAL for Pascal programs.

New files are created with the **ALLOCATE** command. This command allows the user to create new files or change the access to an existing file. Several different parameters involved in creating a new file allow the user to specify how much space the file can use, a particular disk on which the file must be placed, and whether or not the file is to be retained at the end of the current session. Another option allows the user to model the characteristics of the file after another file that already exists.

The ALLOCATE command can also be used to change the access granted to an existing file. The access granted is only for the duration of the current job. It is in three levels. The first level is to share the file with other users. The second level is for exclusive access, and the third level, which requires exclusive access, allows additional records to be added to the file. The ACCESS command can also concatenate two data sets; the concatenated data sets are not linked, but they can be referenced with a single name.

Whenever a file is created, the disposition of that file at the end of the access must be specified. The system allows the user to retain the file (KEEP), to erase the file (DELETE), to keep the file and put the file name into a catalog for future reference (CATALOG), or to remove the file name from a catalog (UNCATALOG).

A wide variety of file types is available in the MVS file system, including ISAM, VSAM, sequential, and partitioned. Discussing and understanding some of these file types such as VSAM can take up an entire book, so only the simpler file types are discussed here.

One rather unusual file type that is available on both batch and TSO is the library. This is called a partitioned data set or **PDS** and is used to store programs similar to UNIX libraries discussed in chapter 14.

PDSs are normally used to store related program source files or object files. A partition in a PDS is called a **member.** A particular member of a PDS is specified by following the PDS file name with the member name, enclosed in parentheses. For example:

```
MYUSER.PDSFILE(MYMEMBER)
```

The PDS file name is "MYUSER.PDSFILE" and the member name is "MYMEMBER".

Files can be renamed or copied in quite simple ways. The RENAME command just requires that the old and new file names be specified in order to change the name of a file (or files, if wild-card specifiers are used). The COPY command is used to copy files, and also just uses the old and new file names. It can be used to change some of the characteristics of a file by copying it to a new file with different characteristics. It can also be used to copy only selected portions of a file.

Several different types of information can be displayed about any file. The primary command to display this information is the LIST command. There are four different variations of the LIST command. The simple LIST has as an operand the name of a file, and it displays the contents of that file on the terminal. The LISTALC command shows a list of files currently allocated for that userid. The LISTCAT command shows which programs are currently in a specified catalog.

When using the LIST command to display the contents of a file contained in a PDS, it is necessary to specify the member name as well as the PDS name. If the member name is not specified, the contents of each file in the PDS are displayed. Many files can be displayed with the LIST command by specifying the file names surrounded by parentheses and separated by commas. The LIST command can also be used to display specific lines or columns in a file.

The LISTDS command is used to display specific information about a file or group of files. Wild-card specifiers can be placed in any qualifier of a file name to be displayed, so that all files fitting the criteria are displayed. The following are some of the items that can be displayed with the LISTDS command:

- The member names in a PDS
- The date the file was created
- The name of the volume that contains the file
- The structure of the file (record length, block size, etc.)
- The type of file (ISAM, PDS, etc.)

Files can be erased rather easily by using the DELETE command. The person issuing the DELETE command must, of course, have ownership of the file to be erased. If the file is cataloged, care must be taken to ensure that the file name is removed from the catalog; otherwise, the catalog may fill with names of files that no longer exist.

Files can have a **retention period** specified when they are created. The retention period is the length of time that file is scheduled to be needed. The creator of the file can specify that the file is to be automatically erased at the end of the retention period, with no intervention from the user required. Files are not usually erased during their retention period, although it can be done by specifying an option on the DELETE command. The date of the end of the retention period is called the expiration date.

Some file system security exists, and can be used without requiring any additional security software. The complete level of security is available with commercial software packages such as RACF.

The PROTECT command is used to specify the level of security desired for a particular file, to assign a password to the file, to change the password, or to report the number and type of accesses to the file. There are four levels of security available. The user can allow read access with no password, read access with a password, write access with a password, or no write access at all, or various combinations of these accesses. Curiously enough, the condition of read with no password in combination with no write access is not allowed. If it is specified, then the system changes it to read with no password and write with password.

The number and type of accesses to any protected file can be reported by using the LIST command. It requires the file name and file password to provide the information. The PROTECT command can also be used to add or replace a password on a file. If the password is to be replaced, then the old password must be specified. The add and replace functions require the ADD and REPLACE operands on the PROTECT command.

File Backup

There are a multitude of packages designed to perform file backups and restores on MVS. The newest and best is the package called **Data Facility Data Set Services** or **DFDSS.** DFDSS provides backup and restore functions as well as disk compaction to reduce fragmentation.

The backup and restore operations are set up so that many different combinations of dumps and restores can be done. Many options are available in order to reduce the amount of data dumped. Some options include:

- Dump the entire volume
- Dump only the files that have changed since the last backup
- Dump only the space used instead of all space
- Dump only specified files with various criteria
- Compress the data when dumping
- Dump only a specified area of the disk

Most of these options are self-explanatory; however, a further look at the criteria possible when specifying which files to be dumped is useful. Some of these criteria are:

- Dump by creation date
- Dump by expiration date
- Dump for changed files
- Dump by last referenced date
- Dump by name with wild-card specifiers allowed in file qualifiers.

The restore operation has many of the same options as the dump operation. It allows a subset of the dumped data to be restored so that a full dump can be completely restored or only specified areas on the disk can be restored. A partial dump can be completely restored or only a subset of that partial dump can be restored. A dump done by file names can restore any one or group of files. Just one area out of a particular file can be restored if that area on the disk is known.

A very useful feature of the restore operation is that files can be restored with a new name. There are many cases when an old copy of some file is needed, but the current copy is also needed and the name of the current copy cannot be changed. Restoring the file with a new name allows both copies of the file to exist simultaneously on the disk without requiring that the current copy be renamed.

The DEFRAG command can be used for either reducing or reporting fragmentation on a disk volume. The reporting facility shows the number and size of the free areas on a volume. If the sizes of the free areas are small, and the number of such areas large, then fragmentation is a problem on that volume.

Fragmentation can be corrected by using the DEFRAG command to move files around on the volume. A file that has several pieces scattered across the volume is moved so that those pieces are grouped into one contiguous location. If this is done for each file on the volume, then the remaining free space must also be grouped into one contiguous area which allows any new files to be allocated in one contiguous area.

Some files are tied to a particular location on a disk volume. This is a relatively unusual occurrence, but it does happen. These files cannot be moved, so the DEFRAG operation cannot be run on them. The DEFRAG command, however, allows certain files to be excluded from the consolidation operation, so that any file that cannot be moved is not affected.

MULTIPROGRAMMING

MVS has complete support for running many programs at once. Some of the features that support multiprogramming are also used to support the multiprocessing requirements, since both require careful management of resources.

Each task that is in the MVS queues, whether or not it is paged in at the time, has an **address space** allocated to it. An address space is the allocation of memory that is necessary for any task to be executed. This includes both areas used by the program itself, and areas used by the operating system but included in the space allocated to the task.

Each virtual address space can be a maximum of two billion bytes in size. It is divided into two or four parts, depending upon whether any of it extends above sixteen megabytes in memory. The common area is shared by many address spaces and is not physically part of the address space. This area contains system values such as queues and pointers that are necessary to actually execute the task. The private area contains the application as well as any system areas that are unique to that particular task, and therefore cannot be shared with other address spaces.

Address spaces that extend above sixteen megabytes have a part both above and below that line. The common and private areas exist below the line, as is usual, but there are also extended common and private areas above the line. These areas are configured very similarly to the areas below the line. The same information is usually not duplicated, but the same areas are.

Example 16-5:

ADDRESS SPACES

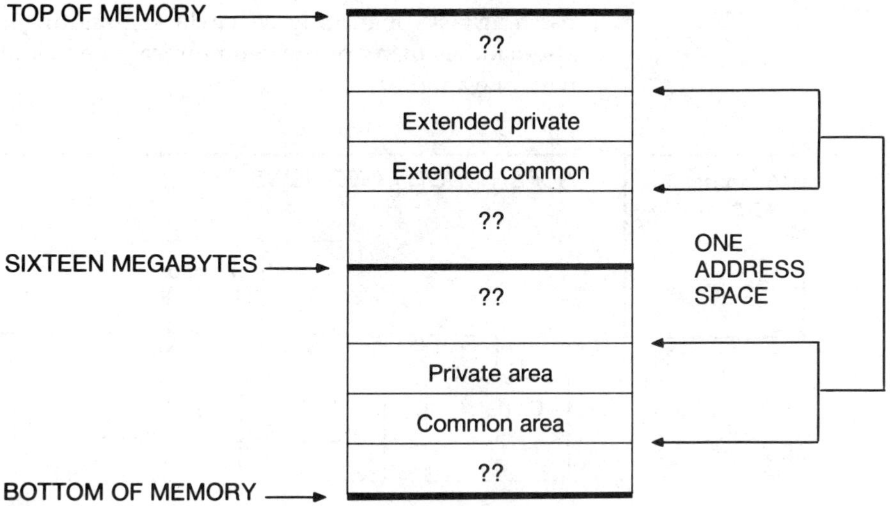

The system queues that control the scheduling of tasks are concerned with address spaces instead of with individual tasks, since the entire address space must be available before the individual task can execute. There are several times during the discussion of MVS where the terms "address space" and "task" can almost be used interchangeably.

A request or program is submitted to be executed (this program is called a job). Each job is divided into smaller jobs, each of which is called a "job step" or just "step". An example of a job is the compilation, linking, and executing of a program. Each of the parts of the job (the compiling, the linking, and the executing) is a job step. This job step is usually, but not always, explicitly called out by the user.

One of the primary characteristics of the XA version of MVS is its support for much larger virtual addresses than with non-XA versions of MVS. Previous versions of MVS were restricted to addresses that could be contained in twenty-four bits (sixteen megabytes), but the XA version supports addresses of up to thirty-one bits (two billion bytes).

Tasks in MVS/XA can run either in the older, 24-bit mode, or in the newer, 31-bit mode. Tasks running in 24-bit mode can only address memory up to sixteen megabytes. If any resources are required from memory areas above the sixteen megabyte line, the operating system must provide a way to get those services without requiring the task to address that memory.

These operations, as well as other internal operations in the MVS operating system, are handled by a group of programs that can loosely be called the **supervisor**. Some of the functions performed by the supervisor include dispatching tasks, managing system locks, handling interrupts, and scheduling. It also handles many of the communications that allows tasks to communicate with one another.

Example 16-6:

SUPERVISOR FUNCTIONS

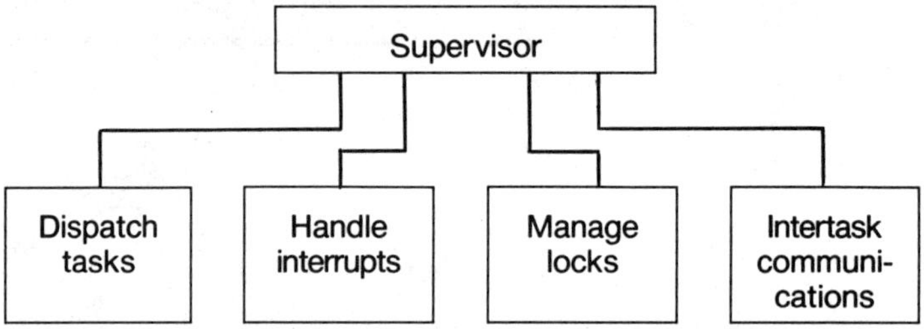

The group of supervisor facilities designed specifically to implement multiprogramming and multi-processing is called **service management.** Service management is concerned with providing requested services by setting up service requests and processing them as quickly as possible.

The service request is actually a control block called a service request block or **SRB.** The SRB contains enough information to allow the request to be satisfied. It is presented to a scheduler, which enters it into a queue of requests to be serviced. When the request has been filled, it is purged from the system.

Interrupt handling

The way interrupts are handled is important to the overall performance of the operating system. Many events within MVS are driven by interrupts, so any inefficiencies in this area quickly become critical. Several different routines are used to process interrupts. There are five different major types of interrupts used in the MVS system.

Program interrupts are very common. They are generated by a program, whenever a page fault occurs, event monitoring is requested, or a program error occurs. The type of program interrupt is determined first, and then appropriate routines are called.

I/O interrupts are also very common. An I/O interrupt is generated whenever an I/O device changes status, such as when it completes a data transfer.

MVS's I/O supervisor handles I/O operations. The I/O interrupt handlers generally just identify the type of the I/O interrupt and branch to the I/O supervisor with the appropriate information.

External interrupts are primarily interrupts generated for processor timer synchronization and processor failures. Each of the different interrupt sources has its own routine, and the external interrupt handler branches to the appropriate routine as soon as the cause of the interrupt has been determined.

SVC interrupts are generated each time the SVC call instruction is executed. The interrupt handler determines the type of service requested, and then branches to the appropriate routine to provide that service.

Restart interrupts are generated whenever the computer operator uses the computer restart command, or whenever the operating system restarts one processor in a multi-processor configuration. This interrupt is only used to start a processor after the system has been inoperational for some reason. The interrupt handler branches to the recovery management routines.

Example 16-7:

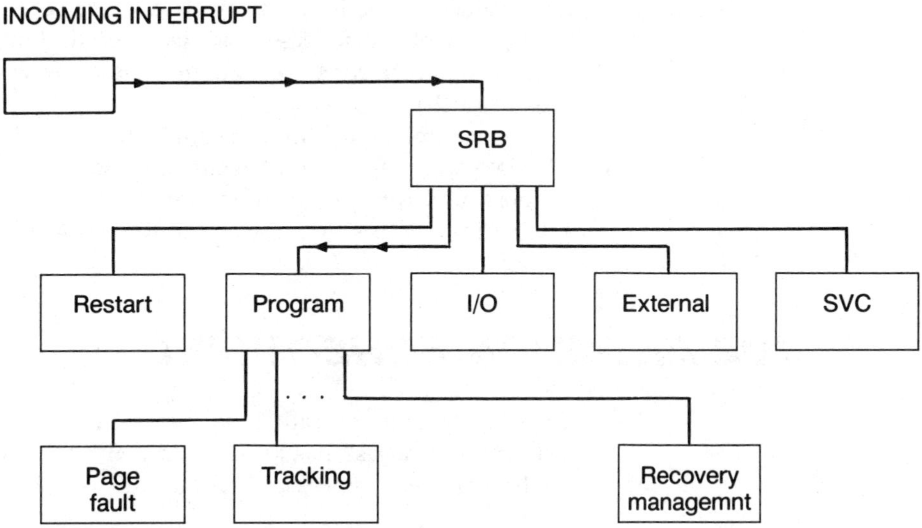

Locking resources

MVS uses locks on critical system resources in order to force serial use of those resources. The potential deadlock problems are much more severe in MVS than in many systems since it is designed to run on computers with more than one processor. The same locking mechanisms that are used to prevent deadlock in the multiprogramming case with a single processor are also used for the same purpose with multi-processors.

Priorities

Much of the management of tasks in the MVS system is done by assigning priorities to each task. Most of the priority changing is handled by the **system resource manager** or **SRM** which also handles many other critical functions such as swapping. SRM is one of the most important parts of the MVS operating system since it handles virtually all critical system resources.

Each address space has a priority assigned to it. A fixed priority is where an address space is initially assigned a priority and that priority is never changed. The range of priorities is 0 to 255. The more common case is to have the priority vary as the task and system characteristics change. Three different algorithms are used for calculating priorities in MVS.

The **mean-time-to-wait algorithm** is frequently used, particularly for interactive tasks. This algorithm lowers the priority for an address space as the task in that address space uses a higher percentage of processor time. The system records the length of time each task uses the processor before entering a wait state. That value is considered the mean-time-to-wait, and the average of those values is used in the mean-time-to-wait algorithm. As the value goes up, the priority of the address space is lowered. Since interactive users use relatively little processor time, and are frequently waiting, they tend to get very high priorities.

The second algorithm is a simple system called **rotate priority,** where an address space is allowed to execute at certain specified time intervals. This is a simple round-robin algorithm where each address space in that group is given a turn in the processor at the end of some time period.

JOB AND TASK SCHEDULING

The MVS scheduler is called the **dispatcher.** The processors do not execute any task unless that task has been scheduled by the dispatcher. The dispatcher is used whenever a processor becomes idle or whenever a task needs processor time.

Three basic types of requests are presented to the dispatcher, each of which requires some processor time. The first type is **special exits** which usually relate to a processor or timer condition. The second type is service requests which are indicated by SRBs. The last type is tasks which are indicated by **task control blocks** or **TCBs.** Whenever the dispatcher dispatches the next element of work, it must check several queues which correspond to these three types of work.

The top priority item of work is any of the special exits. The dispatcher does not have a queue for special exits, since they are really just a flag that tells the dispatcher to perform some special function. When the flag corresponding to a particular special exit is set, the dispatcher takes that exit which causes some action to be performed (such as bringing a processor online).

There are two system queues relating to **global service requests,** which are service requests relating to more than one address space. The two queues are called "global service management queue" and "global service priority list". An element of work is represented in one of these queues by an SRB. SRBs normally go first into the management queue, and from there into the priority list. The dispatcher only takes SRBs from the priority list for access to the processor, so a SRB must be moved into the priority list before actually being dispatched to the processor.

Local service requests can be handled after the global requests have been satisfied. There is a **local service management queue** or **LSMQ** that is available primarily for compatibility purposes. Any SRBs on the LSMQ are moved into the queue in the address space in which those requests are to be dispatched.

The current release of MVS/XA has a separate LSMQ for each address space. Each address space also has a **local service priority list** or **LSPL** which is the queue from which the tasks are dispatched to the processor. These two queues, the LSMQ and LSPL, are exactly analogous to the similar global queues.

The order used by the dispatcher is to first handle special exits, then global SRBs, then moving any local SRBs from the special LSMQ to the appropriate address space LSMQ. Once this has been done, the highest priority address space which has work waiting is actually dispatched.

Example 16-8:

DISPATCHING ORDER

1) Special exits

2) Global SRBs

3) Move local SRBs from special LSMQ to an address space

4) Dispatch highest priority address space

Each address space has a hierarchy of possible work that is somewhat similar to the overall order of dispatching. The first queue checked is the LSPL. If there are any service requests in this queue, they are dispatched before anything else. If there are no requests in the LSPL, then the LSMQ is searched. The highest priority request in it is then dispatched.

If no dispatchable work exists in any of the queues, the next candidate is any local resource lock holders. Since the local lock may be held by a task in another address space, that task may be the one that is dispatched. The holder of the local lock may not be ready to execute, or there may not be a holder of the local lock, in which case the dispatcher continues to the next step.

The next step is to search for any work that does not already have a local lock. The TCBs in that address space are searched to find any TCBs that are ready to execute but have not yet been allowed to execute. If the TCB selected requires the local lock, the dispatcher will attempt to get it, and give it to that TCB.

Example 16-9:

ADDRESS SPACE DISPATCH ORDER

1) LSPL
2) LSMQ
3) Local resource lock holders
4) Executable TCBs

Once the list of TCBs in that address has been searched without finding any work waiting, the dispatcher then drops that address space, and begins the same sequence again with the address space having the next highest priority. If all address spaces are searched without finding any work waiting, then another search is made of all the SRB queues.

After the second search of the SRB queues has been made without finding any work, it is safe to assume that no work is waiting anywhere in the system, so then the **wait task** is dispatched. The wait task is basically a null task that does nothing more than serve as a place-holder while the system is waiting for some work to become available.

MVS dispatcher summary

There are three levels of action in the dispatcher. The first level is to handle any special exits, the highest priority elements of work in the system. The next level is to process any global service requests. After the special exits and global service requests, the local request and tasks in specific address spaces can be handled. Each address space has a priority, and the highest priority address space is dispatched first. Within the address space, service requests are handled first, followed by normal tasks. If no work exists anywhere in the system, then the system is placed in a wait state until work becomes available.

Address spaces are given a priority that is used to determine when that address space is given control of the processor. The range of priorities available is from 0 to 255. These priorities are divided into sixteen sets of sixteen each. The sixteen priorities within each set are further sub-divided into three more categories, based on the performance characteristics of the address spaces. The three categories are mean-time-to-wait, rotate, and fixed. The categories are given different priorities, with the mean-time-to-wait having the lowest priority, and the fixed having the highest priority. Within the category, of course, the priorities still vary in a normal fashion.

VIRTUAL MEMORY

The real memory in a computer running MVS is controlled by the **real storage manager** or **RSM.** The RSM is a virtual storage system that tries to optimize usage of the physical memory available. The paging I/O is done by the **auxiliary storage manager** or **ASM.** Many of the paging activities are initiated by the system resource manager, when some group of pages must be paged out in order to better utilize system resources.

Memory management functions in MVS are dedicated almost exclusively to the virtual memory system. All real memory is handled by the virtual memory system. Real memory is handled somewhat differently above the sixteen megabytes than it is below.

A certain amount of the real memory must be dedicated to the operating system itself. The nucleus, along with certain critical system tables, comprises the fixed portion of system memory. Each address space also has associated tables, and these tables (along with any pages fixed in memory that belong to that address space) comprise the variable amount of memory requirements that must always be in memory.

The virtual memory system in MVS uses both paging and swapping algorithms. Either pages or whole address spaces can be paged in and out. When the complete address space is swapped out, the pages freed up can either be used for normal paging or for an address space that was previously swapped out.

Paging

The memory system in MVS/XA is divided into pages with 4096 bytes. A term that is encountered frequently in studying the MVS paging system is **page backing.** This is the process of placing the correct values in the control blocks and setting the protect key in a page frame to validate the page that has just been placed in that frame. The page is not recognized until the backing has been completed.

The process of paging requires extensive tables of information be maintained about each of the pages in memory. Each **page table** contains entries for

256 pages. The page table itself is exactly one page in length. The information contained in the page table is sufficient to allow a reference to a virtual page to be translated into an access to a physical page.

Since each page table refers to 256 pages, each of which is 4096 bytes in length, the amount of memory referred to by a page table is one megabyte. This one-megabyte piece of memory is called a **segment.** A segment fault occurs when a reference is made to a page contained in a segment, and the page table for that segment is not ready for use.

Segment faults are usually caused by an inability to find all necessary page tables. Since the page tables themselves are contained in virtual memory, there is no guarantee that a given page table will be in memory when an access is made to the segment controlled by that page table.

There are three different levels of page tables available in the system. The **lower page table** follows the normal concept of a page table, that is, it contains the entry for the page in question. The **higher page table** is the page table which has the entry for the page containing the lower page table. The **top page table** contains the entry for the page containing the higher page table. Any access to a page may not be possible if the lower page table containing the entry for that page is itself paged out, and it may not be possible if the higher page table containing the entry for the lower page table is paged out.

In the following example, page table "A" is the lower page table, page table "B" is the higher page table, and page table "C" is the top page table.

Segment table entries are regarded as valid or invalid depending upon whether it is possible to actually access the page table for the page in question. If the page table is not accessible, it is usually because the page containing it is paged out or is in the process of being paged out.

Segment faults result from a page fault where the page table needed is not available. The system attempts to find the page table needed. The page table is usually found, however, and made available to the requesting task. Control is then returned to the task that generated the segment fault, and a new attempt is made to access the page needed. A page fault, instead of a segment fault, occurs this time, and is handled by normal page processing.

Example 16-10:

PAGE TABLES

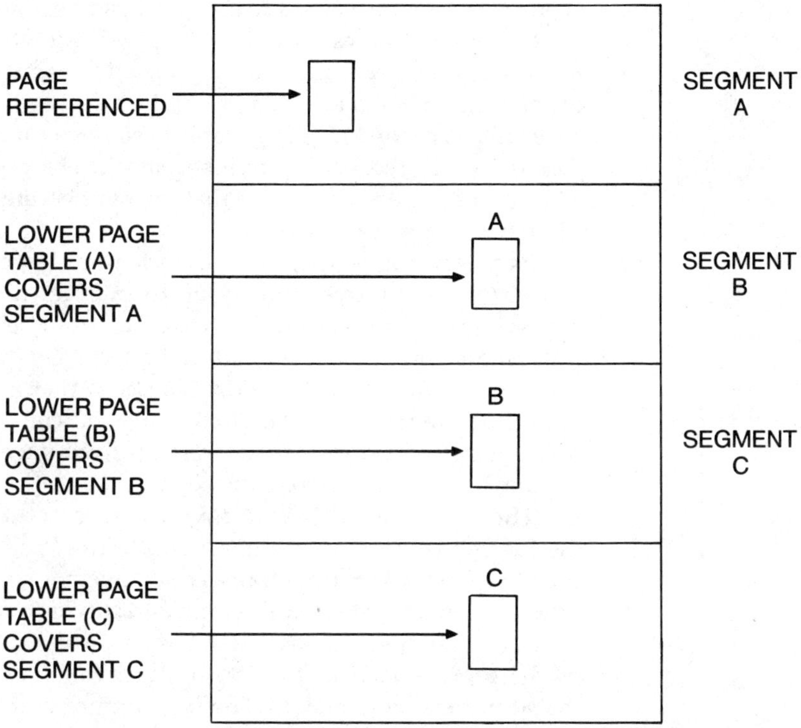

Segment faults must be kept to a minimum in order to optimize system performance. One way to do this is to reduce paging for any page that contains page tables. Top page tables are normally never paged out. Higher page tables are also rarely paged out, although they may become temporarily unusable. A higher page table may not be accessible if the lower page tables it references do not contain any entries pointing to pages actually in memory. Lower page tables, however, are subject to the usual paging algorithms.

Lower page tables should not be paged out when they point to pages that are being referenced. Each lower page table has associated with it a **page fix count,** which is used to keep track of the number of active pages for which that page table is needed. The page table becomes a candidate for paging when the page fix count associated with it becomes 0. The page fix count is incremented whenever a page referenced in that segment becomes active, and decremented whenever pages cease activity.

Page stealing is the process of reclaiming page frames that currently contain pages. Page frames containing fixed pages cannot be stolen, since those pages cannot be paged out. The page frames to be stolen are chosen with the LRU algorithm. The calculations that select page frames are explained below.

The working set of an address space is that group of pages that must be available in memory in order to optimize efficiency. MVS builds the working set for a specific address space from all fixed pages and any non-fixed pages that have been recently referenced.

The paging algorithms in MVS use several different functions to achieve the highest possible performance level. The "page replacement" function is used to keep track of page frames that have not been referenced recently. This function runs at fixed time intervals and checks for page frame references since the last time it ran. Any page that has been referenced has its counter reset to 0 by the page replacement function. Pages that have not been referenced have their counters incremented. The page frames with the highest counter values (those which have not been referenced for the longest time) are flagged as candidates for replacement.

The paging algorithms attempt to maintain a list of available page frames. When this list gets too short more page frames must be added. The "real page shortage prevention" function is designed to maintain the list of available page frames. When the list falls below the minimum amount, this function steals page frames from users and the system areas. The page frames stolen are those that have been identified by the page replacement function as having been unreferenced for the longest time. It continues stealing page frames until the available page frame list is above minimum size.

The "pageable real storage shortage prevention" function is designed to prevent the amount of pageable page frames from getting too small. It calculates a ratio of fixed page frames (those which cannot be paged out for some reason) to the total page frames in the system. When this ratio becomes large it means that a significant percentage of the page frames in the system cannot be paged out, which may lead to thrashing in the remaining page frames.

This function can do several things to alleviate the problem of too many fixed page frames. A common thing is to swap out the user with the highest number of fixed page frames. These page frames cannot be paged out, but usually can be swapped out with the entire user. The function can also prevent new address spaces from forming or swap out other users.

Swapping

There are several terms used by MVS to characterize aspects of the swapping process. A **domain** is a group of address spaces that have similar performance characteristics. One example of a domain is all the TSO users. The number of users in a given domain who are occupying real storage at any given time is called the **multi-programming level** or **MPL.**

Each domain has an MPL and there is a separate MPL value for the overall system. The resource monitor function of SRM runs periodically and determines the correct MPL values for each domain and for the overall system based on the characteristics of the address spaces and the configuration of the computer. The actual MPL values are then adjusted accordingly.

The resource monitor part of SRM determines the best MPL for each domain, and then the swapping algorithms attempt to maintain that MPL. The decision of whether or not to swap a specific address space is made after analyzing the MPL, the performance characteristics of each address space, and system resource consumption for each address space.

The swapping analysis has a sequential list of options. Each option is tried, and the first option that results in a swap being performed terminates the list. The first option considered is to swap in deferred tasks. Deferred users are those users who should have already been swapped in, but were not because of insufficient available pages.

The second step is to swap out some users. Any domain that has more users than its MPL is eligible to have some of those users swapped out until the number of users matches the MPL. Those users that are selected to be swapped out are those with the smallest **recommendation values** (RVs), which shows those users most suitable for swapping out.

The third step is to attempt to swap in **express users,** which are those users who have a greater need to access the processor. The first express user swapped in is the one who has been swapped out for the longest time. If no storage is available, the parameters allowing pages to be stolen from other address spaces' working sets are temporarily increased, which may make more page frames available. The swap-in candidate user is then placed on the defer list to give it the first consideration during the next swap analysis.

The fourth step is to try to swap users into each domain which does not have enough users to meet its MPL value. If insufficient storage is available, the same steps as above (changing the page stealing level and deferring the user) are performed for those users who would have been swapped in.

The last step is to swap in a user to replace another user currently in memory. This is only performed for those domains that already have a number of users matching the MPL value for that domain. The address space with the lowest recommendation value (RV) in memory is the one to be swapped out and the address space with highest RV on the swap device is the one to be swapped in. Before the swap is actually performed, the two RVs are compared, and the swap is only done if the difference between the two RVs is greater than a certain minimum amount. In other words, the swap is only performed if something significant is to be gained by it.

One of the factors in deciding whether or not to swap out a particular address space is the activity level of that address space. The more active address spaces are usually not swapped out, since they would just need to be swapped back in again. SRM has a "workload manager" that monitors the resource consumption rate for each address space. This rate is then compared to the defined normal value for that installation to determine whether that address space is more or less active than the specified rate. The recommendation value is then adjusted based upon this activity rate.

V=R

Certain programs may have requirements that prevent them from being pageable. These programs tend to be much less common under MVS than under VM since many of the programs running under VM that are non-pageable are operating systems. Such programs do occasionally exist under MVS, however, usually when fast response is critical to that application.

Programs that must run in a non-pageable area under MVS can be allocated real memory to run in instead of virtual memory. The memory allocated is called V=R memory. Such memory should be used only if absolutely necessary, since it removes a part of real memory from the paging pool.

Any V=R area that is to be included in the system should be allocated when the system is first initialized. Such regions must be contiguous, and if normal paging activity is allowed in the system, a large contiguous area of real memory is not likely to become available. The only way to avoid this is to allocate the V=R region when the system is initialized, before the virtual regions have been allocated.

V=R regions must be allocated in the lowermost sixteen megabytes of real memory. Any memory available on the system above the sixteen megabyte line is not available for V=R regions.

PERFORMANCE MEASUREMENT AND TUNING

The MVS operating system heavily emphasizes performance measurement and tuning. Several parts of the operating system are involved in gathering performance information. A generalized format for storing any performance information is used so that any module that gathers performance information can provide that information to any other module.

System Management Facilities

Almost all of the information used to provide performance reports is handled by the **system management facilities** or **SMF.** All parts of the operating system that report performance information report that information in a format suitable for processing by SMF.

There are two general categories of information processed by SMF. The first category is information about the operating system, such as scheduling, paging, etc. The second category is information about specific jobs in the system, such as the amount of processor time used, the amount of I/O generated, etc. This information can also be used to generate billing reports for users who are billed for their computer use.

SMF collects vast and detailed information about the activities of the system. Almost all of the other subsystems within MVS which produce reports on system activity gather the data for those reports from SMF. SMF maintains detailed information on every aspect of a job's execution, from the time it started to a list of the files it accessed. SMF also has information on other MVS subsystems such as JES, CICS, and RACF. Disk accesses are monitored, as is processor activity, paging activity, and scheduling activity.

SMF collects and formats the various performance information, but it does not have reporting routines for that information. In order to produce the reports, some other program must read the SMF data. Some subsystems, such as RACF, do that upon request. Various commercial programs are also available to produce the reports, but the data is collected and formatted well enough so that it is not a major task for the reporting routines to be written at a customer installation. Writing the reporting routines also allows the installation to get the reports in the format desired instead of taking the format that is available.

SMF is not a real-time monitor. The information gathered by SMF is designed for long-term analysis. Much of the information is not available until after the monitored event has completed. Very complete statistics are available for long range planning but the reporting programs are usually not designed to display the information in real time.

Job monitoring

The information available on specific jobs is quite detailed. It includes the name of the job, the total time the job was in the system, the processor time used, and a listing of many of the priorities used within the system to execute that job. Much of this information is created by combining the information available for each step within that job.

The step information includes the following:

- Date the step finished
- Time the step finished (in hundredths of a second)
- The job name of which this step was a part
- Date when the job entered the system
- Time when the job entered the system
- Userid submitting the job
- Date the step began executing
- Time the step began executing
- Step completion status (normal, System ABEND, etc.)
- Step name
- Processor time used
- Number of page-ins, page-outs, swap-ins, swap-outs, number of pages swapped in or out, etc.

Disk monitoring

One of the most important parts of the system for tuning is the way it handles disk accesses. This is an important part of any system, but it is probably a larger part of the MVS system than of most other systems. One reason is that MVS usually runs on large computers, and as the processor power grows it becomes more and more difficult to tune the I/O subsystem to make optimum usage of all the available processor power. Another reason is that most internal parameters in MVS are usually well tuned by default, and the I/O subsystem is the most likely area to lack tuning.

SMF collects a tremendous amount of information about the way the system is handling the disk drives. This information allows almost any disk tuning problem to be easily located. An SMF record is generated each time a disk volume is mounted. This record contains information on the amount of space free on that volume, as well as the number and size of the contiguous blocks of free space.

SMF also provides a large amount of detailed information about the file activity on disk drives. Some of the information available includes:

- Usage count for files
- Block sizes used for files
- Record lengths used for files
- Type of disk device used for each file
- Date the file was accessed
- Time the file was accessed
- Whether the file is permanent or temporary
- Number of records processed
- Physical location of the file on the device
- Physical volume name
- Number of extents used (secondary allocations)
- Number of logical records in the file primary area
- Number of logical records in the file secondary area

The I/O activity for individual jobs and job steps can also be determined by reporting on the data in the job monitoring records. Accumulating these records allows the installation to produce a report of the overall activity, categorized by specific jobs.

Paging monitor

The SMF records that track the paging activity are also detailed. Both paging and swapping performance is tracked. The data is available for job steps and can be accumulated for longer periods of time by adding the job step data. Most installations do not need the paging information displayed in the detail that is available, so the reporting programs frequently accumulate the detail information into summary reports.

The paging information available is recorded during a specified time interval. It includes:

- Date and time the currently recorded event occurred
- Number of page-ins

- Number of page-outs
- Number of pages swapped in
- Number of pages swapped out
- Number of page frames available in memory
- Number of page frames in the nucleus
- Average number of unused page frames
- Minimum number of unused page frames
- Maximum number of unused page frames
- Beginning date and time of data sample
- Length of sample time interval

Processor monitoring

The data collected about the processor performance tells not only how busy the processor was, but what functions were being performed during the busy times. Processor usage can also be reported by analyzing the job and job step information. The processor information is collected in two general categories: the amount of time spent on service requests, and the amount of time spent on tasks. The information available on processor utilization is collected over a specified time period, just like the paging information.

The information available includes the following:

- Date and time the record was produced
- Length of time the processor was in a wait state
- Count of wait users *
- Count of TSO users *
- Count of batch users *
- Count of ready value *
- Count of users in the queues *
- Count of users out of the queues *

Items marked with an asterisk represent information counted in a rather unusual way. These items each represent several different fields in the record. Each individual field is a count of the number of times that item was at a specific value. An example is that of TSO users. The individual fields are as follows:

```
Number of times TSO users were 1 or 2

Number of times TSO users were 3 or 4

. . .

Number of times TSO users were 31 - 35

Number of times TSO users were greater than 35
```

The first field indicates how many times there were one or two TSO users, the second field shows how many time there were three or four TSO users, etc. Values that are gathered in this fashion also have fields defined which show the average, minimum, and maximum values during the sampling interval.

Resource Measurement Facility

The information that has been gathered and processed by the SMF system must be displayed somehow. One method is with the **Resource Measurement Facility** or **RMF.** RMF is a comprehensive system that measures and reports on various aspects of system performance. It consists of three parts, each with a different function. "Monitor I" and "Monitor II" measure performance over a period of time and collect the data in SMF records. Monitor II also provides real-time reports on the data that is being collected. "Monitor III" displays information on resource contention.

RMF data can be used either for real-time displays with Monitor II or long-term reports with Monitor I. Monitor III's contention reports are primarily designed as real-time reports. Many of the reports that Monitor II and Monitor III generate are based on information gathered by Monitor I, so if Monitor II or Monitor III usage is desired, Monitor I should also be running.

RMF has several different types of reports, both printed and display, such as reports on disk usage, or paging activity. Reports can also be developed for a current view, for a specified time interval, or summarized over a long period of time.

A very nice feature of RMF is the ability to produce **exception reports.** Most monitors produce reports that show either real-time data, or data that is averaged over some period of time, and the systems programmer must then study the reports to determine if any system performance parameters were poor during that time period. The exception report from RMF contains only those cases where system performance exceeded some previously defined boundary during the time in question. It is a very quick and easy way to see the problem areas in the system.

Another nice feature of RMF is the ability to provide plots of performance data. These plots are relatively simple plots drawn on a normal line printer. These plots are another way of quickly finding any problem areas in the system. The following is an example of such a plot.

Example 16-11:

RMF PLOT REPORT

```
  OS/VS2          SYSTEM ID xxxx     START 05/31/85-17.00.00
  RELEASE 3.8     RPT VERSION 10     END   05/31/85-23.00.00

     TOTAL PAGING RATE
     0               100.0                200.0                300.0

17:00 ************************************                 .
17:15 *********************************.                   .
17:30 ******************************   .                   .
17:45 **************************       .                   .
18:00 *****************************    .                   .
18:15 *********************************.                   .
18:30 *********************            .                   .
18:45 **************************       .                   .
19:00 ************************************                 .
19:15 *******************************************          .
19:30 ***********************************************      .
19:45 *****************************************            .
20:00 ***************************************************  .
20:15 ***********************************************      .
20:30 **************************************************   .
20:45 ************************************************     .
21:00 ***********************************************      .
21:15 ***********************************************      .
21:30 **************************************************   .
21:45 ******************************************           .
22:00 *************************************                .
22:15 ****************************     .                   .
22:30 *************                    .                   .
22:45 ***         .                    .                   .
23:00 **          .                    .                   .
```

CPU Activity Report

One of the reports available from RMF shows the CPU activity. This report has the following format:

Example 16-12:

CPU ACTIVITY

```
   OS/VS2          SYSTEM ID xxxx       START 05/31/85-17.00.00
   RELEASE 3.8     RPT VERSION 10       END   05/31/85-23.00.00
CPU MODEL      3081

CPU             WAIT TIME        WAIT TIME         I/O TOTAL
NUMBER          HH.MM.SS.TTT     PERCENTAGE        INTERRUPT RATE

0               00.47.32.876       13.05              983

2               01.22.15.348       22.78              315

TOTAL/AVERAGE                      17.92              649

SYSTEM ADDRESS SPACE ANALYSIS       SAMPLES =   674
           NUMBER OF ASIDS      DISTRIBUTION OF QUEUE LENGTHS
TYPE       MIN  MAX  AVG         0     1             14+
IN
READY        0    5  3.2      84.3   18.2            0.0

IN           2    6  4.5       0.0    0.0            0.0

OUT
READY        0    0  0.0       0.0    0.0            0.0

OUT
WAIT         1    4  2.1       0.0   97.0            0.0

BATCH        0    8  1.4      17.4   23.0            0.0

TSO          0    9  5.3      14.2   63.0            0.0
```

The first three lines show the date of the report, and the levels of the software involved. The next line shows the computer model, in this case an IBM 3081. The next few lines show the overall activity for the CPUs on that computer, (the 3081 has two processors, which are numbered 0 and 2). These lines show the total amount of wait time and the percentage of wait time, for each processor, and the average of the two processors. The last entry on those lines shows the average number of I/O interrupts received each second, which is a good measure of the amount of I/O activity. Both the total wait times, and the wait time percentages, are taken from the period that the data was collected.

The next section of the report shows activity for address spaces in the system. Each line shows the maximum, the minimum, and the average number of address space IDs in the system. It also shows the way the address spaces are distributed in the system queues. The first line, IN READY, shows the number of address spaces in real memory and ready to execute. The next line, IN, shows the total number of address spaces in memory. The OUT READY line shows the address spaces that are ready to execute but are currently not in real memory. The OUT WAIT line shows the address spaces that are not in real memory, and are not ready to execute.

The final two lines on the report, BATCH and TSO, show the number of address spaces devoted to batch and TSO users. These numbers are very helpful in determining the orientation of the system, since the tuning goals differ somewhat between a majority of batch, or a majority of TSO, users.

Disk Activity Report

RMF also has a report that shows disk device activity. This report has the following format:

Example 16-13:

DIRECT ACCESS DEVICE ACTIVITY

```
   OS/VS2        SYSTEM ID xxxx       START 05/31/85-17.00.00
   RELEASE 3.8   RPT VERSION 10       END   05/31/85-23.00.00

TOTAL SAMPLES =  674
```

DEV NUM	VOLUME SERIAL	LCU	DEVICE ACTIVITY RATE	AVG RESP TIME	AVG IOSQ TIME	% DEV CONN	% DEV UTIL	% DEV RESV	AVG DS OPEN
240	PAGE01	01	5.078	57	0	5.31	8.44	0.0	0.0
241	PAGE02	01	6.043	32	0	7.73	7.35	0.0	0.0
242	PAGE03	01	7.063	46	0	5.84	7.23	0.0	0.0
243	PAGE04	01	3.145	58	0	3.37	8.48	0.0	0.0
250	TEMP01	01	1.098	45	1	4.16	2.67	0.0	2.3
251	TEMP02	01	0.123	23	0	6.57	0.35	0.0	5.8
252	TEMP03	01	3.756	31	2	8.35	3.74	0.0	6.5
253	TSOFIL	01	4.423	78	12	9.13	3.42	0.0	7.7

This report is designed to cover just disk drives. The heading of the report, as usual, provides the release numbers of the operating system and RMF, along with the time the data was collected. The total number of samples collected immediately follows the heading.

The first column in the report is DEV NUM, which shows the physical address of the device being reported. The second column, VOLUME SERIAL, shows the internal label, if any, written on that device. The third column, LCU, gives the logical control unit for each device. The fourth column, DEVICE ACTIVITY RATE, shows the number of successful I/O operations on that device each second. The fifth column, AVG RESP TIME, shows the average response time for the device. This number is reported in milliseconds, and represents the length of time required for the device to complete an I/O request. The sixth column, AVG IOSQ TIME, shows the average time that each request waited in the software queue before being serviced. This number is also reported in milliseconds.

The next three columns are all percentages. They represent the percentage of time the device was in a particular condition during the sampling time. % DEV CONN shows the percentage of time that the device was logically connected to the channel and processing an I/O request. % DEV UTIL reports the percentage of time that the device was not available for new software requests. The device is not available for new requests if it is currently servicing a request, or if it is reserved. % DEV RESV shows the percentage of time that the device was actually reserved, and thus not available for access. The last column, AVG DS OPEN, shows the average number of data sets open on that device at any one time. The number of open data sets should be relatively small, since otherwise the device may become too busy for good response.

Paging Activity Report

Several different reports are available on paging activity. The example given here is the one that is available to report on the paging and swapping data set activities. The format is as follows:

Example 16-14:

PAGE/SWAP DATASET ACTIVITY

```
   OS/VS2          SYSTEM ID xxxx       START 05/31/85-17.00.00
   RELEASE 3.8     RPT VERSION 10       END   05/31/85-23.00.00
TOTAL SAMPLES =    674
                              PAGE DATA SET USAGE
VOLUME    DEV  DEVICE SLOTS   SLOTS USED     NUMBER
SERIAL    NUM  TYPE    ALLOC  MIN  MAX  AVG  IO REQ DATA SET NAME
PLP001    780  3380    3600   900  1900 1463   87    SYS1.PRMPAGE
PAGE01    781  3380   24000     1  8703  345   23    SYS1.PAGE01
PAGE02    782  3380   24000    23   478   89   15    SYS1.PAGE02
PAGE03    783  3380   24000   153   243  215   47    SYS1.PAGE03
PAGE04    784  3380   24000    35   468  259   34    SYS1.PAGE03
```

The first column, VOLUME SERIAL, reports the volume label of the disk device containing the data set. The second column, DEV NUM, reports the attachment number of that device. The third column, DEVICE TYPE, has the type of device. The fourth column, SLOTS ALLOC, shows the number of page frames allocated in that particular data set. The fifth, sixth, and seventh columns, SLOTS USED. MIN, MAX, and AVG, show the distribution of the slots used in that data set. NUMBER IO REQ shows the number of I/O requests that have been made to that data set. The last column, DATA SET NAME, shows the actual name of the data set used for paging or swapping.

General Information

RMF has a vast number of reports in addition to those few that were shown here. In particular, the activity of most of the system queues can be reported. This is particularly helpful in tuning the system since many performance problems are manifested by excessive numbers of jobs in queues or by excessive time spent in queues by a few jobs. The biggest problem with the RMF reports is not in obtaining the information, but sorting the vast abundance of information available to determine what is actually useful.

Performance tuning

Performance tuning under MVS falls into the same general areas as on other large operating systems, that is I/O and paging. Such tuning is probably more important on MVS than on most systems, because MVS tends to be more complex than most systems, and because it usually runs on very large computers, where performance is very important.

Paging tuning

There are three different types of data sets maintained to support paging on MVS: common, PLPA, and local. The common page file is used to write pages from shared areas of memory. The PLPA page file contains pages from the **PLPA, (Pageable Link Pack Area**) an area of memory that contains critical system modules. The local file is used to contain the remainder of the pages, such as from user applications.

Each of the three categories of page files must be large enough to contain all necessary pages for that category of usage. Overflow between the common and PLPA page files is possible, but doing so may degrade paging performance and should be avoided.

Each of the three types of page files should be placed on different physical devices if at all possible. The paging algorithms can optimize performance on any one page file on one physical device, but not on more than one type on the same physical device. Severe paging degradation could result from placing more than one type of page file on the same physical device.

The local page file is by far the largest of the three categories of page files, since it contains the largest area of memory. It should be broken into multiple physical page files. Each of these page files then should be placed on different physical devices, so that the time required to wait while pages are fetched from disk drives is reduced. This is accomplished by having the paging algorithms place all the devices containing local page files in a round-robin queue, and write to each of them in sequence. Such sequencing breaks up the paging between the devices, and therefore no one device is busy as often. The round-robin sequence only works, of course, for page files that have free space, so steps should be taken to prevent those files from filling.

There are three types of devices that are used for paging. Each type of device has a different speed; the faster devices are favored for paging. The fastest device type is one attached with a caching control unit.

The next fastest device type is known as a **fixed-head device.** This is similar to a normal disk drive, except that it is designed so that no mechanical movement is necessary to read the data from disk. Such devices are much slower than cache devices, because the data must actually be read from disk, but it is still faster than normal disk drives. The slowest device type is just a normal disk drive.

The paging system tries to maintain active page files on the fastest devices available. The most active files are therefore on cache devices, then fixed-head devices, then moving-head devices. Most installations do not have all three types of devices, but may have two different types. In these cases, those device types that are available are used.

Another type of paging file, which is really just a special case of the local page file, is the swap file. This is a local page file that is used exclusively for swapping. Performance is enhanced if such files are available and are big enough so that swapping need not be done to the normal local page files. IBM recommends a total size of three to four times the total address space available plus a fudge factor of twenty to fifty percent.

Page files should be allocated generously so that more space is available than is expected to be used. The paging algorithms attempt to write pages sequentially into the page files, which enhances performance since the mechanical movement of the disk drive is reduced if the pages are adjacent. Writing the pages sequentially is only possible if large amounts of free space exist in the page file, which in turn is only possible if those files are somewhat over-allocated.

One approach that is rather extreme is to allocate only one file, the paging file, on devices used for paging. This greatly enhances the likelihood of that device being available when needed for paging, but is extremely wasteful of disk space. A more usual way is to allocate a paging file in the middle of the device and surround that file with other, very low-activity files. A busy paging device is the perfect location for those files that should remain on-line, that use a large amount of disk space but are rarely accessed. An example of such files might be the source for the operating system, which is usually only referenced a few times per month.

I/O tuning

Maintaining optimum I/O performance on an MVS system can be a very complex task. A very high percentage of the work is done by the SRM so the part necessary from the systems programmer tends to be relatively simple. MVS/XA and the whole XA computer architecture have been greatly enhanced in the area of I/O optimization so that many of the functions that would otherwise be either done by the systems programmer (or not be done at all) are done by the computer hardware or the operating system.

The primary tool MVS uses to tune the system is swapping. Address spaces that are in I/O wait are frequently swapped out. Swapping is also used to balance the overall system I/O and paging load, so that a balance between paging, I/O, and CPU-bound jobs is achieved. Such a balance is not always possible, of course, but is achievable as long as a normal mix of jobs are in the system.

Most of the I/O tuning necessary from the system programmer has to do with the placement of files on disks and with the arrangement of disk drives, control units, and channels. The principles used are the same basic principles discussed in chapter 9. Files that are very active should be placed as near as possible to the center of the disk, and multiple active files should not be placed on the same disk.

Disk devices with active files should be equitably divided between different disk control units, and those control units should in turn be divided among the available channels. The XA I/O subsystem is very good at utilizing alternative paths to disk devices, so such paths should be made available whenever possible.

SYSTEMS SECURITY

The basic MVS system has security similar to that of most commercial operating systems. A password is required before accessing the system, and again to access most files.

The enhanced level of security on the MVS system is provided by the Resource Access Control Facility or RACF, similar to the package on CMS.

System access

The system access under RACF is still password controlled, but some features are added to enhance the normal password checking. Each password is encrypted so that it cannot be deciphered by another user, even if that user were to manage to gain access to the file containing the password. There is also an optional feature which can be required to allow terminal interactions.

The password assigned when a userid is installed on the system is a temporary password. It allows the user to log on once and change the password. Once the password has been changed, it is known only to RACF and to the user.

There are several options available to the RACF administrator to provide additional features on the passwords. The administrator can require each user to change passwords before a certain amount of time elapses. The maximum length of this interval can be set by the administrator, and the individual users can set a shorter length for their own userids.

RACF also allows the administrator to set up syntax rules that the passwords must follow, such as the maximum and minimum length allowable, or the types of characters allowed. A password history file option causes RACF to keep a file containing a certain number of previous passwords for each userid. When the user changes passwords the new password is checked against the older passwords and not allowed if it was used before. This prevents a user from alternating between only two or three total passwords, or worse yet, from simply changing the old password to a new password that is identical to the old password.

RACF has an option that can be used to require that all batch jobs have a userid and password just like a logon attempt. It is sometimes possible for system security to be circumvented by accessing the system in batch mode, instead of as an interactive user. Most users are interactive, and in particular, most would-be system security violators are interactive, so many systems guard the interactive access very carefully, but pay little attention to batch access. A violator can then set up a batch job that performs the desired task, or that locates security information that allows the violator to then logon interactively.

File access

The area that probably receives the most attention in RACF is controlling access to files and file devices. Access to disk drives, magnetic tapes, and terminals can all be controlled. This level of control may not be considered necessary in all installations, so options exist that allow the RACF administrator to tailor the exact level of access control to be used.

In order for RACF to protect files, the file names must follow certain conventions. The high-level qualifier of the file name must be a valid userid. Any files not following this naming convention will not be protected. The userid chosen may be either a single user userid or it may refer to a group of userids. In either case, it must be defined as such to RACF.

Not all installations are willing or able set up all file names so that they begin with the userid name, particularly those installations with hundreds or thousands of files created before RACF was acquired. RACF has an option designed to allow these installations to protect their files also. It internally assigns the userid to the beginning of the file name, and then subsequently uses that name to refer to the file, even though the user still uses the original name to refer to the file. Another option allows RACF to show the original, instead of the internally updated, file name on any reports.

The userid in the file name for protected files may be either a real userid or it may be a group name. A group data set is then available to all members of that group, but is protected from access by any userid that is not defined as part of that group.

The file access privilege granted to each group or individual userid can be defined separately for each file or group of files. Any userid without an explicitly defined access privilege may or may not be able to access the file. This is determined by the **universal access authority** or **UACC.** The UACC defines the access level to be granted to any userid not explicitly defined on the access list. This access may be any of the above levels.

A data set profile is used to define the access allowed to files. A data set profile may be defined for each file (a **discrete profile**) or for groups of files (a **generic profile**).

The generic profile is used to apply the same RACF control to large groups of files, without requiring a separate profile for each file. The generic profile specifies a list of the files to be protected. This list need not be updated each time a new file is created, however, since wild-card characters are acceptable when defining the file names to be protected. The high-level qualifier of a file name cannot contain such wild-card characters, but any other part of the file name can.

For example, all of the files for a specific userid can be given the same level of access control by specifying the file names in the generic profile using wildcards for all parts of the file name except the userid, as in:

```
CHRISN.*
```

A generic profile can be over-ridden with a discrete profile because the search order for a profile is done by looking for discrete profiles first, and then looking for generic profiles. If more than one generic profile exists, then the most specific of the generic profiles is used.

RACF can also be used to control access to specific disk drives and magnetic tapes. Magnetic tapes must use standard labels in order for the protection to be effective. Tapes that bypass label processing cannot be protected. Tapes with non-standard labels can be protected, but doing so requires that special routines be provided to RACF.

Access to terminals can be controlled with RACF by specifying the terminal location and authorization. Only authorized userids can then use that terminal. Userids can be authorized either individually or as part of a group. It is not necessary to include all terminals in the controlled group, since installations frequently have only a certain group of terminals that should have access controlled.

Monitoring access

RACF has extensive monitoring and reporting features. Almost every item in the system can be monitored and reported on, and every item which has access controlled by RACF can have accesses and access attempts monitored and reported. The reports provided are designed to provide information on different characteristics of the system, and different levels of access.

RACF reports contain the userid that attempted the access. They show all unsuccessful attempts, as well as all successful attempts. This allows the person monitoring the activity to determine whether any given accesses were valid or not.

RACF also produces a report that shows the amount of activity for any userid, or group of userids, in accessing RACF-protected resources. It also can be used to show the amount of activity on various system resources if those resources are protected by RACF.

The RACF system administrator has access to additional data about various aspects of RACF resources. Several commands allow inspection of all resource profiles in the system, both generic and discrete. These commands can be used to show the owner of the resource, the date it was protected, the userids and groups authorized to use it, and the activity it has received. There are additional commands available for displaying various types of detailed information about RACF and resource activity.

A very useful option in RACF allows on-line, real-time monitoring of attempted access violations. This option causes RACF to send a message to a particular terminal whenever an access violation is detected. The access violations reported this way usually only include those violations that are considered potentially more serious, such as access to the system.

Installing RACF

Most of the difficult aspects of installing RACF, or any other security system, are not the technical aspects of the installation, but the political aspects of getting acceptance from users and management that the security system is necessary. Any security system adds a slight amount of overhead to the user's interface with the system. This overhead may be transparent to the user, but it is definitely noticeable to the RACF administrator. The amount of time involved in being RACF administrator varies depending upon the size of the installation and the degree of protection desired, but the minimum amount is still a significant part of one person's time.

The most important aspect of any security system is acquiring the full support of company management. The management must supply the manpower necessary to administer the system, and must also encourage the users to accept the restrictions imposed on the user by the system. Security systems that are not fully supported tend to be circumvented regularly by the users, and may cause management to think they have security when there is actually no more security than before the system was installed. Any password-driven system, such as RACF, is only as good as the concern of the users in keeping their passwords secret. If the users freely distribute their passwords, and only set up the precautions that RACF forces, there is little more security than before the installation of the security system.

An installation and support team should be defined for RACF before it arrives at the installation. The size of the team may vary between installations, but certain functions should be represented. There should be a systems programmer who is responsible for the physical installation of RACF. An RACF administrator must be defined who will be in charge of overseeing the ongoing operation of RACF after it is installed. An auditor should be available to guide the administrator and the systems programmers in setting RACF up to follow sound auditing principles. A representative of the users should be part of the team, in order to communicate user's needs and desires to the RACF team and to communicate necessary operational changes back to the other users.

The installation team must decide which resources are to be protected and lay out the organizational structure of the groups before RACF is made available. RACF can protect many resources, but not all of this protection may be necessary or desirable at that particular installation. The structure of the organization is necessary in order to set up the group access, and to determine which userids should be in which group.

It is seldom a good idea to institute a new security system overnight. The users must be warned well in advance, at least one month before the system is actually operational. Even after the advance warning, the phase-in of the system should be done as gently as possible. Many users may be accustomed to doing things that, although innocent, are prohibited by a security system.

These users, since they are not deliberately attempting to violate security, are probably going to be surprised when RACF prevents some of their requests.

RACF should be set up so that security violations are only reported during the initial period. Reporting the violations to the users allows those users time to become accustomed to the idea that they must either stop doing some things, or get proper authorization for them. After an initial period, RACF can be put in full operation, at which time access violations are prevented.

The best way to do the phase-in process is to have an initial period during which all access violations are reported to the systems administrator but not to anyone else. After reviewing the number of violations, the administrator is then able to decide what the next step of the phase-in should be. One option is to run in a mode where RACF still does not prevent access violations, but it notifies the user attempting the access, as well as the systems administrator, that the access is violating the security setup. This phase can then be followed by the final phase where all access violations are prevented. The other option is to immediately go to the final phase, without using the warning mode at all. This might be more appropriate when deliberate violations are suspected and the administrator might not wish to give warnings.

A major part of the work necessary in installing RACF is to ensure that each of the groups involved understand what will be necessary with the new system. Each user must become aware of the changes in accessing the system itself, and various system resources. Particular efforts are required from CICS/VS or IMS/VS administrators, since both of those systems have security features that must be integrated with the security features of RACF. The users who either maintain or wish to access RACF-protected files must be aware of the new procedures. Last, but far from least, the RACF system administrator must be prepared to quickly process all requests for setting up or changing RACF access privileges.

MULTI-PROCESSING

MVS is designed to run on computers with one, two, or four processors. It is perhaps the best of the major commercial operating systems at achieving optimum performance from multiple processor configurations. Most tasks running under MVS do not execute in true parallel fashion (on all processors simultaneously). Most tasks are scheduled to run on a single processor and the other processors are used to run other tasks.

Some tasks, however, can be run in true parallel fashion under MVS. A multi-processor FORTRAN compiler exists that compiles FORTRAN programs to run in true parallel under MVS. The programs should be carefully chosen, since some programs lend themselves well to parallel processing while others do not. Even among the better programs, however, some processor power is lost to overhead. The throughput achieved by running a parallel task on four processors simultaneously is about 3.3, according to IBM.

Resource locking

There are two different types of locks used in the MVS system: spin locks and suspend locks. MVS has a mechanism that causes a timeout if a processor has been spinning for an excessive period of time. No processor should maintain a resource for more than about twenty seconds. Before a processor enters a spin loop, it calculates how many loops it must execute in order to let twenty seconds elapse. If it then remains in the spin loop for the full number of loops, it automatically exits and tries to determine why the other processor is still holding the required resource. The system operator is notified whenever spin loops are held for the full loop time, and he has the option of requesting that the processor begin spinning again or manually releasing the required resource from the other processor. The usual reason for one processor to hold a critical resource for more than twenty seconds is a failure which may require that the offending processor be removed from normal functioning.

There are two general types of locks that are available: global locks and local locks. There is a very carefully designed hierarchy for the locks, which is designed to prevent a deadlock condition from arising. The global lock hierarchy is as follows:

- Real storage management
- Virtual storage management fixed subpools
- Auxiliary storage management
- Various locks for specific parts of real storage management Dispatcher
- I/O system unit control block (UCB)
- System Resource Manager
- Processor
- Cross memory services

Some of these locks are called **class locks,** which means that more than one actual lock is defined at that level. All locks of the same class are at the same level in the hierarchy, and are considered one for the above list. Some of the global locks are spin locks and some are suspend locks.

Cross memory services refers to any function that is performed between address spaces. Any function performed from one address space on another or across several address spaces simultaneously requires locking mechanisms. Both the global and local locks list have entries for cross memory services.

Local locks are locks for resources related to only one address space. They can be of two different types, either LOCAL or cross memory. If the task in an address space holds the local lock for it, then that lock is known as a LOCAL lock, or a LOCAL local lock (which tends to be rather confusing). If a task in another address space holds the local lock, then that lock is known as a **cross memory local lock** or **CML.** Each address space has only one local lock associated with it, and any task can hold only one local lock at any one time.

There are several rules that apply to the lock hierarchy discussed above. A task cannot obtain a lock lower in the hierarchy than one already held. A task can request a lock higher in the hierarchy, but not lower. A task cannot hold two locks of one type. A local lock must already be held before any of the global locks is requested, and if the requested lock is for cross memory services, then the local lock must be held until the global cross memory services lock is ended.

It is not usually possible to hold more than one lock at the same level; the processor lock is the exception to this rule. It is a spin lock that allows the processor to become disabled to the system. Once it is in use, no suspend locks are available.

NETWORKING SYSTEMS

MVS has several products to support networking needs. IBM is clearly attempting to have completely integrated networks, but the age and wide diversity of the various IBM networking products have made it very difficult to integrate all the pieces while maintaining compatibility with the old levels of networking. Networking products under the MVS system have reached the highest level of integration of any of the IBM networking products.

The basic strategy of IBM networking is tied to their Systems Network Architecture or SNA. SNA is a comprehensive approach to networking all of IBM's communications products. Some of the older products did not support SNA for many years, but newer products and new enhancements to the older products usually support SNA. The SNA approach is an attempt to provide a total networking solution. It defines every component and level of networking necessary. Not all these levels and components are yet in place in all products, but when they are SNA will indeed be a total networking solution.

SNA is designed in three different layers, where each layer has a distinctly different function. These layers closely approximate some of the layers in the seven-layer networking standard discussed in chapter 12. The layer that is closest to the user is the **application layer.** The middle layer is the **function management layer** and the lowest level layer is the **transmission subsystem layer.**

The application layer performs no functions that relate to actually setting up the link, or to determining how the data is routed between locations on the network. The function management layer is accessed by requests for services from the application layer. It is primarily concerned with serving as an interface between the application layer and the transmission subsystem. Many of the features in this layer are concerned with monitoring and managing the flow of data through the network.

The transmission subsystem layer is the most basic level of the network, and is the one that is concerned with implementing the network functions on the hardware available. There are three primary parts to this layer. The data link control handles the links connecting the nodes of the network. The path control handles the paths available to transmit data over various nodes. The transmission control handles the way data moves into and out of the path and data link controls.

The data link control element of SNA can become quite complex. Implementing it requires a thorough understanding and definition of the protocols used to link devices. The two most common protocols used in SNA networks are the System/370 channel and **Synchronous Data Link Control** or **SDLC.** The System/370 channel is the very-high-speed, short-range connection between peripheral devices and the computer. This is used by communications devices that link directly to a computer. SDLC is the protocol normally used over communications links such as telephone lines.

There is a wide array of software products available to implement SNA under MVS. The major problem, in fact, may very well be that there are too many products. The number of products makes it very difficult to select the correct one for any particular application, and it also makes it very difficult to understand all the products available.

A partial list of basic networking products is:

- ACF/VTAM — Basic networking system
- ACF/VTAME — Basic system for the 4331 computer
- ACF/TCAM — Older basic networking system
- ACF/SSP — System support for basic systems
- ACF/NCP — Control program for FEP
- EP — Control program for FEP

- NTO — Extends the functions of ACF/NCP
- NPSI (X.25) — A packet switching interface
- NSI — Transport of non-SNA data

The ACF/VTAM product is a current, basic networking product that serves to illustrate most of the issues of SNA networks. There is a wide variety of other software packages available to perform many features not included in the basic systems, such as monitoring the network or certain utility functions.

ACF/VTAM provides a network between peripheral devices, front-end processors, and host computers. The network can be between multiple hosts (each host must run ACF/VTAM or its equivalent) or on only one host. It provides the complete network control. A network between multiple hosts with ACF/VTAM requires the optional "multisystem networking facility" be added to ACF/VTAM.

The basic function of ACF/VTAM is to provide an interface between application programs and terminals. Doing this requires managing a large number of items in between the two, but the basic function remains unchanged. An ACF/VTAM domain is that portion of a network in one host that is controlled by ACF/VTAM. Multiple hosts then become multiple domains. A domain usually consists of a host, a front-end processor, multiple cluster controllers, and a large number of terminals or communications links.

One of the important features of ACF/VTAM is that it distributes much of the processing work from the host to the front-end processors or to the terminals. This greatly reduces the processor power required to support the network. Handling a network in a host processor tends to be quite wasteful of processor power, since the load typically consists of many interrupts requiring a small amount of service. Such a load can be handled by a small processor, but if it is placed on a large processor that is attempting to process other jobs at the same time, a disproportionate amount of processor time is spent being interrupted and recovering from being interrupted.

Application programs that are allowed to use specific facilities of ACF/VTAM must identify themselves to ACF/VTAM before actually using the services available. The identification allows ACF/VTAM to set up the necessary control blocks. These applications then use ACF/VTAM macro instructions to handle the communications with the terminals.

There are two different ways that ACF/VTAM communications can be set up. The "primary role" is usually held by the application program that is directing the session, while the "secondary role" is held by the terminal being controlled by the application program. It is also possible, however, to have an application program acting in the secondary role, although it must then interact with another application program as though it were a terminal. The interaction is started when the terminal logon is received by ACF/VTAM. When the secondary role is held by another application program, the request from it is handled the same way as a logon request from a terminal.

ACF/VTAM has two ways of communicating with terminals. "Record mode" transmission is used whenever possible. It is always possible with SNA-compatible terminals, and sometimes with terminals that are not SNA-compatible. "Basic mode" transmission is used whenever record mode is not available.

Record mode transmission requires the application program to set up, or enable, the transfer between the terminal and the application program. Once that transfer has been set up, either the terminal or the program can begin transferring data. The data transfer must then be explicitly disabled. This is very good when terminals (or applications emulating terminals) need to transfer a relatively large amount of data, since the transfer remains immediately available.

Basic mode is a polling strategy. The application program issues a general statement to the terminals on the network, which allows any of them to respond with a data transfer. The first terminal responding gets accepted. As soon as that transfer has been accepted, the general polling continues on the rest of the network. The application program can continue reading data from that one terminal until the transfer is complete, or it can go back to general polling and allow that terminal to take its place with the other terminals requesting data transfer.

Basic mode is not as suitable for networks with a large number of terminals, since the number of terminals may overwhelm the polling mechanism. It is also not as suitable in cases where a large amount of interaction is necessary between the terminal and the application program since a new polling sequence may be necessary with each interaction.

Probably the most important part of setting up and maintaining ACF/VTAM is defining the domain. Errors in the domain may lead to failures of varying degree. The failure could be as simple as a terminal feature not working or as severe as a complete failure of the entire network. The usual error is to accidentally specify one device or line incorrectly, which results in only that device or line not working. Great care must be taken to ensure that the domain definition correctly represents the actual physical network configuration. It is not necessary to define all possible items, but any item that is physically present must be defined.

The following is a partial list of the items that may be included to define the domain.

- Local SNA terminals
- Local non-SNA terminals
- Front end processor programs

- ACF/VTAM application programs
- Links to other domains
- Physical paths to other domains
- Resources available in other domains

ACF/VTAM uses a **front-end processor (FEP)** which is usually the IBM 3704, 3705, or 3725 communications controller. This FEP is very useful in handling many of the tasks necessary in managing the network. It also has a small operating system, called **network control program** or **NCP** which must be set up and configured to handle the devices actually attached to that FEP. These devices are usually terminals. The location, type, and number, of terminals attached must be specified. The non-terminal devices are usually physical lines, and these must also be specified.

The events that can be monitored are primarily concerned with authorizing logon requests, collecting accounting information, and handling non-SNA logons. Each event has a special exit specified in ACF/VTAM. The ACF/VTAM administrator can set up routines to perform special functions by specifying those routines in the appropriate exit. This allows special installation-defined handling for any of the above cases.

The functioning of the network can be modified and various aspects changed while it is running. Special privileges are required to make network changes, but at least one userid (the network operator) should be available that has those privileges. The network operator functions are normally handled at the same location, and by the same person, that handles the normal operating system operator duties.

The network operator can do any of the following functions:

- Monitor the functioning of the network
- Change the configuration of the network
- Start and stop terminals
- Start paths between domains
- Request a logon between a terminal and an application
- Start the network
- Stop the network
- Modify the monitoring of the network
- Start or stop NCPs
- Communicate with other network operators.

SUMMARY

The MVS operating system has evolved tremendously from its beginnings as a primarily batch-oriented system. It still has a very highly developed batch system, and many of the jobs run are batch jobs, but it also supports many interactive users through a variety of subsystems available.

MVS is only used on relatively large computers since the system is so large and complex that there is a significant amount of overhead involved in running it. This overhead becomes insignificant on very large computers, since the additional sophistication extracts more performance from the computer than is lost to the system overhead. Small computers just do not have sufficient processor power and memory size to allow the necessary overhead involved in running MVS. The primary change in the extended architecture is to the addressing modes used in both the hardware and the software.

Another major change for MVS/XA is greatly increased performance in the I/O system. Many changes have been made in both the hardware and software to improve I/O performance. Much of the processing necessary to handle I/O were previously done only in the primary processor. Many of these functions have now been off-loaded to subsidiary processors dedicated just to I/O. Other changes improve the way I/O is handled on computers with multiple central processors, so that an I/O operation started on one processor may sometimes complete on the other processor. This reduces the wait time necessary to actually complete the operation.

EXERCISES

DISCUSSION QUESTIONS

1. Briefly describe the primary characteristics of the MVS system.
2. Discuss TSO and TSO/SPF.
3. Briefly describe the primary function of CICS and list the three primary parts of it.
4. Describe the function of SMP/E.
5. List and briefly describe the four types of system modifications.
6. List eight features provided by the DFDSS program.
7. Briefly describe the functions of the MVS supervisor.
8. List and describe three types of interrupts.
9. Describe the three categories of priorities used for scheduling tasks.
10. Explain how the MPL affects swapping.

11. List five types of information collected by SMF about jobs.
12. List five types of information collected by SMF about I/O.
13. Briefly describe the functions of RMF.
14. Describe the primary tool used by MVS to tune system I/O.
15. Describe the file access levels in RACF.
16. Describe the most important consideration when installing RACF.
17. Briefly describe the locks used by MVS to manage resources.
18. Discuss how MVS avoids the deadlock problem.
19. Briefly describe SNA.
20. Describe the primary functions of ACF/VTAM.

VMS Version 3.6

17

KEY TERMS

Digital Command Language (DCL)	*File version number*
Image file	*Global symbols*
System images	*Shareable images*
Executable images	*Symbolic debugger*
SYSGEN utility	*AUTOGEN utility*
Files-11 Structure Level 1	*Files-11 Structure Level 2*
Index file	*Bad block file*
Pending bad block file	*File headers*
Volume set list file	*Master File Directory (MFD)*
Storage bit map file	*Continuation file*
Bad block locator (BAD)	*Volume set*
Disk Save and Compress (DSC)	*BACKUP command*
Logical names	*Device name*

KEY TERMS

Unit number	*Context switching*
Asynchronous system traps (ASTs)	*Local event flag*
Condition handlers	*Detached processes*
Subprocesses	*Process mailbox*
Global sections	*Process mailbox*
Lock value blocks	*Blocking AST's*
Real-time processes	*Time-slice*
Resident system area	*Working set limit*
Balance set area	*Working set extent*
Working set quota	*Modified page area*
Free page area	*Memory sharing*
Global page table	*Monitor utility*

Hardware Process Control Block (Hardware PCB)

Automatic Working Set Adjustment (AWSA)

KEY TERMS

Voluntary decrementing	*Target node*
Ancillary Control Processes (ACP)	*Protection mask*
User Identification Code (UIC)	*Group access*
Owner access	*World access*
System access	*Stack*
Stack pointer	*Point-to-Point network*
Multipoint network	*Control station node*
Tributary nodes	*Non-routing nodes*
Routing nodes	*Executor node*
DECnet VAX configuration database	*Command node*
Digital Data Communication Message Protocol (DDCMP)	

INTRODUCTION

DEC operating systems have traditionally been oriented toward interactive users instead of the batch usage for which early IBM operating systems were designed. This tradition is continued in the VMS operating system. In many respects, the relative youth of the operating system is an advantage, since it was designed with modern concepts in mind, and hence was not tied to older, sometimes inefficient designs.

The VMS system runs only on VAX computers, so it was designed with the architecture of those computers in mind, which allows it to make efficient usage of the hardware features available. The VMS system is very similar to VM, in that it runs on a range of computers from microcomputers to mainframes from the same vendor. DEC does not manufacture mainframes as large as some of those IBM manufactures, but the largest computers available for VMS, the VAX 8600, are significant mainframes.

VMS may very well be the best current compromise between all the necessary features of an operating system, such as performance, user-friendliness, interactive and batch applications, and a wide variety of available applications. It seems to be one of, if not the primary, operating system that DEC will make a mainstay for years to come.

OPERATING SYSTEMS SERVICES

VMS provides many useful tools and services that are accessible by the user. It does not include a wide variety of tools with the operating system, as UNIX does, but such tools are available. The tools available on VMS tend to cover an extremely wide range of applications. VMS is used for everything from a software development system to a production system, so every area has many tools available. The tools range from software control systems to manufacturing systems.

The trend in VMS seems to be to offer even more tools. The vast majority of DEC's software development effort seems to be going into VMS, and this effort is paying off with a rapidly evolving, sophisticated product. Probably the only significant area where VMS could be enhanced would be for it gain the software development tools used in UNIX, such as "lex" and "yacc", and it would seem from observing the evolution of VMS that this could happen in the near future.

User interface

The primary interface to VMS is the **Digital Command Language** or **DCL.** This is the command interpreter that accepts any normal communications from users. It signals readiness by displaying a "$" prompt. DCL commands can be entered whenever the prompt is showing.

VMS has a HELP facility to provide on-line information about various aspects of the system. Entering just "HELP" brings up a list of the different subjects on which information is available. Entering "HELP subject", where "subject" is selected from the list, displays information on that particular subject. This allows a user to progressively select more and more detailed information. Those users who already know the specific subject may go immediately to a display of information about that subject by entering the name of the desired topic following the keyword HELP.

DCL allows all commands to be abbreviated or spelled out in full. All commands can be abbreviated to no more than four letters. The actual number of characters necessary is that number that makes the command unique, which is frequently only one or two.

DCL has many more features that just accepting commands. It can actually be used as a programming language, although it is not appropriate as a language for large applications. One of the most useful features of DCL is the ability to set up substitutions for commands or command parameters. Almost any character string may be defined as a substitute for almost any other character string, so commands or parameters that are used frequently can be abbreviated by defining a character string that is equivalent to that command.

Another powerful aspect of DCL is the ability to set up command **procedures** which are files that contain a series of DCL commands. All of the commands in the file can be executed by just executing the file, which allows a significant savings in time and effort in cases where a series of commands are frequently executed.

There are several command procedure constructs that are very similar to those of high-level languages, and can be used in the same way. Symbols can be defined and used as variables, which can be modified arithmetically. Branching statements allow control to be transferred to another location in the command procedure. Comparison of strings and values is possible, with various actions conditionally invoked, depending upon the result of the comparison. Interactive communication with the terminal is possible, which allows messages to be written to the terminal, and values or strings picked up from the terminal and used subsequently in the procedure.

Editors

VMS supports four different editors. Two of the editors are designed to function in a batch mode. Batch mode editors use as input a file which contains a list of editor commands. These commands are then used to create or modify a specified file. The actual job runs in the batch system.

The other two editors are interactive editors. The primary editor on the VMS system is the "EDT" editor. It functions as either a line or full-screen editor. The line editor mode is primarily available to allow EDT to be usable on hard-copy terminals. EDT provides the normal functions of a good editor when functioning in full-screen mode. Characters that are displayed on the screen may be changed by merely moving the cursor with cursor movement keys to a location on the screen and typing in the new characters.

Many EDT functions can be performed with only one keystroke by using the keypad, the group of keys on the right side of the keyboard on DEC terminals. Virtually all of the EDT commands can be issued from this keypad, which greatly reduces the keystrokes necessary. If, for some reason, issuing the commands from the keypad is not satisfactory, each command can be issued from a command line that EDT provides.

The commands available provide for such functions as inserting and erasing portions of a file, locating specific character strings, moving and copying pieces of the file, and replacing one character string with another. There are also several advanced features available, such as changing the values of the keys in the keypad, or defining macros. Editor macros are also available. These are collections of normal editor commands that are grouped together in some buffer, and executed as a group by EDT.

Software tools

The VMS operating system has a very large number of software tools available. The operating system itself has many tools and many additional tools are available from DEC or other vendors.

The VMS operating system supports a wide variety of compilers that are supplied by DEC. Some of these are BASIC, BLISS, C, COBOL, FORTRAN, Pascal, and PL/1. There is also the VAX assembler, called MACRO-11. According to DEC, there are more than thirty compilers available on VMS.

Once the compilers or the assembler have created an object module, that module may be converted into an executable module, called an **image file,** by running the VAX-11 Linker. The linker resolves external references between modules, allocates memory to the image, and initializes its contents.

Symbols that are used between different modules (external references) are called **global symbols.** The linker inserts the correct values for any global symbol references. It searches all of the modules supplied with the LINK command, any module libraries supplied with the LINK command, any default user libraries, and the default system libraries. If the external reference cannot be resolved by searching these four sources, then an error message is generated.

Three different types of images are used on the VMS operating system. These are system images, shareable images, and executable images. System images are executable images that are part of the operating system. Shareable images are executable images that can be shared among several different processes. Executable images are load modules that can be executed by a process.

VMS has a **symbolic debugger** which can be used with all VMS compilers and the MACRO-11 assembler. It allows the execution of a program to be carefully monitored, by single-stepping the instructions, stopping at a particular location, viewing or changing memory, and setting up mnemonic symbols.

VMS is designed to serve primarily as an interactive system, but batch processing is also supported. Almost any program that can be run interactively can also be run in batch mode. The program, commands, and data necessary to run are combined in a file and submitted to the batch system. The jobs are placed in a batch queue. The next batch job in the queue begins executing whenever there are fewer batch jobs than the maximum allowable on the system. The systems programmers define the number of different batch queues available and the number of jobs that can execute at the same time.

VMS has a SORT/MERGE utility designed to perform various types of sorting operations. It also allows files to be selectively combined. The PATCH utility is used to change the contents of various files that cannot be changed by a text editor, such as an executable module.

A tremendous variety of other software tools are also available for VMS. These range from accounting and financial packages to engineering CAD/CAM packages. The VMS system has been available for a long enough period of time, and has been widely enough accepted, so that virtually any package is available from some vendor.

Systems generation

The systems generation process for VMS is similar to that of other systems. There are various systems parameters that must be modified properly to reflect the correct computer configuration and desired options. Much of this process is automated and is performed by the "SYSGEN" utility program.

The first step in generating a new copy of VMS is to load the starter version of the system from the vendor distribution tapes onto a disk drive. The tapes have standalone utilities on them that can be loaded into the system, and are used to initially format the disk drives that are to receive the system. Another standalone utility is then used to load the system from the tapes onto the disk drives. When this is done, a usable system exists, but that system must usually still be configured for that particular installation.

There are two basic ways to configure, or reconfigure VMS systems. One way is via the "AUTOGEN" program, which automatically adjusts all system parameters to match the current configuration. The other way uses the SYSGEN utility to manually adjust various system parameters. AUTOGEN should always be used unless there is a specific reason for bypassing it, since the AUTOGEN-supplied default values are usually better choices than manual ones, except when specific problems are being addressed.

AUTOGEN can be used at any time to reset the system parameters, although they will only be changed if something in the system configuration has changed, so it should be used whenever the system configuration changes. The system configuration can also be determined with AUTOGEN. When AUTOGEN is called with the "CONFIG" parameter, it checks the physical devices attached to the computer, and then creates a file called "CONFIG.DAT", which contains the physical configuration, such as the model of the processor, the size of real memory, and how many disk drives, tape drives, terminals, printers, etc., are attached to the system. It also specifies the speed of the disk drive used as the system disk. A potential problem exists if the configuration file is created while some of the devices attached to the system are not operational, since they may not appear in the configuration file.

The CONFIG.DAT file is then used as input to AUTOGEN for the next step in the system configuration process. This step is performed by invoking AUTOGEN with the "GENPAR" parameter. This file is called "PARAMS.DAT". It contains the same configuration information as CONFIG.DAT, but it also contains initial guesses at some system parameters, such as the maximum number of processes or pages available.

After the initial parameters have been determined, AUTOGEN can be used to update the system files, and to start using those files. Invoking AUTOGEN with no parameter causes the contents of the last PARAMS.DAT file to be used to update the necessary system parameters and files. The "SHUTDOWN" option causes the system to be shut down after the system files are updated. The "REBOOT" parameter causes the system to be loaded (booted) after the system files have been updated.

AUTOGEN can also be used to manually update some system parameters. Other system parameters require the SYSGEN utility, but those that can be updated through AUTOGEN should be done that way, since it will automatically update any related parameters to match. SYSGEN is almost completely manual, so if some related parameters must be updated, it is up to the systems programmers to remember those parameters and to select appropriate values for them.

The system parameters can be updated with AUTOGEN by editing the PARAMS.DAT file and changing or adding values to it. This file is used as input by AUTOGEN when actually updating the system files, so any new or added values in it are used to modify the system files. AUTOGEN should be used to change the size of the primary dump, paging, or swapping files, but cannot be used to handle secondary dump, paging, or swapping files.

SYSGEN can be used to modify system parameters to create secondary dump, paging, and swapping files, and to add in unusual device drivers. SYSGEN is used by issuing commands to it and writing out the modified files. System parameters can be modified with the "SET" commands in SYSGEN. After these parameters have been modified, a new system image can be written to disk, and this new system image will be used the next time the system is started.

Example 17-1:

SIMPLE SYSTEMS GENERATION PROCESS

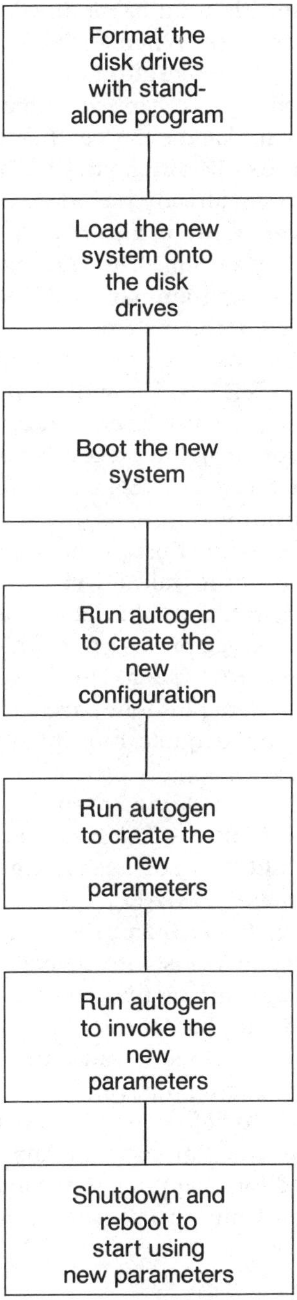

SYSGEN can also be used to modify some system parameters while the system is running. Not all system parameters can be modified this way, since some of them set up structures that cannot be modified while the system is running. Those parameters that can be modified while the system is running are called **dynamic** parameters. When SYSGEN is used to modify dynamic parameters, the changed values take effect immediately, but only in the copy of the system that is in memory. An explicit command is required to have the system image file on disk updated to reflect the new parameter values.

All common devices can be automatically configured in the system, because their device drivers are already included. Unusual devices, which must have custom device drivers written, also require that those device drivers be included in the operating system. The inclusion of these drives requires explicit action by a systems programmer. SYSGEN is the means by which such device drivers are included in the system.

VMS uses files for dumps, paging, and swapping. Those files are called "SYSDUMP.DMP", "PAGEFILE.SYS", and "SWAPFILE.SYS". They are normally created automatically, but can be created manually with SYSGEN whenever the automatic creation or sizing process is not adequate.

The CREATE parameter in SYSGEN is used to create new primary copies, (or extend the old copy), of the dump, paging, and swapping files. These files do not replace the old files while the system is running; it must be shut down and rebooted before the new files take effect.

The size of these system files can be determined manually. The paging file should be as large as the average process, multiplied by the maximum number of such processes allowed in the system. The dump file should be as large as the internal memory on the system plus four pages. The swapping file should be as large as the average working set quota, multiplied by the maximum number of processes on the system.

The latest versions of the dump, paging, and swapping files are used whenever the system is initially loaded. If secondary paging or swapping files are to be used, they should be made available after the system is loaded, by using the SYSGEN parameter INSTALL.

Secondary files can be larger than primary files, and they do not have to reside on the system disk. Systems with several disk drives should normally use secondary paging and swapping files, since any significant activity to those files will create a performance bottleneck if they are all on the system disk.

Nothing explicit need be done to cause the system to use the secondary files. The largest available paging file is always used for any new processes, although any processes created before that file was available will continue to use the same paging file that they started with. Any swapping file that has space available in it can be used for swapping, so secondary swapping file usage can be forced by either not creating a primary swapping file, or by making it very small.

FILE SYSTEMS

The VMS file system actually consists of two different file systems. The file system native to VMS is known as **Files-11 Structure Level 2,** but it will also accept the file structure native to the DEC RSX family of operating systems, called **Files-11 Structure Level 1.** All of the discussion in this section will center around the file structure native to VMS.

The VMS file system is divided into sections, called **volumes.** Volumes are usually disk drives. Volumes can be either public or private, with public volumes accessible to almost all users, and private volumes accessible only to a specific group of users. Volumes must be **mounted** before they are available to be used. Mounting a volume allows the operating system to access it to determine that it does indeed contain a valid VMS file structure.

It is possible to create a logical volume that encompasses several physical volumes. This allows very large files that span more than one physical volume. It is the option of the systems programmers to create such a **volume set** or not. It is possible to add a newly initialized physical volume to a volume set, but it is not possible to join two current volumes into one logical volume set. The system disk should never be part of a volume set, since this may prevent installing some system components.

The file system is maintained by nine files which keep complete information about the status of the files on that device, the condition of the device itself, and the usage of the space available. These files contain an index of the files in the file system, a map of which blocks are in use, a map of which blocks are defective (and thus unusable), and several other items.

The most critical file used in maintaining the file system is the **index** file. This file contains information that must be available to the system whenever access to any file is required. This file serves as an index to all other files on that volume. It contains the information that identifies that volume to VMS, and a list of all files on that volume, together with the information necessary to access any of those files. This information is kept in the index file as **file headers** which contain the name of the file along with sufficient additional information to allow that file to be accessed.

The **master file directory** or **MFD** contains the list of reserved files used to maintain the file system and the list of users' file directories. The **volume set list file** is used to keep the list of the labels of all volumes in a set. It contains valid information only on the first volume of a set. The **continuation file** contains the applicable file names when a file spans multiple volumes. It contains information only on subsequent volumes of a set, and not on the first volume.

The **storage bit map file** is used to keep track of all the blocks on a volume. Each block on the volume is represented by a bit, and the availability of that block is determined by the state of the bit.

The **bad block file** contains a list of the defective blocks that have been detected on that volume. These blocks will not be used to store data as long as they are listed in the bad block file. The **pending bad block file** is used to maintain a list of blocks that are suspected of being bad, but that are not yet proven to be bad.

A very nice feature of the VMS file system is the ability to use **logical names** to specify files or devices. A logical name is a string of characters that is used as equivalent to another string of characters. They are usually used as mnemonics for device and file names. Device names are fixed, and while file names may be somewhat mnemonic, they also have certain restrictions, but logical names have fewer rules.

Example 17-2:

LOGICAL NAME	***EQUIVALENT NAME***	***MEANING***
ARCHIVE	MTA1:	A specific tape drive
TEMPFILE	DBB2:TEMP.DAT;2	A temporary file

There are three different levels of logical names used in VMS. Each level maintains a logical name table that is searched when a logical name is discovered. Process logical names are maintained separately for each process, and only that process can access those names. This allows each process to identify any desired logical names without worrying about a possible conflict with logical names defined by another process. Group logical names are shared among all the processes in a specific group. These logical names may be used by anyone in the group without requiring a definition by that person. System logical names are defined throughout the system, and may be used by any process.

VMS has a pre-defined order to search for logical name definitions. The process logical name table is searched first, followed by the group table, and the system table is last. This implies that if a process logical name is defined that is identical to a system logical name, the system will actually use the process definition instead of the system definition, since the process table is searched first, and the search ends when the name is found.

The VMS file system provides extensive features in the file naming conventions. It has directories and sub-directories that are very similar to the directories and sub-directories available in UNIX.

A VMS file name consists of three parts: the file name, file type, and file **version number.** The file name is a string of characters, either alphabetic or numeric, from one to nine characters in length. The file name is followed by a period, ("."), which is followed by the file type. The file type is three characters, either alphabetic or numeric, denoting the type of file. The file type is optionally followed by a semicolon and a version number.

Example 17-3:

SAMPLE DIRECTORY STRUCTURE

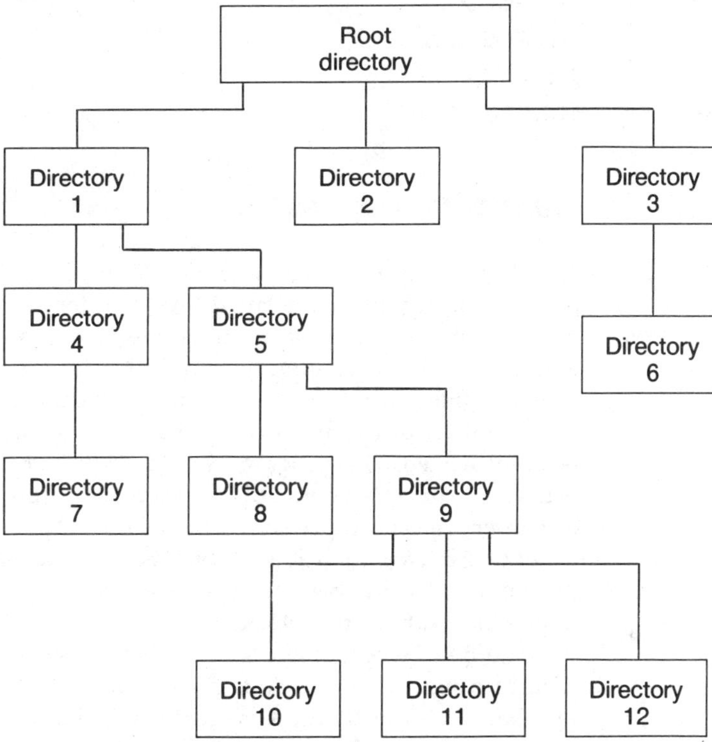

The version number is a number used to keep different versions of the same file. Most operating systems require that different names be used if multiple versions of the same file are to be maintained, but VMS allows multiple copies of the same file, with the same file name and file type, as long as the version numbers are different. When specifying a name without the version number, the default version number is the most recent version. Editing a file creates a new version of the file, and the old version is retained unless explicitly deleted.

Files that are not on the current file device may be accessed by specifying the "device name" and the "unit number", followed by a colon and the normal file specification. The device name specifies the type of device, such as "MT" for a magnetic tape drive. The unit number specifies which of those units is to be accessed, such as "A1" for controller "A" and drive "1".

Example 17-4:

SAMPLE FILE NAMES

MYPROG.ASM
MYPROG.ASM;3
INVENT.DAT;2
MTA1:TEMP.DAT

Bad block locator

The VMS file system is generally quite secure and reliable. If problems arise, there is a utility program called BAD that locates and keeps track of any bad blocks on the device. Most of the problems with an inherently reliable file system (such as VMS) come from physical failures on the disk device, instead of from any failures in the software causing blocks to be lost files to be corrupted.

The BAD program is designed to be run only on disks before they have been initialized. This program should never be run on any disk that has valid data on it, since that data will be destroyed. If problems are suspected with a disk after it has been placed in service, the data on that drive should be copied to another device, such as another disk or a tape backup, before BAD is run on it. After the data has been salvaged, BAD can be run on the disk to determine if it does indeed have bad blocks.

The BAD program checks the disk by writing sample data on the disk, then reading the data back, and checking it to ensure that the data that was read back in is exactly the same as the data that was written out. If the disk has problems, they will show up either as a failure to read or write, or as garbled data when checked against the data actually written.

Whenever an error is detected on a disk, the location of that block is recorded in a file on the disk. This file is maintained after the device is initialized for VMS, so that the file system will not use any blocks that are flagged as bad. The file is located in an area on the disk that is not used by the file system. If that area has bad blocks, the location of the bad block file may be moved slightly.

Most disks have some bad blocks on them, and they are quite usable as long as the number of bad blocks is relatively small. Bad blocks only become a problem on disks if new ones continue forming after the disk has been initialized, since that causes a loss of data.

Verify

The "VERIFY" program is designed to detect and fix those few cases when there is a problem with the file structure. The source of that problem may or may not be traceable to a physical error on the disk drive, but in any case, it is necessary to locate the problems in the file structure and to fix them.

The VERIFY utility searches the file structure on the specified volume to find any cases where files or blocks are in use but are marked in the directory as not used, or that are marked in the directory as in use but are not used. Inconsistencies in the file structure can lead to a completely corrupted file structure if they are not fixed.

VERIFY should be run regularly to determine if any errors exist in the file structure. If such errors exist, then the problems should be analyzed as well as possible before any repairs are attempted. It is also a good idea to cease all updating of that file structure, and to back it up immediately when errors are detected. Such problems can propagate very quickly, and an error that is easily fixable now may become catastrophic in a short time.

After every possible precaution has been taken, the VERIFY utility should be run with the REPAIR option, so that it will attempt to fix any inconsistencies or errors in the file structure. After this run, each of the affected files should be carefully checked to ensure that the repairs were successful, and that the contents of those files are correct. If the file contents are not correct, it may be necessary to restore from the backup just performed, and to recover as much as possible of the files manually before trying the REPAIR option again.

Disk Save and Compress

The **disk save and compress** program (**DSC**) is a hold-over from earlier versions of VMS. There are many VMS systems still using it. It has two different functions: to back up the disks and to rearrange the file structure on the disks.

The DSC program backs up a disk volume either to tapes or to another disk volume. The volume can then be restored to the same or a different disk volume. It also compresses the files when they are restored. The compression function is not necessary when the disk volume has been little used, but if the volume has been used heavily, the files on it may be fragmented, and then the compression will greatly improve the performance when those files are accessed. This program is no longer recommended, since all of it's functions have been superseded by the BACKUP utility program.

Backup system

An extensive backup system is an integral part of the VMS file system. It allows a wide variety of backups to be performed. These backups can be done by a system operator as regular system backups, or can be done by individual users. Both complete volumes and individual files can be backed up and restored.

The BACKUP program has a variety of commands and options that allow the different types of backups to be performed. It can be used to back up data either to tape drives or to other disk drives, and can perform full backups, incremental backups, or individual file backups.

Files that are active when the backup is being performed may or may not be able to be read after they have been restored, so backup programs on different operating systems react differently when attempting to back up an active file. Many backup systems simply choose to ignore the file, and not back it up at all, which is certainly the worst choice, since even a possibly-corrupted backup is better than no backup at all.

The VMS BACKUP utility offers two different choices in backing up active files. The simple choice is to dismount and write-lock the volume to be backed up. This ensures that there will be no active files on that volume. Unfortunately, such extreme measures may not be possible on systems that are in heavy use at the time. In such cases, it is possible to specify that the backup should be performed on active files, as well as inactive files. The backup may not be valid for such active files, but it is better than no backup, since it may be valid.

The IMAGE option in the backup command creates an identical backup of the volume to be backed up. This is most useful for performing full backups, particularly when it may be necessary to restore the entire volume instead of just restoring selected files. A good candidate for such image backups is the system disk.

Individual files can be backed up by specifying the names of the files in the BACKUP command. Whole groups of files can be backed up by specifying directory names instead of individual file names. Wild-card specifiers can also be used in the file names to back up selected groups of files. This is an option that is frequently used by users.

Incremental backups can be done by specifying the option SINCE =BACKUP in the BACKUP command. This backs up all files modified since the last recorded backup. Backups may be recorded by using the "RECORD" option. This causes the current date to be saved as a recorded backup. Each file header has an area for maintaining the date that file was last backed up, and the RECORD option updates that field. Using the RECORD and SINCE=BACKUP options together allow a normal incremental backup to be performed, and leaves the file system prepared for the next incremental backup.

Problems may result if users are using the RECORD option to perform their individual backups. The incremental backup searches only back to the last RECORDed backup. If users are using the RECORD option to back up individual files, the last RECORDed backup will not have been of all changed files in the file system, just that user's.

There are only two ways to effectively implement an incremental backup system. One way is to prevent the users from RECORDing their backups, which is not desirable, but does allow the backup system to be fully automated. The other way is to manually record the date of the last incremental backup, and specify that date in the SINCE= option, in place of the keyword BACKUP. For example use SINCE=08-MAY-1984 instead of SINCE=BACKUP. This circumvents the RECORDing problem, but it is not as cleanly implemented as the other way.

The full backups that are necessary to supplement the incremental backups can be performed by specifying the option "IMAGE" in the backup command. This allows the volume in question to be restored, and ready to use, in one operation.

MULTIPROGRAMMING

VMS is a full multiprogramming system. It supports the simultaneous running of many different jobs. These jobs do not actually run simultaneously, of course, since the VAX computers are not parallel processors, but the jobs seem to the user to be all executing simultaneously. Each job in the VMS system is called a process, similarly to the UNIX system.

Processes can be created in three ways. The most common way is when a user logs on to the system from a terminal. Another way is when VMS starts executing a job in batch mode. The last way is for DECnet, the DEC communications system, to start executing a job for a remote user. Each process may have different execution requirements, but they are all treated similarly by the system, at least until special requirements become evident.

Each process that is in the system has a **hardware process control block** or (**hardware PCB**) which is used to hold the current register values for that process. When a process gives up control of the processor, its register values are stored in its hardware PCB. The processor registers are loaded with the values from the hardware PCB belonging to the next process that is to receive control of the processor. This switching of processes and register values is called **context switching.**

There are several different items used to control the execution of processes. The **local event flags** are used to specify a wait for some function to complete. These are held in 64 bits. A process can specify that some function is to set a particular local event flag bit when it completes, and then the process can either wait until that bit is set, or it can continue running while periodically checking the bit to see if it is set. Such flags are frequently used to show when I/O has completed.

Asynchronous system traps or **ASTs** approximately correspond to interrupt conditions on some systems. ASTs allow a process to request that some routine be executed when a specific event happens such as receiving an I/O interrupt. AST routines may execute at different priorities and security levels than do user processes.

Condition handlers deal with exception conditions, such as hardware or operating system errors. These errors are repaired unless some component of the system fails. Errors caused by an individual process, however, must be handled by that process.

An example of this is what happens when a process executes an instruction that results in a division by 0. A division by 0 is an algebraically undefined operation, and is considered an error by the computer. Such errors are caused by the user process, so the processor or the operating system will not handle the error, but instead just report it to the user process. Such an error usually results in a failure of the process, but that process may have a routine available to recover from that particular error. All that is necessary is to declare that routine to be a condition handler. When the error occurs, the condition handler is given control. It can then continue as necessary, which usually either is to resume execution of the process, or to abort the process in a graceful manner.

There are two ways in which a process can create another process. A **subprocess** is a created process which shares the same system resources as the process which created it. It is essentially just an extension of the original process. **Detached processes,** on the other hand, are separate processes, with a separate set of resources. Almost any process can create subprocesses, but only processes with certain privileges can create detached processes.

One of the most important aspects of running many processes is providing a facility to allow communications between different processes. Several such facilities exist in VMS. **Common event flags** are very similar to the 64 bit local event flag, but can be accessed by multi-processes. They are very useful for telling other processes that a specific event is completed.

A process **mailbox** is a type of temporary file that most processes can access. It is kept in memory instead of on disk. A mailbox is created by a process which can then read any information in that mailbox; other processes can write information into that mailbox. Normal I/O commands are used to read and write mailbox information.

Areas of memory can be set up to be accessible to many processes. Such areas are called **global sections.** One process initially sets up the global section and specifies what type of access (read-only or read-write) will be granted to other processes. Some processes (usually systems processes) can set up global sections that are permanent and remain in memory until explicitly deleted.

VMS uses locks to control access to shared resources. There are six different levels of locks, depending upon the degree of sharing available on that resource. Locking information is passed between different processes with lock **value blocks.** These blocks provide information on the lock status of a requested resource. **Blocking AST's** are used to notify a process which has a resource locked that other processes need that resource.

JOB AND TASK SCHEDULING

The VMS scheduler is similar in many ways to the scheduler used in the VM operating system. The basic algorithm used is the "round-robin" method. This allows each process in the system to have an opportunity to use the processor. The basic algorithm is modified by each process having an associated priority. Processes that are ready to use the processor are called computable, while processes that are waiting for some event are in a wait state.

One of the unique features of the VMS scheduler that is not characteristic of most operating systems is support for real-time events. Real-time events, by their nature, must be handled immediately, so they receive special consideration by the scheduling algorithms. This is accomplished by giving priorities to real-time processes that cause them to be scheduled ahead of anything else, even operating system functions.

The priorities available to processes range from 0 to 31. The higher numbers reflect higher priorities. Real-time processes have the priority numbers from 16 to 31, the highest priorities. Most interactive processes are given priorities of 4. System processes have most of the priorities between 4 and 15.

The scheduler automatically adjusts priorities for processes other than real-time processes. The priorities of real-time processes cannot be altered by the scheduler. The adjustment of priorities is used to modify the normal wait time before a process is allowed access to the processor. For example, a process that has just received a terminal interrupt will have its priority increased, so that a quick response to the terminal request is possible.

The scheduling algorithm allocates an amount of time that is available to each process when it gains control of the processor. This amount of time is called a **time-slice.** A process remains in control of the processor until its time-slice is exhausted, unless some other event occurs. Such events are the process entering a wait state, or another process becoming computable with a higher priority.

Whenever the state of some process changes, such as when a process that is waiting on an I/O interrupt receives that interrupt, the scheduler reevaluates the status of all processes. If any computable process has a higher priority than the process that is currently controlling the processor, that process is removed from the processor and the higher priority process is given control.

None of the normal scheduling algorithms are used with real-time processes. They are not subject to any type of scheduling. Real-time processes remain in control of the processor until voluntarily relinquishing it or being preempted by a higher priority real-time process. The real-time processes in the system must be severely limited if that system is to provide adequate support for time-sharing users as well since each of these real-time processes has the potential of controlling the processor for extended periods of time.

Example 17-5:

PRIORITY STRUCTURE

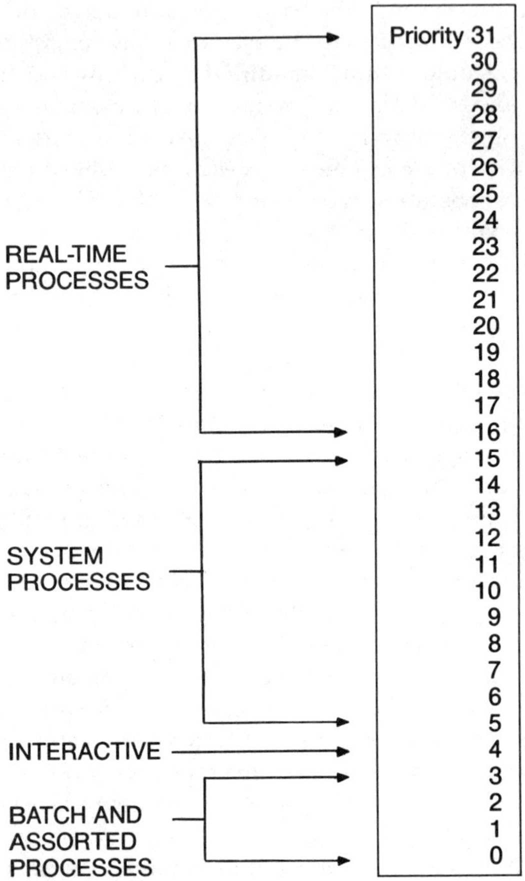

A potential problem with the VMS scheduling system is that one process at a high priority may use a disproportionate amount of processor time. This may not be a real problem if the high priority process actually needs the processor time, but it may indicate a failure to properly assign priorities. If the offending process is at a sufficiently high priority, it may not be possible to solve the problem short of a system shutdown.

VIRTUAL MEMORY

VMS has a very sophisticated and complex memory management system which is designed to provide good support both for computers with large and small internal memories. A large number of parameters can be adjusted to affect the performance of the virtual memory system. Fortunately, the default values for these parameters are well-chosen and they do not often have to be changed.

The memory on the VAX computer is divided into three major sections. One area is the **resident system** area, which contains those portions of the operating system that must be in memory at all times and cannot be paged out. The next area is the **page cache** area, which is where the free pages are maintained. The last area is called the **balance set** area, and is used to maintain the working sets of the executing processes.

Example 17-6:

MEMORY ORGANIZATION

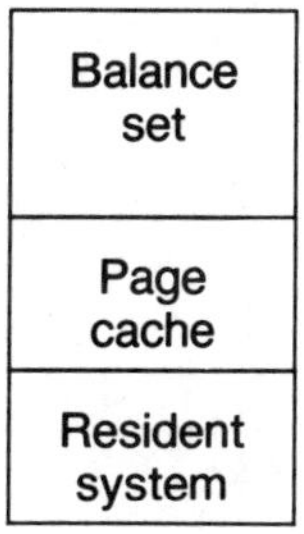

The VMS operating system does both paging and swapping. The page size is 512 bytes, and the swap set size varies depending upon the working set size of the process being swapped. The working set varies in size depending upon the requirements of the individual processes, although minimum and maximum sizes may be set by the systems programmer.

All processes must have a working set. These working sets are maintained in the "balance set" part of memory. Each working set occupies one slot in the balance set. There is a fixed number of slots available in the system, and only as many processes may be in memory at any one time as there are slots available. The number of slots available can also be set by the systems programmer.

If a large number of slots are allocated in the balance set, then the working set size of each of the processes occupying those slots must be quite small. If those processes only need a small working set this is adequate. If they need larger working set sizes, significant degradation if performance may result. Working set sizes set too small leads to excessive paging and swapping of processes, with the resulting increase in systems overhead. Working set sizes set too large, however, leads to wasted memory as the processes fail to utilize all of the memory available.

The number of slots controls the number of working sets available, but it does not control the size of any one individual working set. The average size of the working sets is determined by the number of slots, since a total amount of memory is being divided up among a certain number of slots, but each slot can use as much memory as is needed and available for its working set.

Example 17-7:

BALANCE SET ORGANIZATION

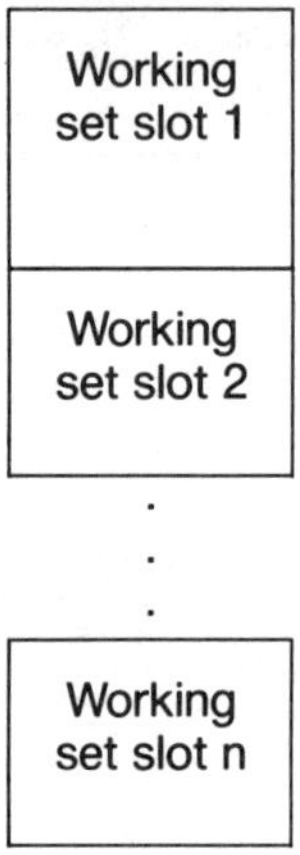

Each process must have a working set before that process is allowed to enter memory. There is no way of knowing in advance how large the working set should be for a process, so each process starts with a certain default number of pages in the working set. Each process is allowed to add pages as needed up to a certain limit called the **working set quota.** Additional pages may not be available beyond this limit, even if the process needs those pages.

A process that reaches its working set quota and needs still more pages may be able to borrow them provided that enough memory is available. There is an additional limit to the number of pages that can be borrowed. This limit is called the **working set extent** and constitutes the final value that the size of the working set can attain.

Working set sizes are changed by the system to reflect the current needs of each of the processes. These changes are made at regular time intervals. The characteristics of the processes' paging are examined, and the working set sizes increased or reduced. The length of time between examinations must be an integral multiple of the processor timeslice.

Two system parameters contain upper and lower values for process paging rates. Any process that has a paging rate outside this range is subject to having its working set size adjusted. Paging rates below the lower value may lead to a reduction in the size of the working set, while paging rates above the upper value may lead to a increase in the size of the working set size. Any adjustments are dependent upon the paging requirements upon the system as a whole, since additional pages may not be available to increase a working set size, or unused pages may not be needed by any other process.

Process working set sizes may grow freely up to the working set quota. When a process has reached its quota, but still needs more pages, those pages must come from the page cache area of memory. This area is divided into two parts, the **free page area** and the **modified page area.** The free page area is an area of memory that is available for use while the modified page area is the part of the page cache that is currently in use by processes.

A process may exceed its working set quota only if enough pages are available in the free page area to satisfy the specified increment in size. If these pages are not available in the free area, other processes in the system have already used up all available free memory and no more can be granted.

DEC has published recommendations on how these values should be chosen. They recommend starting with certain values, and then adjusting those values to fit more correctly after observing the performance of the processes. They recommend a limit of 60 to 200 pages for typical small processing, such as editing and small compilations, and 200 to 500 pages for larger jobs such as compiling large programs.

The VMS virtual memory system supports swapping as well as normal paging. This involves paging out the entire working set of a process, instead of just individual pages. Swapping is a rather extreme measure in the VMS environment, so it is used as a last resort when nothing else is available to improve the performance of the paging system.

When the number of available free pages reaches minimum a value, steps are initiated to recover some memory. The first step is to try to recover, temporarily, some of the pages in the page cache. This is done by checking the modified page list, to see if enough pages are in that area to bring the number of free pages back up to the minimum amount. If enough pages do exist in the modified page area, then those pages are paged out, and those page frames are added to the free page list.

The modified page area is not paged out if this would still not allow the number of free pages to reach the minimum value. Instead, an attempt is made to reduce the size of the working sets. Since this is initiated by the swapper in VMS, it is called **swapper trimming.** The swapper trims until the required number of free pages becomes available.

The first step in swapper trimming is to check for any processes that have borrowed pages. These processes can be reduced back to their quota at the discretion of the system. This may not result in freeing very many pages, however, if only a few pages were borrowed, as in cases where most of memory is used by working set slots and only a small amount is available for the page cache area.

Example 17-8:

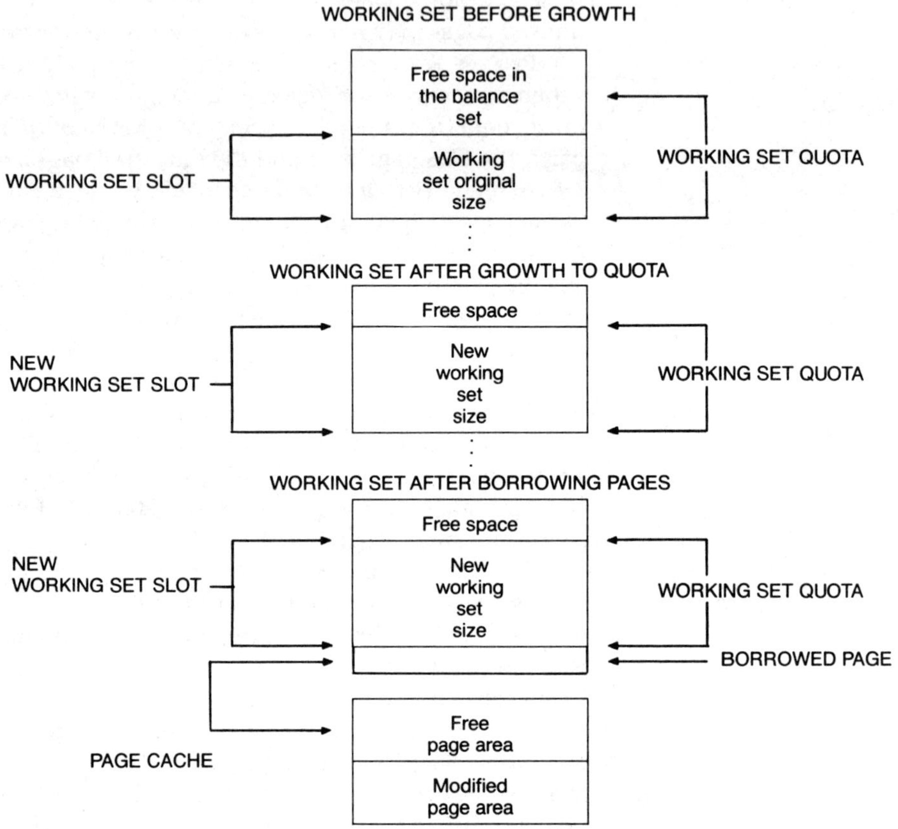

The second level of trimming is selectively reducing the size of the working sets of processes. These are processes that have not exceeded their working set quota, but may not be using some of their pages. No working set is reduced below a minimum level, and only relatively inactive pages are trimmed.

Swapping is instituted when both levels of trimming have failed to produce the minimum number of free pages. Swapping takes the entire working set for a process and pages it out as a block into a swapping file. The swapping files, and sometimes the swapping devices, are maintained separately from the paging files.

The most likely candidates for swapping out are those processes that are waiting on some event to occur. An attempt is made to identify those processes that are least likely to require processor time in the near future.

Most swapping can be avoided by setting the minimum working set size to a small value. If the value is too small, then the working sets may be trimmed so far that the overall paging rate goes up, but it should certainly be smaller than the value needed for best efficiency. A working set should be of a size that allows the best efficiency whenever enough memory is available to accommodate working sets of that size.

Reducing the overall swapping rate is particularly critical on small systems, where one device may be providing the disk space needed for all swapping and paging. It is usually better to have all processes available but running slowly, than to have most processes running quickly while some processes are unavailable until they are swapped back in.

There is a feature called **memory sharing** on the VMS system that greatly reduces the amount of internal memory required. Several different processes can share the same section of memory so that the memory is virtually present to each process.

Any memory that is to be shared by more than one process must be read-only to each of those processes. No process is allowed to modify shared memory. The most usual way to share memory is to set up an image of a program so that it can be shared. Memory sharing must be specified when the image is created.

Programs or data that are used by only one process should not be set up to be shared, but if several different processes may need access to those programs or data, then they should be set up to utilize shared memory. The amount of memory saved by using shared memory is proportional to the number of different processes actually using the shared area.

Shared memory areas do not come completely free; there is a small amount of overhead associated with maintaining the linkage from each process to that shared memory, but the overhead is minimal when compared to the overhead necessary to maintain separate copies of the memory. The mapping of virtual to real memory for shared memory is implemented with the global page table.

The system manager must ensure that the working set size for each shared memory user is large enough to comfortably encompass the shared memory area, as well as any other areas. The shared memory area is considered to be part of each process' working set, even though that memory may not be physically allocated to that process.

PERFORMANCE MEASUREMENT AND TUNING

Many VMS systems run quite well with no intervention necessary to improve performance. When a problem area does arise, great care must be taken when attempting to alleviate the problem, since many of the parameters involved are quite sensitive, and it is very easy to make the problem worse instead of better.

Performance Measurement

Ongoing system performance information can be obtained with the Monitor utility program. It allows the systems manager to monitor various aspects of system performance, such as paging, I/O, and process execution statistics. It produces an immediate display on a terminal and summary information in a disk file, or can simply record the data in a disk file for future display. It can be used to show either a real-time display, or long-term summary information.

The Monitor utility has a variety of options that allow most of the critical system functions to be displayed. The STATES command is used to display the number of processes in each possible state. This is somewhat similar to a general display, and is useful for determining if a problem area exists in some part of the system, without showing great detail on any area.

Example 17-9:

A sample STATES display

```
                            VAX/VMS Monitor Utility
                              PROCESS STATES (%)
                                SUMMARY      From: 21-APR-1985 01:00:00
                                             To:   21-APR-1985 02:00:00

                                         CUR%     AVE%     MIN%     MAX%

Collided Page Wait                       0.0      0.0      0.0      0.0
Mutex & Misc Resource Wait               0.0      0.0      0.0      0.0
Common Event Flag Wait                   0.0      0.0      0.0      0.0
Page Fault Wait                          0.0      0.0      0.0      0.0
Local Event Flag Wait                    0.0      0.0      0.0      0.0
Local Evt Flg (Outswapped)               0.0      0.0      0.0      0.0
Hibernate                                0.0      0.0      0.0      0.0

Hibernate (Outswapped)                   0.0      0.0      0.0      0.0
Suspended                                0.0      0.0      0.0      0.0
Suspended (Outswapped)                   0.0      0.0      0.0      0.0
Free Page Wait                           0.0      0.0      0.0      0.0
Compute                                  0.0      0.0      0.0      0.0
Compute (Outswapped)                     0.0      0.0      0.0      0.0
Current Process                          0.0      0.0      0.0      0.0
```

The status of the paging system can be displayed with the PAGE command in the Monitor utility. The format of the display is as follows:

Example 17-10:

```
                VAX/VMS Monitor Utility
              PAGE MANAGEMENT STATISTICS
                     21-APR-1985
                       01:00:00

                                  CUR     AVE     MIN     MAX
Page Fault Rate                   0.0     0.0     0.0     0.0
Page Read Rate                    0.0     0.0     0.0     0.0
Page Read I/O Rate                0.0     0.0     0.0     0.0
Page Write Rate                   0.0     0.0     0.0     0.0

Page Write I/O Rate               0.0     0.0     0.0     0.0
Free List Fault Rate              0.0     0.0     0.0     0.0
Modified List Fault Rate          0.0     0.0     0.0     0.0
Demand Zero Fault Rate            0.0     0.0     0.0     0.0
Global Valid Fault Rate           0.0     0.0     0.0     0.0

Wrt In Progress Fault Rate        0.0     0.0     0.0     0.0
System Fault Rate                 0.0     0.0     0.0     0.0
Free List Size                    0.0     0.0     0.0     0.0
Modified List Size                0.0     0.0     0.0     0.0
```

The system I/O status can be displayed by the IO command in the Monitor utility. The format of the display is as follows:

Example 17-11:

```
                VAX/VMS Monitor Utility
                 I/O SYSTEM STATISTICS
                     21-APR-1985
                       01:00:00

                                  CUR     AVE     MIN     MAX

Direct I/O Rate                   0.0     0.0     0.0     0.0
Buffered I/O Rate                 0.0     0.0     0.0     0.0
Mailbox Write Rate                0.0     0.0     0.0     0.0
Window Turn Rate                  0.0     0.0     0.0     0.0
Log Name Translation Rate         0.0     0.0     0.0     0.0
File Open Rate                    0.0     0.0     0.0     0.0
Page Fault Rate                   0.0     0.0     0.0     0.0
```

(Continued on page 432)

Example 17-11: *Continued from page 431*

Page Read Rate	0.0	0.0	0.0	0.0
Page Read I/O Rate	0.0	0.0	0.0	0.0
Page Write Rate	0.0	0.0	0.0	0.0
Page Write I/O Rate	0.0	0.0	0.0	0.0
Inswap Rate	0.0	0.0	0.0	0.0
Free List Size	0.0	0.0	0.0	0.0
Modified List Size	0.0	0.0	0.0	0.0

There are several other displays also available from the Monitor utility. These include DECNET statistics, file statistics, processor mode operation, the non-paged dynamic memory pool, and the status of all processes. Each of these displays may be useful for locating or solving a particular performance problem.

Performance Tuning

The VMS system is similar to other modern systems in the areas in which performance can be improved. The basic problems are usually I/O or paging. Sometimes problems may develop in other areas, but these are the most common areas, and the first place to look when a performance problem is suspected. The large number of system parameters available in VMS can make tuning somewhat more complex than on some systems, but most of these parameters need not be modified.

Paging Tuning

Two different paging areas are used in the VMS system. The best source is the page cache area. This is a fast and efficient source for pages. In the cases where this area is too small, the primary paging area becomes the disk drives, which are much slower than the paging cache. In such cases, the system performance can be increased by just increasing the size of the page cache.

The opposite of this problem is when the page cache is too large. This case is not as severe, since it is not necessary to do extra paging to the disk drives, but there is still some unnecessary overhead. The primary symptom of an oversized page cache area is a very high overall paging rate when most of the paging is coming from the page cache. An oversized page cache takes away much of the available memory from the process working sets, thus causing those working sets to be much smaller, so that the processes must borrow pages from the page cache. A good rule of thumb is for the page cache to be about 15% of the total memory size.

Excessive paging may also be caused by having the working set sizes too small. The normal paging system parameters are set correctly so that this will not happen, but there can be occasions when the normal system parameters are not adequate, particularly if some of those parameters have been modified previously.

The first place to look when processes are paging excessively is at the values set for the working set quotas and the working set extents. It is important to look at all the processes that have a high paging rate, but it is also necessary to look at all the other large processes, since they may be keeping more memory than is necessary. If the working set quotas are too large for some processes, then those processes will be keeping more memory than they really need, and thus not allowing other processes to use that memory. On the other hand, some processes may actually require larger values in order to avoid excessive paging.

The **Automated Working Set Adjustment** or **AWSA** normally adjusts the process working sets for the optimum sizes, within the constraints set by the values for working set quotas and extents. There are cases, however, where the AWSA may not be functioning correctly. In these cases, the overall paging rate may become excessive.

Sometimes the working set size requirements are changing so fast that the AWSA is unable to keep up. This can lead to AWSA increasing the working set size just after the increased size is no longer needed, or decreasing it just as a larger size is needed. The second problem occurs less often, so the most important problem is the first. This can sometimes be cured by increasing the amount by which the working sets are incremented, so that even though the increments do not come any more quickly, each increment is larger. It is also possible to decrease the time between each working set adjustment, but this step should be considered carefully before being implemented, since it causes an increase in system overhead.

There is an ongoing condition called **voluntary decrementing** where any process which has a paging rate below some minimum can automatically give up some of the pages in it's working set. Voluntary decrementing, in combination with AWSA, may lead to severe problems. The particular problems depend upon the characteristics of the workload at that installation.

In some installations, voluntary decrementing should be disabled when AWSA is used, since otherwise the working set sizes tend to oscillate. This decision should be made after observing the working set activity at that installation. AWSA may increase the working set size just in time for voluntary decrementing to reduce it, whereupon AWSA increases it again, etc. The opposite case is where voluntary decrementing has been disabled and should be turned back on. In these cases, AWSA increases the working set size to some large value, then the process retains that large working set size even though many of the pages are not being used. Enabling voluntary decrementing will cause these working set sizes to gradually decrease back down to a correct value.

Some cases exist where the values for swapper trimming and swapping must be adjusted. Some swapper trimming and swapping is desirable, but it should not be continuously applied to all processes. The VMS system is set up so that it operates most efficiently when no swapping is occurring, so attempts should be made to minimize the swapping. The entire paging and swapping system tends to be most efficient with some paging activity, but with no swapping.

One potential cause of excessive swapping is an inadequate number of balance slots defined in the system. If there is a large amount of free memory available while processes are being swapped, then it is possible that more balance slots should be allocated. Not so many balance slots should be allocated as to leave some of them unused, but any number up to that is appropriate, as long as a sufficient amount of free memory remains available.

I/O Tuning

I/O tuning probably plays less of a part with VMS than with other operating systems such as MVS or VM, since computers running VMS tend to have far fewer peripheral devices than do the very large computers that frequently run VM or MVS. Nevertheless, it is still quite important, particularly on the larger configurations. I/O problems may also sometimes be masked as paging or swapping problems, since a large percentage of the total I/O may sometimes come from paging or swapping.

The first area to check is the existence of a queue of I/O requests for any particular device. If no such queue exists, then it is probable that nothing need be done to improve the I/O system. If such a queue does exist, then it may seriously hamper the overall system performance. A queue for a particular device does not necessarily imply that that device is the problem, however, since the problem may be with the path to that device.

Many of the problems in the I/O system stem from the **Ancillary Control Processes** or **ACPs** that are used to manage the file system. A common problem is to have the same ACP servicing both a fast and a slow device, where the slow device is heavily loaded with I/O. This tends to make it very difficult for the faster device to receive adequate servicing, since the ACP is tied up servicing the slower device. If this is a problem, it may require setting up more than one ACP and dedicating an ACP to the slower device.

The ACPs use a memory cache to improve performance, but this cache only becomes effective if a large percentage of the I/O performed is able to come from the cache, instead of from the disks. If the cache is not working well enough, the ACP process will have a very high I/O rate. The cache should be large enough to maintain the critical read-only file information, such as directories or file headers, but should not be so large that it uses an excessive amount of memory.

VAX computers do not use channels like IBM computers. Instead, they use busses that serve the same purpose. If several devices are attached to the same bus, an I/O bottleneck may exist on the bus and not on any of the devices. This can be alleviated by moving some of the devices to a different bus. The devices on a bus should be grouped by speed, which can usually be done by grouping similar devices. For example, tape drives have a very high data transfer rate, so if tape drives are sharing the same bus with disk drives, the disk drives may not have adequate access to the bus. In this case, the tape drives and the disk drives can be separated onto separate busses.

One of the most common causes of I/O overloading on a disk drive is using that drive as the system disk, and keeping both paging and swapping files on it. Whenever possible, either or both of the paging and swapping files should be offloaded to another device(s). A minimal paging file must be maintained on the system disk, but all of the swapping file, and the bulk of the paging file, can be moved to another device.

Sometimes the problem is from directory access; in this case it may be appropriate to create many directories, and place some of them on other devices. Another factor that contributes to poor disk performance is fragmentation of the file system. If the disk has a large number of files written on it, and has not been reorganized recently, then the file system may have become fragmented. This can be cured by doing a backup, and then restoring the files, which compacts the file system.

Processor Tuning

Most systems do not require as much processor tuning as they do paging or I/O tuning. There may be several causes for processes not gaining access to the processor. The processor may be overloaded by some system process, such as paging or I/O. These cases can be solved by improving the paging or I/O, which is the real cause of the problem.

The processor may be tied up servicing a real-time process. This case can be solved by limiting the number or scheduling of real-time processes on the system. If it is not possible to limit the real-time processes, then there is little that can be done to solve this problem.

The processor may be locked up by a higher-priority process that is not real-time. The extreme case of this leads to a complete lock-out, where a very high priority process occupies the processor constantly, and allows no other processes access. This may occasionally force a system crash if the priority of the offending process cannot be modified. The usual case requires a systems programmer to use a process at an equally high priority to modify the priority of the process that is occupying the processor. This new process is able to gain access to the processor, since it is of equal or higher priority, and the offending process will not use as much of the processor time once its priority has been lowered.

The most common type of processor scheduling problem is when the processor is simply not able to adequately service all the processes competing for processor time. If the processes are not receiving adequate processor time, but they are all of similar priority and no other performance problem can be identified, then the problem is usually too much work for the available processor power. This problem can only be fixed by reducing or rescheduling the workload, or by acquiring a more powerful processor.

The real processor tuning comes in the cases where the processes are not receiving adequate servicing, but there is no easily discernible cause for the lack of processor performance. One possibility is too much activity on the interrupt stack. Each device on the system generates interrupts which must be serviced by the processor. When too many interrupts are generated, the processor may spend a large amount of time servicing them. The MONITOR utility can be used to display the amount of time the processor spends on the interrupt stack. If this value is significantly greater than 10%, then something should be done to modify the interrupt rate on the system. This may require removing some devices or changing some device or controllers to a different type.

A common solution in cases where the processor is overloaded and several different processes are competing for the processor is to modify the priorities on some of processes. Some processes tend to be more processor-bound and can usually survive receiving a lower priority. This allows the other processes, particularly interactive ones, to receive more of the processor time. The processes with lowered priorities are, of course, slowed by this, but such processes are usually less affected by slower execution than are interactive processes.

A very common source of interrupts on VAX systems is terminal activity. This tends to use an unusually high amount of processor time, since the interrupts are generated constantly. One way of reducing the interrupt problem from this area is to change the terminal controller to one that transfers more data each time. This allows the same data transfer rate, but significantly reduces the number of interrupts received.

Sometimes the processor is completely busy, but not enough of that time is being given to the user processes running in the system. This frequently points to excessive processor time being used up in servicing operating system overhead. This can usually be detected by using the MONITOR utility to display the kernel activity. If a significant percentage of the total processor time is spent in kernel mode, then it is probable that the operating system overhead is excessive.

The most common causes of excessive operating system overhead are problems in the paging and I/O systems. An acceptable overall level of performance in these areas may actually be masking an unacceptable performance level for some specific circumstances. For example, the overall I/O performance may be good, since this is an average, but if the system is having to wait to create spool files, then an excessive amount of processor time will be spent in the spooling system. This problem might only become visible on the rare occasions when very large files must be spooled, but on those occasions the system might degrade significantly. Another example is the case where an unreasonably high level of swapping is occurring. The swapping itself may be functioning quite well, but the processor may be burdened with constantly swapping.

If there are no other reasons for the operating system overhead, the problem might lie in the number chosen for the timeslice value, particularly if it has been modified at that installation.

Sometimes there is nothing that is possible to further tune the system to get more performance from the processor. In these cases, it is necessary to add more processor power. Additional processor power can be added in two different ways with the VAX and VMS environment. Additional computers can be added and configured in a VAX CLUSTER arrangement, where each computer is linked to all other computers in the cluster. The other alternative is to move to a more powerful computer.

The choice of alternatives is determined by the types of jobs running on the system. A job mix that contains many small jobs is ideally suited for running on multiple computers. A cluster arrangement provides increased uptime, since the cluster can continue running even after one or more computers in the cluster fail. Unfortunately, the individual components of the cluster are all relatively small computers, so the turnaround time for any one individual job is not improved by adding computers, except as excess load is removed.

A job mix that consists of a relatively few, large jobs tends to require going to a more powerful processor. The overall system throughput gain may be the same as with adding another small computer, but the individual turnaround times for the large jobs may be much less. Once the maximum size processor has been reached, of course, there is no alternative but to add additional computers. When the overall performance level of the cluster is the same as that of the larger model computer, the overall system throughput will be the same. A fully loaded cluster will turn around large jobs at the same overall rate as a large processor with the same load and performance level, but a partially loaded cluster will not turn those jobs around as fast as a large processor of the same size and load.

SYSTEMS SECURITY

The VMS system has extensive security features. There are many more than the standard levels of access provided by most operating systems. There are two major ways of providing security: through the **user identification code** or **UIC,** and through a **protection mask.** The UIC is originally assigned to a userid, and subsequently is propagated to any files or processes created by that userid. The protection mask is assigned to objects, usually files.

The UIC consists of two numbers, each in the range of 1 to 377 (octal notation). The first number is a group number to control group access. The second number is the member number, which is used to specify different members within a particular group.

All ownership is divided into four different levels. The highest level is that of the owner, who created the object being protected. A userid with a UIC identical to the UIC of an object is said to be the owner of that object. Group access is available to all users whose UIC group number is the same as that of the object being protected.

System access is available to users with a group number that is in a certain range, usually from 1 to 10. World access includes anyone who is not already included in one of the other groups.

Within each access group there are several different levels of access provided, including read access, write access, execute access, and delete access. Several lesser access privileges are also available, such as allocating files, performing logical or physical I/O on non-VMS file formatted volumes, looking up directories, and creating directories.

Objects that require protection, such as files or volumes, have a protection mask associated with them. The protection mask has four fields in it, one each for owner, group, system, and world accesses. Each field has four indicators, which are used to specify the level of access available to users in that particular category. These fields and indicators provide sixteen different bits that can be manipulated to grant a different level of access.

A file normally has the same UIC as the user who created it, but the access levels can be explicitly set on any owned file. This is done by specifying:

```
/PROTECTION=(S:RWED,O:RWED,G:RWED,W:RWED)
```

The different user accesses is specified by the S: for system access, O: for owner access, G: for group access, and W: for world access. The RWED gives read, write, execute, and delete privileges to that category of users. The above example gives full privileges to each group.

It is possible to completely remove the possibility of file deletion from all users, even the owner. In this case, no one can delete that file. This is done by default for directories, in order to prevent their accidental deletion. If such a file is to be deleted, its protection must first be changed to allow deletion, usually by the owner.

In order to provide complete file access protection, both the directory containing those file names and the files themselves should be protected. In particular, if read access is to be prevented, it is not enough to merely protect the directory, since a user who knows the appropriate file name can still access those files. It is also possible to write a program that randomly guesses file names until a file is found.

Example 17-12:

SECURITY FEATURES

```
                      UICs

                GROUP      MEMBER
                NUMBER     NUMBER
                   |          |
                  (nnn,mmm)
                  (377,377)
                  (10,50)   = >GROUP NUMBER ALLOWS
                               SYSTEM ACCESS

                PROTECTION MASKs

          SYSTEM OWNER GROUP WORLD
             |      |     |     |
          (bbbb,  bbbb,  bbbb,  bbbb)

READ   WRITE   EXECUTE   DELETE
```

Care should be taken when a file is to be copied to another user to ensure that that user has full access to the file. When a file is copied between directories, it is written with a UIC matching that of the user who did the copying. If the sending user does the copying, the receiving user may not be able to write to or delete the file. Sometimes this is desired, but more often the receiving user should have full control of the file. The easiest way to ensure this is to have the receiving user do the copying, so that the receiver then becomes the owner of the file.

Each process running in the system has an access mode defined that determines what level of system resources that process can access. There are four different levels of access mode. The least privileged is the user access mode, which is given to all users. The next is the supervisor access mode, which is normally given only to the less privileged components of the operating system. Next is the executive access mode, which is given to more privileged components of the operating system. The highest privilege is the kernel access mode, which is only available to the kernel of the operating system.

Each process owns a "stack" and a "stack pointer". A stack is a set of memory areas in which information can be stored. A stack operates in a LIFO fashion. The stack pointer is used to point to the next piece of information in the stack.

A user process is not allowed to access many areas, or facilities, of the computer. Allowing this access would bypass much of the security needed to protect one process from another. User processes are also not allowed to change to a higher access level, since this would also allow a security breach, yet many process requirements are such that a higher access level may be necessary.

A user process can perform certain approved privileged operations by requesting that those operations be performed by elements of the operating system. The stack belonging to the user process is used by the operating system while it is performing such a service for the user process. This allows the user process to communicate with the system process with the data in the stack without the two processes actually sharing a system data area.

MULTIPROCESSING

VMS does not have extensive support for multiprocessor configurations. Most of the conditions where multiple processors are advantageous are handled by the VAX CLUSTER instead of by placing multiprocessors in one computer. The only current VAX that has multiprocessors is the VAX 11/782. The VMS implementation on the 11/782 is not as multiprocessors, but is instead an "attached processor" configuration.

One of the two processors on the 11/782 handles all system-related work and the other processor is used just for additional computing power. The closest comparison is with PC-DOS and the attached numeric processor, (the 8087). When the system is booted, the primary processor must be available, and the operating system must be running in it, since the secondary processor cannot handle any systems tasks. The secondary processor cannot run any process that needs to execute in kernel mode, since that access level allows system-related activities, which are not allowed on the secondary processor.

All I/O operations, scheduling, paging and swapping operations are handled only by the primary processor. No peripheral I/O devices can be accessed if they are attached to the secondary processor. The secondary processor only runs processes that are completely processor-bound.

The scheduling algorithms are almost identical to those used for single processor systems. Processes are still scheduled by the same criteria. Each process receives a slice of time in the processor, unless interrupted by a higher priority process, or voluntarily relinquishing the processor. The next process is scheduled into the processor in priority order, so that the highest priority process is the next one dispatched to the processor.

The distinction is scheduling is always done for the attached processor before the primary processor, so that the scheduling algorithms first try to dispatch a process to the secondary processor, and then one for the primary processor. Processes are not scheduled to run on the attached processor if they are to run in kernel mode since that is not allowed.

Processes running on the attached processor are not allowed to either page, swap, or do I/O. Whenever such a process requires a new page, or some I/O operations, the attached processor interrupts the primary processor to request the specified service. The process running on the attached processor is suspended, and a new process is scheduled to run on that processor. The primary processor acquires the requested service for the process that was running on the attached processor. When that service is acquired, the process is rescheduled to run. It may continue execution on either processor, depending upon the normal scheduling criteria.

Example 17-13:

PROCESSOR JOB ALLOCATION

PRIMARY	CO-PROCESSOR
Compute Paging I/O Swapping	Compute

The attached processor is only used to perform processor-bound jobs, so the value of the multi-processors varies depending upon the specific job mix at that installation. Jobs that require a large amount of paging or I/O cannot run on the attached processor, so unless a sufficient number of jobs is available that require only processor time, the attached processor may be completely useless. For those installations that do have a large number of processor-bound jobs, however, the attached processor configuration may work quite well.

NETWORKING

VMS does not have an exclusive networking system, but instead implements the Digital Equipment Corporation DECnet networking system. This is the universal DEC networking system, and it is quite extensive. This same networking system is supported by virtually all DEC operating systems, and connections to it are available from several other vendors.

The DECnet network is a decentralized network with no central node. Each node is a peer with all other nodes. It is not necessary that all nodes in the network be computers running the VMS operating system; they can instead be computers running any of several different operating systems. The decentralized network is such that communication with other nodes is achieved with the nodes that are between the two nodes wishing to communicate. These nodes relay any necessary data on to the intended recipient.

DECnet provides a variety of different possible connections. Probably the most common connection method is with the **Digital Data Communications Message Protocol** or **DDCMP.** Connections are also possible to Ethernet networks.

The DDCMP protocol provides control and management for data blocks during transmission. It also detects any errors in the data transmission, and requests retransmission of any data blocks that have errors in them. DDCMP networks are usually set up as either **point-to-point** or **multipoint** configurations. A point-to-point configuration consists of two nodes that are linked with a single connection, and both nodes have equal access to the link. A multipoint configuration has two or more nodes linked with one or more connections, where one of the nodes on the network serves as the control station and the other nodes are called "tributaries".

This type of multipoint network is a polled network where the control station can access the communications link at any time. The tributary nodes, on the other hand, can only access the link after the control station grants specific permission for them to do so. All transmissions between tributary nodes must pass through the control station node.

DECnet also supports connection to Ethernet networks for local area networks. The Ethernet protocol was discussed in chapter 12 and the DECnet implementation follows the normal Ethernet standard. **Routing nodes** send and receive data, but they also retransmit data from other nodes. Routing nodes can also retransmit from non-Ethernet nodes that may be connected to an Ethernet network. **Non-routing nodes,** also called end nodes, can send and receive data, but cannot retransmit data.

The individual DECnet nodes have the responsibility of defining and maintaining the network environment at that node. Particularly in the case of a VAX/VMS computer serving as a node in the network, there may be several functions necessary at the node. The network hardware and software must be properly configured and tested to ensure proper functioning. It is also necessary to set up userids to allow access to the network.

The DECnet interface in VMS is integrated into the system so well that many of the functions performed with DECnet are as easy and simple as performing those same functions on the host VMS system. The transparent communication features of the interface allow users to perform standard systems service calls, do I/O in the usual fashion, and use the same interface to system commands across the network. The only requirement for transparent access to files residing on a remote node is to specify the node name as part of the file specification. That file can then be accessed as though it existed on the local node. The node specification determines the node on which the file resides, and is placed just before the device name in the file specification, as in:

```
node::device:[directory]filename.type;version
```

Some DECnet nodes may not be VMS systems. These systems may also be accessed, although the syntax is not transparent in this case. Non-VMS systems may have file specifications that are not legal VMS file specifications, so a special way of writing those file specifications is necessary. This is accomplished by enclosing the unusual file specification in double quote marks, as in:

```
node::''unusual file specification''
```

A link to a task running on another system can also be accomplished by using the same format, but specifying a task name in place of the file specification.

Configuring DECnet

There are four major parts in the DECnet configuration database. The node database defines all the nodes in the network. Both the local node, and all other nodes, must be specified in this database. The circuit database defines each circuit that is available to the local node. The logging database defines the locations where records can be kept of certain events. The line database is used to specify each communications lines accessible to the local link. Two copies of these databases are maintained (one in memory, and one on disk). The copy in memory can be modified dynamically in order to change the network configuration while the system is running.

The node database is used to maintain a record of all nodes in the network. Any node that is not listed in this database is not accessible, so the usual practice is to keep a list of all nodes in the network. Each node is defined by an address and name. The node address is a number that is unique for each node in the network. This is the way that nodes are identified to the network, so the number must not be duplicated for any nodes. The node name is an optional name that can be attached to the node address. It allows the node to be referenced by a mnemonic name, instead of just by a number. The node name is used only at the local node, so there are no restrictions on using the same name at different nodes to define different node addresses. It is strongly recommended that an effort be made to use the same node names to refer to the same node addresses at each node.

There are many parameters that can be specified on the node definition. These are used for controlling the way the physical links function. This is done by setting the buffer sizes, setting the maximum number of buffers, and setting the maximum number of circuits. The buffers used should all be of the same size; otherwise some data may be lost during transmissions.

Circuits are the logical connections between nodes. They provide a high-level communications path, whereas the lines provide a low-level path. Circuits provide either a point-to-point or multipoint connection between nodes. The three types of circuits available are point-to-point, multipoint control, and multipoint tributary. The multipoint control circuit refers to the controlling node on a multipoint link, while the multipoint tributary circuit refers to the tributary node on a multipoint link.

Circuits have names somewhat similar to node names, although the format is slightly different. The name format is:

```
dev-c-u.t
```

where "dev" is the device name. This is the name of a physical device, and must follow the normal DEC device names. The "c" is a number that designates the device controller attached to the device. The "u" is a unit number to specify which unit is referenced, if there is more than one unit attached to that controller. The "t" is a number which specifies the tributary number on a multipoint circuit.

Circuits are also similar to nodes in that there are many parameters available to more completely specify their characteristics. Most of these parameters set functions such as the number of buffers, the number of transmissions to be made under different circuit conditions, etc. Most parameters are universal for all circuits, but there are some parameters that are unique for particular types of circuits, such as Ethernet circuits.

The communication between nodes is done with lines. There are four types of lines; each of which supports a particular type of network protocol. The types are CI, DDCMP, Ethernet, and X.25. CI is used primarily for very high-speed links. DDCMP, Ethernet, and X.25 support each respective network protocol.

Lines are named almost identically to circuits. The only distinction is that the "t" for tributary is not available. The format is:

```
dev-c-u
```

where "dev" is the device name, "c" is the controller number, and "u" is the optional unit number.

The parameters available for line specifications are the same general type as the parameters for circuit specification. Many of the parameters are concerned with timing information on the various parts of the link. Others refer to such things as the number of buffers available, the type of protocol used on that line, and the condition of the line.

The logging database contains the names of locations where logging data is stored. Monitoring a network is necessary in order to ensure the continued functioning and performance of that network. Computer systems tend to be kept in one small contained area, there are many ways of monitoring and maintaining the health of that system. Networks, on the other hand, tend to be spread over vast distances, using a wide variety of dissimilar equipment, under a wide variety of conditions. Such a configuration may be subject to frequent failures or performance degradations, and the only way to detect problems is with monitoring. The monitoring system tends to generate a large amount of data, which must be stored in the files specified in the logging database.

The information logged consists of such things as any circuits or lines that are not functional, the amount of activity at nodes, any change in state for nodes, lines, or circuits, and data error levels. Most events that are logged specify the network layer where the event occurred, and the type of event that occurred. There are pre-defined classes and types of events and the reporting is a set of numbers that specify the class and type of event.

Example 17-14:

CONFIGURATION COMPONENTS

NODE DATABASE

Node address
Node name
Node parameters

CIRCUIT DATABASE

Circuit name
Circuit type
Circuit parameters

LINE DATABASE

Line name
Line type
Line parameters

LOGGING DATABASE

Logging file names
Logging specifications

Network Access

Access to the network is controlled on several different levels. The primary levels are node-level access to remote nodes, route-level access to remote nodes, and system-level access that creates a local process. Node-level access to remote nodes is controlled at the remote node. Access control information must be supplied from some source, in order to allow access. This information may come from the process requesting the access, the local node control software, or from the remote node control software.

System-level access that creates a local process requires an access control string. Privileged access to a remote node requires that the requesting process have sufficient privilege itself. Both local and remote nodes maintain a database which specifies access control codes. If the requesting process has a privilege level to match the access level requested, then the appropriate access control code is generated automatically by the node. A default access control code is defined at both the remote and local nodes. These default access levels are used by most processes, which do not require any special privilege levels.

The links between nodes are initialized when the system is booted or when that circuit is first turned on. These links may or may not require passwords before they are set up. There are both receive and transmit passwords. The receive passwords are used to validate an incoming initialization request, while the transmit password is sent out to request initialization. The transmit password sent out must match the previously specified receive password for that link.

Node-level access controls whether a transmission can be accepted from, or sent to, a remote node. If that node is specified in the local node database, then the access specified there is used, otherwise the overall default access is used. Node accesses, either specific or default, can allow either no connections to be made, links from the remote node, links to the remote node, or both.

There are a few simple rules that should be followed in order to prevent problems with the configuration. The first, and probably the most important, is to ensure that the same list of remote node names is used at each node. Few problems are more disastrous, yet more difficult to find, than problems arising from naming the same node differently at different locations. This can cause a variety of problems, such as lost or misplaced files. These problems tend to be intermittent, that is, they occur under some conditions, and not under other conditions, and thus very difficult to solve.

Each node in the network should have a unique address. This is easy to achieve if the list of node names is kept at each node, since that list should also have the node addresses. A quick glance at the list shows which node addresses are already in use. This implies, of course, that the list is ordered by node address. A good way of maintaining the list is to have it sorted both by node address, and by node name. This makes locating a given node address or name very simple.

Forcing the routine tables and buffer sizes to be the same at each node also tends to prevent problems. These steps can be achieved by specifying the same maximum value for the node addresses at each node, and by specifying the same receive buffer size at each node. They are not absolutely necessary, but problems with lost or misrouted data may occur if they are not followed.

System management via DECnet

True systems management cannot be done over a network for any large or complex installation, but some facets can be performed, particularly on small installations. For example, many nodes on a network may consist of one small computer at some remote location. It is not usually cost-efficient to have one or more operators at each such remote location, so some means of doing some necessary functions from a central location is very useful.

A feature of the VMS DECnet that is sometimes quite useful is the ability to boot one computer system from another computer system. The system image file is transmitted via the network, and loaded into the other computer. The network node that controls the loading is called the **executor node,** and the node that is being loaded is called the **target node,** and the node that reqested the load is called the "command node".

There are two primary ways in which this process can occur. One way has the target node also serving as the command node, that is, the node that is to have the system loaded also initiates the load operation. This is normally done by activating, probably manually, the built-in bootstrap function on the target computer. The bootstrap function then sends the load request to the executor node, which responds by sending the system image.

The other method is to have an operator, usually on the executor node, sending a network command that triggers the system load. The target node may be loaded by sending a copy of the system image across the link, or by just invoking a load routine, which then loads the system image from a disk drive attached to the target node.

Some obvious difficulties arise with the whole concept of downline loading of operating systems. The load is not possible unless the network circuit between the two nodes is available, yet that circuit is usually not available until after the target node has an operating system running. This typical "chicken and egg" problem is solved by utilizing the circuit in its maintenance mode. DECnet communications lines have maintenance modes available that are used to test the functioning of the hardware circuit. The service mode does not require an operating system at the target node, although some software must be running there. The minimal amount of software required at the target node is the bootstrap loader built into the computer.

Another useful and somewhat unusual feature provided by the VMS DECnet system is the ability to upload a memory dump from a failing system to another node. Whenever an operating system experiences a catastrophic failure, it shuts down completely. The last function performed is an attempt to dump a copy of the memory contents. System failures are very serious, and every effort should be made to prevent them, so analyzing why the failure occurred is necessary. The only means of analyzing the cause of failure is usually a dump of memory.

Memory dumps can only be uploaded on the network from a target node, called a **slave node** here. They are uploaded to an executor node. The memory upload uses the same line service protocol for communication as is used by the system image download procedure.

There are four steps needed in order to have a memory dump uploaded. The first step is when the slave node detects a system failure. It then sends a message to the executor node, requesting a memory upload. Various physical information may be included with the request, such as the memory size on the slave node (which determines the size of the dump).

The executor node checks for a valid disk area to contain the dump, the beginning memory location to be dumped in the slave node, and the number of memory locations to be dumped. This information may either be uploaded from the slave, or it may be stored in the network database at the executor node. The dump address defaults to the beginning of memory if no value is supplied. Once the executor node has verified these values, it sends a message back to the slave node validating the upload, and specifying how much of the dump is to be sent at each transmission.

The slave node then begins transmitting blocks of data, each of which is a part of the memory dump. It continues until the specified amount of memory has been dumped and transmitted. As soon as the dump is completed, an attempt is made to re-load the slave node's operating system. This is done with a downline system load. A message is sent to the slave node, which triggers the bootstrap procedure on that system, which in turn requests a new system image from the executor node.

Several requirements exist that must be met before either the system can be downloaded or the dump can be uploaded. The first step, of course, is to set up the network so that the links are available. The second step is to ensure that the operating system for the slave node is generated properly. For example, a systems generation parameter is required in order to allow a system to do an uploaded memory dump. Finally, the circuit between the two nodes must be able to perform in the service mode, since otherwise the upload or download cannot be transmitted.

SUMMARY

The basic approach of the VMS operating system is to provide good support for interactive usage, but it also has incorporated batch processing and real-time features. The VMS file system has many of the nice features of the UNIX file system, although not as many tools are provided.

The kernel of the operating system provides the complex performance features needed to provide a high level of performance, but these features are not carried to the level that would require a large computer to support the necessary overhead. The networking system is quite thorough and complete, but it does not require the vast amount of supporting resources that are required by some systems, such as MVS.

VMS is a very good compromise as an operating system. It does not emphasize any one particular area at the expense of other areas, unlike most systems. The primary thrust of VMS is to support the interactive user, but the primary strength of VMS is that all types of usage are supported well. It is a very well-rounded system.

EXERCISES

DISCUSSION QUESTIONS

1. Briefly describe the primary functions of DCL.
2. Describe the functions of the AUTOGEN program.
3. Contrast the usage of AUTOGEN with SYSGEN.
4. Briefly describe the function of logical names in the VMS file system.
5. List some of the functions available with the BACKUP program.
6. Describe how processes are created.
7. Describe how process priorities are allocated.
8. Describe the lockout problem caused by real-time processes.
9. Describe how the physical memory on VAXes is organized.
10. Describe how the working set limit, quota, and extent are used.
11. Explain the importance of the page cache in performance tuning.
12. Explain how voluntary decrementing works with AWSA.
13. Discuss the most common causes of excessive operating system overhead.
14. Explain how the UIC is used for security.
15. Explain how the protection mask is used for security.
16. Briefly describe how VMS implements multiprocessing.
17. Briefly describe the organization of the DECnet network.
18. Discuss how a user accesses a remote node via DECnet.
19. Briefly describe the major parts of the DECnet configuration database.
20. Briefly describe how DECnet can be used to downline load an operating system.

APPENDIXES

ANALYTIC MODELING

A

KEY TERMS

Source	*Birth and death processes*
Service time	*Arrive*
Interarrival time	*Server*
Traffic level	*Poisson process*
Markov process	*Discrete states*
Transient state	*Recurrent state*

INTRODUCTION

Analytic modeling is the process of setting up a mathematical model that is a representation of part or all of a computer system. Some parts of an operating system are more amenable to a mathematical representation than are other parts, so the value of the model tends to vary somewhat depending upon the part of the system that is being modeled.

Analytic models involve some relatively sophisticated mathematics. Since the text is not designed as a text on mathematics, no attempt has been made to derive or justify the mathematics involved. All that is intended is to provide enough information so that the basic elements of analytic modeling become understandable.

Analytic models are primarily used to test the effects of new algorithms for various system functions. Many internal algorithms, such as scheduling or paging algorithms, can have a significant affect on the performance of an operating system, so such algorithms are very important. It is quite difficult, however, to test many of these algorithms, since the testing requires that the algorithm be fully developed and placed in a functioning operating system under a heavy load. Analytic models can be a way of testing the effects of a new algorithm without requiring it be placed in a complete operating system.

Analytic models can be very useful in certain areas of system development, but it is not easy to develop a model that is both accurate and relatively simple. Much care must be taken when developing the model to ensure that it accurately reflects real system performance. Errors in the model could easily cause algorithms to be developed incorrectly, so that they do not perform well in a real system.

Models should be as simple as possible, but as systems and system loads become more complex, models must also become more complex in order to accurately reflect those complex systems. If the models become too complex, however, then developing and evaluating the results from the models may become impractical, so some limit must be placed on model complexity.

The normal way to use models is to develop a variety of relatively simple models that are used to model various parts of a system, and then to evaluate the results of those models as a group. No one model is usually accurate enough to provide conclusive results, but when the results of a group of models all point to the same conclusion, then that conclusion is probably accurate.

QUEUEING THEORY

One of the most common areas of operating system performance to be modeled is the queueing process. This is both because the queueing process tends to lend itself well to a mathematical representation and because it is not always easy to understand without the aid of mathematics. The basic idea of queueing theory is that each entry in a queue arrives at some time, stays for some length of time, and leaves at another time. Although this seems quite simple, the reality tends to become rather complex.

Queue entries come from a **source,** when they enter the queue they have **arrived,** and each requires some **service time** from one or more system **servers.** The source for queue arrivals can be either finite or infinite. A finite source implies that only some maximum number of entries can possibly arrive in the queue, while an infinite source implies that an infinite number of entries can arrive. If the queue can have an infinite number of arrivals then, of course, the size of the queue also becomes infinite. For most operating systems the number of possible entries is finite, but quite large, so most models assume an infinite source, which makes the model somewhat simpler.

Poisson processes

Queue arrivals are normally assumed to occur at random intervals. The time between queue arrivals is thus also random, and is called **interarrival time.** Most queueing theory assumes that queue arrivals can be described mathematically by a **Poisson process.** Poisson processes model a theory that the interarrival times for queue entries are identically distributed, exponential random variables. This basically means that the arrival times of the queue entries can be described with exponential variables.

The arrivals can be described mathematically by:

$$\frac{e^{-Lt}(Lt)^n}{n!} \qquad (\text{for } n=0,1,2,\ldots)$$

where "L" is the constant average arrival rate, "n" is the number of entries arriving, and "t" is a time interval of a certain length.

Traffic level

The amount of service that a queue provides to the entries in it is defined as the "traffic level" of that queue. It is defined as the ratio of L to m, where "L" is the rate at which new entries arrive, and "m" is the rate at which those entries are serviced. The traffic level is dependent upon both the rate at which new entries arrive and the level at which current entries are serviced.

Queue servers

Each entry in a queue is, of course, waiting for some type of service. The speed with which the service is provided depends primarily upon the number of entries in the queue and the number of servers servicing the queue. Queues have either a single server, as a process queue on a single-processor computer, or multiple servers, as a process queue on multiprocessor computers.

The use of the servers is defined mathematically as:

$$P = \frac{u}{c} = \frac{L}{mc}$$

where "u" is the traffic level, "c" is the number of servers, "L" is number of entries in the queue, and "m" is the average rate at which service is provided by one server.

Steady state

One of the important assumptions made in almost all analytical models is that the queues, as modeled, are in a **steady state** at the time of the modeling. A queue in a steady state is much more amenable to modeling than that same queue in a state of transition. Queues are normally only in a state of transition when some part of the operating system is beginning or ending operation.

MARKOV PROCESSES

One technique that sometimes makes system modeling easier is to break the system performance down into a series of individual, frozen states. Such states are called **discrete states,** and a complete model can be made up of a series of such discrete steps. This type of modeling can be compared with movie films, in that they also consist of a series of discrete steps, and the apparent movement is caused by viewing a series of still pictures. A particular type of model, called a **Markov process,** uses a series a discrete steps to model the system.

A Markov process is a set of mutually exclusive and collectively exhaustive discrete states. This means that each discrete state is different from all other discrete states in the model, and that all of them taken together completely describe the system.

A discrete state is **recurrent** if it can occur more than once in the system, that is, whenever the system has changed to another state it can still at some future time return to the original state. This can be stated mathematically by letting the initial state be S_i and the second state be S_j. State S_i is then recurrent if, when the system moves from state S_i to state S_j, the state S_i is still reachable. If it is not, then state S_i is called a **transient state** instead of a recurrent state.

A particular type of Markov processes, called **birth and death processes,** is frequently used in computer modeling. Birth and death processes refer to to transition of a model from one state to another. The birth process is when the transition is to the next state in the model, and the death process is when the transition is to the previous state in the model.

A continuous Markov birth and death model states that, for any random state, the transition is just as likely to be to the previous state (the death process), as it is to be to the next state (the birth process).

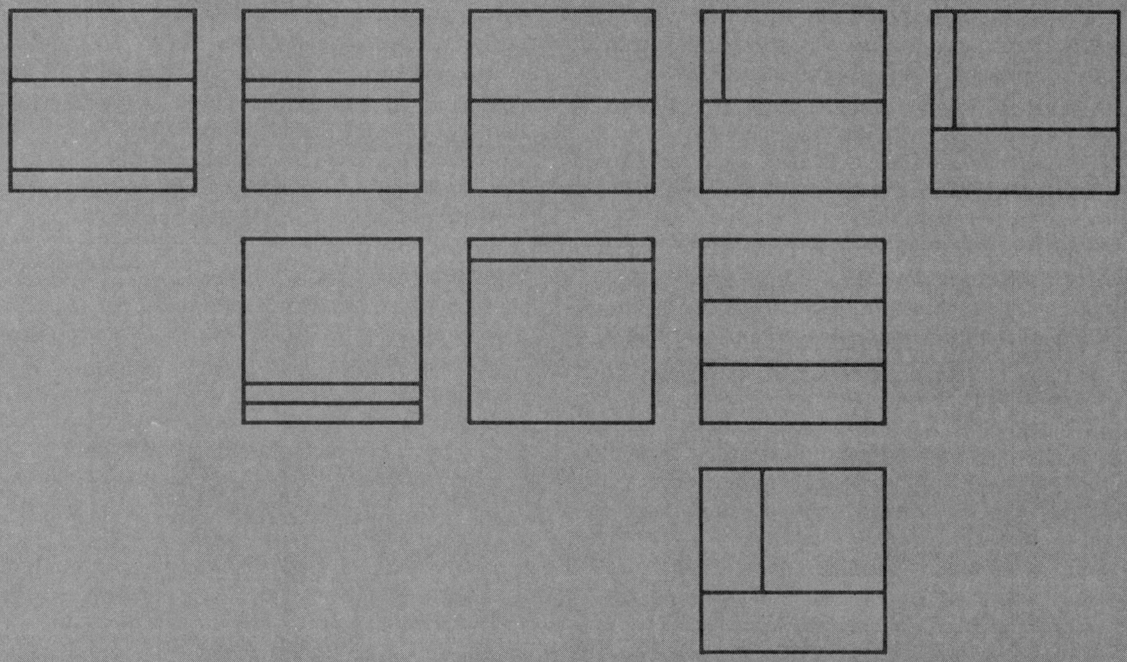

REAL MEMORY ORGANIZATION

B

KEY TERMS

Bits	*Bytes*
Words	*Fullwords*

Many of the strategies and algorithms used in operating systems directly relate to managing memory. The memory management algorithms are only concerned with managing memory, but many other algorithms, such as many of the scheduling algorithms, also make heavy use of memory management constraints. Because of the importance of memory management, it is important to understand how most computer memories are organized.

At its lowest level, computer memory consists of huge quantities of elements that can be thought of as switches. Each of these switches may be in one of two binary states, off or on, 0 or 1, etc. These switches are called **bits.**

Bits are grouped together in groups of eight. Each group of eight bits is called a **byte** (pronounced like "bite").

The length of any memory area is determined in bytes. The addresses of consecutive areas are determined by their lengths. If the address of a given memory area is four less than that of a second consecutive area, it means that there are four bytes between the two memory areas. These four bytes may be the actual length of the first memory area, or there may be other areas in between the two. No memory area can be less than one byte in length.

Memory addresses are specified in several numbering systems. The decimal numbering system is very good for humans, but it does not work as well with computers, which use the binary (base 2) numbering system. Binary numbers are quite difficult for humans to use, so shorthand methods of binary arithmetic have been developed. The two most common methods are octal (base 8) and hexadecimal (base 16).

Both the octal and hexadecimal numbering systems are somewhat similar to decimal, so arithmetic in those systems is not too difficult for humans. The nicest part of these systems is that each digit in either octal or hexadecimal can be converted to or from binary by inspection. The ease of conversion stems from the fact that both eight and sixteen are powers of two, so that numbering systems based on eight or sixteen are also ultimately based on two.

Example B-1:

NUMBERING SYSTEMS

DECIMAL	OCTAL	HEXADECIMAL	BINARY
0	0	0	0
1	1	1	1
2	2	2	10
3	3	3	11
4	4	4	100
5	5	5	101
6	6	6	110
7	7	7	111
8	10	8	1000
9	11	9	1001
10	12	A	1010
11	13	B	1011
12	14	C	1100
13	15	D	1101
14	16	E	1110
15	17	F	1111
16	20	10	1000 0000
17	21	11	1000 0001
18	22	12	1000 0010
19	23	13	1000 0011
20	24	14	1000 0100

GLOSSARY

Attached processor The secondary processor in a multi-processor configuration. It usually does not perform many of the system-related activities in the configuration.

Central processing unit (CPU) The part of the computer that executes the instructions provided by the system or a program.

Command interpreter The part of the operating system that accepts and deciphers commands entered by the user. These commands are translated into work units for the computer.

Concurrency The technique of maintaining several programs simultaneously in memory and executing them in such a manner that it appears to the user as if they are executing simultaneously.

Co-processor One of several processors in a multi-processor configuration.

CPU-intensive Using the CPU as a primary resource.

Critical sections A section of the operating system that is a resource and must be serially shared among several tasks. These critical sections are managed just as are other serially shared resources such as disk drives.

Data Encryption Standard (DES) A standard adopted by the National Bureau of Standards that specifies the ways in which data should be encrypted.

Data set A file of logically related data. The name is primarily used in IBM batch-type operating systems.

Deadlock A condition that can arise when trying to schedule requests for locked resources. Two jobs are attempting to access the same two resources, and each job locks one of the resources and begins waiting for the other resource. Neither job is normally able to stop waiting.

Direct access storage devices (DASD or disk drives) Peripheral I/O devices that are used to maintain data.

Directory A central index of the files in a given file system. It usually contains a variety of information about those files, some of which is available to the users.

Disaster recovery The process of planning for recovery from severe and unusual problems in the data center. These problems can range from natural disasters (such as earthquakes) to such common events as accidental erasure of a file.

Dispatcher The part of the operating system that determines which job is to receive access to the system resources, the order in which the resources are made available, and the amount of resources made available.

Dynamic address translation Hardware that facilitates virtual memory. It translates memory references into commands that locate and make available memory locations.

Feedback queues A method of segregating jobs into queues with other jobs that have similar CPU requirements. Job execution is tracked, and that information is used to place the job in the queue most suited to its resource requirements.

File A collection of logically related data.

Fragmentation A condition in file systems and RAM memory where small blocks of unused space become interspersed among larger blocks of used space. These spaces are unusable because of their small size.

HELP facilities A way of providing online information to the user about a particular feature or command. Such information should be sufficient in most cases but is not detailed as in the manual.

Image backup A complete and exact copy of the disk drives is backed up to tape.

Incremental backup A copy of the files that have changed since the last backup.

Interrupts Signals to the operating system (usually from some external source) indicating that the source needs immediate attention from the operating system.

ISO network standard An international standard for developing compatible networks. It specifies the parts of a network in seven different layers. Each layer provides a certain network function.
I/O-intensive Using the I/O system as a primary resource.
Kernel The "heart" of the operating system. The part of the operating system that contains such functions as dispatching and memory management.
Local area network (LANs) A network designed to cover a small contiguous area such as one department.
Locking resources A way of managing serially reusable resources. Each resource is dedicated entirely to one task until that task is finished. It then becomes available to the next task.
Loosely coupled A multi-processing environment where each CPU usually contains memory and/or peripheral devices. This is in contrast to a tightly-coupled arrangement where all processors share all resources.
Memory-intensive Using the RAM memory as a primary resource.
Multiprogramming The process of allowing many programs to reside in memory simultaneously and to run in a manner that appears to the user to be simultaneous.
Multitasking The process of allowing many tasks to reside in memory simultaneously and to run in a manner that appears to the user to be simultaneous.
Overlaying A memory management technique which requires the programmer to designate which areas of that program may take turns residing in the same area of memory. The overall memory requirement is reduced by sharing memory between certain areas of the program and loading each area into that memory when it is needed.
Packet A collection of data transmitted over some networks. It is usually a small fixed size and contains both data and control information.
Pages A small area of memory (used in virtual memory implementations) which may be moved into or out of real memory in one piece.
Parallel processing A technique of using more than one processor to simultaneously work on separate parts of a single job. The job must be divided into parallel instruction streams in order for parallel processing to be efficient.
Polling The process of having a central node in a network serially check the other nodes in the network to allow any of those nodes the ability to transmit a message. Only one node can usually transmit at any one time.
Priority A number that is dynamically assigned to all tasks in the system. It is used to determine the dispatching state of tasks relative to one another. The task with the highest priority usually gets dispatched next.
Private branch exchange (PBX) An electronic communications switch, usually designed to be placed in a single building in an installation. It handles and routes all local calls within that area without forcing the calls to be routed outside the area.
Process The smallest complete work unit in the system. This term is frequently used interchangeably with the term "task".
Round-robin A queueing method wherein the job at the top of the queue is allowed to execute, then rejoin the queue at the bottom, and the next job is allowed to execute. The first job executes again only after all other jobs in the queue have had a turn.
Scalar processing A system where each computer instruction is executed after the previous instruction. This is distinct from parallel processing where several instructions may be executed simultaneously.
Scheduling The process of determining the relative priorities of jobs waiting to execute. These priorities are then used to determine the order in which tasks receive access to various needed system resources.
Semaphores Flags that are used when scheduling resources to determine if the resource is available, or if it is already in use by another task.
Spinning on locks A technique of resolving access to resources. A task that requires a particular locked resource will continue to actively seek that resource until it is available.

Swapping A paging technique where entire groups of pages are paged in or out as a block, instead of individually.
Systems generation The initial setup that is necessary before any operating system can be used. It normally involves preparing disk drives to receive the system and configuring and building the system to match the requirements of the local installation.
Systems services That group of functions that must be supplied by the operating system but are not part of the kernel of the system. An example is the facilities necessary to compile programs.
Task The smallest complete work unit in the system. This term is frequently used interchangeably with the term process.
Thrashing A condition where the memory of the computer is over-allocated, the paging rate becomes unacceptably high, and almost the entire computer system is devoted to doing paging.
Tightly coupled A way of creating a multiprocessing environment where each CPU shares one central set of memory and peripheral devices.
Trojan horse program A seemingly innocent program, incorporated into a system, which contains secret features that allow unauthorized access to the system.
User friendly A user interface environment that is easy to use for people who are not sophisticated computer experts. It should contain simple commands and clear instructions.
Vector processing A technique where the instructions are processed in groups instead of singly. The term is frequently used in place of the term "parallel processing".
Virtual memory A way of allowing each user in the system to have access to very large memory sizes. It is done by supplementing the real memory with disk drives, and only reading the data into real memory when it is actually needed.
Working set That group of pages for a particular user that must always be contained in real memory in order to optimize performance.

INDEX